The Archidamian War

BY DONALD KAGAN

The Outbreak of the Peloponnesian War

The Archidamian War

The Peace of Nicias and the Sicilian Expedition

The Fall of the Athenian Empire

The Great Dialogue: A History of Greek Political Thought from Homer to Polybius

Great Issues in Western Civilization, editor with Brian Tierney and L. Pearce Williams

Problems in Ancient History, editor

Hellenic History, with G. W. Botsford and C. A. Robinson, Jr.

The Archidamian War

DONALD KAGAN

Cornell University Press

ITHACA AND LONDON

Cornell University Press gratefully acknowledges a grant
from the Andrew W. Mellon Foundation that
aided in bringing this book to publication.

First published 1974 by Cornell University Press.
Reissued, 1987, by Cornell University Press, with corrections.
Third printing 1991.
First published, Cornell Paperbacks, 1990.
Second printing 1992.

Printed in the United States of America

Library of Congress Cataloging-in-Publication Data

Kagan, Donald.
    The Archidamian war / Donald Kagan.
        p.   cm.
    "First published in Ithaca by Cornell University Press in 1974".
    Includes bibliographical references.
    ISBN 0-8014-0889-X (alk. paper)
    ISBN 0-8014-9714-0 (pbk. : alk. paper)
    1. Greece—History—Peloponnesian War, 431–404 B.C.   I. Title.
DF229.3.K33   1990
938'.05—dc20   89-28639

For Myrna

Preface

❦

This book is a sequel to *The Outbreak of the Peloponnesian War* and is part of a general history of that war which will require another volume or two to complete. The subject has not been treated on a large scale since the turn of the century; the important scholarship that has intervened and the continued interest in the war amply justify an attempt at a new history.

The present volume deals with the first ten years, the Archidamian War. That struggle, beginning in 431, deserves a volume of its own, for to contemporaries it appeared to be a war complete in itself. Only hindsight and the special perception of Thucydides placed it, together with the diplomatic maneuverings of the Peace of Nicias in 421 and with the events from the resumption of hostility after the Sicilian expedition to the surrender of Athens in 404, as a single war of twenty-seven years and separated it from the war between the Peloponnesians and Athenians of 461–445. The Archidamian War, moreover, was the war planned by the Peloponnesian and Athenian strategists, and so the one that tested their skill and prescience. Because the conditions and character of the war could be foreseen, as far as such things are ever predictable, it is possible to make some judgment of the wisdom of each policy and the effectiveness of its execution. The main purpose of this volume, however, is to attempt a general history of the Greek states in their conduct of the war that does justice to military, political, diplomatic, and economic developments and shows how closely they were related.

My views about the use of ancient sources other than

7

Thucydides, the interpretation of the speeches in Thucydides, and the problem of the composition of his history remain those I set forth in the Preface to *The Outbreak of the Peloponnesian War*. Since these matters remain controversial, I have argued for my opinion at appropriate places in this volume.

I have chosen to organize the book annalistically, as Thucydides organizes his. This method has shortcomings, for which Thucydides has been reproached. It leads to the artificial division of continuing events and prevents their most effective presentation; it may lead to repetition or confusion. I have consciously run these risks in an attempt to avoid the paralyzing force of hindsight, to present the events in the contexts in which they appear to the participants. I hope in that way to emphasize the choices open to them and their lack of any sense of predestination. I hope the gain in immediacy and reality will offset the loss in fluidity and grace.

Most readers will quickly recognize my debt to three great German historians, Georg Busolt, K. J. Beloch, and Eduard Meyer, and of these my debt to the wise, sober, and judicious Busolt is the heaviest. Among the scores of modern historians who have helped to shape my knowledge and understanding of the period, I must single out for special mention A. W. Gomme and the continuators of his splendid commentary on Thucydides, A. Andrewes and K. J. Dover; also Russell Meiggs and David Lewis, whose fine edition of the Greek inscriptions has done so much for historians, and B. D. Meritt, H. T. Wade-Gery, and M. F. McGregor, whose publication of *The Athenian Tribute Lists* initiated an era in the study of Greek history.

I am grateful to B. M. W. Knox and to Ronald P. Legon for reading the manuscript and for their encouragement. Thanks are due also to the two anonymous publisher's readers, who made many valuable suggestions and helped to eliminate a number of errors. I also want to thank Janalyn Gibb for typing the manuscript and John Hale for helping to prepare the maps. Finally, I wish to express my thanks to the National Endowment for the Humanities and to Yale University for providing me with time to complete this volume.

DONALD KAGAN

New Haven, Connecticut

Contents

Maps

❧

Abbreviations and Short Titles

❦

AClass	*Acta Classica*
AFD	B. D. Meritt, *Athenian Financial Documents*
AJA	*American Journal of Archaeology*
AJP	*American Journal of Philology*
ASI	E. Badian, ed., *Ancient Society and Institutions*
ATL	B. D. Meritt, H. T. Wade-Gery, and F. M. McGregor, *The Athenian Tribute Lists*
BCH	*Bulletin de correspondance hellénique*
BSA	*Proceedings of the British School at Athens*
Beloch, *Bevölkerung*	K. J. Beloch, *Die Bevölkerung der griechisch-römischen Welt*
Beloch, *GG²*	K. J. Beloch, *Griechische Geschichte*, 2d ed.
Bengtson, *GG*	H. Bengston, *Griechische Geschichte*, 2d ed.
Bengtson, *Staatsverträge*	H. Bengtson, *Die Staatsverträge der griechisch-römischen Welt von 700 bis 338 v. Chr.*
Busolt, *GG*	G. Busolt, *Griechische Geschichte*
CAH	*Cambridge Ancient History*
CIA	*Corpus Inscriptionum Atticarum*
CP	*Classical Philology*
CQ	*Classical Quarterly*
CR	*Classical Review*
Delbrück, *Strategie*	H. Delbrück, *Die Strategie des Perikles*
Duncker, *GdA*	M. Duncker, *Geschichte des Altertums*
FGrH	F. Jacoby, *Die Fragmente der griechischen Historiker*
GHI	R. Meiggs and D. Lewis, *A Selection of Greek Historical Inscriptions*
GRBS	*Greek, Roman, and Byzantine Studies*

Gomme, *HCT*	A. W. Gomme, *A Historical Commentary on Thucydides*
Grote	George Grote, *A History of Greece*
HSCP	*Harvard Studies in Classical Philology*
Henderson, *Great War*	B. W. Henderson, *The Great War between Athens and Sparta*
Hignett, *HAC*	C. Hignett, *A History of the Athenian Constitution*
IG	*Inscriptiones Graecae*
JHS	*Journal of Hellenic Studies*
Kagan, *Outbreak*	D. Kagan, *The Outbreak of the Peloponnesian War*
Meyer, *Forsch.*	E. Meyer, *Forschungen zur alten Geschichte*, II
Meyer, *GdA*	E. Meyer, *Geschichte des Altertums*
PA	*Prosopographia Attica*
PACA	*Proceedings of the African Classical Association*
PW	Pauly-Wissowa and others, *Realenzyklopädie der klassischen Altertumswissenschaft*
REG	*Revue des études grecques*
TAPA	*Transactions of the American Philological Association*
Sealey, *Essays*	R. Sealey, *Essays in Greek History*
Westlake, *Essays*	H. D. Westlake, *Essays on Greek Historians and Greek History*

The Archidamian War

1. Plans and Resources[1]

✻

In the spring of 431 a band of more than three hundred Thebans, under cover of darkness, launched a surprise attack on the neighboring city of Plataea. Because Thebes was an ally of Sparta and the Plataeans were allied to Athens, this action was an open breach of the Thirty Years' Peace of 445. So began the great Peloponnesian War, which lasted, with several interruptions, for twenty-seven years. Since ancient times the first ten years of the great war, concluded by the Peace of Nicias in 421, have been regarded as a unit and called, after the name of the Spartan king who led its early campaigns, the Archidamian War.

Examination of the Archidamian War as a unit apart from the events that followed is useful and revealing. Although many surprises took place in the decade of its course, the war was fought essentially within the framework established by those who embarked on it. Departures from the original strategies were necessary, but none compared with the great changes that followed the Peace of Nicias. The sending of an Athenian army into the heart of the Peloponnese in 418, the invasion of Sicily, the shift of the center of warfare from the mainland to the Aegean and the Hellespont, all were unforeseen by the men who began the war. They could not have anticipated what happened after 421, when conditions and personnel presented a completely new situation. Although most of the events of the Archidamian War itself do not in retrospect seem entirely surprising, it is

[1] This chapter owes much to the intelligent and fully detailed account of Busolt (*GG* III: 2, 854–902).

interesting for us to ask how well the several states and their leaders anticipated the course of action. How promising were the strategies followed by each side? Did the Athenians' and Spartans' estimation of the situation in 431 justify their decisions to run the risks of war?

A successful strategy must rest on a clear understanding of the aims for which a war is undertaken and an accurate assessment of one's own resources and weaknesses and those of the enemy. It aims at employing one's own strength against the enemies' weakness. It makes use of, but is not bound by, the experience of the past. It adjusts to changes in conditions, both material and psychological. It considers in advance that its first expectations may be disappointed and has an alternate plan ready. Rarely, however, has a state or statesman embarking upon war been well enough prepared strategically.

Sparta's declared aim in breaking the Thirty Years' Peace was "to liberate Greece," [2] that is, to restore autonomy to the Greek states subject to Athens.[3] Thucydides tells us that the Spartans' true motive was their fear of Athens' growing power.[4] Although the Spartans were always slow to go to war, Athens' use of her power against Sparta's allies made the situation unendurable, "and the Spartans decided they must try with all their might to destroy that power if they could and to launch this war." [5] Whether the Spartans made war to free the Greeks, to defend their allies against Athens and thus to continue to enjoy the security provided by the Spartan alliance, or to restore the uncontested primacy that Sparta had enjoyed in the time of the Persian War, or for all these reasons, makes no difference. Each of these goals seemed to the Spartans to require the destruction of Athenian power, that is, of Athens' walls, which made her secure against the power of the Spartan army, of her fleet, which gave her command of the seas, and of her empire, which provided the money that supported her navy. A strategy aiming

---

[2] 2.8.4. All references are to Thucydides unless otherwise indicated.
[3] 1.139.3. By far the best account of Sparta's strategy in the Archidamian War is provided by P. A. Brunt in *Phoenix* XIX (1965), 255–280.
[4] 1.23.6; 88.   [5] 1.118.

at a peace that left these intact was of no value. Sparta's war aims required that she must take the offensive.

When the war began, the Peloponnesian forces included all the states in the Peloponnese with the exception of the neutral states, Argos and the towns of Achaea other than Pellene.[6] Outside the Peloponnese the members of the Spartan alliance included the Megarians, Boeotians, northern Locrians, and Phocians,[7] and in the west the Corinthian colonies of Ambracia, Leucas, and Anactorium. In Sicily the Spartans were allied to Syracuse and all the Dorian cities except Camarina, and in Italy to Locri and their own colony Taras.[8] The great strength of the Spartan alliance lay in its splendid, heavily armed infantry made up of Peloponnesians and Boeotians. This was two or three times the size of the Athenian hoplite phalanx and universally regarded as abler and more experienced.[9]

At the beginning of the war Pericles had to admit that in a single battle the Peloponnesian army was a match for all the rest

[6] 2.9.2.

[7] 1.9.2; Gomme, HCT II, 11. Busolt (GG III:2, 854) believes that the alliances with central Greek states were made immediately before the outbreak of the war: "Während sie [die Lakedaimonier] mit den Athenern verhandelten." There is no evidence for such an assumption, and we may believe that some of the treaties, that with Thebes, for instance, go back to the time of the First Peloponnesian War.

[8] 3.86.2; 6.34.4; 44; 104.

[9] Pericles announced that the Athenians had 13,000 hoplites fit for combat and not engaged in garrison duty at the beginning of the war (2.13.6). Thucydides does not supply us with figures for the size of the Peloponnesian army, but Plutarch says that 60,000 hoplites invaded Attica in 431 (Plut. Per. 33.5). Since only two-thirds of each contingent took part in the invasion, Plutarch would have 90,000 hoplites available to the Spartan alliance, and that figure is much too large. Busolt believes that the invading army consisted of 22–23,000 Peloponnesians and 7,000 Boeotians, for a total of 30,000, and his calculations are persuasive (GG III:2, 858–861). Beloch (Bevölkerung, 152), Meyer (GdA IV:2, 26 and n. 2), and De Sanctis (Pericle [Milan and Messina, 1944], 257) agree. Other modern estimates are: Duncker (GdA IX, 425) and Bengtson (GG, 221) 40,000, Adcock (CAH V, 193) 34,000, Hammond (History of Greece to 322 B.C., [Oxford, 1959], 345) 50,000, Henderson (Great War, 29) 60,000. The figure given by Androtion (Frg. 39 in FGrH) is corrupt and has been read as either 100,000 or 200,000. Either figure is impossible.

of Greece,[10] and recent history had shown that the Athenians had long been aware of the relative weakness in their hoplite army. In 446 a Spartan army had invaded Attica. Instead of fighting, the Athenians made a truce which soon led to the end of the First Peloponnesian War with the Thirty Years' Peace. The Athenians abandoned their land empire in central Greece and conceded Spartan hegemony on the Greek mainland.[11] The Spartans had good reason to believe that they would be invincible in a land battle against Athens. Such considerations were behind the eagerness of the Spartan war party to undertake the war and their unwillingness to heed the cautious warnings of their King Archidamus. To them the proper strategy was obvious and success inevitable: the Spartans needed merely to invade Attica during the growing season. Almost surely the Athenians would not stay behind their walls and watch their crops, homes, and property destroyed. Either they would yield as they had in 446, or, if their courage allowed, they would come out to fight and be destroyed. In either case the war would be short and Spartan victory certain.

To be sure, the Spartans realized that the Athenians might choose neither to fight nor to surrender immediately, for Athens was like no other Greek city—it was defended by stout walls, as was its port, Piraeus, and the two were connected by the Long Walls, no less strong. Greek armies rarely took a fortified place by assault, and the Spartans were less skillful at siege warfare than most.[12] The Athenians, because of their navy and their empire, could hold out by bringing supplies from abroad even though deprived of their own lands. Still, the Spartans did not believe that any people could put up with such conditions for long: the Athenians might hold out for a year or two, but certainly not more. When the war began the Spartans expected that "they would destroy the power of the Athenians in a few years if they wasted their land."[13] Nor did that expectation seem rash, for the Athenians themselves were in a pessimistic mood,[14] and Thucydides tells us that at the beginning of the war the Greeks in general shared their view: if the Peloponnesians

[10] 1.141.6.   [11] See Kagan, *Outbreak*, 124–130.   [12] 1.102.2.
[13] 5.14.3.   [14] 6.11.5.

should invade Attica, "some thought that Athens could hold out for a year, some for two, but no one for more than three years."[15]

King Archidamus was more cautious. He expected that Athens could hold out indefinitely without either giving battle or surrendering. In such circumstances superiority in arms and numbers would be of no use. The Spartans would need another strategy, but what could it be? The only alternative was to incite rebellion among the allies of Athens and thereby deprive her of the men, ships, and money she needed to survive. But, since the Athenian Empire was chiefly maritime, this strategy required that Sparta have the ships necessary to encourage and support rebellions of the islanders, and these, in turn, required money. As Archidamus pointed out, the Peloponnesians were vastly inferior in financial resources, "having neither money in the public treasury nor being able readily to raise money from taxation."[16]

On the eve of the war the Peloponnesians had a fleet of about 100 triremes,[17] most of these recently built by Corinth for the war against Corcyra. These required rowers, steersmen, and captains skilled in the maneuvers of modern naval warfare which had been perfected by the Athenians. Such men were in short supply in the Peloponnese; for their war against Corcyra the Corinthians had been forced to hire rowers at high pay from all over Greece.[18] Most of these must have come from the Aegean, the Athenian sphere of influence, and they would no longer be available to the Peloponnesians in a war against Athens. At the battle of Sybota both the Corinthian and Corcyrean fleets had employed archaic tactics.[19] In a naval war the Peloponnesians would be inferior in ships, sailors, and tactics.

Conscious of these weaknesses, Archidamus advised the Spartans to consider the Athenian offer of arbitration rather than go to war immediately. If negotiation failed he urged them at least to wait until they had repaired their naval and financial deficiencies.[20] The Corinthians, eager for war, tried to make light of the difficulties described by Archidamus, because of the Peloponnesian superiority in numbers, military experience, and discipline.

[15] 7.28.3.   [16] 1.80.4.   [17] Busolt, *GG* III:2, 863–864.
[18] 1.31.1.   [19] 1.49.   [20] 1.82, 85.

They believed that the fleet could be paid for with funds from the Delphic and Olympian treasuries and with money contributions from the Peloponnesian allies themselves. One victory at sea would destroy Athenian power, for it would lead the allied rowers, mere mercenaries, to defect to the winning side. If, on the other hand, the war continued, time was on the Peloponnesian side for it could be used to acquire the naval experience which, combined with superior courage, would guarantee victory. Besides, the Corinthians argued, they could persuade the Athenian allies to revolt, erect permanent forts in Attica, and use all "all the other such devices as cannot now be foreseen." [21]

The last few words tell how little conviction the Corinthian arguments carried for Spartans like Archidamus. They emphasized the vagaries of war which "least of all follows fixed rules and itself contrives its own devices to meet events," [22] but Pericles also knew the vanity of Corinthian optimism. He pointed out that the Peloponnesians were farmers, without naval skills and unable to leave their fields for long. They would face difficulty in recruiting experienced sailors from the Athenian Empire even with the offer of higher pay, for the sailors would be reluctant to risk exile from home when the chances of victory seemed slight. The prospects of the Peloponnesians acquiring naval skill were dim, for this required much practice, and the overwhelming preponderance of the Athenian navy guaranteed that few Peloponnesian sailors who had the experience of a naval battle against the Athenians would survive to benefit from it.[23] Naval training, moreover, required money which the Peloponnesians did not have and could not get. Pericles saw little possibility of "contributions." Most of the Peloponnesian states were poor; they were unable or unwilling to make such contributions. Besides, "accumulated wealth, not forced contributions, sustain a war." [24] The suggestion that money could be obtained from the sacred places was chimerical. The Eleans, who controlled Olympia, would not have allowed it, nor were the priests there or at

---

[21] 1.122.1; the Corinthian argument is presented in 1.121–122.
[22] 1.121.1.
[23] 1.141.4; 143.2; 142.6; see Brunt, *Phoenix* XIX (1965), 259.
[24] 1.141.5.

Delphi likely to have approved. To seize the treasures by force would be sacrilege and might alienate the Hellenic good will so necessary for Spartan success. The suggestion was never acted upon during the war, even in moments of the greatest need. Brunt may be right when he says that the Corinthians made the suggestion because "they were more exposed to the sophistic *Aufklärung* than the majority of the Peloponnesians." [25]

The Spartans and their friends hoped, no doubt, for help from abroad, but with little justification. At the start of the war, the Spartans ordered their allies in Sicily to provide them with a fleet and money, but they should not have been surprised when it was not forthcoming. The Greeks of the west had not intervened in the affairs of mainland Greece in the past and they would not do so during the Archidamian War.[26] Nor should the Spartans have expected a favorable reply from the Great King of Persia. They found it difficult even to get a messenger safely through to the court at Susa, and when they did they found themselves irreconcilably at odds with the Persians. The Great King, of course, had good reason to fear the might of the Athenian navy. He would have been glad to see Athens humbled, but he was not likely to run the risk of a war as long as her fleet was intact. In any case, the king's major interest in such a war was the recovery of the territory inhabited by the Greeks of Asia Minor. The Spartans who were fighting "to bring freedom to the Greeks" could hardly have agreed to his terms.[27]

We can see, and the Spartans should have realized, that Archidamus was right. At the beginning of the war Sparta was with-

---

[25] Brunt, *Phoenix* XIX (1965), 261.

[26] Thucydides (2.7.2) tells us that the Spartans asked for 500 ships at the start of the war. Diodorus (12.41.1) gives the figure of 200. Both numbers are impossible, for no such fleet was available nor were the Sicilians likely to build one. Busolt (*GG* III:2, 866) thinks that Thucydides gives this figure ironically, but Gomme does not think so (see Gomme, *HCT* II, 7). It is difficult to explain the passage. Perhaps the optimistic request was made by the war party in full knowledge of its absurdity, with the intention chiefly of responding to the arguments of Archidamus and reassuring hesitating Spartans with visions of powerful naval support.

[27] Brunt, *Phoenix* XIX (1965), 262–263.

out a fleet or the prospect of getting one large enough to attack the Athenian fleet and so was unable to attack her empire or encourage defections from it. The Spartans had to face the fact that their only plan of warfare was likely to founder on the Athenian unwillingness to give battle, even if the Spartans invaded and destroyed their crops and homes. If the Athenians were willing to follow such a policy the Spartans could not defeat them, yet the Spartans went to war. The reason is not far to seek. For all the good sense of Archidamus, his countrymen did not want to believe him. They were moved by fear, anger, and their memory of the past. In 446 when the Spartans invaded Attica, the Athenians had chosen not to fight, but to accept a reduction in their power rather than destruction at the hands of the Spartan phalanx. At that time, too, the Athenians had walls, ships, and money, yet no more than other Greeks could they stand by and see their fields wasted. But even if Archidamus were right and the Athenians were not now like other enemies, they might hide behind their walls for a year or two, possibly three, but then they must surrender. What did it matter if alternate strategies were defective? They had no need of other strategies. So thought the Spartans and the rest of the Greeks as well.[28]

The war aims of Athens under Pericles were completely defensive. She had no ambitions for territorial gain and no intention of destroying Spartan power or hegemony in the Peloponnese. Pericles himself made this clear when he spoke to the Athenians on the eve of war: "Many other things, too, lead me to expect victory if you will agree not to try to extend your empire while you are at war and not to expose yourselves to dangers of your own choosing." [29] He spelled out his meaning in greater detail shortly after the war had begun,[30] and Thucydides recapitulates the policy he advocated when he speaks of the death of Pericles: "He said that if the Athenians would remain quiet, take care of their fleet, refrain from trying to extend their empire in wartime and thus putting their city in danger, they would prevail." [31] Precisely what victory might mean is not, of course, clear. The success of Pericles' plan would lead to a stale-

[28] See above, pp. 20–21.   [29] 1.144.1.   [30] 2.13.2.   [31] 2.65.7.

mate that would at least guarantee the security of Athens and her empire. Brunt, however, points out that "a stalemate might be more than a defensive success. If Sparta failed in her published aims and real designs, the reaction might be momentous. The shock to her reputation might dissolve her confederacy. Athens might recover control of the Isthmus, and even displace Sparta in the hegemony of the Peloponnese." [32] These expectations seem far too optimistic. Sparta had suffered Peloponnesian defections in the past and always managed to put the rebellions down. She would do so again in 421. Athens could only hope to produce such grand results if she were prepared to send an army into the Peloponnese to face the Spartans, and this Pericles was unwilling to do. Whatever the value of these speculations, we have no reason to believe that they played any part in the thoughts of Pericles. He never mentions such notions in his speeches even though they might have helped win support for his unusual strategy. We may believe that his aims when the war began were to restore the status quo as of 445, a world in which Athens and her empire and Sparta with her league, realizing that they had no way of imposing their will on Athens, would live peacefully, each respecting the integrity of the other.

The achievement of these moderate war aims seemed to Pericles well within the capacity of Athens. At the outbreak of the war the Athenians could boast of free allies like Chios, Lesbos, and Corcyra, who provided ships of their own to add to the Athenian fleet, and the Plataeans, the Messenians who inhabited Naupactus, the Zacynthians, and most of the Acarnanians, who supplied infantry and money when called upon.[33] They could also count on the cavalry of the Thessalians [34] and, if it should be necessary to counter the western allies of Sparta, they had their own allies in the west, Rhegium and Leontini.[35] In addition they could call on the considerable resources of their tribute-paying imperial allies for money and men. That empire included, as Thucydides tells us, the seaboard cities of Caria,

[32] Brunt, *Phoenix* XIX (1965), 259.
[33] 2.9.4–6; Gomme, *HCT* II, 12.   [34] 1.102.4, 2.22.4.
[35] 3.86.3, *GHI*, nos. 63 and 64.

Ionia, the Hellespont, and Thrace, as well as all the islands "which lie between the Peloponnesus and Crete toward the east, except Melos and Thera." [36]

The power and hopes of Athens rested on 'her magnificent navy. In her dockyards lay at least 300 seaworthy triremes; to these could be added a number of older ships which could be repaired and used in case of need.[37] In addition Chios, Lesbos, and Corcyra could provide ships, perhaps over 100 in all.[38] The men who steered and rowed these ships, both Athenian citizens and allies, were far more skilled than their opponents, as the battle of Sybota had already shown and as the whole course of the Archidamian War would continue to demonstrate.[39]

The Athenians had strong financial resources to maintain the ships and pay their crews. In 431 the annual income of Athens was 1,000 talents, of which 400 came from internal revenue and 600 from the tribute and other imperial sources.[40] Although the considerable sum of about 600 talents annually was available for the costs of war, it would hardly be adequate. Athens would need to dip into her capital, and here, too, she was uniquely well provided. In the spring of 431, Pericles encour-

[36] 2.9.4-5. By 430-429, Thera was paying tribute to Athens, although Thucydides does not tell us how she came to do so. See Gomme, *HCT* II, 12.

[37] 2.13.8; Busolt, *GG* III:2, 868 and n. 1.

[38] Busolt, *GG* III:2, 869-870. Meyer (*Forsch.*, II, 169 and n. 3) and Miltner (*P.W.* XIX [1937], s.v. "Perikles," 781) following the Old Oligarch (3.4) set the figure of Athenian triremes at 400. Xenophon (*Anab.* 7.1.27) and Andocides (3.9) give the same figure. Aristophanes (*Acharnians* 544) and Aeschines (2.175) support the figure 300. Meyer and Miltner resolve the contradiction by adding the 100 ships which were set aside as a reserve force after the Spartan invasion of 431 to the original 300. They may be right.

[39] Brunt, *Phoenix* XIX (1965), 259-260.

[40] The figure for the annual revenue comes from Xenophon (*Anab.* 7.1.27). Thucydides tells us that an average of 600 talents came from tribute (2.13.3). Since the tribute lists show that so high a figure is impossible, it is generally agreed that Thucydides is speaking loosely and means "all the revenue contributed by the allies" (Gomme, *HCT* II, 17; see also *ATL* III, 333-334). The other 400 talents, coming from such sources as rents, customs duties, market taxes, and court fees, went to pay for current expenses and provided no surplus (Busolt, *GG* III:2, 876; *ATL* III, 333; cf., however, Gomme, *HCT* II, 19. For another view see A. French, *Historia* XXI [1972], 1-20).

aged his fellow citizens by pointing out that there were in reserve on the Acropolis 6,000 talents of coined silver remaining from the maximum figure of 9,700 which had been reached some time before.[41] In addition there was uncoined gold and silver worth at least 500 talents on the Acropolis as well as no small sum in other temples. Finally, if the Athenians were in desperate straits they could melt down the gold plates with which the great statue of Athena on the Acropolis was covered. These were removable and worth 40 talents.[42] Such an income and such a reserve fund were unexampled among the Greek states and certainly not to be matched by all the Peloponnesian allies together.

These resources would be needed also to support the land forces of Athens which, though not equal to those of the enemy, were far from inconsiderable. These included 13,000 hoplites of an age and condition suitable for service in the field. There were also 16,000 others who were metics and men too young or too old for the battlefield; these troops were capable of defending the border forts of Attica and the city walls of Athens and the Piraeus as well as the Long Walls connecting them.[43] The Athenians also had available 1,200 cavalry including mounted archers and 1,600 bowmen on foot.[44] These were ample for the defensive strategy Pericles had in mind.

But what, precisely, was that strategy? Most scholars agree that the aims of the Athenians were defensive and did not include conquest, but how were those aims to be achieved?

[41] 2.13.3. I accept the figures given in the manuscripts rather than those provided by a scholiast to Aristophanes' *Plutus* 1193 which are defended by the authors of *ATL* (III, 118–132). Their arguments appear strained and not weighty enough to support the scholiast against the unanimous evidence of the MSS as well as Diodorus (12.40.2) and Isocrates (8.69 and 15.234). Gomme makes an effective attack against the *ATL* arguments (*Historia* II [1953], 1–21, and *HCT* II, 16–33).

[42] 2.13.4–5; for a discussion of the disagreement among ancient authors on the value of the gold on the statue see Gomme, *HCT* II, 24–25.

[43] 2.13.6–7. Diodorus (12.40.4–5) gives the figures as 12,000 hoplites for the field and 17,000 garrison troops. Although the Thucydidean figures have been challenged they stand up well and I accept them. They are ably defended by Gomme in *CQ* XXI (1927), 142–150, and again in *HCT* II, 34–39.

[44] 2.13.8.

Thucydides' account of the words of Pericles as well as his own summary of the Periclean strategy [45] make it plain that the Athenians were to reject a battle on land, abandon their fields to devastation, retreat behind their walls, and wait until the exhausted enemy was ready to make peace. Just how the enemy was to be exhausted is not clear. It would be annoying, of course, to march out each summer and spend a month or so ravaging the Attic countryside, but not exhausting. Pericles mentioned two possible means of doing damage to the Peloponnesians: building a fortified camp in the Peloponnesus and launching seaborne attacks upon the Peloponnesian coast. [46] The scheme of planting a fort in the Peloponnese need not be taken seriously, for it was not seriously intended by Pericles. The suggestion was made as part of a hypothetical situation: "Suppose the enemy does establish a fort in Attica and damages our land with raids and receives our deserters, still he will not be able to prevent us from sailing to his land where we can build a fort, nor from attacking him by sea." [47] The fort in the Peloponnese was suggested merely as a possible response to a possible Spartan action. The Spartans did not take that action until well after the Archidamian War was over, so that Pericles did not need to think of the fort again unless it formed a part of his original plan. In fact, he never mentioned the idea again so far as we know. More telling yet, he made no attempt to establish such a fort in the first year of the war, although he did engage immediately in seaborne raids on the Peloponnese. We may therefore disregard the construction of a fortress on the Peloponnese as part of the offensive element of the Periclean strategy.

It remains to decide what part the Athenian fleet was meant to play in forcing the Spartans to make peace. Some scholars, critical of Pericles' strategy in greater or lesser degree, consider his employment of the fleet of no value whatever. [48] Others see

---

[45] 2.65.7.   [46] 1.142.4.   [47] Ibid.

[48] Beloch (GG² II: 1, 300, n. 1) speaks of "die unfruchtbare Flottendemonstration"; De Sanctis (Storia dei Greci [Florence, 1963], II, 267–268) says that the Athenians' reaction to the Peloponnesian invasions "non poteva consistere che nel dannagiare i commerci e nel operare piccoli sbarchi sulle coste del Peloponneso." Henderson (Great War, 62) believes that "these naval parades round the Peloponnese were extraordinarily futile."

coastal landings and raids as having had some purpose as countermeasures to the Peloponnesian invasions of Attica; these might
have had some strategic value, if only in raising Athenian
morale.[49] But there is more general agreement that the naval
campaigns urged by Pericles were neither pointless nor trivial
in their aims. One view that has won considerable support is that
the main task of the Athenian navy was to impose and maintain
a blockade of the Peloponnesus.[50] In its most ambitious form this
view suggests that Pericles intended to cut off the grain supply
to the Peloponnesus by closing off the Gulf of Corinth through
control of Naupactus.[51] Such a scheme was impossible. In the
first place it is far from clear that imported grain was necessary
for the survival of the Peloponnesians and that the deprivation
of imported grain would have been more than an annoyance.
More important, a blockade of the entire peninsula could not
have been achieved. "The Peloponnese has a long coastline containing many harbours easily accessible to ancient ships, and
whereas triremes, not being designed to carry large quantities of
food and water, normally hugged the shore and did not remain
long away from their bases, merchant ships did not share these
limitations and could, if necessary, cross the open sea." [52]

A blockade of coastal states on or near the isthmus, such as
Corinth, Megara, and Sicyon, might have been more serious and
more successful.[53] However dependent on imports the Peloponnesians may have been, there can be no doubt that their economic prosperity would have been severely damaged if these
areas were cut off from markets in the Aegean, Asiatic, and
Hellespontine areas by Athenian domination [54] or if an Athenian

[49] Bengtson, *GG*, 222, speaks of the landings as "Gegenaktionen";
Grundy, *Thucydides*, 331, gives some support to the notion of Athenian
morale as the point of the raids. See the discussion of Westlake, *Essays*,
91–92.
[50] Some version of this theory has been held by Busolt (*GG* III:2,
899–900) and Miltner ("Perikles," 781).
[51] Miltner, "Perikles," 781.   [52] Westlake, *Essays*, 88.
[53] The Corinthians mention the danger of Athenian naval power to
the economy even of inland states, 1.120.2.
[54] Busolt (*GG* III:1, 588) and Miltner ("Perikles," 781) make a great
point of Athenian control of grain shipments passing through Byzantium
that permitted even allies of Athens to obtain grain only under special
conditions (*IG*² 57 = *GHI* 65, 11.35ff.). There is no evidence that these

squadron at Naupactus cut them off from important markets in the west. The establishment of an effective blockade would have done great harm to states like Corinth, which depended on the export of bronze work, pottery, textiles, and other goods for much of its prosperity. We may perhaps believe that, "if Athens were successful in the blockade, or even in interrupting trade to a large extent, a pressing state of distress would gradually grow in the Peloponnese, then the unfailing economic ruin of the coastal states, especially Corinth, would also involve the hinterland," [55] but such a blockade was not part of Pericles' plan at the outbreak of the war. The most crucial element of such a blockade would have been the location of a fleet at Naupactus and this the Athenians did not carry out until the winter of 430/29.[56] Two campaigning seasons were permitted to go by before Pericles even attempted to seal off the Gulf of Corinth. He could not, therefore, have been thinking of a blockade as part of his battle plan in 431.

Still other historians, making no use of the notion of an Athenian blockade, nonetheless believe that Pericles planned a vigorous use of the fleet in an offensive strategy. "If the strategy of Pericles was defensive by land, it was offensive by sea." [57] The navy would force encounters on the sea and make landings on the Peloponnese; "and if occasion arose, it might establish fortified posts on enemy territory." [58] Another version says, "If Pericles recognized the necessity of conducting a defensive war and avoiding any battle, that did not mean that Athens should sink into passivity. On the contrary, if the Peloponnesians devastated Attica, Athens, with its fleet and landings and devastation of their coastal territory, could do at least equal damage." [59] We have already seen that Pericles did not intend to establish forts in the Peloponnese, and it is also plain that the devastations of the

provisions were part of any blockade, in fact it is likely that they were intended chiefly to guarantee the grain supply of Athens. In any case the inscription belongs in 426/5, so we have no reason to believe that a policy of blockade at the Hellespont was part of the Periclean strategy at the start of the war.

[55] Busolt, GG III:2, 900.   [56] 2.69.1.
[57] Hammond, *History of Greece*, 348.   [58] *Ibid.*, 347.
[59] Meyer, *GdA* IV, 32.

Peloponnesian coast could not have done as much damage as the leveling of Attica.[60]

Westlake offers the most plausible explanation of Pericles' offensive intentions: "The devastation of enemy territory, which was the chief achievement of these operations, was also their chief object, being designed to cause so much economic distress that political consequences would ensue and the Peloponnesian League would have no heart to continue the war." [61] This suggestion has the advantage of not projecting onto the Periclean strategy actions which were never taken during the lifetime of Pericles and of assuming that the actions that were undertaken in that period has a purpose connected with their results. Seaborne raids might cause distress "both physical and psychological"; political opposition, typically democratic, within the affected city would try to bring in the Athenians and to overthrow the pro-Spartan oligarchs.[62] Unfortunately, three instances adduced by Westlake to support his suggestion come from a period well after the death of Pericles, when policy was in the hands of the successors whom Thucydides found so unworthy, and the fourth, the attack on Epidaurus in 430, will not bear scrutiny. Thucydides tells us nothing about the internal condition of Epidaurus when Pericles attacked it, nor does any other ancient authority. Westlake's inclusion of that incident is based on an unsupported conjecture by Adcock.[63]

The other three instances offered by Westlake in support of his thesis are the attempted seizure of Megara and the alliances Athens made with Troezen and Halieis.[64] In Troezen and

---

[60] See Beloch, *GG*[2] II:1, 300; De Sanctis, *Storia di Greci* II, 268, and Westlake, *Essays*, 94.

[61] Westlake, *Essays*, 99–100.   [62] *Ibid.*, 95.

[63] *CAH* V, 200, cited by Westlake, *Essays*, 95. Delbrück, who may have been the source of Adcock's speculation, makes the same suggestion, and his reason is clear. He is trying to explain why Pericles did not launch so potentially important a campaign in the very first year of the war, and as one of two lame attempts at explanation he invents a revolutionary party in Epidaurus which was ready to support Athens in 430 but not yet in 431 (*Strategie*, 121–122). We have no reason to believe that the attack on Epidaurus was prepared by negotiations with dissidents within the city or that it was anything but a simple assault.

[64] Megara: Thuc. 3.51; 4.66–74; Troezen: Thuc. 4.45.2, 118.4; Halieis: Thuc. 4.45.2; *IG* I[2], 87, Bengtson, *Staatsverträge* II, 184.

Halieis there is evidence for Athenian raids followed by a treaty; there is no evidence for political strife in the cities or for a domestic upheaval. In all three cases, the final Athenian action —treaties concluded in two cases, an attack aided by treason in the other—the ground had been prepared by the establishment of a fortress in the vicinity—Minoa, an island near Megara, and Methana, a town in the region of Troezen and Halieis. That is, the final stroke came as a result of the policy eschewed by Pericles in the years he was in command. None of these actions took place until after 425, in the seventh and eighth years of the war. It should not surprise us that one of the demands made by Cleon, the devotee of an active and aggressive strategy, was the restoration of Troezen to Athens.[65] We have no reason, therefore, to attribute so aggressive a policy to Pericles at the outbreak of the war.

The fact is that the Athenian failure to prosecute the naval war more actively has led to criticism of Pericles not only by those who deplore the defensive strategy in general [66] but by those who approve the general strategy and try to defend it and Pericles. Busolt, for instance, judges Pericles' plan "fundamentally right" but concedes that it was "somewhat one-sided and doctrinaire, and in its execution it was lacking in energetic procedure and in the spirit of enterprise." [67] Bengtson, too, while defending the Periclean plan against its critics, admits "that the carrying out of the offensive part of the plan appears to modern viewers as not very energetic and resolute." [68] By far the ablest and most influential defender of Pericles' strategy is Delbrück; he vigorously rejects those who would have had the Athenians launch an aggressive war on land and awards Pericles a place "among the greatest generals in world history" for his ability to impose upon a free people the difficult, unpopular, but necessary strategy of exhaustion.[69] Still, he too is troubled by the Athenian failure to use the navy more aggressively to help bring about that exhaustion.

---

[65] 4.21.3.   [66] E.g., Beloch, Duncker, Pflugk-Hartung.
[67] GG III:2, 901.   [68] GG, 221, n. 5.
[69] Geschichte der Kriegskunst I, Das Altertum (Berlin, 1920), reprinted 1964, 124–133.

Delbrück's defense of Pericles is based upon a comparison with the strategy of Frederick the Great during the Seven Years' War. Frederick was able to win a great and difficult war by use of the strategy of exhaustion. But that war was finally decided by major battles which Frederick undertook when he was ready. Where were the equivalent actions of Pericles and how did he hope to win his war? [70] Delbrück argues first that we should not look for precise parallels where historical circumstances are different. Frederick was weaker than his opponents but had forces of the same kind, a land army; thus he could use the strategy of exhaustion to bring about a decisive battle on his own terms. Pericles faced a situation where neither side could bring the other to battle since one was a naval power and the other military; thus he had to plan to damage the enemy in other ways. Delbrück lists first the wasting of the enemy's land by raids and grossly overvalues their effect. Next Pericles could create a secondary theater of war, such as the one later established in Acarnania, where a partial force might dare to fight limited land battles under certain conditions. Also, he could establish forts on the enemy coast, such as the one later established at Pylos in Messenia. "Finally, the conquest or the taking by surprise of enemy coastal states: Epidaurus, Hermione, Gytheum, perhaps even Megara or Troezen." [71] Then he confronts the difficult question: if the physical exhaustion of the enemy was intended and these tactics were suitable for bringing on that exhaustion, why did not Pericles employ them all in the first year of the war instead of contenting himself with coastal raids and devastations which appear to have had little effect? Here Delbrück's answer is unconvincing: "The greatest power in the strategy of exhaustion is time, and hence one of the fundamental laws, the economy of resources. However much might be achieved even in a first campaign with the indicated stratagems, they would still not have brought the enemy to defeat or to peace." [72] But we must ask if it would not have been far more effective to begin immediately to do real damage to the Peloponnese instead of being satisfied with trifling annoyances? Would it not have had a great effect on Athenian morale to bring off a real achievement

[70] *Strategie*, 101, 108.   [71] *Ibid.*, 112–113.   [72] *Ibid.*, 113.

on the offensive side and thus help justify the difficult strategy
of passivity in Attica? If the enemy were to be worn down, the
first year of the war would seem to be a splendid time to begin
in earnest.

Delbrück is keenly aware of the weakness of his argument for
he returns to it more than once. Why, he asks, did Pericles not
decide on such a powerful blow as the attack on Epidaurus in
the first year of the war instead of waiting until 430? "If such a
conquest had succeeded, any success in Acarnania, any campaign of devastation, however intensive, any fortification of a
coastal spot in Messenia would disappear in comparison." The
possession of Epidaurus would have faced Troezen, Hermione,
and perhaps Sicyon with the prospect of a similar fate. If it did
not bring peace immediately it would at least help diminish the
eagerness for war of the Peloponnesian states. He is compelled
to answer, "We do not know." [73] All he can do is to offer two
attempts at explanation which are unsupported by the evidence
and unpersuasive.[74] Delbrück also considers the fact that the

[73] *Ibid.*, 121

[74] One, which suggests that the Athenians delayed the attack for a
year because they were waiting for a dissident faction in Epidaurus to be
ready, we have discussed above in n. 63. The unlikelihood of the suggestion is plain when we consider not only that the ancient sources make
no mention of internal dissension in Epidaurus in 430 but also that they
make no mention of any civil strife there at any time during the Peloponnesian War. This is true even though the territory of Epidaurus was the
scene of fighting for much of the war and the Athenians built a fort in
the region on one occasion. These are the classical conditions for bringing on internal rebellion, yet Thucydides gives us no hint of any in
Epidaurus, though he tells us of such a rebellion in neighboring Argos.
The argument from silence here is very strong. Delbrück's second argument is that Pericles waited until 430 to attack Epidaurus because he did
not want to entrust the campaign to another general, and he, himself,
could not afford to leave Athens in 431. This is even weaker than the
first. In the first place, Pericles often entrusted important difficult campaigns to trusted generals. The fact is that after the attack on Epidaurus
had failed, the Athenians put the fleet and army into the hands of
Hagnon, a reliable associate of Pericles, and sent him to try to take
Potidaea. Besides, if it was not politic for Pericles to leave Athens in
431 it was even less so a year later when the plague had broken out,
the people were restless, the opposition powerful, and the need for
Pericles' influence at home enormous.

Athenians sent a fleet to Naupactus only in the autumn of 429, although the closing of the Corinthian Gulf was one of the most important Athenian weapons of war. "This measure appears so natural that we ask why wasn't it hit upon the first day of the war?" Conceding that no positive answer is possible, he suggests that the cost of maintaining 20 ships the year round, which he places at 240 talents, more than half the annual tribute collected from the allies, deterred Pericles. The ships were finally sent out in connection with the establishment of a new theater of warfare in Acarnania. This double function, presumably, justified the expense.[75] If Pericles could not afford to send a fleet to close off the Corinthian Gulf, particularly in the first year of the war, the whole strategy of exhaustion was absurd. Nothing was more likely to cause economic damage to the Isthmian states and to bring home to them the high price of fighting the Athenians.[76]

This discussion is designed to show that no theory, not even those argued so intelligently and learnedly by Westlake and Delbrück, that tries to see in the strategy employed by Pericles at the start of the war an aggressive attempt to exhaust the Peloponnesians physically by the use of the fleet alone or in conjunction with the army will hold. Pericles failed to take the offensive vigorously in the first year of the war not because he lacked the ability or daring as a commander to execute the measures he had planned as a strategist; his strategy did not include a serious attempt at offense. The fact is that Pericles did not intend to exhaust the Peloponnesians physically but psychologically. He meant to convince the Spartans, the important enemy, that they could not win a war against Athens. When convinced, they must make peace. The strategy of Pericles, both its major defensive and slight offensive aspects, was aimed at this goal, and Adcock has put it well: "[Pericles] must first prove that the existence of Athens and of the Athenian Empire could not be destroyed and then that Athens, too, could harm her enemies. . . . It was a reasonable calculation that the nerve and

[75] Delbrück, *Strategie*, 132–133.
[76] For a discussion of other, less thorough and less persuasive, arguments for an aggressive Periclean policy see the concluding chapter.

will-power of her opponents might well be exhausted before the treasures on the Acropolis, and that they might admit that the power and determination of Athens were invincible." [77]

An important question remains: how long did Pericles expect the Spartans to hold out? The question is generally not asked by those who regard the outcome of the Archidamian War as the justification for his strategy, but their implicit reasoning is that a war of ten years was not outside his calculations. No doubt this view rests in part on Pericles' speech to the Athenians on the eve of the war. The Peloponnesians, he says, "have had no experience with wars overseas or extended in time; they only wage brief wars against each other because of their poverty." [78] As men who farm their own lands (*autourgoi*), they cannot stay away from their farms and must bear the cost of expeditions from their own funds. Such men will risk their lives rather than their property, "for they have confidence that they will survive the dangers but they are not sure that they won't use up their funds first, especially if the war lasts longer than they expected, which is quite likely." [79]

Pericles rightly argued that the Peloponnesians lacked the resources to launch the kind of campaign which would have endangered the Athenian Empire, but nothing prevented them from continuing to undertake annual invasions and devastations of Attica. This is essentially what they did until the taking of Spartan hostages at Sphacteria in 425 put an end to such invasions. Pericles could not have foreseen this fortuitous benefit and must have counted on such campaigns as a regular feature of the war, for there was no material reason why the Peloponnesians could not continue them for an indefinite time. A better test of Pericles' expectations is to ask how long he thought Athens could continue the war pursuing the strategy with which she began it. Busolt seems to be alone in having studied this question in some detail.[80] He calculates that "the available money supply was sufficient to carry on the naval war against the

---

[77] *CAH* V, 195–196.   [78] 1.142.3.

[79] 1.141.5–6. The key clause is τὸ δὲ οὐ βέβαιον μὴ οὐ προαναλώσειν, ἄλλως τε κἂν παρὰ δόξαν, ὅπερ εἰκός, ὁ πόλεμος αὐτοῖς μηκύνηται.

[80] *GG* III:2, 876–878. 893 with n. 3; see also III:1, 551, n. 1.

Peloponnesians energetically and with superior power, without exhausting all reserves, for about four or five years." [81] He reasons that the experience of the Samian War would justify an estimate of about 1,500 to 1,600 talents annually to support the war; if it lasted five years it would cost 7,500 to 8,000 talents. The Athenians began the war with a reserve fund of 5,000 talents, excluding the 1,000 that they set aside for extreme emergency, "in case the enemy should attack the city with a fleet." [82] To this sum should be added 3,000 talents for five years, revenue from the empire at 600 per annum, bringing the total fund available to Athens for five years of war to 8,000 talents. The Athenians would be unable to pay for the sixth year of such a war.[83]

These calculations certainly do not overestimate the cost of the war; in fact the expense Pericles could expect to incur by the strategy we have described might well have come to over 2,000 talents annually. Epigraphical evidence shows that the Athenians borrowed 1,404 talents from the treasury of Athena for the war against Samos and the suppression of Byzantium connected to that war.[84] Busolt uses this figure as the basis for arriving at his estimate of the total cost of the war. But that is to assume that the Athenians did not employ the full 600 talents that they received as income from the empire before borrowing whatever they needed in addition, a most unlikely assumption. Thus we may conclude that the cost of the Samian War, on which Pericles might have based his expectations of the cost of the Archidamian War, was probably about 2,000 talents annually.[85]

[81] GG III:2, 878; on page 892 he says that Pericles "could not conceal that the war would last for some time, but he probably expected it to end victoriously within five years."

[82] 2.24.1.

[83] Busolt, GG III:2, 893, n. 3. Busolt's calculations of the cost of the Samian War are to be found in GG III:1, 551, n. 1.

[84] IG I², 293 = GHI, 55.

[85] Duncker (GdA IX, 215 and n. 1). already had pointed out that the annual tribute should be added to the borrowed sum, but Busolt ignored the argument. There is no need to refute Isocrates (XV, 111), who gives the figure 1,000, or Nepos (Timotheus 1) and Diodorus (12.28.3: τιμησάμενος αὐτὰς ταλάντων ⟨χιλίων⟩ διακοσίων, with the insertion of chiliōn before diakosiōn), who set it at 1,200, for the inscriptions make a higher figure for the total cost of the war necessary.

A reasonable estimate of the actual cost of the first few years of the Archidamian War, moreover, shows that 2,000 talents annually cannot be far from the truth.

This conclusion is well supported by an examination of the cost of the first year of the war, which was as unadventurous as any year could be while Athens was still in good fighting condition.[86] When the Peloponnesians invaded Attica in the spring of 431 the Athenians sent 100 ships round the Peloponnese.[87] At the same time they sent a squadron of 30 ships to Locris, where they were to operate and at the same time protect Euboea.[88] There were already about 70 ships blockading Potidaea from the sea.[89] This gives a total of 200 Athenian ships in service for the year. If we accept the usual estimates of about one talent as the cost of maintaining a trireme at sea for a month, and eight months as the period that a fleet could be kept at sea, we arrive at a figure of 1,600 for naval expenses.[90] To this must

[86] Succeeding years in the lifetime of Pericles saw such undertakings as the sending of 4,000 hoplites and 300 cavalry to Epidaurus in 430 and the sending of Phormio with 20 ships to Naupactus in 429.

[87] 2.25.1.   [88] 2.26.1.

[89] Thirty had been sent with the first expedition under Archestratus (1.57) and an additional 40 under the command of Callias (1.61). We are not told if any triremes were sent with the reinforcements led by Phormio (1.67), but there probably were some.

[90] The figure of a talent a month for each trireme is arrived at by multiplying the 200 men who manned a trireme by thirty days in an average month by the salary of one drachma per sailor (the salary attested by Thucydides [3.17.3, 6.31.3]) yielding 6,000 drachmas or one talent per month. The figure of eight months is given by Plutarch (*Per.* 11.4) for the peacetime navy. Probably the ships blockading Potidaea and those guarding Euboea remained in service throughout the year, in which case our figure must be raised considerably. For a slightly lower estimate of the cost of maintaining a trireme see S. K. Eddy, *GRBS* IX (1968), 142–143. The figure could be cut in half by setting the pay of rowers at three obols. That is what A. Boeckh (*Die Staatshaushaltung der Athener*, 3d ed. [Berlin, 1886], I, 344) did, and he was followed by Gomme, among others. In 6.31.3, however, Thucydides says flatly that in 415 rowers were paid a drachma a day; in 3.17.3 he says that in Potidaea even the servants of the hoplites received that wage. In 6.8.1, he tells us that the Segestans brought to Athens sixty talents as a month's pay for sixty ships, which comes to a drachma per man each day. The evidence for a salary of a drachma during the war and even before is solid. See the excellent discussion by Dover and Andrewes in Gomme, *HCT* IV, 293.

be added the military costs, of which the greatest portion was spent at Potidaea. There were never fewer than 3,000 hoplites engaged in the siege there, and to that number Phormio added 1,600 who did not, however, remain throughout the whole siege. We may conservatively set the average number of troops at Potidaea at 3,500. These men were paid a drachma for themselves and one for a retainer each day, so that the daily cost of the army was at least 7,000 drachmas, or one and one-sixth talents. If we multiply this by 360 days, a round number for a year, we arrive at 420 talents. In addition, whenever the Spartans invaded Attica, 16,000 men were needed to man the fortifications of Athens, Piraeus, and the Long Walls.[91] We do not know whether they were paid; if they were, it was probably not at the full rate for fighting men. We also know that the Athenians launched annual invasions of the Megarid and stayed long enough to ravage the country.[92] In 431 the invasion force numbered 10,000. Once again, we do not know whether or how much they were paid nor precisely how long they stayed, but there must have been some cost. Even if we include only the naval costs and the expenses for Potidaea we arrive at a sum over 2,000 talents.[93]

A similar conclusion can be arrived at by quite a different kind of calculation. Inscriptions give us the accounts of the Athenian *logistai* recording loans to the state from the sacred treasuries during the Archidamian War.[94] They show that in the seven years 433 to 426 the Athenians borrowed almost 4,800 talents from the sacred treasuries. Beyond that, the interest figures recorded show that the bulk of the borrowing fell in the period 432–429. The epigraphers have made a reasonably accurate estimate of annual borrowing and suggest a figure of

[91] 2.13.6–7.   [92] 2.31.1–3.

[93] Thucydides gives the figure 2,000 talents as the total cost of the siege of Potidaea (2.70.2). Since the siege took about two and one-half years, the average annual cost is about 800 talents. Isocrates (15.113) gives the figure as 2,400. If he is right the average would be 960 talents annually. If we are right in calculating the cost of soldiers at 420 and if we add to it 560 talents for 70 ships in service eight months a year we get very close to the Isocratean number. This reckoning, thought inexact, seems to lend some support to our previous calculation.

[94] *GHI*, 72.

1,370 talents for the first year of the war.[95] If this figure is approximately right and we add to it the 600 talents annually received from the empire, we once again, by a different route, come close to the figure of 2,000 as the cost of the first year of the war.

Clearly, Pericles must have expected to spend at least 1,500 but probably 2,000 talents a year to carry on the war. Three years of such a war would probably cost 6,000 talents. If we add to the usable reserve fund of 5,000, three years of imperial income, 1,800, we get 6,800.[96] Pericles could thus maintain his strategy for three years, but not for a fourth. No more than the other Greeks should he have believed that Athens could hold out for more than three years.[97] But even if he expected it to last only three years we may wonder why he did not take so obviously effective a step as sending a fleet to Naupactus immediately at the start of the war.

A closer examination of Pericles' expectations and a more precise expression of them shows that his hope was to bring about a change of opinion in Sparta, the true decision maker in the Peloponnesian League in matters of war and peace.[98] Such a hope should not seem unreasonable when we remember with what reluctance Sparta was drawn into the war. She had tried to persuade the Corinthians to arbitrate their quarrel with Corcyra, fearing that it might lead to a conflict with Athens.[99] The Spartans had not sent aid to beleaguered Potidaea even after their ephors had promised it.[100] Their vote that Athens had broken the Thirty Years' Peace was powerfully influenced by a concerted campaign of propaganda executed by Corinth, Aegina, Megara, and, perhaps, other allies. Even then a strong Spartan faction led by no less a figure than King Archidamus had opposed the motion, which seems to have carried by a close margin.[101] Still later, after a state of war had been recognized,

[95] ATL III, 341–342; GHI, 217, accept the figure in general "without claiming literal accuracy for it."

[96] See Appendix A.   [97] 7.28.3.   [98] See Kagan, Outbreak, 9–30.

[99] Ibid., 225.   [100] Ibid., 279–280.

[101] Ibid., 286–316. In Outbreak, I argued that both votes called for at the Spartan assembly showed a large majority for war and that the second was called only to emphasize the size of the margin. I am now per-

the Spartans tried to negotiate a peaceful settlement, at least once, it appears, sincerely.[102] Finally, the Spartans allowed many months to elapse between their vote for war and their first bellicose action. The fact is that Sparta was moved to fight at last as the result of a Theban action which forced its hand. It is plain now as it must have been in 431 that the proponents of peace in Sparta, who had controlled its policy since 445, were still numerous and might regain control. To persuade the Spartans to consider making peace only required winning over three of the five ephors. To persuade them to accept peace the Athenians needed merely to help restore the natural majority which kept Sparta conservatively and pacifically inside the Peloponnese most of the time.

Confronted by these facts the plan of Pericles and the hopes he entertained for its success make excellent sense. Archidamus had warned the Spartans that their expectations about the nature of the projected war were mistaken, that the Athenians would not fight a land battle and be defeated, and that no other strategy was at that time available. They did not believe him. The plan of Pericles was to prove to the Spartans that their king had been right. The main tactical problem for Pericles was the defensive one of restraining the Athenians and preventing them from offering battle in Attica. The offensive actions were deliberately unimpressive, for they were intended only as evidence that an extended war would be damaging to the Peloponnesians. To engage in offensive actions which were more vigorous would, in fact, conflict with the plan. Offensive actions, while unable to bring about victory, might enrage the enemy and prevent the reasonable policy of Archidamus from winning the upper hand. But a policy of restraint both at home and abroad would likely bring the friends of peace to power in Sparta sooner or later.

Pericles might have expected such a change in Spartan opinion to come about very quickly, perhaps after only one campaigning season. Perhaps it would take two years of similar actions,

---

suaded by the argument of E. Will (*Revue historique* CCXLV [1971], 120, n. 5) that the first vote was close.

[102] Kagan, *Outbreak*, 321–324.

surely not more than three, for what could it profit Sparta to beat its fist against the stone wall of Athenian defensive strategy? There can be no certainty, of course, that Pericles had no alternative plan for increasing offensive activities should the Spartans prove stubborn. All we can say is that such actions would have meant a reversal of the strategy with which he began the war and that Thucydides tells us nothing of such a plan. On the contrary, he tells us without qualification that the Periclean strategy, from which his successors departed with disastrous results, was "to remain quiet." [103] Certainly that was the plan Pericles followed at the outbreak of the war.

[103] 2.65.7: ἡσυχάζοντας.

2. The First Year of the War

In August of 432 the allies of Sparta voted to go to war against
Athens, yet as the winter of 432/1 came to an end the Spartan
alliance had taken no action. In fact, the Spartans in some of the
intervening time had sent embassies to Athens to offer several
plans for keeping the peace.[1] The Spartans, divided about the
wisdom of fighting Athens, secure from attack by land, and
having devised a strategy that bade them wait until the Athenian
crops were full grown, were in no hurry to begin hostilities. Far
different was the attitude of the Thebans. They shared a long
border with the Athenians and had much to fear from them.
Thebes had long wished to unify and dominate all of Boeotia.
Before the Persian War, as president of the Boeotian League,
Thebes had come close to achieving her goal. Her disgrace in
that war shattered her power and virtually dissolved the league.[2]
During the First Peloponnesian War the Athenians, by defeating the Boeotians in battle and establishing democratic governments in the Boeotian towns, had dominated the Theban homeland for some years. The Thebans did not know that the strategy of Pericles was wholly defensive and expressly ruled out
campaigns on land. They and their friends clearly expected an
Athenian attack on Boeotia, for at the outbreak of the war the
citizens of several unwalled towns left their homes and went to
Thebes for safety.[3] If war should come, whether or not accompanied by an Athenian invasion, it was essential for Thebes
to possess Plataea.

[1] 1.125–139; Kagan, *Outbreak*, 315–341.
[2] E. M. Walker, *CAH* V, 79.   [3] *Hellenica Oxyrhynchia* XII, 3.

Plataea was a small town, with fewer than one thousand citizens.[4] Its size, however, was a poor indication of the threat it would pose to Thebes in case of war with Athens. Its democratic government had always resisted incorporation in the Boeotian League dominated by oligarchic Thebes. Since the sixth century Plataea had been allied to Athens and remained steadfastly loyal.[5] The Plataeans could be expected to continue that loyalty and to make use of their strategic position to help the Athenians and harm Thebes. Their town lay less than eight miles from Thebes, immediately flanking the road from Thebes through the pass of Dryoscephalae, by Eleutherae, to Athens. It also flanked the other, more direct path to Athens from Thebes by way of Phyle.[6] In the hands of Athens, Plataea could serve as a base for attacks on Thebes and Boeotia and as a threat to any Boeotian army entering Attica. Even more important, perhaps, Plataea flanked the only road connecting Thebes with Megara and the Peloponnese which did not pass through Athenian territory. "An active enemy in Plataea not only threatened any Theban invasion of Attica, but imperilled the whole cooperation of Athens' northern and southern enemies." [7] For these reasons the Thebans determined to seize Plataea while there was still peace and the Plataeans were unprepared.

In the early part of a cloudy night, either the sixth or seventh of March,[8] over three hundred Thebans commanded by two Boeotarchs were secretly admitted within the walls of Plataea by Nauclides and his traitorous partisans. Nauclides and his supporters were oligarchs who wanted to destroy the democrats who were in power and then put their town under the control

---

[4] Beloch, *Bevölkerung*, 166, sets the number of grown men at "kaum unter eintausend," while Busolt (*GG* III:2, 905, n. 1) argues for only five hundred.

[5] Hdt. 6.108; Thuc. 3.55. See specially Dem. *Against Neaera* 94–99.

[6] See map 1.

[7] Henderson, *Great War*, 73. Busolt (*GG* III:2, 905) and Henderson (*Great War*, 72–73) give good accounts of the strategic importance of Plataea. G. B. Grundy, *The Topography of the Battle of Plataea* (London, 1894), is very useful.

[8] Unless otherwise indicated the chronology followed is that of A. W. Gomme, which is conveniently set out in tabular form on pages 716–721 of the third volume of his *Commentary*.

Map 1. Attica and Boeotia

of oligarchic Thebes.[9] The Theban connection in the conspiracy
was Eurymachus son of Leontiadas, a man well suited to the
task, being one of a line of traitors and scoundrels. Leontiadas,
his father, had betrayed the Greeks at Thermopylae, and Leontiadas, his son, later betrayed Thebes to the Spartans in 383/2.[10]
The Thebans imagined that once they had entered the town and
made their armed presence known the Plataeans would surrender. They expected to take over the city peacefully and made
a proclamation accordingly. They threatened no reprisals but
offered alliance to all Plataeans who would accept it. Clearly an
allied Plataea under a friendly oligarchic government would be
better for Thebes than one decimated by executions and burdened with exiles waiting for revenge.

The traitorous oligarchs, on the other hand, urged the Thebans
to lay hands on their democratic opponents immediately. The
chief goal of these Plataeans had been to destroy their domestic
enemies, and they must have been eager to begin the slaughter.
They did, however, more accurately estimate the mood of
their fellow citizens, believing they would surely attempt to
resist the Thebans once the shock of the coup had worn off.
Their advice was ignored.[11] At first the Plataeans were frightened
into accepting the Theban proposals, but as they were discussing
the terms they came to see how few the Thebans were. Spurred
on by their loyalty to Athens and, no doubt, by their hatred of
Thebes and their own oligarchs, no less by their desire for
autonomy, they decided to resist. To avoid detection, they dug
through the common walls separating their houses and came together to plan their counterattack. Just before dawn they fell
upon the Thebans, who found themselves caught by surprise in
the dark in an unfamiliar town.

By this time a heavy rain had begun to fall, and discomfort
turned to danger when the Plataean women and the slaves,
screaming for blood, climbed to the rooftops and threw stones
and tiles at the confused Thebans. The Thebans were panicked
and fled for their lives, but they were in a strange town pursued
by natives. The gate by which they had entered was closed again,

[9] 2.2–2.3.   [10] Thermopylae: Hdt. 7.33; Thebes: Xen. *Hell.* 5.2.25.
[11] 2.2.4.

and before long the survivors were forced to surrender without condition.

The Thebans had not counted on the surprise coup alone to bring Plataea into their power. Their plan included the dispatch of the entire Theban army, which was to help the three hundred within Plataea in case they ran into trouble. The plan must have provided for the main army to arrive shortly after the three hundred were admitted, but it went wrong. The heavy rain had slowed the progress of the Theban force; even more serious, it had swollen the Asopus River which separated Theban from Plataean territory and made it difficult to cross. As a result the army arrived too late to help the Thebans in Plataea.

The Plataeans, however, were not out of danger. Many of their citizens, surprised by an unprovoked attack in peacetime, were still at their farms in the countryside and at the mercy of the Theban army. The Thebans planned to seize them as hostages to exchange for the men in the city, but they were forestalled. The Plataeans threatened to put their prisoners to death unless the Thebans withdrew from the country immediately. Thucydides reports two different versions of the Plataean message. The Thebans said that the Plataeans promised to restore their prisoners in safety if the Thebans withdrew and that this promise was sealed with an oath. The Plataeans claimed they had taken no oath and promised to restore the prisoners only if a general agreement were negotiated. The practical difference is small, for since the Thebans, like most Greeks, were reluctant to abandon any considerable number of citizen-soldiers, they would certainly have withdrawn, whatever the Plataean promise. When the Thebans had withdrawn and when the Plataeans were safe, they put to death their captives to the number of 180, including the infamous Eurymachus.[12]

The Plataeans had sent a messenger to Athens as soon as the Thebans broke into the city. The Athenians immediately gave orders to arrest any Theban found in Attica. A second messenger

---

[12] The account of the affair at Plataea is that of Thucydides (2.2–5). Herodotus (7.233) and Demosthenes (*Against Neaera* 99–100) add nothing of importance. The account of Diodorus (12.42.1–2) differs on a few points and in each case Thucydides is preferable.

was sent to Athens after the Plataeans had regained control of
their city and taken the Theban prisoners but before their fate
was determined. The Athenians had quickly seen the immense
value of these prisoners as hostages. The Thebans may or may
not have valued the lives of their hoplites as highly as the
Spartans did, but their behavior at Plataea proves they did not
take their capture lightly. One of the captives, moreover, was
Eurymachus, a leading politician and a person of influence with
the ruling faction. The 180 captives might have included other
important men. These men in the hands of the Athenians would
have been an invaluable prize, and possibly, used as hostages,
they might have prevented any Boeotian invasion of Attica, as
the capture of a similar number of Spartans in 425 prevented
any further Spartan invasion. The Theban coup at Plataea had
already turned out contrary to expectation.[13] Holding the captives as hostages might have had the consequence, disastrous for
Thebes and the Peloponnesians, of beginning the war at the
same time as it tied Thebes' hands. The Athenians swiftly sent a
herald to Plataea asking that no harm be done to the captives
until the Athenians were consulted. The message arrived too
late; passion had overcome, perhaps even prevented, calculation.
The Athenians could do nothing but bring food and a contingent
of eighty Athenian hoplites to help garrison the city against the
inevitable attack. They removed the women and children and
"the least efficient of the men," presumably all but hoplites,
leaving a total garrison of 480 plus 110 women as cooks.[14]

The attack on Plataea had clearly broken the peace, and when
word of it reached the Peloponnese the Spartans ordered their
allies to send two-thirds of their fighting force to gather at the
Isthmus of Corinth for the invasion of Attica. The other third
was conventionally held at home to guard where it could against
Athenian landings. The grand army was to be led by King
Archidamus who, ironically, had opposed the vote for war and
had argued vigorously that the strategy of invading Attica would

[13] For an analysis of the affair at Plataea and Thucydides' interest in
demonstrating its unforeseen and unforseeable character see Hans-Peter
Stahl, *Thukydides* (Munich, 1966), 65–74.

[14] 2.6.4; 2.78.3–4.

be unavailing. But Spartan armies were customarily commanded by a king, and in 431, Archidamus was the only king available. Pleistoanax had been banished in 445 for allegedly accepting a bribe to evacuate Attica.[15] His son Pausanias was too young for service and it was unthinkable that his uncle, the regent Cleomenes, should command when a king was available. Archidamus may not have approved of his task, but patriotism and honor bade him do his best. They did not, however, compel him to rash actions when delay might avoid the war he feared Sparta could not win.

After a speech to his officers warning them to be careful in the unlikely event of an Athenian attack on the march, he sent an ambassador to inquire if the Athenians would yield now that they saw the great Peloponnesian army actually on the road to Attica. Pericles, however, had anticipated such a maneuver. Fearing that the Athenians might lose heart in the face of the frighteningly large invading force, he had proposed a decree passed by the assembly forbidding the admission of any herald or embassy from the Peloponnesians while their army was in the field. The Spartan envoy was seen out of the country under guard, his mission unaccomplished. When Archidamus received the news he had no choice but to advance into Attica.

The swiftest route from the isthmus to Attica was by way of the coastal road through the Megarid, to Eleusis, past Aegalius, and into the fertile plain of Athens, but that is not the road Archidamus took.[16] He did not, in fact, move swiftly at all, but delayed at the isthmus, marched in a leisurely fashion, and, when he passed through Megara, did not turn south toward Athens but marched north to besiege the town of Oenoe, an Athenian fortress on the Boeotian border.[17] Oenoe was a powerful little fort defended by stone walls armed with towers, and it might have had strategic importance for some purposes: it lay on the main road from Athens to Plataea and held an important position in regard to the pass leading from the Athenian fort of

---

[15] Plut. *Per.* 22–23. See Kagan, *Outbreak*, 124–125.   [16] See Map 1.
[17] 2.18. For the location and importance of Oenoe see A. Milchoefer, *Karten von Attika, Heft VII–VIII* (Berlin, 1895). N. G. L. Hammond, *BSA* LXIX (1954), 112, identifies it with the modern Villia.

Eleutherae, slightly to the northwest between Cithaeron and Megalo Vuno, which secured the connection with Parnes. Late in the war, for instance, the Athenians used the fort to ambush some Corinthians returning home from Decelea.[18] Busolt believes that its taking was very important to the Peloponnesians and Boeotians: "In so doing they would open a wider road between Boeotia and Megara, facilitate a Boeotian inroad into Attica, sever the main connection between Athens and Plataea, and make it very difficult for the Athenians to interfere with an army besieging Plataea." [19]

Though these considerations explain why the Spartans might have wanted to take Oenoe at some time, they do not make clear why that should have been the first order of business for the invading army. Oenoe presented no threat to such an army and interfered with no immediate Peloponnesian plans. Taking it, moreover, proved to be no easy matter and would have required an extended siege and the abandonment of the main purpose of the expedition, the ravaging of Attica. The conclusion is attractive that Archidamus' motives for the attack on Oenoe were less strategic than political, that he still had not abandoned all hope of avoiding war. A year earlier he had argued that the Spartans should be very slow to ravage the land of Attica. "Do not think," he said, "of their land as anything but a hostage for us, and the better it is cultivated the better hostage it will be." [20] As long as it was unravaged the Athenians would have something valuable to lose and might make concessions, but once destroyed they would be desperate and enraged. The Spartans, blaming him for the delay which permitted the Athenians time to prepare for the invasion and remove their cattle and property to safety, suspected him of just such a purpose.[21]

At last Archidamus was compelled to abandon the siege of Oenoe and to turn to the major purpose of the Peloponnesian invasion: the devastation of Attica. Eighty days after the Theban attack on Plataea, toward the end of May when the grain of Attica was ripe, the Peloponnesian army moved south and began to ravage Eleusis and the Thriasian plain. They were chal-

[18] 8.98.   [19] GG III:2, 927.   [20] 1.82.   [21] 2.18.5.

lenged by the Athenian cavalry but easily beat it off and continued their march. The obvious next step was to proceed
directly into the plain of Athens through the pass at Daphne.
Instead Archidamus moved east to Acharnae, where he made
camp and spent some time ravaging that territory. He knew
that Acharnae was a large deme which provided many hoplites
to the Athenian army,[22] and it must have contained enough
farmland to make the excursion worth while. Still, we should
expect the Spartans to have gone first to the fertile plain of
Athens where the lands of the nobility of Athens were to be
found[23] if they meant to do the greatest damage. Busolt suggests that Archidamus' fear of the superior Athenian and Thessalian cavalry caused this slow and cautious advance,[24] but there
is no evidence that the cavalry presented a serious problem to
the Peloponnesians. At the first contact it had been routed and
it did the Spartans no important damage at any time.

Thucydides reports an explanation current in his time. In this
version Archidamus ravaged Eleusis and Thriasia in the hope
that the sight would be unbearable to the proud and powerful
Athenians, who, like their grain, were just then at their peak,
with numerous youth and well prepared for war.[25] When the
Athenians did not fight he moved against Acharnae because the
deme was large and its citizens numerous, "inexorable, tough as
oak"[26]; they at least would not look on quietly but would be
outraged and urge their fellow citizens to come out and fight.
If even this failed the Peloponnesians could move more safely
into the plain of Athens and up to its walls. This would be safe,
the argument ran, because the Acharnians, "deprived of their
own property, would not be so zealous to run risks for the lands
of others," so that discord would appear among the Athenians.[27]
This explanation is not persuasive. If Archidamus wanted to put
the greatest possible pressure on the Periclean policy of restraint
he should have marched into the Athenian plain immediately

---

[22] Thucydides (2.20.4) says 3,000. This figure has seemed too large to
most scholars and emendations have been suggested. The number has
provoked much controversy, but the precise figure is not significant
here. See Gomme, *HCT* II, 73–74.

[23] Gomme, *HCT* II, 73.   [24] *GG* III:2, 930.   [25] 2.20.2.

[26] Aristoph. *Acharn.* 180.   [27] 2.20.4–5.

where his proximity and his attack on the best land of Attica would be most provocative. We must reject it, and we should reiterate that Thucydides does not adopt it as his own but merely reports it. Perhaps his intention was ironical. Thucydides and his readers must have had before them the picture of the Acharnians painted by Aristophanes in the comedy he produced ·in 425. Even after six years of war they are depicted as the Athenians most zealous for war, unwilling even to hear of peace, furious with any man who speaks of a truce with the Spartans:

> Let's follow him! Let him not jeer at us, old
> Acharnians that we are, as he flees after making
> a treaty, by Zeus the father
> and the gods, with the enemy against
> whom I want the war to grow in revenge for my
> ravaged lands. And I will not let up until I
> pierce deep into them like a sharp arrow
> so that they may never again trample my vine-
> yards. Come, we must seek the man out and look
> for him with stones in hand and hunt him from
> place to place until we find him. I could
> never have enough of throwing stones at him.[28]

Clearly Archidamus' understanding of the psychology of the Acharnians was flatly contradicted by events. Perhaps Thucydides meant his readers to understand that the vicissitudes of war could not be predicted by a man like Archidamus even though his prediction of the course of the war in general was largely correct. However that may be, the most plausible explanation of Archidamus' actions is that he had not yet given up hope that the Athenians would see reason at the last moment, that as long as possible he wanted "to hold as a hostage" the most prized fields of Attica.

If that was indeed his hope he was disappointed, for the thoughts of the Athenians were of a different sort. On hearing of the Spartan invasion the Athenians had followed Pericles' plan and begun to move from their beloved countryside. Wives and children were sent to the city, sheep and oxen to Euboea. Most Athenians lived in the country and few were still alive who

[28] *Acharn.* 221-236.

had seen it devastated by the army of Xerxes. "They were dejected and angered at having to abandon their homes and the temples which had always been theirs, ancestral relics of the ancient polity, at facing a change in their way of life, at nothing less than each man having to abandon his own *polis*." [29] What they found when they arrived in the city did not improve their mood. At first they were all crowded within the city of Athens itself. Every vacant space was occupied; even sanctuaries to the gods were not exempt. The Pelargikon at the foot of the Acropolis was occupied in spite of an oracular curse from the Pythian Apollo to the scandal, no doubt, of the pious. The very towers of the city walls were used by squatters. Later the displaced Athenians were spread to Piraeus and to the territory between the Long Walls, but for the moment the discomfort was extreme.[30] It was made more bearable, however, by hopes arising from recent memory. As long as the Peloponnesians were confined to ravaging Eleusis and Thriasia the Athenians did not believe in serious invasion and a thorough devastation of all Attica. In 445 another invading Peloponnesian army had gone as far as Eleusis and Thria but no further. In 431 they thought, quite unreasonably, that the same thing would happen again.

When the enemy appeared at Acharnae, however, and began to lay waste its land less than seven miles from the Acropolis, the mood in Athens changed to fury. The anger was directed, of course, at the Spartans, but not less at Pericles, who was held responsible. It did not matter that Pericles had predicted these events or that the sufferings were a necessary part of the strategy they had accepted. His careful explanations of why Athens had to avoid great battles on land were forgotten in the anger and frustration of the moment, and they accused Pericles of cowardice because he would not lead them out against the enemy.[31] Of these attackers one was surely Cleon, who had opposed Pericles for some years.[32] Hermippus makes that clear in his comedy the *Fates*, produced probably in the spring of 430. He addresses Pericles as follows: "King of the Satyrs, why won't you ever lift a spear but instead use dreadful words to wage the

[29] 2.16.2.   [30] 2.17.   [31] 2.21.3; Gomme, *HCT* II, 75–76.
[32] See Kagan, *Outbreak*, 199, 200, 242, 319, 326.

war, assuming the character of the cowardly Teles? But if a little knife is sharpened on a whetstone you roar as though bitten by fierce Cleon." [33] But Cleon was only one of the enemies who attacked him and even some of his friends urged him to go out and fight.[34]

The intensity of the uproar may have surprised Pericles but not the clamor itself. From the first he had recognized that restraining the Athenians would be the great difficulty in his strategy.[35] We can understand Pericles' decision to go out and face the invading Spartans in 445, even though the Long Walls were complete and offered security, only if we realize the immense task it was to get the Athenians to abandon their fields to the enemy. In 445, Pericles did not have the power to persuade and restrain them; in 431 he did. By that time his personal prestige had risen to the point where Thucydides could speak of him as "the foremost among the Athenians and the most powerful in speech and action," [36] and of Athens he could claim that it was "in name a democracy but really a government by the first citizen." [37] If he had achieved such a position, it was not by virtue only of his wisdom, rhetorical skill, or his famed patriotism and incorruptibility. Pericles was a shrewd politician and had built up over the years a group of soldiers, administrators, and politicians who formed "a circle of like minded colleagues-in-office whose ability had been proven, for the most part, in a colleagueship of many years." [38]

Our record of the generals of Athens is incomplete, but the evidence indicates that Pericles could usually count on his colleagues. We have the names of only ten of the twenty generals who held office in the year 431, one group of ten leaving and another taking office at midsummer. Pericles, of course, was in both groups; the others include Phormio, Hagnon, Socrates son of Antigenes of Anagyros, Proteas son of Epicles of Aexone, and Callias son of Calliades.[39] Phormio had fought with Pericles

[33] Hermippus frg. 46 in Plut. *Per.* 33.4.   [34] Plut. *Per.* 33.6.
[35] 1.143.   [36] 1.139.4.   [37] 2.65.9.
[38] G. Gilbert, *Beiträge zur innern geschichte Athens im zeitalter des peloponnesischen krieges* (Leipzig, 1877), 105.
[39] Beloch, *Attische Politik* (Leipzig, 1884), 290, 299–300; *GG*[2] II, 262–263; Fornara, *The Athenian Board of Generals* (Wiesbaden, 1971), 52–53.

in the Samian War, had been sent with an army to Potidaea, and was a colleague of Pericles in 430/29 and 429/8. Hagnon was an old associate of Pericles, fought alongside him in the Samian War, had been selected as founder of Amphipolis during a period of Pericles' unrivaled ascendancy, and had helped defend him from political attack.[40] Proteas had been one of the generals sent to Corcyra in 433. Socrates had fought with Pericles during the Samian War, and Callias probably was the mover of the famous financial decrees passed in 434. To the others who held office in 431, Carcinus, Eucrates, and Theopompus, we might add the name of Xenophon son of Euripides of Melite, who was a colleague of Pericles during the Samian War and again in 430/29. We do not know that he was a general in 431, but it is probable that he, like the others, held office in the years for which we have an incomplete list. Further evidence that Pericles was surrounded by supporters in the *strategia* may be gleaned from the fact that the death of Pericles seems to have interrupted the careers of all these men. For the four years after Pericles' death we have the high number of thirty names for the forty generals who served. The list does not include a single colleague of Pericles for 431; none of their names appear on the list of generals again, although we hear of the death of only five of them and we know that at least two, Hagnon and Proteas, lived on for some years.[41] There can be no certainty, but it is hard to disagree with Gilbert that we must consider these generals "special partisans of Pericles who disappeared from the political life of Athens with his death." [42]

The support of such men makes it possible to understand how Pericles was able to withstand the storm of criticism he encountered and to restrain the hot-blooded and inexperienced youth of Athens who, along with others, urged him to attack the Peloponnesian army. Thucydides tells us that Pericles refused to call a meeting of the Athenian assembly or any informal gathering fearing that if they met they might "make a mistake by obeying their anger instead of their judgment." [43] We may wonder how Pericles could prevent the meeting of the assembly,

[40] Kagan, *Outbreak*, 193–202, especially 195 and 201.
[41] Gilbert, *Beiträge*, 105–109.   [42] *Ibid.*, 109.   [43] 2.22.1.

since the *ecclesia* had regular meetings and did not depend on the actions of the generals,[44] and, in any case, Pericles was only one of ten generals. Some scholars have suggested that Pericles was a kind of *generalissimo* or that the Athenians had given him special wartime powers, but there is no good reason to think so.[45] Part of the answer must be that Athens was under siege, and strategic necessities must have given the generals more power than usual de facto. The citizens were under arms, guarding the walls. If they were called to assembly the city walls would be undefended; if they stayed at their posts the assembly would be peculiarly unrepresentative. Thucydides clearly implies that Pericles did not merely fail to call an assembly himself but prevented the calling of one. Even he and the other generals combined had not the power to do this, for meetings of the assembly were convened by the prytanies.[46] We must believe that the prestige of Pericles, supported by his influence with the other generals, prevailed on the prytanies to avoid a meeting. In Roman terminology Pericles achieved his purpose not through any special *imperium* but by his *auctoritas*.[47]

While political life was suspended Pericles was free to hold to his strategy, responding to the Spartan devastations only by sending cavalry detachments to deter the Peloponnesians from ravaging too close to the city. Archidamus, seeing that the Athenians would neither fight nor yield, abandoned his camp and moved eastward to ravage the demes between Mounts Parnes and Pentelicus. From there the army continued on to Oropus, laying waste the district of Graïce, and went on home-

[44] Arist. *Ath. Pol.* 43.

[45] For a list of those believing Pericles had special status within the *strategia* see the excellent article of K. J. Dover, *JHS* LXXX (1960), 61, n. 2. The theory that the assembly had given Pericles special powers in the crisis is put forth by Busolt (*GG* III:2, 917). Both of these views are properly discredited by Dover. More recently Fornara (*Athenian Board of Generals*) has put forward a persuasive argument for the legal equality of all the generals.

[46] Arist. *Ath. Pol.* 43.3.

[47] This view was put forward by U. Kahrstedt, *Untersuchungen zur Magistratur in Athen* (Berlin, 1936), 268. It is accepted by Gomme, *HCT* II, 76, and C. Hignett, *A History of the Athenian Constitution* (Oxford, 1952), 246–247.

ward by way of Boeotia. Archidamus had not yet destroyed the rich fields of the Attic plain, but persisted in his plan to hold it hostage as long as possible.[48] The invading army had been in Attica for a month and withdrew when its provisions were exhausted.[49] The Spartans had little cause for satisfaction. The strategy with which they entered the war had thus far proven faulty. The Athenians were essentially unharmed and were even now engaged in avenging what damage had been done.

After the withdrawal of the Peloponnesians, Pericles took several steps to strengthen the defenses of Athens. Permanent guards were posted to watch for sudden incursions by land or by sea. In addition the Athenians took the extraordinary measure of setting aside in a special fund 1,000 talents from the treasury on the Acropolis. This money was not to be used for the ordinary expenses of the war, but if Athens were itself attacked by an enemy fleet. Moreover, if anyone should propose the use of this fund for any other purpose, the penalty was death. The Athenians also set aside each year 100 of their best triremes to be used only for the same purpose.[50] Scholars have differed in their evaluations of these actions. Those who regarded Pericles as insufficiently aggressive have attacked them as indicative of Pericles' timidity, of his unwillingness to seek victory by a decisive blow.[51] Others praise them as evidence of his wisdom and prescience. Busolt goes so far as to suggest that Pericles even foresaw the intervention of Persia at this early date.[52] Such an assumption seems excessive, for there was no chance that the

[48] Busolt (*GG* III:2, 930) argues that fear of the Athenian and Thessalian cavalry explains his action. There is little reason to believe it. On the one occasion when the cavalry met a significant Peloponnesian force they were routed by a combination of Boeotian cavalry and a hoplite phalanx. See 2.22.2.

[49] Busolt (*ibid.*, 931) estimates the time as 25–30 days. Gomme (*HCT* II, 79) guesses 30–35. Diodorus (12.42.7–8) attributes the withdrawal of the Peloponnesian army to the fleet which Pericles sent to the Peloponnese at that time. He is surely wrong because he contradicts not only Thucydides but common sense. If all Pericles needed to do to get the Peloponnesians out of Attica was to send out a fleet, there would never have been an invasion.

[50] 2.24.

[51] Pflugk-Hartung, *Perikles als Feldherr* (Stuttgart, 1884), 98.

[52] *GG* III:2, 932.

Persians would intervene while the Athenian fleet was intact and no chance that the fleet would be lost under the strategy of Pericles.

Whatever the judgment of his purpose, we must ask why the Athenians waited until the Peloponnesian withdrawal to enact these measures. The answer must be sought in the intervening events. One possibility is that Pericles might have feared that the Peloponnesians would employ their navy at the outbreak of war, perhaps to attack Euboea or even Athens. If so the securing of Thronium, Atalante, and Aegina, together with the Peloponnesian failure to act, may have relieved that fear and enabled Pericles to take the prudent course he liked. There may, however, have been another reason. The behavior of the enemy had denied any hope of a swift end to the war; the war would be extended, and the Athenians must carefully husband their resources.

Pericles' sense of prudence may have been sharpened by the attacks on his policy made by Cleon and others. He knew that as time passed the demand would increase for aggressive expeditions, with large and expensive fleets and contingents of soldiers, expeditions which would be risky. He may well have proposed his measures in direct response to these attacks. While he still was in full control of the situation he could guarantee at least a portion of his defensive strategy against a time when his political power might be weaker.

While the Peloponnesians were still in Attica the Athenians sent out a fleet of 100 ships with 1,000 hoplites and 400 archers on board under the command of Carcinus, Proteas, and Socrates.[53] It was supplemented by 50 ships from Corcyra and some from the other western allies. This considerable force could easily defeat or drive from the seas any enemy fleet it might encounter, make landings and ravage enemy territory, even capture and sack small enemy cities. More than this it could not do, but no more was intended. The purpose of the expedition was to avenge the ravaging of Attica and bring home to the Peloponnesians the cost of such a war as they had chosen to fight. The Athenian force made landings on the Peloponnesian coast, probably in the

[53] 2.23.2–3.

region of Epidaurus and Hermione; [54] then it landed at Methone in Laconia (see Map 2). The Athenians ravaged this territory, attacked the poorly defended walled town, and might have sacked it. Methone was saved by the enterprise and bravery of Brasidas, a Spartan officer who took advantage of the scattered disposition of the Athenian forces to dash into the town and reinforce its garrison. The Spartans rewarded him with a vote of thanks.[55]

After Methone the Athenians sailed to Pheia in Elis. There they continued their depredations for two days, defeating an opposing native army of three hundred. The next action gives us an idea of what was intended at Methone. A storm came up that endangered the fleet which had no safe harbor. The ships sailed around the nearby promontory to safety leaving behind the Messenian contingent and some other troops who could not get back to the ships. These men marched to the town of Pheia and took it, but as soon as the Athenian ships came into view they abandoned the town and sailed away, "for the entire Eleian army had come to the rescue." [56] Clearly the Athenian force was not of a number or of a mind to hold even a coastal city in the Peloponnese against a full assault. We may be sure that if Brasidas had not arrived to save Methone the Athenians would have sacked it and sailed off.[57]

After further devastation of the western coast of the Peloponnese the Athenian armada sailed northward, past the mouth of the Corinthian Gulf, to Acarnania.[58] This was no longer Peloponnesian territory but within the Corinthian sphere of interest, and Athenian behavior was strikingly different. They took Sollium, a town belonging to Corinth, and kept it throughout the rest of the war, giving it to some friendly Acarnanians to occupy. The town of Astacus, ruled by a tyrant Euarchus, they took by storm and incorporated into their alliance.[59] Finally,

[54] Thucydides (2.25.1) says merely ἄλλα τε ἐκάκουν περιπλέοντες, but Diodorus (12.43.1) gives us more detail, naming the region of Acte. He is probably accurate here. See Gomme, HCT II, 82–83.

[55] 2.25.1–2.   [56] 2.25.3–5.   [57] See Gomme, HCT II, 84–85.

[58] See Map 3.

[59] In the following winter Euarchus, aided by 40 Corinthian ships and 1,500 Corinthian hoplites, retook Astacus. Their other attempts to undo the Athenian successes failed.

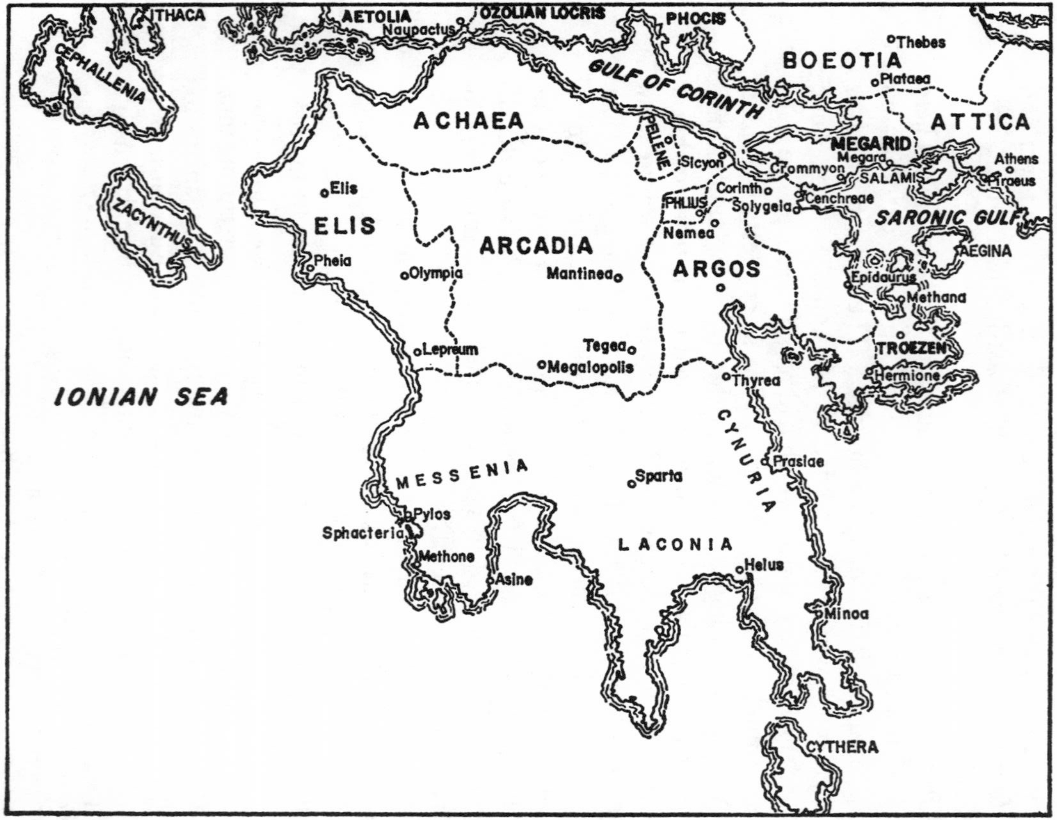

Map 2. The Peloponnesus

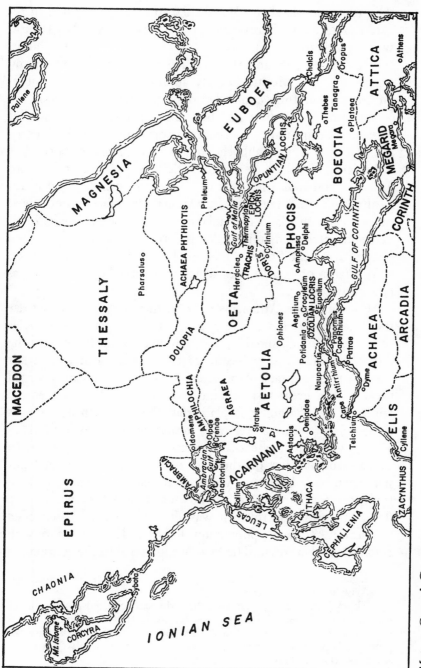

Map 3. Central Greece

they took the island of Cephallenia, strategically located in regard to Acarnania, Corcyra, and the Corinthian island of Leucas,
without a battle.[60] After these successes the fleet sailed home,
stopping at Aegina and then joining the main Athenian army
which attacked Megara in early autumn. It had carried out its
limited and carefully controlled mission with great success.

While this great fleet had been engaged in its task a smaller
force of 30 ships under Cleopompus was sent to Locris to harry
the enemy in that neighborhood and to safeguard Euboea. The
Athenians ravaged some territory, defeated a force of Locrians
in battle, and took the town of Thronium, well situated in regard to Euboea.[61] Later in the summer the Athenians occupied
the uninhabited island of Atalante off the Locrian coast, fortified and garrisoned it in order to prevent predatory raids on
Euboea from the hostile shores of Locris.[62] These two actions
were vital to protect Euboea which now served the Athenians as
pasture and refuge.

Meanwhile, the Athenians took further measures to increase
their security. Aegina, "the eyesore of the Piraeus," as Pericles
called it,[63] was inhabited by a people long competitive with the
Athenians and bitterly hostile to them. They had helped stir
the Spartans to attack Athens, and now the Athenians charged
them with a great responsibility for the war.[64] Whatever the
truth of the charge, it is plain that the Athenian action was
strategic, not judicial. Aegina is located in the Saronic Gulf, in
a position to dominate that waterway and the approaches to
Piraeus, and also just off the coast of the Peloponnesus. A Peloponnesian navy based on Aegina could interfere with Athenian
trade, threaten Piraeus, and tie down a large Athenian defensive
fleet. Athenians control of it was vital. The Athenians expelled
the entire Aeginetan population and resettled the island with
colonists of their own. The Spartans, grateful to the Aeginetans

[60] 2.30.   [61] 2.26.   [62] 2.32. See map 1.
[63] Arist. *Rhet.* iii.10, 1411 a 15.

[64] Thucydides (2.27.1) says that the Athenians claimed οὐχ ἥκιστα τοῦ
πολέμου σφίσιν αἰτίους εἶναι. οὐχ ἥκιστα is usually translated "most" and it
is possible that the Athenians magnified the Aeginetan responsibility for
propaganda purposes. The words, however, may mean simply "not least,"
and I take them so here.

for past favors and well aware of their hatred toward Athens, settled them in Thyrea, a borderland between Laconia and the Argolid.[65] Those Aeginetans who accepted the Spartan invitation could be counted on to keep a close watch on democratic Argos and to resist fiercely any Athenian landing in that region. Their homeland, however, was securely in Athenian hands.

In this first year of the war, too, the Athenians brought off a diplomatic coup that promised greater security in the important northeastern region of their empire. They won over the formerly hostile Nymphodorus of Abdera. He was brother-in-law to the powerful Thracian king Sitalces and had great influence with him. The Athenians made him their *proxenus*, and he performed wonders. He came to Athens, bringing an alliance with Sitalces and also the king's son, who was given the rare award of Athenian citizenship. Athens' main problem in the Thraceward region was Potidaea that was draining the Athenian treasury beyond expectation. Nymphodorus promised to get Sitalces to lend the Athenians cavalry and peltasts and bring the war to an end. As if this were not enough, he reconciled the Athenians with Perdiccas, king of Macedon, and they gladly restored Therme to him in return for his friendship. Perdiccas immediately joined Phormio's army in attacking Potidaea's Chalcidian allies.[66] Perdiccas had previously proved to be an unreliable ally [67] and would do so again, but the Athenians could not be fastidious. They needed help against Potidaea, and for the moment they seemed to have it.

As the autumn of 431 approached Pericles himself took all the Athenian army not occupied elsewhere, some 10,000 hoplites, 3,000 metic hoplites, and a large number of light-armed troops, and invaded the Megarid. Thucydides tells us this was the largest Athenian army ever brought together, and with it Pericles ravaged the Megarid.[68] This invasion may well have been the result of the decree proposed by Charinus in revenge for the alleged murder of an Athenian herald, a serious religious violation. The decree, as Plutarch reports it, provided that "there be irreconcilable and implacable enmity on the part of Athens towards them and that whosoever of the Megarians should set

[65] 2.17.   [66] 2.29.   [67] Kagan, *Outbreak*, 276ff.   [68] 2.31.1.

foot on the soil of Attica be punished with death; and that the generals, whenever they should take their ancestral oath of office, add to their oath this clause, that they should invade the Megarid twice during each succeeding year." [69] The Athenians did invade the Megarid twice annually [70] until the capture of the Megarian port of Nisaea in 424 made it unnecessary, and the decree may be authentic. If so, it was passed in the summer of 431, not earlier where Plutarch puts it.[71]

If the decree was genuine, it added religious fervor to the zeal with which the Athenians attacked Megara, but religion was not the motive for the invasion. The Athenians, of course, wanted to devastate Megara's fields and hoped that their embargo on Megara's trade and the invasions would bring her to her knees. But the size of the invading force shows that there was more to it. A smaller army could have produced the same results in safety after the Peloponnesians had withdrawn and scattered. Pericles was well aware of the price the Athenians paid in morale for his defensive strategy. The sight of a powerful enemy army ravaging Athenian soil unchallenged was both a frustrating and intimidating one. The grand scale of the Megarian invasion was intended both to relieve frustration and to demonstrate visibly the might of Athens. We cannot doubt that this satisfying expedition, along with the successes of Athens' marauding fleet, the diplomatic victory in the northeast, and the occupation of Aegina, reaffirmed Pericles' position among the Athenian people. When the Athenians held funeral rites for those who had fallen in the first year of the war Pericles "was chosen by the city as the wisest and most esteemed" to deliver their eulogy.[72]

We need say little about the most famous speech of antiquity, but must reaffirm what should be obvious: that the speech re-

[69] *Per.* 30.3, translated by B. Perrin.   [70] 4.66.1.

[71] W. R. Connor, *AJP* LXXXIII (1962), 225–246, has argued for a fourth-century date for the decree, but his argument has been effectively refuted by G. L. Cawkwell, *REG* LXXXII (1969), 327–335. Cawkwell, like Busolt and Beloch, places the decree after the attack on Plataea. Connor's response to Cawkwell and other critics, (*REG* LXXXIII [1970], 305–308) does not seem to me persuasive.

[72] 2.34.6.

ported by Thucydides is close in content, and in some degree in form, to the one actually delivered by Pericles. As Grote has put it: "The speech of Pericles was a real speech, heard reproduced, and doubtless dressed up, by Thucydides." [73]

It is possible to believe that the speech reflects the ideas of Thucydides no less than of Pericles and that the reason for its reproduction lies in that identity of opinion.[74] But at the most limited and obvious level the inclusion of the speech is a neces-

[73] Grote VI, 152, n. 2. See also Gomme (*HCT* II, 104, 126, 129–130, 136) for a good understanding of the problem. We may wonder why Thucydides, after the fall of Athens in 404, chose to reproduce this speech at length, but we may not ignore Thucydides' promise to stay as close as possible to the general purport of what the speaker really said (1.22.1). Whoever can believe that the Funeral Oration of Pericles is a free composition of Thucydides is free to believe that there was no public funeral in Athens in 431 or that the Spartans never invaded Attica during the war. The error of treating the history of Thucydides like a drama, poem, or oration and therefore subject to the criticism deserved by the work of a poet or an orator is at least as old as Dionysius of Halicarnassus, who blamed Thucydides for composing so grand a speech for such a paltry occasion. This error has continued to the present and will, no doubt, go on as long as Thucydides is studied by men accustomed to view his work as part of classical literature, pure and simple. A recent student of the question, therefore, has said that we must consider the role of Thucydides in the composition of the speeches to be very significant, that it even, "bis zur Erfindung ganzer Reden oder der Konzentration mehrerer Reden in eine gehen kann" (Hellmut Flashar, "Der Epitaphios des Perikles," *Sitzungsberichte der Heidelberger Akademie der Wissenchaften* [Heidelberg 1969], 6) without embarrassment by or reference to Thucydides' promise to hold ὅτι ἐγγύτατα τῆς ξυμπάσης γνώμης τῶν ἀληθῶς λεχθέντων.

[74] Most students of the speech have regarded it as a Thucydidean invention, and the majority of these have taken Thucydides to be in close accord with the ideas of Pericles. Mme de Romilly, for instance, says that "the Funeral Oration was written as a highly sympathetic expression of Pericles' ideas . . . which implies a kind of collaboration between the historian and the orator" (*Thucydides and Athenian Imperialism*, tr. Philip Thody [Oxford, 1963], 137). This could be taken to mean that Thucydides was trying to reproduce what Pericles said, but de Romilly plainly regards the Thucydidean role as paramount, saying that the historian gives the ideas of Pericles "an elevation of tone and an intensity of analysis which are very different from those which Pericles could in fact have reached when speaking before the people" (*idem*). E. Lange, on the other hand, argues that the Funeral Oration reproduces the ideas of Pericles and that they could only be put forth as we have them by a historian who shared them (*Philologus* LII [1894], 624).

sary part of the history of the war because it illustrates a Periclean quality which made his peculiar strategy possible. As Thucydides reports Pericles saying later, a statesman must not only plan his course correctly in accord with a good sense of what is likely to happen; he must also present it persuasively.[75] Pericles' special attribute, indeed a unique one according to Thucydides, was that "when he saw that the Athenians were unreasonably confident to the point of arrogance, he would speak so as to frighten them, but when they were frightened beyond reason he knew how to restore them to confidence." [76] The Funeral Oration, at the very least, shows how Pericles could hope to succeed at the monumental task of holding the Athenian people to a painful strategy for the necessary time.

Pericles' speech has had a continuing impact, but it was addressed to his contemporaries and was intended to have a particular effect on them. It is as unlike the standard Athenian funeral oration [77] as Lincoln's Gettysburg Address was unlike the weary rhetoric spoken at length the same day by Edward Everett.[78] But Pericles, like Lincoln, was not engaged in delivering a mere memorial address in honor of the dead. Instead he intended to explain to the living in the midst of a difficult war why their sufferings were justified and why their continued dedication was necessary.

The Funeral Oration brought the first year of the war to a close. Its power and brilliance must have encouraged the Athenians and stiffened their resolve to carry on the war; indeed to many it must have seemed that the war was going well. Even so hostile a modern critic as Beloch has written as follows:

Taken all in all [Pericles] had reason to be satisfied with the results of this first campaign. If no great military successes had been produced at least any serious misfortune had been avoided. The enemy invasion remained limited to the northern district of Attica; the enemy had not dared to move forward under the walls of the

[75] 2.60.5, γνῶναί τε τὰ δέοντα καὶ ἑρμηνεῦσαι ταῦτα.

[76] 2.65.9.

[77] Such as those of Lysias, Ps.-Demosthenes, Isocrates' *Panegyricus*, Plato's *Menexenus*, and the speech of Hypereides.

[78] The comparison with the Gettysburg Address is aptly made by Henderson, *Great War*, 83–84.

capital, still less to leave Athens on the flank and move into the Paralia. And, what was more important, in the face of the foreign threat all internal quarrels were stilled. More closely than ever the citizenry rallied round the man who now again stood at the head of the state.[79]

A more balanced view nonetheless does not paint the condition of Athens in the winter of 431/0 in somber colors. Busolt's account is judicious and typical:

If Pericles balanced the books for the first year of the war, he found on the one side a moderately extensive devastation of the Peloponnesian and Locrian coastal regions, victorious engagements with the Eleans and Locrians, the devastation of the greater part of Megara, the capture of Sollium and Thronium, the winning of Cephallenia, the seizure of Aegina, the fortification of Atalante, finally, the treaties with Perdiccas and Sitalces. On the other side stood the considerable devastation of Attica, the failure at Methone, the continuation of the Chalcidian rebellion and the costly siege of Potidaea, the expenditure of from three to four hundred talents for the operating fleet, the damage to the Athenian sea trade, and the growing bad temper of the citizenry. Athens had neither suffered a serious defeat nor gained a striking victory. This had been expected in the Periclean system of war, but from the experiences of this year, which really had the character of a war of devastation, the end was not in sight.[80]

The end, to be sure, was not in sight, but the cost of the first year of the war had been great and the prospects for victory were not what they had been. "In a war of attrition," as Brunt says, "the side that does all the damage must win in the end." [81]

[79] GG^2 II:1, 307.

[80] GG III:2, 938–939. Busolt cites in support of his evaluation the conclusion of Grote (6.153) which give us a clue to the precise meaning of his own somewhat ambiguous remarks. Grote makes it clear that, although nothing decisive had been accomplished by either side and the relative strength of the two sides was not changed, "no progress was yet made towards the fulfillment of those objects which had induced the Peloponnesians to go to war." The Athenians had not been forced to raise the siege of Potidaea, and "the result of the first year's operations had been to disappoint the hopes of the Corinthians and the other ardent instigators of war, while it justified the anticipations both of Pericles and of Archidamus."

[81] *Phoenix* XIX (1965), 270.

The damage to Athens had been considerable. In addition to the psychological price of watching their crops cut down, their vines and olive trees destroyed, their houses torn or burned down, the Athenians had lost grain needed for food. It could be replaced by imported supplies, but at some cost. The exports usually employed to maintain a balance of trade were the olive oil and wine that had been destroyed. The imported foodstuffs might be paid for entirely from private funds or be subsidized in some part by the state; we do not know. In either case the resources of the Athenian commonwealth would be reduced and the capacity of Athens to persist curtailed.[82] By comparison, the attacks on the Peloponnesians, apart from extra-Peloponnesian Megara, were mere pinpricks, irritating but not really damaging. Sparta herself was untouched; in all her territory of Laconia and Messenia only Methone had been attacked. Corinth had lost a little town in Acarnania; that was annoying but not important. She was excluded from trade in the Aegean, but her main commercial areas were in the west, and they were undisturbed. Megara continued to be excluded from Aegean ports and her land was seriously devastated. There is no doubt the Megarians suffered badly, but not badly enough to make them seek peace even after ten years.

For Athens, on the other hand, the first year of the war was very costly. Her victories—the capture of Thronium, the fortification of Atalante, the capture of Sollium, the winning of Cephallenia, the occupation of Aegina—had all improved her defensive posture. They helped safeguard Euboea, guaranteed control of the Saronic Gulf, and improved communications with Corcyra and the west. They had not, however, damaged the enemy's capacity or will to fight. Athens, moreover, had suffered a serious disappointment: the Chalcidian rebellion and the expensive siege of Potidaea continued. If we have calculated correctly, the Athenians had been compelled to borrow from the sacred treasuries some 1,300 to 1,400 talents in the first year of the war, more than one-fourth of their disposable war chest.[83]

[82] Lysias 7.6 speaks of the destruction of olive trees, and Aristoph. *Acharn.* 221–236 gives evidence for damage to grain and vines. See Brunt, *ibid.*, 266, n. 41, and 267.

[83] See above, pp. 38–39.

The Peloponnesians showed no sign of discouragement, but would return the next year with spirit to destroy the large portion of Attica they had left untouched. We have no evidence of any dissension within the Peloponnesian League and no growth in influence of the advocates of peace in Sparta, on whom Pericles must rely. In Athens, however, tensions had come to the surface. Cleon's complaints at the inefficacy of the Periclean strategy might still be a subject for comic poets, but they were merely the tip of the iceberg of dissent which was bound to reveal itself as the suffering continued. For the moment the occupation of Aegina, the attack on the Megarid, and the eloquence of Pericles might quiet the opposition, but it was sure to burst forth if the situation did not improve. As the first year of the war came to an end the pressure on Pericles and his strategy increased.

3. The Plague and Its Consequences

🔹

In the seventh prytany in February or March of the Attic year 431/30 Pericles was re-elected to the generalship and with him his associates, Hagnon, Phormio, Xenophon, and Cleopompus.[1] The election was further evidence of his success in calming the Athenians and convincing them of the wisdom of his strategy. With steadfastness and reasonable luck they might expect to carry the war to the Peloponnesians somewhat more vigorously and to withstand their ravages with patience. Toward the beginning of May, about a month earlier than the previous year's invasion, Archidamus again led two-thirds of the Peloponnesian hoplites into Attica to complete the destruction.[2]

The Spartans had not been there for many days when it became clear that Pericles and the Athenians could not rely on a reasonable supply of luck. A plague broke out and raged with unprecedented ferocity during the years 430 and 429 and, after

---

[1] Grote VI, 168, and Beloch, *Attische Politik*, 300–301, among others, think that Pericles was not re-elected in that year, believing that elections were regularly not held until the summer, after the Spartan invasion. Aristotle *Ath. Pol.* 44.4, which was not available to them, tells us that the elections took place in the seventh prytany, late winter to early spring. See Busolt, *GG* III:2, 939, n. 4. For the date according to the Julian calendar see Gomme, *HCT* II, 183; Meyer, *GdA* IV, 39, n. 1. Busolt places it about a month later, as he does uniformly throughout this year. For the list of generals see Beloch, *GG*[2] II:2, 263, and Fornara, *Athenian Board of Generals*, 53.

[2] 1.47.2; Gomme, *HCT* II, 145.

a hiatus, it broke out again in 427. Before it was done it had killed 4,400 hoplites, 300 cavalrymen, and an untold number of the lower classes, wiping out perhaps one-third of the population.[3] Thucydides, who suffered from the plague himself, carefully described its symptoms, but scholars do not agree on the name of the disease.[4] In May of 430, however, the plague had barely begun its depredations and had no effect on the plans of either the Spartans or the Athenians.

This time Archidamus was both fearless and merciless, sparing no part of Attica. He ravaged the great plain before the city of Athens then moved on to the coastal regions of Attica, both east and west.[5] He could be bold because this time there was no Thessalian cavalry to oppose him, nor did the Athenian cavalry resist either.[6] By now Archidamus must have known that there was no longer any point holding the land of Attica hostage; the Athenians would not yield to such blackmail. The army remained in Attica for forty days, their longest stay of the war, ravaging the entire country, and left only when their provisions were exhausted.[7]

Toward the end of May, while the Spartans were still ravaging the coastal regions, the Athenians took countermeasures. They sent out a fleet of 100 of their own triremes aided by 50 from Chios and Lesbos. On board were 4,000 hoplites; in addition, there were 300 cavalry in transports especially pre-

[3] For the plague see 2.47–54 and 3.87. The latter passage gives the death toll. The estimate of the percentage of the loss is that of Adcock, *CAH* V, 201.

[4] Among the suggestions have been pneumonic plague, spotted fever, smallpox, measles, and typhus. For references see Bengtson, *GG*, 222, n. 1.

[5] 2.55.

[6] De Sanctis (*Pericle*, 260), who is keenly aware of Athens' financial troubles, suggests that the Thessalians were not there because the Athenians could not afford to pay them. It is more likely that they were absent because they were not needed. Their function in 431 was psychological, not military: to prevent the Peloponnesians from coming too close to the city and thus provoking the Athenians to battle. By 430, Athens did not need to fear such a rebellion and so had no need of the cavalry. It is also possible that the Thessalians were disunited at this time and were unwilling to send a squadron. See Thuc. 4.78.

[7] 2.57.

pared for the occasion. This force Pericles himself led against the Peloponnesus.[8] It was equal in number to the one which undertook the great Sicilian expedition of 415,[9] and we must ask the explanation for and the purpose of so great an undertaking. The account of Thucydides gives little help, but it is worth quoting in all its flatness: "When they arrived at Epidaurus in the Peloponnesus they ravaged most of the land. And when they made an attack on the city they arrived at the hope of taking it, but they were not successful. Leaving Epidaurus, they ravaged the land of Troezen, Halieis and Hermione, which are all on the coast of the Peloponnesus. From there they sailed to Prasiae, a coastal town of Laconia; they ravaged its land, took the town, and sacked it. When they had done this they returned home. They found that the Peloponnesians were no longer there but had withdrawn." [10]

The question immediately arises, why did Pericles undertake so large and expensive an expedition for such meager results? He did not need so large a force to ravage some coastal territory and sack a little town like Prasiae; even if he did, the results hardly seem worth the trouble. Modern scholars have determined that the main target must have been Epidaurus. Adcock's comment is typical: "This was to be no mere raid but a serious attempt to take Epidaurus, thus securing a foothold in the Peloponnese and possibly inducing the Argives to strike in against their old enemies the Spartans." [11] The implication is that the Athenians meant to take the city, place a garrison in it, and hold it against the inevitable attack when the main Peloponnesian army returned from Attica. A large force was sent in order to storm the city, no easy task in itself, and also to leave some troops behind as a garrison.

We should note carefully the important consequences of accepting such a theory, as its proponents have not. If Pericles intended to capure and hold the large and important Peloponnesian city of Epidaurus, he abandoned his original strategy of not

---

[8] 2.56.1–3.   [9] 6.31.   [10] 2.56.4–6.
[11] *CAH* V, 200. Adcock is here following the influential suggestion of Delbrück (*Strategie*, 121ff.). Delbrück is also followed by Busolt (*GG* III:2, 945) and Miltner ("Perikles," 785.1).

trying to extend the empire during the war, thus running needless risks.[12] As Westlake has pointed out, "The occupation even
of small plundering bases is not strictly reconcilable with his
cardinal principle that new conquests should not be attempted
during the war." [13] If this be true of small bases it is plainly
true of a city like Epidaurus. Thucydides mentions no such
shift in strategy. Describing the strategy of Pericles in his final
eulogy, moreover, he continues to speak of the policy outlined
by Pericles at the beginning of the war in which he urged the
Athenians to "remain quiet, take care of their fleet, refrain
from trying to extend their empire in wartime and thus putting
their city in danger." [14] All this does not rule out the possibility
that so great a change really was intended. There are, however,
good reasons to reject it.

We should not accept the suggestion that the Athenians meant
to hold Epidaurus and use it as a base for raids on the Peloponnese and as a refuge for Peloponnesian deserters, in the way
that Pylos and Cythera were used later in the war after the
death of Pericles. Their abandonment of Prasiae after they had
captured it shows they had no such intention. Still, the idea of
establishing closer relations with Argos near by and persuading it
to join in the war may have been tempting enough to make them
try to capture Epidaurus. If such was their intention they
chose a most ineffective strategy to accomplish it. To take a
walled city by storm was very difficult and rarely accomplished
in the fifth century. Typically success against such a city came
as a result of treason after a long siege. To be sure, the Athenian
attack came when two-thirds of the Epidaurian army was away,
leaving the city defended by perhaps 700 men.[15] But Brasidas

[12] 1.144.1, ἢν ἐθέλητε ἀρχήν τε μὴ ἐπικτᾶσθαι ἅμα πολεμοῦντες καὶ κινδύνους
αὐθαιρέτους μὴ προστίθεσθαι.
[13] Essays, 90. Westlake is right in arguing that the conquests of Sollium
and Astacus in the first year of the war do not violate the principle.
Sollium was turned over to the Acarnanians. Astacus, like Thronium on
the Locrian coast and Atalante off it, was so petty and intrinsically un-
attractive that it was plainly meant only as a station for carrying on the
war and irritating the enemy, not as an expansion of empire.
[14] 2.65.7.
[15] Beloch, Bevölkerung, 121–123, estimates the population of the Ar-
golic Acte, including Epidaurus, Troezen, Halieis, and Hermione, at

had saved Methone against 1,000 Athenians with only one-tenth of their force,[16] and the Epidaurian defenders had a better ratio. The only hope the Athenians had of taking the city was by a surprise attack. Yet they threw away that advantage by first ravaging the territory of the Epidaurians, as they had done at Methone and as they would do at Prasiae. As Delbrück put it, "You don't need to be a general to know that if you want to make a surprise attack you don't first set fire to the houses as a signal." [17] If the purpose of Pericles' assault on the city was really to take it and hold it, and if that were the point of the landing, we cannot avoid blaming Pericles for a strategic blunder of the highest order.[18]

Nonetheless, Thucydides and Plutarch tell us that the Athenians came close to taking the city.[19] What would have hap-

---

10,000 citizens. His estimate of the number of hoplites available from the Acte (*Klio* VI [1906], 57) is 3,000. Epidaurus was by far the largest of these towns and probably supplied over half the troops. Beloch's figures are generally too low, and we can conservatively raise the contingent from the Acte to 4,000 hoplites, of whom perhaps 2,100 were from Epidaurus. This would mean that 1,400 went with Archidamus to Attica and 700 were left to defend the city.

[16] 2.25.2.   [17] *Strategie*, 122.

[18] Duncker (*GdA* IX, 451) chides Pericles for his mistake. The statement of Delbrück cited above is a sardonic one that is part of a defense of Pericles against Duncker's charge. The desperate yet eloquent defense is worthy of citation but not of belief: "If the devastation of the land really preceded the attack on the city, the connection must be a different one; some kind of trick of war, an ambush or an attempt of some other kind must be involved. But why speculate on this? We don't know. We don't know whether the undertaking failed because of an error on the part of Pericles or a subordinate, a false calculation or bad luck. It doesn't matter. Let us assume with pleasure that it failed through an error of Pericles himself. The essential thing remains, nevertheless, that only a general of high daring and true enterprise could dare to attempt such a deed. How easily it could have happened that a unit entered and then strolled around as the Thebans did the year before in Plataea, that the Epidaurians gained the upper hand in a street battle, cut them off and annihilated them. We must remember that Epidaurus is a state with a greater territory than Megara." The discussion of Delbrück demonstrates incidentally how risky the operation of taking the city in order to keep it would have been and emphasizes, without intending to do so, the sharp departure that policy would have represented from the Periclean policy described by Thucydides.

[19] Thuc. 2.56.4–5, καὶ πρὸς τὴν πόλιν προσβαλόντες ἐς ἐλπίδα μὲν ἦλθον τοῦ ἑλεῖν; Plut. *Per.* 35.3, πολιορκήσας τε τὴν ἱερὰν Ἐπίδαυρον ἐλπίδα παρασχοῦσαν ὡς ἁλωσομένην.

pened had they been successful? They must prepare immediately for the return of the huge Peloponnesian army and the inevitable siege. Since they would have just overrun a garrison of some 700 men with an army of 4,000 they must leave not fewer than 1,000 Athenians to withstand the much greater army they would face. These men must be paid and supplied, further draining the already strained Athenian treasury.

These considerations fortify the case suggested by the silence of Thucydides that Pericles could not have intended to take and hold Epidaurus, and he does not deserve the charge of military incompetence in his choice of tactics. We still do not know the purpose of so large an expedition if not to take so large a city. The answer may be found by viewing the attack on Epidaurus in the context of the other raids undertaken by the Athenians in the first two years of the war: the attacks on Methone, Pheia in Elis, Troezen, Hermione, Halieis, and Prasiae. In each case the first action was to ravage the territory. At Methone and Pheia in the first year attempts were made to enter and sack the cities, but the attempt to sack seems more due to accident than to the purpose of the expedition. Methone, we are told, happened to be weakly defended by an insufficient garrison, a fact the Athenians could not have known in advance. Pheia, too, was taken as the result of an accident. After two days of ravaging the land, the Athenians were forced to move from their anchorage by a storm. The Messenian contingent and a few others could not get back to the ships and headed overland to make their rendezvous. On the way they took Pheia, obviously almost deserted by the defenders who had to watch for the main body of Athenians on the ships. None of this could have been planned or foreseen.[20] Plainly, the intentions and instructions of the Athenian forces in 431 were to ravage the land of the enemy and to do whatever damage they could beyond that. The purpose of the expedition of 430 was much the same, as we can see from the treatment of Troezen, Hermione, Halieis, and Prasiae. The attack on Epidaurus was merely an intensification of the same idea. The near miss at Methone and the sack of Pheia may have given Pericles the notion to do the same to a larger, more important, and strategically significant city like Epidaurus.

[20] 2.25.3–5.

Success would have brought great rewards. The plague had not reached its peak when the expedition left Attica, but Pericles knew that with it added to the Athenians' woes, the criticism of his strategy during the first year of the war was certain to multiply. Plutarch tells us that Pericles undertook the expedition against Epidaurus "because he wanted to cure these ills and also because he wanted to do some harm to the enemy," [21] a judgment that seems sound enough.[22] The sack of such a city would have had an enormous impact on Athenian morale and would have helped Pericles with his political battle at home. It might also have made a powerful impression on the neighboring cities and made them reluctant to send the usual contingents to join the Peloponnesian army invading Attica. At best such a success might lead some Peloponnesian coastal cities to defect from the Spartan alliance, which would be striking evidence of Spartan weakness, and might even bring Argos into the war. All this might be accomplished, if things went well, without all the disadvantages of trying to hold a Peloponnesian city without a garrison, and Pericles probably never thought of it.

Four times as many troops as in the previous year's army would be needed for an assault on a city which was larger and better defended than Methone or Pheia. The previous year's experience in Elis, moreover, had shown that the ravaging army could expect an attack by a large force once the natives recovered from their surprise. The Athenians could not be sure that a considerable Peloponnesian army would not appear soon after their landing. The size of their army and the corps of cavalry, which was of no use in the assault of a walled city but very helpful in the open field, guaranteed the Athenians against disaster. If they were successful in their assault, well and good. If not, they would at least wreak havoc on the Peloponnesian coastal cities.

[21] Per. 35.1.

[22] Miltner ("Perikles," 782–783) rejects this statement, noticing only the first half of it. Beloch (GG² II:1, 308), of course, is glad to accept the first half, which is damaging to Pericles. De Sanctis, however, who is by no means biased against Pericles, says that the campaign was undertaken "per acquietare con la condotta energetica della guerra maritima la esasperazione degli Ateniese" (Pericle, 261).

Such, we may believe, was the purpose of the second Athenian naval expedition: not the beginning of a new strategy, but the raising of the old one to a new level of intensity. Pericles was compelled to reach this new level because his strategy was not working well enough. The Spartans, as we have seen, gave no evidence of yielding. Archidamus himself, in whom Pericles must put the greatest hope of seeing reason, had now led a second invasion of Attica and was methodically devastating the entire territory. Hopes for a quick victory were dim, while the Athenian treasury was being drained by the unexpected stubbornness of Potidaea. Even before the outbreak of the plague Pericles must have realized that he could not fight the war he had planned but must raise the stakes. He must hurt the enemy enough to make him yield without, however, abandoning the fundamental strategy of a defensive war. The appearance of the plague made this policy even more necessary.

The first year's fleet had sailed all around the Peloponnesus to the Greek northwest. Pericles' force went no further than Prasiae on the eastern coast of the great peninsula and then turned back. We can only conjecture what else might have been accomplished by so mighty a force, joined perhaps by the 50 Corcyraean ships that had served in 431. It could, at least have done great damage to Corinth and her colonies. Why did the mighty armada return, having achieved so little?

Thucydides gives us one clue—the returning Athenians found that the Spartans had already left Attica.[23] Word must have reached Pericles of the Spartan withdrawal immediately after it started, for Epidaurus and the other towns he visited are only a short sailing distance from Athens. The arrival of the main army would force the Athenians out of the Peloponnese where their landings might be met by overwhelming forces, but they could have gone to the northwest as they had the previous year. Plutarch says that the attack on Epidaurus failed because of the plague.[24] That cannot be true, for the fleet and army were well enough to do significant damage after the failure at Epidaurus.

The plague may have broken out in the army at some time

---

[23] 2.56.6.   [24] Plut. *Per.* 35.3.

during the expedition and hastened its return,[25] but the same soldiers and sailors were soon sent off on another campaign, so the infection could not have been widespread nor the reason for return decisive. The likeliest conclusion is that Pericles broke off his expedition and returned in haste because he had received word of the political effect the plague was having in Athens.

Pericles and the expedition returned some time after the middle of June; the plague had been in Athens for well over a month. The Athenians, crowded into the city as a result of Pericles' policy, were particularly exposed to the contagion which was deadly to some and demoralizing to all. The panic, fear, and collapse of the most sacred bonds of civilization were such that many neglected to give proper burial to the dead, the most solemn rite of the Greek religion.[26] The suffering was unbearable, and the people plainly connected it with the war, whose necessity Pericles had urged, and the strategy on which he insisted. They had borne his strategy during the first year, when only part of their land was ravaged and when the Athenian fleet had launched worthy, if indecisive, counterblows. Now, however, "after the second invasion of the Peloponnesians, the Athenians, since their land had been devastated a second time and the plague and the war together pressed hard on them, changed their minds and held Pericles responsible for persuading them to go to war and for the misfortunes that had befallen them." [27] No doubt they were angered, too, by the failure of the great armada commanded by Pericles himself to accomplish anything worthy of such an effort.[28]

In this climate the Athenians sent the force which had returned from the Peloponnese on an expedition to the Chalcidice under Hagnon and Cleopompus. The purpose was to end the resistance of Potidaea and to suppress the Chalcidic rebellion in general. The undertaking turned out to be a disaster. Potidaea held out in spite of the siege engines which the Athenians had brought into play. Worse than that, Hagnon's troops infected the original Athenian besieging army, which had been free of the plague. After forty days of fruitless activity Hagnon took the

---

[25] Such is the opinion of De Sanctis, *Pericle*, 262.   [26] 2.52.
[27] 2.59.1.   [28] Busolt, *GG* III:2, 944.

remnant of his army back to Athens—he had lost 1,050 of the original 4,000.[29] Some scholars have doubted that Pericles was responsible for sending out this expedition, which Beloch calls "an almost unbelievable error." [30] Delbrück, always eager to defend the reputation of Pericles, concludes that not he but his pacifist enemies who were in the midst of peace negotiations with Sparta were behind the expedition. They would have preferred that Potidaea be once again in Athenian hands at the time when the peace they hoped for was concluded.[31] De Sanctis, on the other hand, believes that the expedition sailed before the peace forces gained control and was instead sent out by "those who blamed Pericles for the feeble conduct of the war." [32]

The choice of Hagnon to command the army should be evidence enough that the expedition was supported by Pericles. His enemies would hardly have selected perhaps his closest associate to conduct an expedition that the great man did not approve. Thucydides, moreover, speaks of Hagnon and Theopompus, the commanders of this expedition, as "fellow-generals of Pericles." [33] This is a unique usage, in which Thucydides speaks of generals as colleagues of a man not on the expedition with them. He seems to emphasize that Hagnon and Theopompus were associates of the *generalissimo* and perhaps that they led the army under his aegis.

There should be little doubt why Pericles decided to send this force to Potidaea, although one scholar has taken the expedition as evidence that "the leading men in Athens had obviously lost their heads and no longer rightly knew what they were doing." [34] The political situation in Athens was menacing. Pericles and his policy were under attack from two directions. The peace forces, dormant since the first Spartan invasion, were eager to make terms with the enemy. The advocates of more aggressive warfare could point scornfully to the meager results of the attack on the Peloponnese. A significant victory was needed to meet both challenges and to bolster Athenian morale.

[29] 2.58.   [30] GG²:1, 308.   [31] Strategie, 130.   [32] Pericle, 261.
[33] 2.58.1: ξυστράτηγοι ὄντες Περικλέους.
[34] Pflugk-Hartung, Perikles, 104.

Events had shown that the war would be longer than he had planned and hoped. It could not be maintained at the present rate of expenditure, and the siege of Potidaea was a major item in the budget. If the Athenians could end the siege with a single major effort, Pericles might count on a breathing spell at home and in his conduct of the war. He might well have been conscious of the gamble he was taking, but he had little choice.

Hagnon returned to Athens about the beginning of August. While he was away Pericles felt the wrath of his enemies and lost control of Athenian policy for the first time in many years. As long as the Spartans were in Attica and the Athenians needed to man their walls and forts, the bitterness against Pericles was limited to private complaints, for no formal assembly was called. But when the Spartans retired and the force under Pericles returned from the Peloponnese there was no barrier to such meetings. After their withdrawal there must have been an assembly to vote the expenses and command for the expedition to Potidaea. The departure of that army and its generals weakened political support for Pericles, and it must have been in their absence that the attacks against him were successful.[35] Contrary to his wishes and while he was general, with no greater or lesser powers than he had always had, the Athenian assembly sent ambassadors to Sparta to ask for peace.[36]

[35] The chronology of this period is uncertain. The evidence for the attacks on Pericles and his policy given by Thucydides (2.59 and 65), far from full, is imprecise and chronologically vague. No two scholars seem to put the events in the same order and at the same times. The sequence and dating offered here do not, I believe, violate the evidence and seem to me to make the best sense. Two points of chronology, however, seem to me indisputable: that Pericles had been elected general for 430/29 late in the winter or early in the spring of 431/30, pace Beloch and Grote (see n. 1 above); and that Pericles was still general during and after the peace embassy had gone to Sparta and been rejected. The language of Thucydides makes this latter point absolutely clear (pace Miltner ["Perikles," 785]): καὶ πρέσβεις τινὰς πέμψαντες ὡς αὐτοὺς ἄπρακτοι ἐγένοντο. Πανταχόθεν τε τῇ γνώμῃ ἄποροι καθεστηκότες ἐνέκειντο τῷ Περικλεῖ. ὁ δὲ ὁρῶν αὐτοὺς πρὸς τὰ παρόντα χαλεπαίνοντας καὶ πάντα ποιοῦντας ἅπερ αὐτὸς ἤλπιζε, ξύλλογον ποιήσας (ἔτι δ' ἐστρατήγει). . .

[36] Thucydides is exasperatingly brief and vague at this point, saying merely "they even sent ambassadors to the Spartans" to discuss peace. He (2.59.2) does not say directly that the Athenian ambassadors went to seek peace, though the speech of Pericles which follows makes that

Nothing could indicate more clearly the desperate condition of Athens and the complete collapse of Athenian morale. Nothing, incidentally, disproves more clearly the claim of Thucydides that Athens in the time of Pericles was a democracy in name only but in fact was or was becoming the rule of the first citizen.[37] Pericles vigorously opposed peace on any terms and surely realized that to ask for peace when Athens seemed unable to carry the war further and had no bargaining strength was madness and not in accord with her true power. Thucydides tells us neither what the Athenians asked nor what the Spartans answered. We are at a loss to understand the omission, for a great deal hangs on knowing what was said on each side.[38] Did the Athenian advocates of peace make proposals that a reasonable Athenian would support? If so we must question Pericles' opposition and his failure to offer peace earlier. Were the proposals such that reasonable Spartans should have accepted them? If so we should be critical of the Spartans for rejecting them and, perhaps, less critical of the successors of Pericles for continuing to fight a more aggressive war. Perhaps if we knew the terms proposed by Athens they might seem unreasonable. In that case we would know that the differences between the advocates of war and the advocates of peace were not very great and, perhaps, condemn the pacific group for being so foolish as to seek peace on their terms at an inauspicious moment. Our picture of these negotiations is vital to understand the further course of the war, but since Thucydides chose not to inform us we must try to construct it as well as possible.

---

plain, as does the explicit statement in 2.65.2: οὔτε πρὸς τοὺς Λακεδαιμονίους ἔτι ἔπεμπον ἔς τε τὸν πόλεμον μᾶλλον ὥρμηντο. Diodorus (12.45.5) makes the purpose of the embassies explicit: μετὰ δὲ ταῦτα πρεσβείας ἀποστείλαντες Λακεδαιμονίοις ἠξίουν καταλύσασθαι τὸν πόλεμον.

[37] 2.65.9.

[38] Dion. Hal., p. 843, quite rightly blames Thucydides for the brevity of his account. It is impossible to understand how Eduard Meyer, usually so shrewd and perceptive, can explain Thucydides' omission as follows: "So sollte man zunächst erwarten, dass Thukydides den Perikles entweder bei den Verhandlungen mit Sparta reden liesse—dann hätte er mittheilen müssen, was Athen bot und was Sparta forderte; das aber ist historisch so irrelevant, dass er kein Wort darüber verliert, nur die Taatsache, dass Athen verhandelte aber abgewiesen worde, hat historische Bedeutung" (Forsch. 390).

Probably the Athenians did not suggest peace terms, but, as the losing side usually does, asked the Spartans for theirs. The Greeks could be harsh victors, imposing such severe terms as to force the losers to abandon their city; sometimes they even put the defeated men to death and sold the women and children into slavery. These horrible extremes we may dismiss, for the Spartans did not impose such terms even upon their victory after twenty-seven years of war, when their enemies were helpless. On that occasion they offered peace, "on condition that the Athenians destroy the long walls and the Piraeus, hand over their ships except for twelve, receive back their exiles, have the same friends and enemies as the Spartans, and follow them wherever they lead, by land and by sea." [39] Athens was to be reduced to helplessness and become a satellite of Sparta, like her other allies. Such terms were possible in 404, after the battle of Aegospotami had destroyed the Athenian navy and made further resistance impossible, but in 430, for all their misery, the Athenians were still secure, indeed invulnerable. Their navy was intact and dominant, their treasury still abundant, and the source of income secure. It is hard to believe that even the most warlike Spartan could have thought of such terms in 430.

Perhaps a passage in Aristophanes' *Acharnians* may provide a clue. The poet comes forward to speak humorously of his own prowess and his service to the state. "The fame of his daring has already reached so far that when the Great King was testing the Spartan embassy he asked them first which of the two warring cities was stronger on the sea. And next he asked which had that famous poet who spoke sharp satire. The men who have had his advice have become better by far and will surely win this war. That is why the Spartans offer peace to you and demand Aegina in return. It is not that they care for that island but want it to get hold of that poet." [40] The poet is presumed to have some connection with Aegina, and the comic assumption is that if the island goes over to Sparta so, too, will Aristophanes. The joke can have no point unless at some time before the presentation of the comedy the Spartans had offered peace terms and had mentioned Aegina. Since the play was presented at the Lenaean

[39] Xen. *Hell.* 2.2.20.   [40] 646–654.

festival in the winter of the year 426/5, before the capture of the Spartan prisoners on Sphacteria, the reference cannot be to the peace terms we know the Spartans offered and the Athenians rejected on that occasion.[41] Some scholars have imagined that the lines refer to some peace offer made by the Spartans shortly before the presentation of the play, otherwise unknown to us because Thucydides thought it unworthy of mention.[42] It is unlikely, however, that Thucydides would fail even to mention a peace offer, however little attention he might give one which was unsuccessful. The words of Aristophanes do not require that the Spartan offer be very recent. The likeliest object of the reference is the last occasion when we know that there were discussions of peace terms, the summer of 430.[43]

If the Spartans spoke of Aegina in 430 they probably demanded the restoration of its autonomy, as they had done in the negotiations which preceded the outbreak of war.[44] Possibly the Spartans asked of the Athenians in 430 what they had demanded in their penultimate proposal before the war: to withdraw from Potidaea, restore autonomy to Aegina, and rescind the Megarian Decree. Given the favorable situation, they surely added the demand of the last embassy: restore autonomy to Greece, by which they meant abandon the Athenian Empire.[45]

Some such reconstruction is necessary to understand the Athenian mission and its rebuff. We may conjecture that many Athenians would be willing to abandon the Megarian embargo; some could consider abandoning Potidaea and even Aegina in desperation; few could image surrendering the Athenian Empire, which meant that Athens must sink to minor stature and be vulnerable thereafter to her enemies. The Spartan rejection of the Athenian peace mission was a blow from which the peace party would not recover for some years. Their ill-con-

---

[41] 4.15–22.

[42] Beloch (GG II²:1, 323) connects the reference in Aristophanes with the restoration of King Pleistoanax in Sparta in 427/6. Adcock (CAH V, 226–227) follows him, adding the consideration of an earthquake which hit the Peloponnese that year and prevented the invasion of Attica. Busolt (GG III:2, 1079) puts the Spartan peace offer in the autumn of 426, as a result of the Peloponnesian defeat in Amphilochia.

[43] Gomme, HCT II, 391, regards this as possible.   [44] 1.139.

[45] Ibid.; see also Kagan, Outbreak, 321–325.

sidered proposals had only proved that Pericles was right in his main point: the Athenians could achieve no satisfactory peace until they had convinced the Spartans that Athens would not yield and could not be defeated. For the moment, however, this was not completely clear. The peace party may well have thought that further negotiations would bring success, and the debate continued. The main barrier to continued search for peace was Pericles who even now retained some of his influence and all of his eloquence. The program of seeking immediate peace, at whatever cost in the long run, was halted until the formidable champion of fighting the war to an honorable conclusion had been removed.

The mood of the Spartans can only be inferred from their actions, for Thucydides tells us nothing of it. The rejection of the Athenian ambassadors shows plainly that the group led by Archidamus, which had spoken for a cautious policy and for peace before the outbreak of war, was still out of favor. The Athenians' failure to come out and defend their fields had not proven to the Spartans, as Pericles hoped, that their strategy was useless. Instead it convinced them that the Athenians were cowardly and would yield if the pressure were maintained or increased. The attacks on the Peloponnese had done no serious damage but caused considerable annoyance. The result was not to discourage but to inflame the Peloponnesians. The plague in Athens could only enhance Spartan warlike spirit, for it weakened the Athenians and promised early and easy victory. We may well understand why they should offer no terms but the unacceptable ones with which they had brought on war. We may understand their action but we cannot commend it. The Spartans acted ungenerously and unwisely. The plague hurt Athens badly, but it did not destroy her capacity to fight, to resist her enemies and, if she chose, to do them serious injury. It did, however, weaken her will. For the moment the Athenians were weak, divided, and demoralized; if the Spartans, contrary to their habit, had gathered their forces and invaded Attica a second time in the same summer the Athenians might even have been compelled to accept the harshest conditions.[46] The Spar-

[46] Such is the suggestion of Eduard Meyer, *GdA* IV, 42.

tans, however, missed the opportunity because they feared the plague, could not induce their allies to act, or lacked the imagination. If they were unwilling to take advantage of good fortune and thus end the war, they should have offered more generous peace terms and concluded the war by negotiation. A reasonable examination of the course of the war to that point would have given the Spartans little reason for expecting victory in a long war. If the Athenians could recover from the plague they were again invulnerable behind their fleet and their walls. The Spartans might have persuaded the Athenians in 430 to relieve Megara, to abandon Corcyra, and even to surrender Aegina and Potidaea. The offer of such terms would at least have helped divide Athenian opinion. Eduard Meyer may be right when he says, "If Sparta at that time had a statesman of the sort of Pericles it would have been able to secure the greatest successes." He is certainly right in saying, "But the Spartans believed that Athens already lay prostrate and it was only necessary to help themselves to it. They set conditions which Athens could not accept even in its present condition and thus they themselves compelled the already despondent enemy to pull himself together and carry the war forward." [47]

Athens, however, had not yet decided on a course of action, and the defeatists were still hoping to negotiate for peace, though Pericles continued to bar the way. His enemies, therefore, concentrated increased attacks on him, and at last he arose to defend himself and his policies.

It was difficult, for he spoke when his cause was at its nadir, but the task was easier for Pericles than it might have been for another. He was that rare political leader in a democratic state who had told the people the truth, while pursuing disputed and even unpopular policies. He had led them into a war, presenting the issues clearly and honestly. One could disagree with his policies, but no one could claim that they had not been fully and freely debated or that the people had not been consulted. He had presented the reasons why he expected victory and not exaggerated them; he had examined the enemy's prospects and not depreciated them. If he had underrated the fierceness of Sparta's

[47] *Ibid.*

hatred and determination, the people had been permitted to share or dispute his estimate when they voted on his policies. Men commonly forget their own responsibility and seek a scapegoat when they have suffered misfortunes as a result of miscalculation, and the Athenians were typical. Yet Pericles' previous forthrightness gave his angry listeners no escape, for they could not claim they had been uninformed or deceived. The responsibility, he made plain, was theirs as well as his. "If," he said to the Athenians, "you were persuaded by me to go to war because you thought I had the qualities necessary for leadership at least moderately more than other men, it is not right that I should now be blamed for doing wrong." [48]

The speech is an argument against those Athenians still working for immediate peace in spite of Sparta's recalcitrance. The sufferings of the Athenians and the failure of their recent military attempts gave the peace advocates a large audience, and to them Pericles directed the speech. He reaffirmed that the war was necessary. The choice was either to receive orders from the Spartans and their allies and so to keep the peace or to accept an unwelcome war in order to maintain freedom of action. In such circumstances the man who resists is less culpable than the man who yields. Pericles is the man to whom the people gave their trust and whose policy they supported. He is still of the same mind, but the sudden and unforeseeable misfortune of the plague has made them repent of their previous decisions. That is understandable, but not becoming to citizens of a city whose greatness and character Pericles has described in the Funeral Oration. Private misfortunes must give way to the safety of the city.[49]

That there is no reason to fear the ultimate outcome of the war Pericles has argued on previous occasions.[50] There is, however, another reason for confidence: the greatness and power of the Athenian Empire, which contributes to, but is separate from, the greatness and special character of the city of Athens. That empire, and the naval power on which it rests and to which it contributes, enables Athens to master not only its allies but the entire realm of the sea. No one, not even the Great King, can

[48] See Appendix B.   [49] 2.61.   [50] 1.140–144; 2.13.

limit Athenian movement on the sea, the only limit being the desire of the Athenians. Compared to this the loss of land and houses is nothing, "a mere garden or other adornment to a great fortune. Such things can easily be regained if Athens retains her freedom, but should she lose her freedom all else will be lost as well." [51]

This is a significant departure from the previous attitude taken by Pericles. Since the Thirty Years' Peace of 445 he had advised restraint. He always counseled the Athenians to be satisfied with what they had and not try to extend their empire. He especially emphasized this theme during the war, and we have no reason to think he ever changed his opinion that the Athenian Empire was large enough, that to try to extend it, especially in time of war, was madness. Nevertheless his words in this speech seem to encourage expansionist sentiment. Pericles himself explains his change of tone: "I did not speak of this in my previous speeches, nor would I use such language now—for it seems rather boastful —if I did not see you depressed beyond reason." [52] He is willing to risk rousing such feelings since the menace, for the moment, is from the opposite direction than he expected. The earlier attacks on him came from those forces who wanted to fight more aggressively. In the present calamity their voices were stilled. This statement giving comfort to expansionists might have been calculated to win such Athenians to the defense of Pericles against the attacks of the pacifists.

Pericles was not content to remind the Athenians of their present benefits and future hopes. They should also fear a policy of making peace and withdrawing from empire. Not only would Athens become subordinate to the greater power of Sparta and her allies. The Athenians had a tiger by the tail: "By now the empire you hold is a tyranny; it may now seem wrong to have taken it, but it is surely dangerous to let it go," for "you are hated by those you have ruled." [53] Plainly, the advocates of peace were critical of the empire and talked of giving it up. It stood in the way of peace, if we have approximated the Spartan peace terms correctly. There must have been some Athenians, members of the old faction of Thucydides son of Melesias as

[51] 2.62.   [52] 2.62.1.   [53] 2.63.2; 2.63.1.

well as others, who were hostile to the imperial idea and who were willing to make public their heretofore unpopular views at this seemingly propitious moment.[54]

He surely addresses such Athenians when he says, "It is not possible for you to withdraw from this empire, if any in the present situation out of fear or from love of tranquillity (*apragmosyne*) has decided to become honest. . . . Such men would quickly destroy a state if they persuaded others even if they had an independent state for themselves. For the lover of tranquillity (*apragmōn*) cannot be preserved except in alliance with the active man, and it is of no use for the citizen of an imperial city to seek safety in slavery; that is expedient only in a subject state." [55]

Pericles' remarks indicated that the opposition had revived the moral argument as a weapon against the imperial policy and the war. The supporters of the son of Melesias had complained more than a decade earlier that the empire was tyrannical and therefore immoral because it used funds from the league for the benefit of Athens alone. On that occasion Pericles had rejected the charge of tyranny, but had been glad to emphasize the rewards of empire received by the Athenian people.[56] This time he

[54] Mme de Romilly, among others, takes the mention of anti-imperial sentiment in this speech as evidence for its composition after the war when "the accusations against imperialism had acquired importance, because it was easy to condemn it and needful to defend it" (*Thucydides*, 150). To be sure, Thucydides mentions no such arguments in 430, but he says almost nothing about internal politics in Athens at any time. Yet we know from other sources that political conflict existed, and we should be amazed to learn that it did not even if these sources did not exist. We have every reason to take the remarks attributed to Pericles as directed to real political problems contemporary with the speech in 430.

[55] 2.63.2–3.

[56] Plut. *Per.* 11–12; see also Kagan, *Outbreak*, 142–145. Mme de Romilly (*Thucydides*, 127) correctly identifies the *apragmones* as "the people hostile to the empire, who, through fear, would have liked to act in a virtuous manner," and connects them with the opposition to the empire going back to its origin. Gomme (*HCT* II, 177) has misread her comments and accuses her of speaking of a "small party of extreme oligarchs." This she does not, as she makes plain in a note to her edition and translation of the second book of Thucydides in the Budé edition (Paris, 1962). Her rebuttal is apt (p. 100), and I agree with her that "l'argumentation de Périclès nous semble ici une groupe d'adversaires assez déterminé."

did not reject the charge of tyranny for the empire. Instead he used it as a weapon with which to defend his policy—the time for morality is past; it is now a matter of survival. He therefore urged the Athenians to reject the advice of the *apragmones*, and not to turn against Pericles and his policy either because the enemy did what was expected or because the plague brought suffering that could not be expected. They must act in a manner worthy of their city and bear their misfortunes with courage, for it is a city which has "the greatest name among all men because it has not yielded to misfortunes but has given life and labor in war and possesses the greatest power up to this time." [57]

There follows a section which some believe was not spoken by Pericles but written by Thucydides after the war in the full knowledge of the defeat of Athens. These words, however, do not seem out of character for Pericles in 430:

Even if we should now be compelled to give way to some degree, for all things which have grown also decline, the memory will remain that no Greeks ever ruled over so many Greeks, that we opposed in the greatest wars alliances and individual enemies, and that we have inhabited a city which was both the richest and the greatest. No doubt the *apragmōn* would complain of these things, but the man who wishes to accomplish something will strive after them and whoever does not possess them will be jealous. To be hated and odious for the moment is the fate of all who have tried to rule others, but whoever accepts this jealousy with a view towards the greatest things judges well. For hatred does not last long, but the splendor of the present and the glory of the future remain in memory forever. And with the foreknowledge that you will have a noble future as well as a present free of shame, and that you will obtain both by your zeal at this time, do not send heralds to the Spartans and do not let them know that you are tormented by your present sufferings. For those whose spirits are least troubled in the face of misfortunes and who resist them most in their actions, they are the strongest, whether they be states or individuals.[58]

Pericles won the debate over policy, aided powerfully, no doubt, by the intransigence of the Spartans and the harshness of their terms. The Athenians sent no more embassies to Sparta but

[57] 2.64.3.   [58] 2.64.3–6.

took up the war with renewed vigor.[59] But the advocates of peace had not given up. They still saw Pericles as the chief barrier to success and determined to remove him from the scene and open the road to peace. Unable to defeat him in the political arena, they turned to the law courts. Athenians politicians frequently attacked a man and his policies by charging him with corruption. Pericles had begun his public career with such an attack on Cimon, and Ephialtes had prepared the way for his reform of the Areopagus by attacking individual Areopagites in this way. In the same way now, probably in September, at the principal meeting during the prytany, when the usual vote confirming the magistrates in office was taken, Pericles was deposed from office in order to stand trial on a charge of embezzlement.[60]

The *apragmōnes* were not strong enough to bring this about alone, but the situation played into their hands. The peace negotiations and the assembly at which Pericles spoke against re-

[59] 2.65.1.

[60] It is difficult to speak with confidence of this trial, for Thucydides tells us almost nothing about it, saying merely that the Athenians imposed a fine on Pericles (2.65.3). The slightly fuller account of Plutarch (*Per.* 35) seems to me essentially correct. Even Diodorus (12.45.4) tells us more than Thucydides and, though the amount of the fine he mentions, 80 talents, is far too large, the rest of his account is plausible. My account of the trial comes from these sources, filled out with the technical description of such proceedings provided by Aristotle (*Ath. Pol.* 43.4 and 61.2). I exclude the evidence of Plut. (*Per.* 32) which is used by most scholars to elucidate the trial of 430. This error was apparently introduced by Beloch (*Attische Politik*, 330ff.), who argues that the attacks on Pericles and his friends placed before the war by Plutarch in *Per.* 32 really belong in 430 and that there were no such attacks and certainly no trial before the war. The heart of Beloch's argument is that Pericles was not and could not have been removed from office in the years before the war. I agree, but Plutarch never says he was. He merely says that the proposal was made by Dracontides and passed by the assembly that Pericles should deposit his accounts with the prytanies, and that the trial, when it took place, should be of a special sort. The bill was then amended by Hagnon in such a way as to make acquittal certain. Plutarch never says that Pericles left office or that the trial ever took place. I have argued (*Outbreak*, 193–202) that all this took place in 438. It seems to me that Plutarch is quite right in keeping that occasion separate from the trial of 430 and that his account of both affairs is reliable. For the time of the trial I follow the reasoning of Busolt (*GG* III:2, 955, n. 2) though, as usual, I place events a month earlier than he does. The nature of the charge is revealed by Plato (*Gorgias* 516a).

newal of them probably took place in July. Since then Hagnon and what was left of his decimated army had returned from the unsuccessful attack on Potidaea. The Athenians must have been shocked to learn that not only had they failed to win a victory, but that this great force had been so reduced. This failure must have helped produce the widespread malaise reported by Thucydides: the Athenians "grieved over their private sufferings, the common people because, having started out with less, they were deprived even of that; the rich had lost their beautiful estates in the country, the houses as well as their expensive furnishings, but worst of all, they had war instead of peace." [61] Perhaps the attack on Pericles, brought on chiefly by those weary of war, was also supported by those who wanted to wage the war more vigorously. Such men as Cleon must have realized that Pericles stood in the way of their plans no less than of those of the peace party. They may have calculated that the Spartan attitude made peace impossible, so that the removal of Pericles would put the conduct of affairs in their hands.

The sentiment against Pericles was unprecedentedly strong, for he was convicted and punished with a heavy fine.[62] Pericles had been in office without interruption for many years. We may well imagine that during that time his prestige and reputation for incorruptibility had made the regular investigation of his accounts perfunctory. He must have had no small task in preparing all his accounts for hostile scrutiny in 430. Xenophon told the story of the young Alcibiades, the nephew and ward of Pericles. "Seeing his uncle troubled he asked the cause of his concern. Pericles answered, 'I am asked to defend my use of the public funds, and I am trying to find a way to make an accounting to the citizens.' 'You would do better,' said Alcibiades, 'to seek a

[61] 2.65.2.

[62] Plutarch (*Per.* 35.4) says that his authorities differ on the amount, ranging from 15 to 50 talents. Diodorus (12.45.4) gives the figure as 80 talents. The lowest amount seems the most plausible, though it, too, is an enormous amount for an individual to pay. Plutarch tells us also that his sources differ on the name of the formal accuser, Idomeneus naming Cleon, Theophrastus saying it was Simmias, and Heracleides Ponticus mentioning Lacratides. Since the last two are not famous and therefore are unlikely inventions, they may really have been involved. On the other hand, there is no good reason to reject the name of Cleon.

way not to make such an accounting.' " [63] The anecdote may be apocryphal, but *se non e vero e ben trovato*. Pericles, in fact, seems to have made his defense in his usual Olympian way. When asked to account for certain sums, he replied simply that he had spent them "for a necessary purpose." [64] We must interpret this as a reference to the expenditure of money for purposes that must necessarily be secret, possibly for bribing foreigners in the interests of the state, as our ancient sources say, more likely for the costs of intelligence, spying, and the like. [65]

The jury was obviously not fully convinced of Pericles' guilt, for the crime of peculation might carry with it the death penalty. [66] Still, the conviction and fine appear to have carried with them disfranchisement, [67] which means that the verdict removed Pericles from public life. No doubt Pericles, perhaps

---

[63] Diod. 12.38.3; Plut. *Alcib.* 7.3.

[64] εἰς τὸ δέον. The words are cited by Aristophanes (*Clouds*, 859) which proves they were already a famous public utterance of Pericles.

The scholiast explains them as follows: "Pericles, the Athenian general, when he was asked to make an accounting for moneys he had spent, having given it to the Spartan harmost Cleandridas to make him commit treason; this he did not make plain, but said merely he had spent it for a necessary purpose." The reference must be to the story in Plutarch (*Per.* 22.2) that Pericles secured the withdrawal of the Spartan army from Attica in 445 by bribing Cleandridas. Theophrastus (Plut. *Per.* 23.1) says that Pericles paid the Spartans 10 talents annually to conciliate them and gain time to prepare for war.

[65] The whole affair brings to mind the attacks made upon Marlborough by his enemies in 1712. Like Pericles, the duke was rightly thought to be essential for the continuation of a war which had grown unpopular. Since he could not be brought down by political means, he was charged with peculation. A specific complaint was that he had taken part of the money given him for the pay of foreign troops in English service and not expended it for that purpose. Trevelyan tells us that the accusation was frivolous: "The Duke showed that it was the custom for Commanders-in-chief openly to receive that amount in lieu of secret service money for the purposes of war. He showed that Anne had specifically sanctioned the arrangement in his case; there indeed was the Queen's signature!" (G. M. Trevelyan, *England under Queen Anne* vol. III, *The Peace and the Protestant Succession* [London, 1934], 200). Pericles, we may be sure, was not less well informed than the duke, and the money was certainly spent for the state, but he was not so fortunate as Marlborough. He could point to no authorization, and his enemies took advantage of his restraint.

[66] Lysias 30.25.   [67] Andoc. *de Myst.* 74.

with the aid of his friends, soon paid the fine, but the disfranchisement seems not thereby to have been removed.[68] We have no reason to imagine, with some scholars, that Pericles was swiftly re-elected to the *strategia* by a special election; the likelihood is that he was out of office and less able to influence the conduct of affairs directly from about September 430 until the beginning of the next official year in midsummer 429.[69]

Late in the summer of 430, while the Athenians were hampered by the plague and political dissension and their fleet was occupied in the Chalcidice, the Spartans launched an attack on Zacynthus, an island lying off the coast of Elis and an ally of Athens. The expedition consisted of 100 triremes and carried the remarkably large number of 1,000 Lacedaemonian hoplites, the whole force being commanded by the Spartan navarch Cnemus.[70] This undertaking represented a change in the Spartan strategy. The advocates of a war to destroy Athenian power were plainly in control, for they had rejected the Athenian overtures for peace and imposed unacceptable conditions. But their original belief in an easy victory had been shattered. After two years of seeing their fields and homes destroyed the Athenians had refused either to fight a hoplite battle or to surrender. They remained stubborn in spite of the plague and in spite of the disgrace and dismissal of the leader most responsible for the policy leading to war and for the strategy. The naval attacks launched by the Athenians in the second year of the war, although curtailed by the plague, politics, or both, had been more menacing than the earlier one. The coastal allies of Sparta had been hurt

[68] For the payment of the fine see Ps. Dem. 26.6; on the duration of the disfranchisement see Busolt (*GG* III:2, 955).

[69] For the arguments in favor of a special election see Miltner ("Perikles," 787), who also gives references to the literature on the subject. All the arguments rest on Thucydides' words ὕστερον δ' αὖθις οὐ πολλῷ, ὅπερ φιλεῖ ὅμιλος ποιεῖν, στρατηγὸν εἵλοντο (2.65.4). There is no reason to think that "not much later" must in this context mean a few days or a few weeks, indeed it is hard to imagine such a swift change of opinion. The five or so months between the trial and the new elections in late winter 430/29 seem to suit the language well enough and the situation far better. The Athenians who had deposed Pericles from office and imposed such a heavy fine on him needed some time to recover from their anger, and his opponents needed an equal time to discredit themselves.

[70] 2.66.

and had reason to fear the future. If Sparta could not protect them she must face the danger of defection. Defecting Peloponnesian allies, to be sure, could be brought to heel by the arrival of a Spartan army, but such expeditions would be costly and difficult. The inhibition of Athenian naval campaigns by depriving Athens of the bases it needed in the northwest would be far better. If the western Peloponnese were made safe from Athenian attack the Peloponnesian forces might be concentrated more effectively in the east to deter Athenian raids. The attack on Zacynthus was part of this plan, but it failed. The Spartans could not take the city and were limited to ravaging its territory before sailing home again.[71]

Even had the Spartan plan been successful it would have merely defended the Peloponnese from attack. A new offensive strategy was required if Sparta meant to win the decisive victory upon which the war party insisted. They now turned to the policy which Archidamus had advocated in peacetime—to seek financial and naval aid in the struggle against Athens, even from the barbarians, if need be.[72] Accordingly, after the Zacynthian expedition had failed, the Spartans sent an embassy to the Great King consisting of three Spartans, two of whom had a special relationship with the Persian monarchy, as well as Aristeus of Corinth, Timagoras of Tegea, and Pollis of Argos. Since Argos was neutral, Pollis, unlike the others, went as a private citizen.[73] These men "set out for Asia and the court of the Great King, to try to persuade him to furnish money and to join in an alliance." But the Persians were not the only barbarians who were

[71] 2.66.2. See also 2.80.1 and Brunt (*Phoenix* XIX [1965], 272). Toward the end of the summer the Ambraciotes also tried to take advantage of Athens' preoccupation and attacked Amphilochian Argos. They, too, failed in an assault on the city (2.68).

[72] 1.82.1.

[73] 2.67.1. The two Spartans referred to, Aneristus and Nicolaus, were the sons of Spartans sent to the court of Xerxes during the Persian Wars. They had volunteered themselves to atone for the Spartan murder of Persian heralds who had come to demand earth and water. Xerxes graciously spared their lives (Hdt. 7.131–137). Argos, of course, had been neutral during the Persian Wars and her ambassador might expect a good reception in Susa. Pollis was probably an oligarch who favored Sparta and was glad to lend his good offices. See Kagan (*CP* LVII [1962], 209–217).

the objects of their diplomacy. They stopped on the way at the court of Sitalces in Thrace to try to persuade him to abandon the Athenian alliance and join with the Peloponnesians. They hoped he would send an army to help relieve the siege of Potidaea and give them protection on the journey to Asia.[74]

Word of the plague that had struck Athens and her army in the Chalcidice must have reached Sitalces. Probably he was also aware of the fate of Pericles and the city's weakened condition. The Peloponnesians must have considered the time ripe to suggest he abandon a doomed cause, but their hopes were frustrated. Thucydides tells us that two Athenian ambassadors happened to be visiting Sitalces. Probably the Athenians saw to it that there were always Athenians at the court of Sitalces to maintain communications and keep him loyal to their cause. The Athenian ambassadors persuaded Sadocus the son of Sitalces to arrest the Peloponnesians and turn them over to Athens. When they arrived they were put to death immediately and without a trial. Their bodies were thrown into a pit and denied proper burial. Thucydides says the Athenians committed this atrocity out of fear of Aristeus, lest this daring and brilliant man escape and do them further harm. The official explanation was that the execution was in retaliation for Spartan atrocities. From the time war had broken out the Spartans had made it a practice to kill all persons captured at sea, Athenians, Athenian allies, and neutrals.[75] Both reasons must have played a part; we may also recognize behavior which is all too common when men find themselves affected by fear, rage, and frustration in a war which is extended beyond expectation.

This act of terror and reprisal took place when Pericles was out of power. It could not have been perpetrated by the peace group, since the atrocity could only inflame feelings between the enemies. The finger of responsibility points directly at the advocates of a more aggressive policy. They were the most likely to hate the Spartans, but also the executions further damaged the cause of the advocates of peace, already hurt by Sparta's harsh demands. In fact, the atrocity may have been committed with that intent. Eduard Meyer is right to say that after the collapse

[74] 2.67.1.   [75] 2.67.2–4.

of peace negotiations, "the war must be carried forward, and its leadership fell, for good or ill, to the Radicals. All the evidence in the next months shows that the war party was master of the situation." [76] The title "war party" is intended merely as a convenient shorthand and does not refer to anything resembling a modern political party. Athenian politics typically involved shifting groups which came together, often around a man, sometimes around an issue, occasionally with reference to both. There was little or no party discipline in the modern sense and only limited continuity. During wars, however, the issues tended to become more clear-cut than in peace, and the allegiance of the citizenry to a particular policy more obvious and strong. There were surely nuances in people's positions and no doubt individuals changed their views with changes in the situation. Throughout the early years of the Archidamian War, however, opinion seems to have fallen into three distinguishable categories: (1) the desire for immediate peace with Sparta; its advocates we call the peace party; (2) the determination to wage an aggressive war against Sparta, to run risks, to try to defeat Sparta rather than wear her out; this group we call the war party; (3) the willingness to support the policy of Pericles, avoiding risks, wearing down the Spartans, and working for a negotiated peace on the basis of the *status quo ante bellum;* these men we call the moderates.[77] In the autumn of 430 the moderates were in disgrace, the peace party discredited, and the war party in control.

This group, probably led by Cleon and others, took vigorous steps to deal with Athens' problems. Alerted, no doubt, by Sparta's attack on Zacynthus and the Ambracians' attack on Argos in Amphilochia, they supported the sending of Phormio

[76] *GdA* IV, 46.

[77] These groups should not be associated with economic, social, or even geographical groups in Athenian society, as some scholars have done. The evidence is inadequate to sustain any theories. The usual assumption, for instance, is that the city folk were for the war and the peasants against it, yet the Acharnians, a country people, are pictured by Aristophanes in 425 as unwilling to hear a word in favor of peace. Cleon, a city man, is a leading figure in favor of war, but of the city *demos* we learn nothing useful. Aristocrats, as usual, are found on all sides. Sociological analysis of political behavior, however desirable, is here impossible.

with 20 ships to Naupactus, apparently partly to safeguard the port from sudden attack. The new policy, however, went further than Pericles' plan by attempting to seal off the Gulf of Corinth.[78] At the same time the Athenians took measures to guarantee the revenue and make the empire secure. A reassessment of the tribute was carried out. Although the record is incomplete, we know that the Hellespontine region had its assessment raised from about 74 to about 98 talents.[79] This seems to be evidence for greater pressure in general on those states paying tribute, for the total collected for the year appears to be the same as in 433/2 [80] even though Aegina and Potidaea, who together had contributed 45 talents, were no longer contributing. The rise in the assessment must partly explain the dispatch of Melesander with 6 triremes to Caria and Lycia to collect the tribute, since the force appears to be larger than usual and is one of the few such expeditions noticed by Thucydides.[81] Another purpose of Melesander's mission was to prevent Peloponnesian ships from establishing a base in that region and launching predatory raids on merchant ships coming from the east. The mission turned out badly, for Melesander and his troops, disembarking in Lycia and marching inland, were defeated in battle. The general and part of his army were killed.[82]

This misfortune was easily redeemed by the fall of Potidaea in the winter of 430/29. The failure of the Peloponnesians to win over Sitalces had sealed the city's doom. After a siege of two and one-half years all food was gone and the people were reduced to cannibalism. Finally, they asked the Athenian generals, Xenophon, Hestiodorus, and Phanomachus, for terms of surrender. The generals had little reason to hesitate; their army was exposed to the cold, it had suffered from disease, and some of the men may have been away from home for years. Even more important, the Athenians had already spent over 2,000 talents on the siege, and every day cost at least another talent.[83]

[78] 2.69.1. Phormio's mission was: ὁρμώμενος ἐκ Ναυπάκτου φυλακὴν εἶχε μήτ᾽ ἐκπλεῖν ἐκ Κορίνθου καὶ τοῦ Κρισαίου κόλπου μηδένα μήτ᾽ ἐσπλεῖν.
[79] ATL III, 339.   [80] Ibid.   [81] Ibid., 69–70 and 352.   [82] 2.69.
[83] 2.70 for the cost of the siege up to then. The figure of a talent a day assumes a cost of two drachmas daily for at least 3,000 besieging troops.

Prudence dictated the offer of acceptable terms, and even these were none too generous: "They were to depart with their children and wives and the mercenary soldiers, each with one garment, the women with two, with a stated sum of money for the journey." They scattered, chiefly to the Chalcidic towns, but to wherever they could.[84] Reasonable as this settlement was, and welcome as it must have been to the Athenians, we should not be surprised that the war party at home complained that unconditional surrender could and should have been demanded. They must have pointed out that now the Potidaeans and the Peloponnesian mercenaries were free and helping to increase the forces ranged against Athens in the Chalcidice. Perhaps they even argued, as some would on other occasions, that the lenient treatment would encourage others to rebel.

The war party, then, possibly led by Cleon, brought charges against the generals in a formal trial.[85] The charge seems to have been that they overstepped their authority in making peace without consulting the Athenian council and assembly.[86] There may well have been some substance in the charge, for normally generals in the field were empowered to make truces but not to conclude a peace. But the Potidaeans and mercenaries had been permitted to leave and scatter; the deed could not be undone. The Athenian people had been commited without their consent. There may have been a political motive as well, for the generals had all been elected along with Pericles late in the previous winter, when Pericles had great influence.[87] Probably they were all supporters of Pericles; certainly Xenophon was an old associate. The attack on these generals was an attack on Pericles and his moderate faction, and it failed. The Athenians were relieved to

[84] 2.70.3–4.

[85] Thucydides, as usual, gives us only the skimpiest idea of what took place in this matter of domestic politics. He says merely Ἀθηναῖοι δὲ τούς τε στρατηγοὺς ἐπῃτιάσαντο ὅτι ἄνευ αὐτῶν ξυνέβησαν (2.70.4). The language leaves no doubt that a formal accusation was made. Aristophanes (Knights 438) seems to implicate Cleon in the affair. See Busolt (GG III:2, 962, n. 1) and Gilbert (Beiträge, 122–123).

[86] Gilbert (Beiträge, 122) says the charge was either treason or bribery. Not only are these suggestions pure invention, but they ignore the clear statement of Thucydides, however brief, ὅτι ἄνευ αὐτῶν ξυνέβησαν.

[87] 2.34.6–8.

have the long and costly siege of Potidaea ended; they were not inclined to quibble over technicalities. The acquittal of the generals may also be evidence that the popular feeling against Pericles was abating. A colony was sent out to hold the deserted city, which would henceforth be an important Athenian base in the Thraceward regions.[88]

As the second year of the war came to a close the Athenians were far weaker than they had been a year earlier. The prospects for the success of the Periclean strategy were worse than ever. The Athenians had shown restraint during two invasions. They had permitted their fields and houses to be destroyed without offering battle. Now that all of Attica had been devastated there was little reason for the Spartans to think that future incursions would bring better results. The Athenian fleet, moreover, had shown that it could hurt and annoy the coastal states of the Peloponnese with relative impunity. Now was the time, according to the Periclean plan, for the Spartans to realize that Athens was invulnerable and further fighting fruitless. Now was the time for the discredited war party of Sparta to yield to Archidamus and his reasonable colleagues and offer peace on reasonable terms.

Instead, the Spartan determination was fiercer than ever. Deprived of a land battle, they had turned to the sea, threatening Athenian control of the western seas and even the security of Naupactus. All this flatly contradicted Pericles' confident prediction that the Peloponnesians would be too poor and tied to the land to man any considerable fleet and would, in fact, be "shut off from the sea." [89] The future looked grim. The Spartan embassy to Persia had been intercepted, but there was no guarantee that future envoys would not get through. The Great King might well be persuaded by the Spartans because of Athenian weakness. Should that happen, all calculations based on Athenian superiority in ships and money would be worthless. Encouraged by their prospects, the Spartans had shown themselves unwilling to make peace on any but their own terms.

This situation, though unhappy, need not be disastrous if the Athenians could achieve some striking victory that would un-

[88] 2.70.4–5; Diod. 12.46.7; Gomme, *HCT* II, 204.　　[89] 1.141.2–5.

dermine Spartan confidence. The prospects for such a stroke, however, were worse than ever. The plague was still decimating Athenian manpower and morale. The financial condition of Athens was also a severely limiting factor. Of the 5,000 talents of expendable funds (excluding the emergency fund of 1,000 talents) available at the beginning of the war, almost 2,700, over half, had been spent.[90] The expensive siege of Potidaea was over and its heavy drain on the treasury ended. Spartan activity on the sea, on the other hand, meant that the Athenians might have to spend more to man fleets and protect allies. At the rate of the previous two years they could fight not more than two years more. Even the war party must realize that Athens could not afford a major campaign in the coming year, yet a policy of inactivity was also dangerous. Though Spartan intransigence had restored Athens' will to fight, and though her walls, fleet, and empire were intact, the Athenian future did not seem bright.

[90] *ATL* III, 341–344.

4. The Third Year of the War: Phormio

Early in the spring of 429, Pericles was once again chosen as general of the Athenians.[1] Thucydides explains the reversal of opinion as follows: "Not much later, as the mob loves to do, they elected him general again and turned everything over to him, for their individual feelings were less keen over their private misfortunes whereas for the needs of the state as a whole they judged him to be the ablest." [2] The explanation tells more about Thucydides' view of the Athenian democracy than it does of the reasons for the change of opinion. No doubt the passage of time had accustomed the Athenians to their sufferings and had revealed that the removal of Pericles as scapegoat had no useful result. No doubt, too, they missed his outstanding talents, his experience and confidence, and the security he made them feel. Practical politics, however, may hold part of the explanation for the shift. We have suggested that the condemnation of Pericles was brought about by a unique union of his opponents at opposite extremes of the political spectrum.[3] Such an "unnatural coalition" [4] could not last long. As the significance of Sparta's refusal to negotiate sank in and as the war continued the hopes of the peace party faded. Its adherents had joined with Cleon and men like him to bring down Pericles, but if there could be

[1] For the date see Busolt (*GG* III:2, 963, n. 2).
[2] 2.65.4; Plutarch (*Per.* 37.1) says something very similar.
[3] See above, pp. 89–91.   [4] The term is that of Beloch (*GG* II²:1, 312).

no peace they preferred the moderate strategy and tactics of Pericles to that of his more aggressive opponents. In the elections of 429 they surely voted for Pericles in preference to more dangerous men, for their own chances of election at that moment were nil.

The return of Pericles to office did not restore the steady direction and vigorous execution of policy that had always characterized his guidance of Athenian affairs. By midsummer 429, when he resumed office, Pericles was mortally ill and had only a few months to live.[5] Plutarch tells us that the disease which killed him, probably the plague, did not attack him suddenly but lingered, "using up his body slowly and undermining the loftiness of his spirit." [6] We need hardly be surprised, therefore, that the events of the year bear no mark of his influence. The ancient authors give no clear insight into the political situation, but, besides the effects of the plague, we may guess that there was a vacuum of leadership and a consequent uncertainty in Athenian policy. In 429 no leader or faction was strong enough to control Athens throughout; different groups prevailed on different occasions. For the first time in many years the Athenians experienced the inconveniences inherent in the truly democratic management of a state in time of war.

About the middle of May the Peloponnesians launched their annual campaign. This time, however, they marched against Plataea.[7] There were good reasons not to invade Attica again. The previous year's invasion had been thorough, and there was not much left worth destroying. More important, the plague still raged in Attica, and an invading army ran the risk of infection. The Spartan need for a land campaign is questionable. Plataea was strategically located, but there is no evidence that its possession by Athens had interfered with communications

[5] The generals took office at the beginning of the archon year, at midsummer. See Hignett, *HAC* 347ff. In 429, according to Meritt (*Proceedings of the American Philosophical Society* CXV [1971], 114), that was on July 14. Pericles died two years and six months after the start of the war (2.65.6). If this is taken literally, Pericles must have died early in September. Even if it is taken loosely we must believe that he did not live far into October. He could not, therefore have been general for as much as three months.

[6] *Per.* 38.1.   [7] 2.71.1.

between Boeotia and the Peloponnese and no reason to fear that it would do so in the future. At worst Plataea was a nuisance not worth tying up the Peloponnesian army for a campaigning season. We may well believe that the decision to take Plataea came from Thebes, eager to take advantage of the situation to achieve her own purposes. The Spartans accepted the Theban proposal because they saw the strategic value of Plataea, because the plague prevented their usual activity, but also, no doubt, because of the need to placate the Thebans. In the Spartan alliance, the leader could not dictate to the other members. A state like Thebes was largely independent and could not be counted upon to obey Spartan orders or execute Spartan policy unless it wanted to.[8] The attack on Plataea may have been the price Sparta paid for continued Theban support.[9]

The attack on Plataea was particularly embarrassing for the Spartans, who purportedly launched the war "to free the Greeks." Plataea was an inoffensive small town that had done the Spartans no harm and had for some years maintained its freedom in the face of the rapacious hostility of Thebes. Beyond that the Spartans had themselves pledged to defend Plataea's independence when, after the battle of Plataea in 479, King Pausanias had administered an oath to all the Greeks who had fought in the battle. He restored to the Plataeans "their land and city, holding them in independence," and he swore the Greeks to see to it "that no one should march against them unjustly or for their enslavement; if any one did the allies who were present should defend them with all their might." [10] The Plataeans, of course, confronted Archidamus with this oath when his army appeared before Plataea, poised to ravage its land.

The response of Archidamus, if the words are close to what he really said, shows that sophistry was not foreign to Sparta. He told the Plataeans to exercise the freedom given them by

[8] See Kagan, *Outbreak*, 9–30.

[9] Most scholars have taken the Plataean campaign for granted or, like Busolt (*GG* III²:964) and Adcock (*CAH* V, 211), noticed only the strategic consideration, which I do not find sufficient. Only Duncker (*GdA* IX, 472–473), so far as I know, has suggested that the idea came from Thebes.

[10] 2.71.2.

Pausanias to join in the fight against Athens, the enslaver of the Greeks. Only in that way could the Plataeans keep their oath. Barring that, they should remain neutral.[11] There was, of course, nothing in the oaths taken in 479 that required the Plataeans to abandon their alliance with Athens, which was already in effect. As long as Plataea took no aggressive action against Sparta or its allies they had no excuse to attack her. The offer of neutrality had been made impossible by the unprovoked attack; the Plataeans could hardly "receive both sides as friends." [12] The Plataeans pointed out that apart from the danger of an attack by Thebes, they faced the certainty that Athens, which held the city's women and children, would not accept the arrangement. In either case Plataea would lose its freedom. Archidamus responded with an apparently generous offer: the Plataeans could evacuate their city for the duration of the war; the Spartans would hold their land and property in trust, paying rent for its use, and restore it intact after the war.[13] This offer, like the others, was a charade. Once the city was in Peloponnesian hands the Thebans would never permit its restoration. Thucydides elsewhere makes the Spartan motives unmistakably clear: "The hostile attitude of the Spartans in the whole matter of Plataea was chiefly on account of the Thebans, for the Spartans thought that the Thebans would be useful to them in the war just then beginning." [14]

The Plataeans, however, did not flatly reject the offer but requested a truce while they asked permission of the Athenians. Their plight illustrates the helplessness of small Greek states caught between the great powers. Independence, so highly cherished by the common man, was illusory in a world of powerful alliances. They could only hope for the protection and good will of one of the hegemonal states. On this occasion the Plataeans may have expected the Athenians to grant permission for some arrangement with the Spartans, for the Periclean strategy permitted no way to rescue their city. Any attempt at raising the siege would result in the great battle of hoplite armies that Pericles was determined to avoid. The Athenians, however, called upon the Plataeans to keep their oaths and hold to the alli-

[11] 2.72.1.   [12] 2.72.2.   [13] 2.72.3.   [14] 3.68.4.

ance, promising that as they had never deserted them in the past, "they would not now stand aside and allow them to be wronged, but would aid them with all their power." [15] We may be sure that the Athenians gave no such answer while Pericles was in control. The response must reflect the momentary ascendancy of the war party, taking advantage of Athenian emotions of loyalty to the little state that had sent help to the men of Marathon and anger at the sophistry and hypocrisy of the Spartans. The promise was honestly intended, but it could not be kept.

The Plataeans now had no choice but to reject the Spartan proposal, the answer, no doubt, that Archidamus expected. He was now free to proclaim, calling the gods and heroes to witness, that the Plataeans, not the Spartans, were guilty of wrongdoing, for they had rejected all reasonable offers. The Spartan actions now would not be in breach of the oaths and not, therefore, contrary to religion and law.[16] The Spartans, of course, were a religious people, and were truly concerned that the gods should approve an act which they feared might be sacrilege. But Archidamus also aimed his proclamation at public opinion in Greece in an attempt to justify a simple act of aggression and a violation of the principle of autonomy by the champion of Greek freedom.

The preliminaries over, the Spartans launched their attempt to take the city by ingenious methods of siege warfare instead of the long and expensive process of starvation.[17] All attempts failed, however, and in September the Spartans withdrew, leaving a part of their army to build and guard a wall around the city. Within the city was a small garrison of 400 Plataeans and 80 Athenians as well as 110 women to cook.[18] So well situated was the town that the small force could defend it against assault by the entire Peloponnesian army.[19]

---

[15] 2.73.3.   [16] 2.74.3.

[17] 2.75–77; Thucydides is fascinated by the details of the novel techniques used by the Spartans and the ingenious Plataean responses to them. For a possible explanation see G. B. Grundy, *JHS* XVIII (1898), 218–231.

[18] 2.78.

[19] For a discussion of the site and the Thucydidean account see Grundy, *Topography*, 53–72.

Toward the end of May, shortly after the Spartan attack on Plataea, the Athenians took the offensive in the Chalcidice. The fall of Potidaea had not ended the rebellion against Athens in that region; the release of its defenders had, in fact, added to the number of rebels in the field. The uprising deprived Athens of sorely needed revenue and always threatened to encourage emulation. Both war party and moderates must have supported the campaign led by Xenophon and two other generals commanding 2,000 hoplites and 200 cavalry. Given the Athenian shortage of funds, this was a major undertaking, but there was reason to believe it would be brief and successful. The attack was directed against Spartolus in Bottice and was made by arrangement with a treasonous party within the city. Thucydides does not say so, but this must have been a democratic faction, for such was the pattern throughout the long war. Sometimes patriotism would triumph over factional interest, but when love of party was greater than love of independence democrats betrayed their cities to Athens and oligarchs to Sparta. The Athenians began, as usual, by cutting down the ripe crops, but their hopes for an easy victory were thwarted. The opposite faction had learned of the imminent treason and sent for help to Olynthus. The Olynthians sent troops to serve as a garrison and prevented the betrayal. They forced a battle and defeated the Athenians by means of their superiority in cavalry and light-armed troops. These were arms in which the Athenians were not strong, for they rarely needed them in the hoplite battles they usually fought. This was not the last time in the war that hoplite armies would be defeated when out of their element.

The two Athenian allies in the region, Perdiccas of Macedon and Sitalces of Thrace, sent no help. Perdiccas, of course, was a most untrustworthy ally, and his failure to help should have caused no surprise. Sitalces, however, had behaved well in the matter of Peloponnesian ambassadors, and his absence must have been disappointing. These were alliances of convenience, and Sitalces may not have been eager to see Athens regain her old power on the coast of Thrace. The defeat was costly for Athens. She lost all her generals, 430 men, and the initiative in the northeast.[20]

[20] 2.79.

The Athenian failure at Spartolus may have increased the enemy's daring, but plans were already afoot to challenge Athenian control of the west. Not long after the events in Thrace the Chaonians and Ambraciots proposed that the Spartans organize a fleet of ships and 1,000 hoplites from among their allies and attack Acarnania. Their motives were selfish—they wanted to expel Athenian influence from the region and conquer it for themselves.[21] But they presented the idea to the Spartans as part of a grand strategy to prevent the Athenians from troubling the Peloponnesus: Acarnania would fall easily, then Zacynthus and Cephallenia, perhaps even Naupactus.[22] Here was another of many instances when the Spartans were led into dangerous undertakings on behalf of their allies, and in this case the appeal was persuasive and the prospects seemed good.

The new strategy, heralded by the unsuccessful attack on Zacynthus,[23] had not been fully tried, and the time seemed good to test it. The Athenians still lacked effective leadership and were weakened by the plague and their recent defeat. They had only 20 ships in western waters; the plague and shortage of money put in question how many reinforcements would be available. The invitation of the Ambraciots and Chaonians guaranteed the Spartans enthusiastic allies who knew the territory. Before the war the Corinthians had scoffed at Archidamus' gloomy picture of Athenian naval superiority. The Peloponnesians, they said, would be able to gather a fleet superior to the Athenians' because it would be manned by Peloponnesian citizens and not by hirelings. "In all probability one defeat at sea would finish them." [24] Now was the time to test that theory.

Not surprisingly, the Corinthians vigorously supported the suggestion of their Ambracian colonists. They may even have invented the scheme; in any case, they had good reason to favor it. Corinth was the one city most threatened by Athenian presence in the west. Her influence, defense of her colonies, and access to northwestern Greece and Sicily by land and by sea would all benefit from the success of the plan. Once again Sparta put the navarch Cnemus in charge. He slipped past the fleet of Phormio and sailed to Leucas where he joined the forces of the

[21] βουλόμενοι . . . καταστρέψασθαι καὶ ᾿Αθηναίων ἀποστῆσαι, 2.80.1.
[22] 2.80.1.   [23] See above, pp. 93–94.   [24] 1.121.4.

Leucadians, Ambraciots, and Anactorians. They were strengthened by significant numbers of barbarians from Epirus who
were friendly to Corinth.[25] Corinth and Sicyon were enthusiastically preparing their fleets, but they were not yet ready
when Cnemus and his thousand hoplites sailed. The wily
Phormio may have deliberately allowed the fleet of Cnemus to
go by in order to engage only part of the Peloponnesian force.
Had he tried to stop Cnemus he might have had to deal with
reinforcements from Corinth and Sicyon. When at last he chose
to engage the reinforcing fleet the Spartans were fighting in
Acarnania.

Cnemus did not wait for the additional force still at Corinth
but marched through Amphilochian Argos, sacking a village on
the way. Had he waited he might have been strengthened by
a thousand Macedonians sent by the treacherous Perdiccas, evidently convinced to change sides by the Athenian defeat at
Spartolus. But Cnemus, without reinforcements, attacked
Stratus, the largest city of Acarnania, believing it the key to the
campaign.[26] The Acarnanians were clever enough not to oppose
the Spartans in a pitched battle. Instead, they used their knowledge of the terrain, their skill with the sling, and the poor discipline of the barbarians to rout the attackers. Cnemus was forced
to take up his dead under a truce, leave the field to the enemy,
and return to the Peloponnese.[27]

When Cnemus arrived at Stratus the Acarnanians had sent
word to Naupactus asking Phormio to come to their aid, but he
could not leave his base unguarded while the Corinthian and
Sicyonian fleets were still in the gulf.[28] He could only keep the
reinforcements from getting through, but that was no easy task.
Phormio had 20 ships against the enemy's 47. The Peloponnesians never imagined that the Athenians would challenge them
with such an inferior force, but they reckoned without the dar-

---

[25] 2.80; evidence for Epirote friendship with Corinth is provided
by R. L. Beaumont, *JHS* LXXII (1952), 64ff. Beaumont believes that
Corinth was interested in Acarnania because it was on the land route to
Apollonia in the north. For a discussion of the geography of Acarnania,
Ambracia, and Argos Amphilochia see N. G. L. Hammond, *BSA* XXXII
(1936–1937), 128ff.

[26] 2.80.7–8.   [27] 2.81–82.   [28] 2.81.1.

ing and confidence of the Athenian sailors and their general. The Peloponnesians, moreover, suffered from a disadvantage. Their ships served as transports for the soldiers they were carrying to Acarnania, so their vessels, already slower than the Athenians', were even less suitable for a sea battle of the modern style at which the Athenians were so adept.[29] The great number of hoplites on board would have given the Peloponnesians an advantage in the old style of naval warfare such as the Corinthians and Corcyraeans had fought at Sybota. There both sides carried many hoplites, archers, and javelin throwers on their decks. When ships came together they remained still while their troops fought it out. They did not use the sophisticated naval tactics employed by the Athenians, "but they fought with fury and brute strength rather than with skill." The battle resembled a war on land.[30] Phormio, of course, would not permit such tactics, so the speed and maneuverability of his ships gave him some advantage to offset the enemy's superiority in numbers.

On the very day that Cnemus was marching against Stratus, his reinforcements sailed into the gulf of Corinth. Phormio allowed the enemy ships to sail along the Peloponnesian coast for some distance without hindrance. He wanted them to clear the narrow straits between Rhion and Cape Antirrhion, for his tactics required an open sea (see Map 3). At last, when the Peloponnesians tried to sail across the open water from Patrae to the mainland, they were challenged by the Athenians. They apparently anchored for the night and then tried to slip away under cover of the darkness, but Phormio caught them in midchannel and forced them to fight in open water. The Peloponnesians arranged themselves in a defensive formation very similar to that employed by the Spartan admiral Eurybiades against the Persians at Artemisium in 479;[31] they formed a large circle with the ships' prows facing outward. The ships were placed close enough together to prevent the Athenians from breaking through, and in the center were five of the fastest ships which could bring help to any point where a breakthrough might

[29] 2.83.1–3; Gomme, *HCT* II, 217.   [30] 1.59.
[31] Hdt. 8.11. The similarity was called to my attention by John Hale, a keen student of Greek naval tactics.

occur. This was not a bad plan in the circumstances, and with reasonable skill, confidence, and luck it might work.

Phormio responded to this stratagem by forming his ships in a line and sailing them around the circle formed by the prows of the enemy ships. This could be dangerous, for the vulnerable sides of the Athenian ships were exposed to the metal beaks of the enemy. A swift assault by the Peloponnesians might ram the Athenians and send them to the bottom before they could turn. Phormio, however, sent his ships around the enemy in an ever-shrinking circle, forcing the Peloponnesians into a narrower and narrower space, "always just grazing by and giving the impression that they would charge at any moment." [32] He obviously had complete confidence in the skill of his men and contempt for the enemy. He expected that in close quarters the Peloponnesians would not be able to maintain position and would foul each other's oars. But he knew that toward dawn a breeze usually blew from the gulf and that in the choppy water it would create, the Peloponnesians would have difficulty managing their ships, burdened with many troops on board. We cannot improve upon Thucydides' account of the battle:

When the wind began to come up, the ships, which were already in close quarters, were thrown into disorder both by the wind and by the small boats; [these were a number of light boats, not warships, placed in the center of the circle for safety] one ship was colliding with another while the men tried to push them apart with poles, shouting at one another to watch out and cursing so that they could hear neither the words of their commanders nor the calls of the coxswains. At last, when the inexperienced rowers were unable to clear their oars in the high waves, just at that opportune moment Phormio gave the signal and the Athenians fell upon them. First they sank the ship of one of the generals and then they destroyed any one that they came upon, and they reduced the enemy to such a state that not one of the ships turned to defend itself, but all fled to Patrae and Dyme in Achaea.[33]

The Athenians pursued and captured 12 ships with most of their crews. They set up a trophy of victory and returned in triumph to Naupactus. The surviving Peloponnesian ships crept along the

[32] 2.84.1.   [33] 2.84.3.

coast to the naval base at Cyllene in Elis. There they met Cnemus limping home from his defeat at Stratus. The first major Peloponnesian effort at an amphibious offensive had resulted in humiliating failure.

The news of the defeat of a Peloponnesian fleet in their first naval battle by an inferior force came as a shocking surprise to the Spartans. They were convinced that the fault must be slackness in leadership, "failing to consider the long experience of the Athenians compared to their own brief practice." [34] Enraged by Cnemus' failure, for as navarch he was responsible for the entire campaign, they sent three "advisers," *xymbouloi*, to Cnemus, among them the dashing Brasidas. Their orders were to prepare for another battle and "not to be driven from the sea by a few ships." [35]

They equipped their ships for battle and sent to the allies for assistance. Phormio was immediately aware of these preparations and sent a messenger to Athens both to announce his great victory and to ask for reinforcements, as many and as soon as possible, for a battle was imminent. The Athenian assembly responded swiftly but strangely. They granted a fleet of 20 ships and ordered its commander to sail to Phormio. On the way, however, he was to stop at Cydonia in Crete and take the town, which was hostile to Athens. This diversion was ordered in response to the request of a certain Nicias of Gortys, a *proxenus* of the Athenians. Typically, he had unrevealed selfish motives, but even what Thucydides tells of the public reason for the trip to Crete is puzzling. Why should the Athenians have sent a fleet to Crete at all, and particularly at such a time, merely in the hope of taking an unimportant town? Thucydides gives no clue, for his account of this incident is even sparser than usual; he does not, for instance, tell the name of the commander of the expedition, though he must have known it.

Such an expedition could not have won the support of Pericles, but must have been approved over his objection or, more likely, in his absence. Some scholars, therefore, have concluded that the foolish mob, unrestrained by intelligent leadership merely gave vent to its unthinking and rapacious ambition

[34] 2.85.2.   [35] 2.85.1–3.

to the detriment of the city's security.[36] A military historian goes further: "The imbecility of this order . . . is almost beyond belief. It stands starkly out as the most glaring instance of crass strategical stupidity in the entire war. . . . it may well be that some civilian nincompoop seized his incomparable chance for blundering." [37] The distinction between civilians and soldiers in Athens was not very great, and the Athenians made many blunders during the war, but they usually plausibly explained even their disastrous undertakings. For this one we can only guess the motive. Gomme suggests that the Athenians intervened in Crete out of concern for their trade with Phoenicia and the Levantine regions, "which might be interrupted by privateers based on Crete." [38] Crete, of course, was closely tied to Sparta, and the Athenians may have thought that the exploitation of local quarrels on the island might deprive the Spartans of support and further indicate the high cost of fighting Athens. Perhaps the outbreak of a major revolt on Crete might even divert the Spartans from their naval activities in the west and in the Corinthian Gulf. All of this is conjecture, for no such rising took place, but they may well, as Gomme further suggests, have been trying to kill two birds with one stone.[39] Why, then, did they not send one fleet directly to Phormio and another to Crete, thus dealing with both situations without prejudice to either? Even the 20 ships sent to Naupactus seems too few in light of the number available to the Peloponnesians. We must conclude that the Athenians were unable to do better. Whether it was a shortage of men caused by the plague or of money caused by the shrunken treasury is not clear; probably both played a part. To some scholars this seems a strange time to undertake additional responsibilities. To the Athenian war party, and to most Athenians it may have seemed just the time to divert the Spartans from a concentration of their forces. The Athenians did not choose the moment. The invitation came when it did; it must be immediately accepted or rejected. Nor should the partially unsuccessful outcome of the double mission obscure

[36] Even Grote, the great defender of Athenian democracy, gives some such explanation, 6.203.

[37] Henderson, *Great War*, 103–104.   [38] *HCT* II, 221.   [39] *Ibid.*

its prospects at the time. The Athenians obviously thought the fleet could do both jobs. If we read Thucydides carefully we notice that the fleet was delayed for a long time not because of its activities on Crete but "because of the winds and bad sailing weather." [40] Suppose the Athenians had been able to stir up a major rebellion on Crete that required Spartan attention. Suppose the weather had been favorable and the ships arrived in time to help Phormio. The mission would then be regarded as a stroke of brilliant strategic imagination. Perhaps all this was too much to hope for, but we should not be too completely impressed with the *fait accompli*. The mission may have been a mistake; it was certainly not absurd.

The reinforcements were, however, detained at Crete, leaving Phormio with 20 ships to face the Spartan force of 77. This time the Peloponnesians were not only overwhelmingly superior in numbers but anxious for battle. This time the ships were not slowed and encumbered by passengers. They were commanded more vigorously, imaginatively, and skillfully than before. After gathering and fitting out their ships at Cyllene, they sailed along the Peloponnesian shore until they reached Panormus, just east of Cape Rhium, at the narrowest point in the Gulf of Corinth. There they met their infantry.

Phormio, of course, need not have responded to this threat. He could have stayed at Naupactus, defending his base and refusing to fight a force almost four times the size of his own. That, however, would have given the enemy free access to the west, breaking the Athenian blockade and locking the Athenians in. It would also have destroyed the image of Athens as mistress of the seas, encouraged the enemy, and possibly given the restless subjects of Athens the courage to revolt. Phormio was compelled to confront the superior force of the enemy and attempt to avoid defeat. He took his fleet to Antirrhium, Molycrian Rhium, as Thucydides calls it, less than a mile across the gulf from Rhium in the Peloponnese.[41] There he anchored just outside the narrows. Phormio again wanted to fight in the open sea where the superior tactics of the Athenians would be most effective. The Spartans, more ably led this time, wanted to

[40] 2.85.6.   [41] 2.86; Gomme, *HCT* II, 222.

fight inside the narrows for just the opposite reasons. For a week the enemies glared at each other across the narrow water, each refusing to give battle in an area of the other's strength.

But the Athenians were at a disadvantage in the choice of a battle site. They were outnumbered but, more important, they were compelled to protect Naupactus, their naval base on the gulf. The Spartans, well aware of this, began to sail eastward, along the Peloponnesian coast. On their right wing were their 20 best ships, heading toward Naupactus. Phormio had no choice but to cover them as he sailed back into the narrower portion of the gulf. As he moved, swiftly and reluctantly, he was accompanied on land by the Messenian hoplites, the Athenian allies who lived at Naupactus. All was going as the Spartans had planned. When they saw the Athenian ships hurrying along the north shore in single file the Spartans wheeled about and raced to the attack. Nine of the 20 Athenian ships were cut off and driven ashore as they tried to escape. Eleven remained to face the 20 best Peloponnesian ships on the right wing. Even if the Athenians could defeat or elude them they must still face the remaining 57. Disaster seemed certain.

The Athenian 11 used their speed to get past the enemy. Ten reached Naupactus, waiting there with prows outward, ready to fight the overwhelming numbers which would soon arrive. One Athenian ship had escaped the first onslaught but was still limping home, pursued by the Peloponnesians, who were already singing the chant of victory. A merchant ship happened to be lying at anchor in the deep water off Naupactus; it became the device that produced a stunning reversal. The lone Athenian ship, instead of racing for the protection of Naupactus, whirled, using the anchored merchantman as a pivot, and rammed the leading pursuer, sending her swiftly to the bottom. This unique act of skill and daring completely confounded the Peloponnesians. They had given up all semblance of order in their pursuit, thinking the battle won. Some ran aground in ignorance of the waters. Others, confused, put their oars into the water to stop their ships and wait for the rest of the fleet, a terrible mistake, for it left them motionless and helpless before a moving enemy.

All of this gave the remaining Athenians new courage. They

attacked the enemy who still outnumbered them two to one, but the Peloponnesians had lost all taste for battle. They fled to Panormus, abandoning the 9 Athenian ships they had captured and losing 6 of their own. Each side set up a trophy as a mark of victory, but it was clear who had won. The Athenians retained their fleet, their base at Naupactus, and free movement on the sea. The Peloponnesians, fearing the arrival of Athenian reinforcements, sailed back home, most to Corinth, the Leucadians to their island. Very soon thereafter the 20 ships from Athens arrived by way of Crete, too late for the battle; their coming at least discouraged the enemy from trying again.[42]

The significance of Phormio's victory was great. The Athenians had successfully defended their vital base at Naupactus, thereby making it possible to take swift action in Acarnania and the other western regions and helping to foil the ambitious Peloponnesian plan in that quarter. Even more important, perhaps, was the effect on morale. The Athenians were convinced more than ever of their superiority at sea. So were their enemies and subjects. Spartans undertaking naval campaigns would be more timid; subjects contemplating rebellion might think again and find it hard to win allies. The best way to appreciate the importance of Phormio's victory is to imagine the consequences of defeat. Athens would have lost Naupactus, her position in the west, her chance to damage the commerce of Corinth and other Peloponnesian states trading with the west. Her own confidence, shaken by the plague, by the expense of war, and by the unchallenged destruction of her territory, would be further diminished. The enemy, on the other hand, would be encouraged to undertake greater naval operations, perhaps to challenge the Athenians on the Aegean. The news of an Athenian defeat at sea might have encouraged enemies of Athens in the empire to rebel. All this might have brought the Great King into the picture. No wonder the Athenians remembered Phormio fondly and after his death honored him with burial in the state cemetery on the road to the Academy near the grave of Pericles.[43]

[42] 2.90–92.
[43] Paus. 1.29.3. On the later career of Phormio see the sensible discussion of Gomme, HCT II, 234–237.

The defeated Spartan commanders were reluctant to return home with news of their failure and so were driven to daring. The Megarians suggested that they attack the Piraeus. The idea was incredibly bold, for the Athenians still commanded the sea and had just proven their tactical superiority. But the plan counted on the power of surprise. What was less likely than a sea attack on the very port of Athens, particularly in November, after the sailing season,[44] and especially by the Peloponnesians who had just suffered a humiliating defeat? Besides, the Athenians were overconfident and ill-prepared. The harbor was neither closed nor guarded, "quite naturally," says Thucydides, "because of their great superiority at sea." [45] Such carelessness may be natural, but is not excusable, for superiority was no guarantee against the surprise attack the Peloponnesians planned. The Spartan commanders were convinced of the feasibility of the Megarian scheme, and they prepared for the attempt.

The plan was to send the oarsmen from the fleet at Corinth overland to the Megarian port of Nisaea on the Saronic Gulf. There they would find 40 unmanned Megarian triremes which they would sail immediately to the unsuspecting and unprotected Piraeus. The first step went as planned; the rowers reached Nisaea undetected and found the ships as promised. Then the nerve of the Spartan commanders failed. Thucydides says, "They were thoroughly frightened by the risk—and also there was some talk of a wind having prevented them." [46] Thucydides may be too hard on the Spartans. Brasidas, after all, was one of them, and he was not usually one to be frightened away from the right action. Perhaps the generals were already aware of the obviously poor condition of the Megarian ships.[47] Perhaps, on the other hand, Brasidas was outvoted by his more cautious colleagues.

The Peloponnesians did not sail directly to the Piraeus, but against Salamis instead. There they assaulted the fort, captured the three ships set to guard against an attack from Megara, and ravaged the island. Fire signals warned Athens, which was soon in panic. The Athenians believed that the Spartans had taken Salamis and were on their way into the undefended Piraeus,

[44] Gomme, *HCT* II, 237.   [45] 2.93.1.   [46] 2.93.4.   [47] 2.94.3.

which Thucydides thinks they could have done.[48] At dawn the Athenians took courage, sending a force of infantry to guard the port and a fleet to Salamis. At the first sight of the Athenians the Peloponnesians fled, sailing to Nisaea and going from there on foot to Corinth. Athens was safe and the Athenians took steps to see that no such surprise attack in the future could succeed.[49]

The incident, because it failed, was trivial. Had it succeeded it would have had some material effect on the war; presumably the reserve fleet set aside by Pericles was in the Piraeus, unmanned, and a successful surprise attack might have destroyed it. Much more important would have been the effect on Athenian and Peloponnesian morale; so bold a stroke might have undone the results of the victories of Phormio. The failure, however, was not the result of incalculable chance, any more than the failure of the Spartan victims of Phormio to use their numerical superiority to good effect.[50] In both cases the Peloponnesians failed because their inexperience on the sea caused them to make mistakes and to be fearful. These weaknesses were correctly calculated by Pericles in estimating Athens' chances for success in the war. On the sea she could even afford to make mistakes, so great was her superiority.

Pericles, however, was not able to enjoy the fruits of his predictions. Two years and six months after the outbreak of the war, in September of 429, he died of the lingering disease which had struck him some time before.[51] His last days were not happy. The man who had been the first citizen of Athens had suffered the ignominy of public condemnation, loss of office, the imposition of a heavy fine, perhaps even the loss of his citizenship. All this might be forgotten after his re-election, but some losses could not be repaired. Many of his friends died in the plague, among them some of his closest associates in the administration. Even closer to home were the deaths of his sister and his legitimate sons, Xanthippus and Paralus.[52] Faced with the threat of the disappearance of his line he asked the

[48] 2.94.1.   [49] 2.94.4.
[50] Hans-Peter Stahl (*Thukydides* [Munich, 1966], 86–94) argues that the point of Thucydides' narrative is precisely to show the irony of men calculating what is incalculable.
[51] 2.65.6.   [52] Plut. *Per.* 36.

Athenians for exemption from a law on citizenship which, ironically, he himself had introduced over two decades earlier. It declared illegitimate the offspring of marriages between any but Athenian citizens. The children of the liaison between Pericles and Aspasia, a Milesian woman, were thus illegitimate. Pericles asked that his son by Aspasia, also called Pericles, be exempted from the law, and the Athenians, in their restored reverence for their leader, granted the wish.[53]

Public matters also apparently weighed heavily on the mind of Pericles as his life drew to an end. The man who had tried to turn Athens away from expansion and toward a conservative policy of maintaining the empire and living peacefully with the Spartans had seen his moderate policy explode into war. That war, which he hoped to bring to an early satisfactory conclusion, stretched on with no end in sight. His conservative strategy calculated to save Athenian lives now seemed incapable of winning the war, and the unforeseeable plague had brought unprecedented carnage into Athens. Ironically and, he must have thought, unfairly, he was now blamed for the war and the miseries it brought. This is the context in which we must understand a plausible anecdote reported by Plutarch. Toward the very end of his life some friends who were attending Pericles, supposing him to be asleep, discussed his greatness, his power, and his achievements. They spoke particularly of his military prowess, of the many victories he had won for Athens. Pericles, however, had heard what they said and expressed his surprise at what they chose to praise, for such things were often due to chance and had been achieved by many. "But they had not spoken of the greatest and most beautiful thing. For no one of the Athenians now alive has put on mourning because of me." [54] This was a strange remark for a general who had led Athenian soldiers and sailors into battle where some of them, certainly, had died. It is explicable, however, as the response of a man with a burdened conscience to those who accused him of deliberately bringing on a war which he might have averted.

The death of Pericles was a serious blow to the Athenians. To appreciate his importance, we need not agree with Thu-

53 Plut. *Per.* 37.   54 Plut. *Per.* 38.3–4.

cydides' encomium uncritically; we need not believe that the original strategy with which Pericles entered the war guaranteed victory; we need not believe that Athens in the time of Pericles was something like a benevolent dictatorship or that after his death it was led by selfish incompetents. He was a man of unusual intelligence and vast experience who made a reasonable estimate of Athenian needs and power. He was not infallible, but he was wise and, the attack on Epidaurus appears to indicate, flexible. Probably he would have adjusted his strategy and tactics to the new realities once his original expectations had been disappointed. More important even than these qualities was the unique nature of the power he commanded. He was a military man and strategist of stature, but even more a consummate and successful politician. He had been able to decide on a policy and persuade the Athenians to adopt and hold to it for the necessary time and to restrain them from overly ambitious undertakings. Perhaps the restored Pericles would have had enough power to hold the Athenians to a consistent policy, as no other Athenian could. Inconsistency would haunt Athens throughout the war.

Thucydides gives us a version of a speech in which Pericles enumerates the qualities needed by a statesman: "to know what must be done and to be able to explain it; to love one's country and to be incorruptible." [55] No one had these qualities in greater measure than Pericles himself, and if he made errors from which no mortal is free, he of all Athenians was most likely to put them right. His countrymen would miss him sorely.

While the Spartans were making their attack in the Saronic Gulf a great army was on the march in the northeast. Sitalces, king of the Thracians and ally of Athens, with 150,000 troops, one-third of them cavalry, attacked the Macedonian kingdom of Perdiccas as well as the Chalcidic cities. The attack on Macedon was the result of a private quarrel; its purpose was to enthrone Amyntas, Perdiccas' nephew, in his place. The attack on the Chalcidians fulfilled the terms of Sitalces' alliance with Athens and was undertaken in concert with the Athenians. They sent

[55] 2.60.5, γνῶναί τε τὰ δέοντα καὶ ἑρμηνεῦσαι ταῦτα, φιλόπολίς τε καὶ χρημάτων κρείσσων.

envoys to accompany the king, among them Hagnon, who was to command the fleet and army that Athens was to send.[56] Thucydides' account leaves many questions unanswered. We do not know why the Thracian king had not participated in the Athenian attack on Spartolus during the summer. When the Athenians negotiated with Sitalces for the current campaign, whose idea it was, and why the decision was made to attack at the onset of winter when the campaign would be least effective are all unknown. The answers to these questions might explain still another surprising event: the failure of the Athenians to fulfill their part of the bargain.

Sitalces invaded Macedonia, stormed some fortresses, and accepted the capitulation of others, but his advance was hampered by the resistance of some fortified places and by the Macedonian cavalry. He was soon reduced to the relatively ineffective device of ravaging the territory in the winter and compelled to begin negotiations with Perdiccas. The attack on the Chalcidice was delayed while Sitalces awaited the arrival of the Athenian fleet. Obviously the plan was for the Athenians to attack by sea and the Thracians by land. The Athenian fleet, however, never came. Athens instead sent envoys and gifts, but these were of little use against the stubborn Chalcidians. Thucydides explains that the Athenians thought that Sitalces would not come; perhaps he had been expected to start earlier, even in concert with the attack on Spartolus. By November they may have given up hope that the Thracians would ever move.[57] Most scholars are not convinced by Thucydides' explanation. Their general opinion is that the Athenians were shocked by the size

[56] The campaign is described by Thucydides (2.95–101). Diodorus (12.50–51) is almost completely dependent on Thucydides, although he gives a different figure for the army of Sitalces, 120,000 infantry and 50,000 cavalry. There is also a difference in the figures each gives for the tribute collected by Sitalces; Thucydides says it was 400 talents annually in coin and 400 in goods; Diodorus says simply that it was more than 1,000 talents.

[57] Grote (VI, 220) says, "having probably waited to hear that his army was in motion, and waited long in vain, they began to despair of his coming at all, and thought it not worth while to despatch any force of their own to the spot."

of Sitalces' army, "that Sitalces seemed too formidable and that the plan of joint action with him had been abandoned." [58]

This explanation seems likely, but not adequate, for the Athenians must have had some idea of the power of Sitalces before he mustered his troops. They had been active in Thrace for decades, and such Athenians as Thucydides had property and connections in the region. The terseness of his account and the absence of other evidence permits us only to speculate. The grand campaign in the Chalcidice must have been planned when the Athenians were feeling confident, perhaps when the war party was ascendant, possibly near the time they had promised support to the Plataeans. The choice of Hagnon as commander of the Athenian force is interesting. He was a supporter of Pericles and his moderate policy, and generals were often, though not always, chosen to command campaigns of which they approved. Perhaps, however, Pericles had come to favor this undertaking, which was merely an extension of the fight against Potidaea. Hagnon may also have been chosen for his special qualifications to command in the Thraceward region. He was the founder of Amphipolis and had fought at Potidaea.

Between the formation of the plan, however, and the movement of the Thracian army had come the Spartan attack on Ambracia, the challenge to Naupactus, the unthinkable raid on the Piraeus, and the defection of Perdiccas. Though all Sparta's naval actions had failed, they were frightening. If they could assault the port of Athens, contrary to all expectations, what might they not try? Initiative on the sea had, for the moment, passed to Sparta. The Athenians may have decided that this was no time to undertake large expeditions far from home. Also, manpower and money were in short supply in the autumn and winter of 429/8. The combination of these problems may explain the failure of Athens to meet its commitment to Sitalces.

Whether the assembled might of the Thracians alarmed their Athenian allies, it certainly terrified all the Greeks from the borders of Macedon to the pass at Thermopylae. They heard

[58] Adcock, *CAH* V, 206; much the same view is held by Busolt (*GG* III:2, 973), who in n.1 cites a number of others sharing that opinion.

rumors that the Athenians meant to unleash the barbarians against central Greece and believed them enough to begin preparations for defense. Similar fears were felt by Thracian tribes not under the control of Sitalces. All these fears were needless, for the huge Thracian army ran short of food, which the Athenian fleet might have been expected to supply, and they could not live off the land in the winter. The shrewd Perdiccas won over Seuthes, the nephew of Sitalces and his heir apparent after the death of the Athenophile Sadocus. Seuthes, who had been promised the hand of Perdiccas' sister and a dowry, persuaded Sitalces to withdraw, though we may believe that the failure of the Athenians was a more compelling argument.

The abortive Thracian campaign brought the third year of the war to an end.[59] Though the Athenians had been spared the invasion of their territory and suffered no defeats on land or sea, their prospects were not good. There is much truth in the gloomy assessment by Beloch:

The war had now lasted three years without bringing any decision. But Athens had been able to hold on to its sphere of power only by the most difficult sacrifices, while the resources of the enemy remained almost intact. The war treasury on which Athens' maritime superiority chiefly rested, was already, for the most part, exhausted. The plague had torn frightful holes in the ranks of the men able to fight, more than the worst defeats could have done. Still more considerable was the moral damage Athens' authority had suffered in the eyes of the allies as a result of these things. Thus, if the Peloponnesians also showed no really striking military success, if they were not even able to prevent the loss of Potidaea, if their attempt to try conclusions with the Athenians on sea had been miserably defeated, still, in spite of everything, the power relationship of the two belligerents had shifted very substantially in their favor. The Athenian Empire staggered on its foundations; the crisis approached.[60]

Beloch paints somewhat too dark a picture. The Athenian treasury was not on the point of exhaustion. The Athenians seem

[59] At about the same time Phormio led a minor expedition to Acarnania. Its purpose was to "show the flag" and to bolster the loyalty of the friends of Athens in that region (2.102–103).
[60] Beloch, GG II²: 1, 316.

to have taken only 600 talents from their reserve fund in 429, leaving an estimated usable balance of 1,450.[61] That boded ill for the future, but did not compel an immediate crisis. The Athenians could fight on at full steam, on the level of the first two years, for one more year, or at half speed for two. There is no question, however, that if they meant to fight beyond that they must discover new sources of income. The loss of prestige in the eyes of the allies, moreover, may have been reduced considerably by the impressive victories of Phormio and the pusillanimous conduct of the naval war by the Spartans; still the allies could not fail to see the weakness of Athens. Busolt clearly saw the Athenians' predicament: "It was a doubtful omen for the Athenian conduct of the war that they abandoned the offensive on the sea to the enemy. To be sure, the continuation of the plague and the great diminution of the funds in the treasury must have a crippling effect on operations, but if the Athenians limited themselves to the defensive on the sea, too, . . . one cannot see how they could compel the enemy to make peace." [62]

[61] *ATL* III, 343.   [62] Busolt, *GG* III:2, 984.

5. The Revolt at Lesbos

The death of Pericles left a vacuum in Athenian political life. No towering figure stood ready and able to exercise the enormous influence he had held. "Those who followed him," said Thucydides, "were more equal with one another" and so not able to provide the unified, consistent leadership necessary in a war. Pericles has often been criticized for failing to provide a successor of equal stature, as by Beloch: "The personal regime, as it does everywhere, in Athens, too, allowed only mediocrities to arise. Pericles' tools were intellectual zeroes who had no capacity for independent initiative." [1] That judgment depends on Thucydides' famous statement that under Pericles "what was in name a democracy was becoming the rule of the first citizen in fact." [2] Busolt has formulated that claim so as to make its full implications most clear: it was "a regime that was popular government in name but one ruled by the first citizen in fact, a monarchical leadership on a democratic base, which frequently resumed the traditions of the democratic monarchy of the Peisistratids." [3] Let us put aside for a moment the question of whether Thucydides' description of the Athenian politicians who followed Pericles is accurate. First, the notion of the constitution of Athens in his time as a monarchy where the leader could pass on the command to a successor is completely false.

The analogy with Peisistratus is particularly instructive. Un-

---

[1] Beloch, *GG* II²: 1, 313. The same view is expressed by Bengtson, *GG*, 224.

[2] 2.65.9.

[3] Busolt, *GG*, III: 1, 499.

like Pericles, who depended on repeated election to office in an atmosphere totally free of coercion and who was subject to examination and recall at least ten times a year, Peisistratus seized power by military force after defeating the Athenian army in battle. Thereafter he disarmed the citizenry and controlled them with the only military force in Athens, his own band of armed mercenaries. Pericles, of course, had no armed force of his own, while the people all possessed arms. The laws bound Peisistratus so little that he could indulge a whim and free a particularly plucky farmer from the tax that he himself had imposed.[4] Pericles, of course, could do nothing without the approval of the assembly; he could be removed from office, tried, and punished—and he was. Peisistratus was a tyrant famous for his mildness, but the incident reported by Aristotle to prove it shows the vast gulf between kindly tyranny and true democracy. "Once, when he was called before the Areopagus on a charge of homicide, he even came forward in person to defend himself, but the man who brought the charge became frightened and stayed away." [5] In such a regime it was possible for the popular tyrant to hand on his power to his sons, as Peisistratus did. For Pericles such a thought was impossible.[6]

In the direct democracy of Athens, where "policy was really determined by mass meetings of the citizens on the advice of anyone who could win the people's ear," [7] a politician had less influence on the choice of his successor than presidents or prime ministers in modern representative democracies. They, at least, can use the weapons provided by organized parties, the discipline they provide, and the patronage they offer. Pericles had no comparable political organization, and the Athenian people dispensed all patronage themselves. Still, even in the Athens of Pericles, a prestigious political leader had influence and none

[4] Arist. *Ath. Pol.*, 16.6.   [5] *Ibid.*, 16.8.

[6] It is surprising that so sober and perceptive a historian as Busolt could have spoken of Periclean Athens as a "monarchy" of any kind. Eduard Meyer goes even further to suggest that if Pericles had lived he would have established in Athens the rule of the Alcmaeonid family like the later rule of the Magos in Carthage and Medici in Florence, with Alcibiades as his immediate successor (*GdA* IV, 48ff.).

[7] A. H. M. Jones, *Athenian Democracy* (Oxford, 1957), 132.

more than he. If he could not designate a successor he could at
least tell his friends and supporters in what men he had confidence. There is some reason to think that Pericles did so.

Aristophanes, though his evidence is difficult to use with
confidence, may provide a clue to the political situation in
Athens just after the death of Pericles. He speaks of two men
who "manage the affairs of the state" before Cleon, the first a
seller of hemp and the second of sheep.[8] An ancient commenta-
tor on the passage tells us that the hemp seller is Eucrates. Other
ancient sources tell us that he ran a gristmill and was called either
the Bear or the Wild Boar of the deme Melite.[9] Eucrates is also
the name of a general sent to Macedonia in 432/1, and there is
every reason to think he was the same man.[10] Probably he was
the father of Diodotus, who opposed Cleon in the debate over
Mytilene.[11] The sheep seller is identified as Lysicles, general for
the year 428/7. The ancient commentators tell us that he married
Aspasia after the death of Pericles, and his election along with
such associates of Pericles as Nicias and Asopius, the son of
Phormio, makes it likely that he, too, was close to Pericles.[12]

Aristophanes' indication that these men were the precursors of
Cleon, combined with the belief derived from Thucydides,
Aristotle, and other ancient writers that Cleon was a demagogue
and Pericles was not, has obscured the likelihood that they were
Pericleans, and, most probably, the men expected to carry forward his policy.[13] But the sharp distinction between Pericles and
the politicians who succeeded him was, so far as we know, made
first by Thucydides and not generally accepted by the other
ancient writers. Aristotle, though he does not use the term

---

[8] *Knights*, 128–137.

[9] For the ancient references to Eucrates see *PA* 5759.

[10] The general is named in *IG*, I^2, 296, line 5. Arguments for his
identity with the hemp seller are given by West, *CP* XIX (1924), 130–
132.

[11] West, *idem*.

[12] References to Lysicles may be found in *PA* 9417 and Busolt, *GG*
III:2, 988, n. 1. For arguments in favor of a connection with Pericles,
see West, *CP*, XIX (1924) 132–134.

[13] I accepted the usual interpretation of Eucrates and Lysicles as
demagogues hostile to Pericles in *Outbreak*, 200, though I should have
known better. West had already shown the way to a more correct
understanding.

demagogue and regards the time of Pericles as better than what
came later, classifies Pericles as one of the "leaders of the demos"
against those who led "the nobles," "the better sort," "the
wealthy." He places him in a line with Solon, Peisistratus,
Cleisthenes, Themistocles, Ephialtes, Cleon, and Cleophon in
opposition to such worthies as Isagoras, Miltiades, Thucydides
son of Melesias, Nicias, and Theramenes.[14] We need not take
that rather arbitrary list, lacking in nuance and detail, too
seriously, but it indicates what an intelligent and well-informed
man of the fourth century believed. With the perspective given
us by Aristotle, we can believe Eucrates and Lysicles were
followers of Pericles even though Aristophanes places them on
a plane with Cleon.

Nor should we be troubled by their designation as merchants.
Most politicians of the past, to be sure, had landed wealth, but
in the latter part of the fifth century things were changing.
Callias son of Hipponicus, "The Treaty-Maker" and close
associate of Pericles,[15] scion of an old and noble Athenian family,
nevertheless earned his nickname "pit-wealthy" and his money
came from mining and the leasing of slaves.[16] Nicias, whose
qualifications as an associate and successor to Pericles are not
questioned, made his money in the same way.[17] Clearly Pericles,
without abandoning his ties with the old landed aristocracy, and
while continuing to seek the support of the lower classes, was
quite ready to ally himself to politicians of a new sort, wealthy,
able men without noble lineage, men like Eucrates, Lysicles, and
Nicias. What united such men with Pericles and led them to
oppose men like Cleon and Hyperbolus, so far as we can tell,
was not class, wealth, nor education but differences of opinion
on policy based on the usual differences among men.

We know little of Eucrates and Lysicles but these obscure
references in a joke of Aristophanes. We know nothing of the
fate of Eucrates,[18] but Lysicles was killed while commanding a

---

[14] *Ath. Pol.*, 28.   [15] See Kagan, *Outbreak*, 108 and n. 27.

[16] W. R. Connor, *The New Politicians of Fifth Century Athens*
(Princeton, 1971), 153, n. 38.

[17] Plut. *Nic.* 4.2.

[18] Gilbert (*Beiträge*, 125–126), with great ingenuity, invents a trial
which removed Eucrates from public life, and Busolt (*GG* III:2, 988)
hesitantly adopts the invention. It does not bear scrutiny.

fleet of 12 ships and in the company of four other generals in Caria. His mission was the traditional one of collecting money from the empire; the number of generals suggests it was important, and the fact that Thucydides names him alone suggests that he was the leading figure.[19] Had he lived he might have succeeded to the leadership left vacant by the death of Pericles, although there is little reason to think that Thucydides would have thought better of him than he did of the other politicians who followed Pericles, for the forces which made Pericles great were partly accidental and not readily reproduced.

Two men dominated Athenian politics from the end of the Persian War to the beginning of the great Peloponnesian War, Cimon and Pericles, respectively. The key to the extraordinary influence held by these two, apart from their talents, is that each was thrust into a leading position at a very early age. Cimon began his career as a young and successful soldier who did more than anyone to build the Athenian Empire. In the normal course of events he would have faced vigorous opposition for Athenian leadership, but Themistocles, a formidable opopnent, was removed from the arena when his opponents joined to have him ostracized. The other leading men, Xanthippus and Aristeides, were from an earlier generation and soon passed from the scene, leaving Cimon in a commanding position because of his early start and great popularity.[20] Pericles began his career as an opponent of Cimon in an appropriately minor role. Two circumstances projected him early into a position of leadership. The Spartans insulted the Athenians by rejecting the help they themselves had requested, discrediting the Laconophile Cimon, and making it possible for his opponents to have him ostracized. Then, before he could enjoy his victory, Ephialtes, leader of the democratic faction, was assassinated, leaving a free road for Pericles. He proved to be an able leader and brilliant politician, consolidating his influence until he was "first among the Athenians and most powerful in speech and action," [21] at the outbreak of the great war. For as long as any Athenian alive in 429 could remember, Athens had been under the leadership of a single powerful and popular politician, yet that was hardly a natural

[19] 3.19.   [20] Kagan, *Outbreak*, 57–65.   [21] 1.139.4.

condition in a democratic state. Accident and good fortune had
provided the Athenians with remarkably stable government for
a long time, but it was inevitable that the situation would one
day revert to the more competitive, equal, and unstable condition more typical of democracies. The successors of Pericles
necessarily suffer from comparison, but the fault need not be
theirs. The political world they inherited did not permit a Cimon
or a Pericles.

The death of Lysicles brought to the fore two politicians who
played the leading roles in Athens to the end of the Archidamian
War, Nicias son of Niceratus and Cleon son of Cleaenetus.
Thucydides and most scholars since have judged Nicias and
Cleon to be very different from one another: Nicias a follower
of the policy of Pericles, an advocate of peace, a man of probity
and reserve, a gentleman; Cleon an opponent of Pericles, an advocate of war, a demagogue, a vulgarian; both men, of course,
immeasurably inferior to Pericles. Neither was ever as effective
as Pericles, and neither achieved anything great and lasting; both
are associated with serious defeats for Athens. But these facts
contribute only partly to the comparison. Not only did Pericles
have the inestimable political advantages we have described; his
successors inherited problems that were all but insoluble. Instead
of the Athens growing in wealth, men, power, and confidence he
had found, they came to a city whose military strength and
morale had been riddled by a still-raging plague, a depleted and
shrinking treasury, a war being fought by a strategy which had
failed and with no alternative in view. Surrender was unthinkable; the enemy refused a negotiated peace; the strategy of exhaustion was exhausting Athens more rapidly than the enemy.
We need not wonder that under these men Athens failed to win
a glorious victory and a lasting peace; rather should we marvel
that they found a way to avert disaster and achieve a respectable
peace, however transient it proved be.

We need also to consider whether the two men were as
different as they usually are depicted. Both come from the same
class of "new men" without noble lineage as did Eucrates and
Lysicles. Nicias, as we have seen, made his money from the
rental of slaves to work in the silver mines of Attica. Cleon's

father owned a tannery which made hides into leather, and he did well enough at it to become quite rich, for only a rich man could afford to be a *choregus* at the dramatic festivals, as Cleaenetus was in 460/59.[22] Neither source of wealth was aristocratic. In each case the father is the first member of the family known to us.[23] Connor has traced each man's genealogy and concludes: "The two genealogies show a similar pattern. Nicias and Cleon are the first members of their families known to have won any great distinction; their fathers were probably both wealthy but not especially prominent in the city. Although Cleon and Nicias rose to success, the families into which they married seem not to have been very distinguished, but in the next generation or two their descendants began to marry into houses which, if not themselves especially famous, were at least tied to old and prestigious families." [24] Nor were the men as different in their attitude toward the war as is usually thought. Neither favored the peace negotiations with Sparta which Pericles also opposed. Both, therefore, tried to find a way to win in the years following the death of Pericles, Nicias usually as a general. There is no clear record of any disagreement between the two until the Pylos affair in 425,[25] but the usual assumption that Nicias must have opposed the harsh measure proposed by Cleon in 427 which would have put the Mytilenean rebels to death is probably right.

Nicias, in fact, seems to have been the most active general in the Archidamian War: in 427 he commanded an Athenian force that took Minoa, an island off the Megarian coast,[26] in 426 he led an attack on Melos, attacked Tanagra, and ravaged the Locrian seacoast,[27] in 425 he led an attack on Corinth,[28] in 424 he took the island of Cythera,[29] and in 423 he recovered Mende and tried

[22] IG II²:2318, line 34.

[23] There is a tradition that Nicias had an ancestor who brought Epimenides from Crete to Athens in the sixth century, but there is reason to discount this tale. As Connor, *The New Politicians*, 162, says, "this story is most probably a piece of pseudo-history promulgated by the fifth century Nicias to bolster his reputation for piety and religious devotion."

[24] *Ibid.*, 162.

[25] 4.27.5. Thucydides says in 425 that Cleon was an enemy of Nicias, but not when the enmity began nor why.

[26] 3.51.   [27] 3.91.   [28] 4.42.   [29] 4.53–54.

to take Scione from Brasidas.[30] No other Athenian general
fought as many diverse campaigns; and the attack on Corinth,
at least, went beyond the original strategy of Pericles. The
Athenians could not regularly have chosen a man to lead campaigns in which he did not believe.[31] It is not easy to distinguish
between Nicias and Cleon on the basis of their different strategies before Pylos, and that fortunate event changed the balance
of power so much as to justify a reconsideration of one's plans
and aims. We should not allow their quarrel on that occasion to
dominate our view of the two men.

All this is not to say that Cleon and Nicias were cut from
the same cloth. Cleon had been a public critic of Pericles and
his moderate policy probably before and certainly since the outbreak of the war.[32] Nicias, we may be sure, was not. Few men
could have been more different in personality, character, and
style. In 428, however, their interests were identical, since a
negotiated peace was impossible. The empire must be kept safe
for Athens, the Athenians must be imbued with the spirit to
carry on the war, resources must be husbanded and new ones
found, some way must be found to resume offensive operations
if the war was ever to be brought to a successful conclusion. The
two men had a motive to cooperate, and there is no reason to
think that they did not.

The generals who were elected early in the spring of 428, such
as are known to us, seem all to have been men with Periclean associations, direct or indirect. Nicias had served alongside Pericles
as general,[33] Asopius was the son of Phormio, Pericles' frequent
colleague,[34] Lysicles married Pericles' beloved Aspasia, and
Paches is usually associated with the views of Nicias, though the

[30] 4.129–131.
[31] The choice of Nicias to lead the Sicilian expedition of 415 was
plainly an extraordinary exception that Thucydides explains in great
detail. At no time does he hint that Nicias was reluctant to undertake
the earlier commands.
[32] Cleon was probably among those who were critical of Pericles for
sending Lacedaemonius to Corcyra with too few ships (Plut. *Per.* 29.3
and Kagan, *Outbreak*, 242). A fragment from Hermippus (Plut. *Per.*
33.4) proves that Cleon was a public critic of Pericles after the war
began.
[33] Plut. *Per.* 2.2.   [34] 3.7.

evidence is slender.[35] Apparently the swing back to Pericles which restored him to power continued after his death. The peace party remained shattered and the critics of moderation could not demand a more aggressive policy while Athens had all it could do to recover its strength.

The campaigning season of 428 began in the usual way, with a Spartan invasion of Attica about the middle of May. The invaders made camp and engaged in systematic devastation. The Athenians confined themselves to harassing the enemy with cavalry. After about a month, when their supplies were exhausted, the Peloponnesians withdrew.[36]

During that month, however, a plot far more menacing to Athens was brewing on the island of Lesbos.[37] By far the most important and powerful city on Lesbos was Mytilene. The lesser states of Antissa, Pyrrha, and Eresos followed her lead, but Methymna, a small town on the northern coast of the island, pursued an independent and sometimes hostile policy (see Map 4). Mytilene was unusual among the allies of Athens, apparently

[35] Beloch (*Attische Politik*, 30 and 33, n. 1) and Busolt (*GG* III:2, 1002), who follows him, call Paches "ein Gesinnungsgenosse" of Nicias. Their judgment is probably right, but Beloch's arguments in support of the association are not weighty. Beloch (*GG* II²:2, 263) lists Eurymedon and Nicostratus as generals for this year, but without evidence. As West, *CP* XIX (1924), 134, n. 2, points out, there is absolutely no evidence for Eurymedon. Beloch cites Thucydides 3.75 where Nicostratus commands the Athenian fleet at Corcyra in 427 as evidence that he was general for 428/7. Nicostratus "hat das geschwader bei Naupaktos offenbar seit Anfang des Jahres befehligt." But the events at Corcyra took place after the beginning of the official Athenian year 427/6. Fornara (*Athenian Board of Generals*, 56) omits Nicias, wrongly, I think.

[36] 3.1; Gomme, *HCT* II, 252.

[37] The first important monograph on the rebellion on Lesbos was written by W. Herbst, *Der Abfall Mytilenes* (Cologne, 1861). Since then the matter has received a great deal of attention, but until recently most of it centered on the debate at Athens in 427 on the disposition of the defeated island. (For bibliography see D. Gillis, *AJP* XCII [1971], n. 5.) The debate over the nature of the Athenian Empire inspired by the provocative article of G. E. M. de Ste. Croix, *Historia* III (1954), 1–41, has led to a more careful study of the causes and course of the revolt. (For a good bibliography of the literature to this point see again D. Gillis, *ibid.*, n. 4.) The keenest insight into these questions is provided by R. P. Legon, *Phoenix* XXII (1968), 200–225, and I accept most of his conclusions.

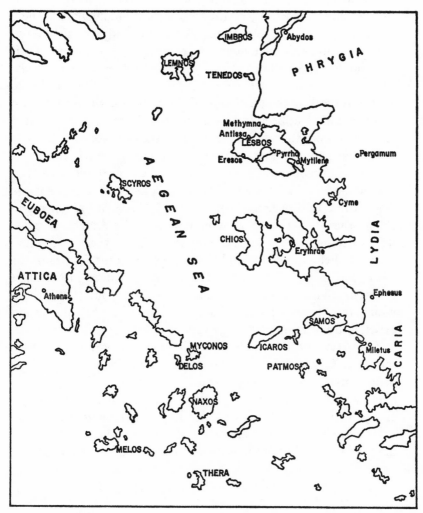

Map 4. The Aegean

governed by an oligarchy. The three satellite towns appear to have been oligarchies, too, and Methymna democratic.[38] These Lesbian towns were exceptional also in that, along with Chios, they still provided ships instead of tribute as their contribution to the confederation.[39] They were regarded by themselves, Thucydides, and, presumably all the Greeks as autonomous, and there is no reason to believe that the Athenians had ever interfered with their independence in any way. In spite of its favored position, however, Mytilene had considered withdrawing from the Athenian alliance even before the war,[40] but had been deterred by the refusal of the Peloponnesians to accept them into their alliance. That had been in peacetime, but during war a rebellion on Lesbos would surely be welcome to the enemies of Athens.

The time for such an uprising could hardly have been better. The Lesbian rebels, themselves, manned a considerable fleet. The Peloponnesians had shown that they could put to sea a large fleet, if not an especially skillful one. A successful revolt might bring other defections that would weaken the Athenians while strengthening their enemies. This time, moreover, cooperation from the Peloponnesians and their allies was almost certain, for the Boeotians as well as the Spartans were involved in the plans for an uprising.[41] Most encouraging was the condition of Athens which, the Mytileneans said, had been "ruined by the plague and expenditure of money." [42]

The Mytileneans presented their reasons for rebellion in a speech at Olympia before the assembled Peloponnesians.[43] The main motive, they alleged, was fear that at some time the Athenians would reduce them to subjection like all the other allies except Chios. They had seen the league gradually become an empire as one state after another had been deprived of its autonomy, and they believed it was only a matter of time and oppor-

---

[38] Legon, *Phoenix* XXII (1968), 200.   [39] 1.19; 2.9.5.

[40] 3.13.1; 3.2.1. For the date see Busolt, *GG* III:1, 545, and n. 3; Kagan, *Outbreak*, 172, n. 1.

[41] 3.2.3.   [42] 3.13.3.

[43] 3.8. Thucydides was surely not present at this meeting, and we cannot know his source for the speech. Thucydides may have departed from what the speaker really said, but there is no reason to doubt that he gives us something not too far from the kinds of arguments used.

tunity until Athens treated Lesbos in the same way.[44] There was another motive for the rebellion, which the Mytileneans were careful not to mention. They intended to unify all the cities of Lesbos under Mytilenean leadership, but needed to do so in conjunction with rebellion from Athens because the Athenians would certainly not permit it. The Athenians were in general opposed to the creation of larger units in their domain and in fact tried to break them up into smaller ones. The presence of Methymna on the island, a city which was hostile to Mytilene and unwilling to join with her, compelled the Athenians to intervene. Athens, distracted by war, might have permitted a voluntary union at this time and dealt with it after the war if necessary, but could not allow one ally to coerce another—unification meant war.[45] There is every reason to think, as Diodorus does, that the unification scheme was the chief motive for the revolt.[46] The Mytilenean oligarchs, long eager to break with Athens and to control their island fully, seized the moment of Athenian weakness to achieve their ends, acting, so it seems, more from hope than from fear.

Even before the Peloponnesian invasion of Attica the Mytileneans had put their plan into action. They quietly began to build defensive walls, block up their harbor, increase their navy, and send to the Black Sea regions for grain supplies and mercenary bowmen.[47] They hoped to delay the rebellion until all these preparations were completed, but could not keep the secret, for there were too many eager to betray it. Methymna and the island of Tenedos, presumably democracies and certainly hostile to Mytilene, were quick to tell Athens what was going on and to urge quick action to prevent the rebellion. They were assisted and, probably, informed by some citizens of Mytilene who were *proxenoi* of the Athenians and not members of the government.[48] Thucydides says they acted from political motives (κατὰ στάσιν) while Aristotle [49] tells us that the *proxenus* Doxander became a leader of the opposing faction for personal

[44] 3.9–12.
[45] The situation is something like the one which compelled Athens to intervene in the quarrel between Samos and Miletus. See Kagan, *Outbreak*, 170–171.
[46] 12.55.1.   [47] 3.2.2.   [48] 3.2.3, ἰδίᾳ ἄνδρες.   [49] *Pol.* 1304a.

reasons when his son was rejected as a suitor for the hand of one of the daughters of the wealthy Timophanes, presumably a member of the oligarchic regime. The two explanations need not be contradictory. The disclosure forced the rebels to act before they were ready.

When word reached the Athenians, already distressed and worn out by the war and their sufferings, they at first refused to believe it, "giving greater weight to the wish that it was not true." [50] But the embassy they sent to see what was really happening soon found that the rumors were true: the Mytileneans were carrying out the unification and their other preparations and refused to stop. They may not yet have been fully committed to rebellion but may have hoped that the Athenians, eager to avoid trouble at this difficult time, would accept the unification if faced with a *fait accompli*. Their previous negotiations with the Boeotians and Spartans had not been formal or binding, and if the Athenians had acquiesced, the Mytileneans might have been content to stop there. But the early Athenian discovery of the plan put an end to such hopes if they existed. Athens had prepared a fleet of 40 ships for the annual cruise around the Peloponnese. The small size of this force, compared with the 100 ships put to sea on the same mission in 431 and 430, speaks eloquently of the strain on Athenian resources. These ships, commanded by Cleippides and two others, were diverted from their original course and sent quickly to Mytilene. A religious festival was in progress there, and the Athenians thought they could take the rebels by surprise. They seized the 10 Mytilenean ships which were serving with the Athenian fleet and arrested their crews to prevent the news from reaching Lesbos, but secrecy was impossible in the Athenian democracy, where every decision of policy had to be made in the full assembly on the Pnyx, and a messenger got through. The Mytileneans, forewarned, abandoned their celebration and prepared their defenses. The Athenian generals ordered them to give up their ships and tear down their walls. When the order was refused the Athenians attacked.

Neither side was fully ready to fight. The Mytileneans had

[50] 3.2.1.

been caught before their supplies and archers had arrived, their
defenses completed, and their Peloponnesian and Boeotian alliances made formal and effective. The Athenians, on the other
hand, knew the weakness of their own force and reserves, "fearing that they were not strong enough to fight all of Lesbos." [51]
The Mytileneans, therefore, put up only token resistance with
their fleet before asking for an armistice so that they could try
to obtain a reasonable agreement with Athens. Thucydides tells
us that they "wanted, if they could, to get rid of the Athenian
ships for the present." [52] No doubt their plan was to delay until
the Spartan alliance came to their assistance. Cleippides, fully
aware of his own weakness but probably unaware of the Spartan
involvement, agreed to the request.

A mission was sent to Athens, and among its members was one
of the men who had informed the Athenians of the Mytilenean
plot who, Thucydides says, was now repentant. We may pre-
sume that he was one of the Athenian *proxenoi*, just the man to
plead the city's case. The Mytileneans asked that the Athenians
withdraw their fleet on condition that the island would remain
loyal to the alliance and foment no rebellion. Nothing was said
about the forcible unification of the island, which must have
gone some way toward completion, for it was already under
way when the Athenian ambassadors had unsuccessfully asked
the Mytileneans to stop.[53] The Mytileneans were asking that
Athens accept the unification in return for future loyalty. Realizing that Athenian approval was at least doubtful, they secretly
sent an embassy to the Spartans to negotiate for aid from their
alliance,[54] a sensible action, for the Athenians refused. To permit
their will to be flouted, to abandon Methymna to the mercy of

[51] 3.5.4.

[52] 3.4.2, βουλόμενοι τὰς ναῦς τὸ παραυτίκα, εἰ δύναιντο, ὁμολογίᾳ τινὶ
ἐπιεικεῖ ἀποπέμψασθαι.

[53] 3.3.1.

[54] Legon, *Phoenix* XXII (1968), 206, says that the *proxenos* must have
been unaware of the mission to Sparta. It seems to me, however, that
the terms he asked for were likely to produce an Athenian refusal,
though there was at least some hope that they would not. In case of
the war that must follow such a refusal, help from Sparta was essential.
I see no reason why he would not be informed of and approve so
prudent an action as the mission to Sparta.

Mytilene, would have abdicated the leadership and refused the protection which guaranteed and justified their command of the empire. The Athenians would have invited and justified rebellions elsewhere and completely jeopardized their security. It is important to emphasize, for Thucydides does not do so, that the request of Mytilene and the rebellion that followed its refusal were completely unjustified and the Athenian response necessary by any reasonable judgment.

The Athenian response forced the Mytileneans to begin their rebellion in earnest, though they were not ready. They were joined by their satellites on Lesbos and opposed by the Methymnians, the Athenians, and some of their allies. The rebels launched an attack on the Athenian camp but, lacking the confidence to follow it up, withdrew from the field. They decided not to risk another campaign until they had received reinforcements and sent off new ambassadors with the Laconian and Theban envoys who had arrived after the battle to speed the arrival of help. The Athenians were encouraged by the inactivity of the rebels and so were their allies. They quickly established an effective naval blockade of the island. On the island itself the Mytileneans had almost a free hand, for the Athenian land force was far too small to prevent them from controlling the entire island except for Methymna and the small bit of land around the Athenian camp.[55]

Athens considered the situation on Lesbos under control. The blockade would sooner or later starve out the rebels and compel them to submit. Meanwhile the Athenians were free to resume their naval harassment of the Peloponnese. The enemy's recent naval undertakings required that the Athenians reassert their supremacy of the sea. When the Acarnanians asked the Athenians to send a son or other relative of Phormio to help them, since Phormio himself was no longer available,[56] they sent his

[55] 3.6.2. Thucydides says that the Mytileneans and their Lesbian friends τῆς δὲ γῆς τῆς μὲν ἄλλης ἐκράτουν without mentioning Methymna, but his narrative is clear that it was independent and hostile to Mytilene.

[56] Thucydides, in another of his inexplicable omissions, tells us nothing of Phormio's fate or the reasons for his unavailability. He may have been sick or even dead, but the story that he was out of action because he had been attacked in court, fined, and deprived of his citizenship does not make sense at this time. See Gomme, HCT II, 234–237.

son Asopius with 30 ships. He ravaged the coast of Laconia, tried to capture Oeniadae with the Acarnanians, and was finally killed fighting on Leucas. The shortage of Athenian resources is once again demonstrated by the fact that after the attacks on Laconia, Asopius sent 18 ships back to Athens and carried out the rest of his mission with the remaining ships based at Naupactus.[57]

While Asopius was on his travels the first Mytilenean envoys arrived in Sparta, probably about mid-July,[58] but the Spartans took no immediate action. To be sure, the envoys said that negotiations with Athens were under way and that the Athenians had not yet taken military action, but the point of the mission to Sparta was the expectation that the negotiations would fail and fighting ensue. The second envoys must have arrived not much more than a week later with the news of the fighting and the blockade, but still the Spartans waited until the second week in August [59] to take action. Even then they merely told the Mytileneans to appear at the Olympic games and tell their story to the assembled members of the Spartan alliance. The Spartan hesitation is not hard to understand. The rebellion had not been their idea, but was suggested by the Boeotians and eagerly seized upon by the Mytileneans. Here was another instance of a state seeking to embroil Sparta in dangers for that state's private interests. To help Mytilene would mean manning a large and expensive fleet and fighting at sea. The memory of the recent disgraceful battles in the Corinthian Gulf must have made that an unappealing prospect. To be most effective the naval campaign should be accompanied by a second invasion of Attica in the same year, which would be an unusual and unwelcome burden on Sparta and her allies. For these reasons Sparta was in no hurry to act, especially without the agreement of the allies.

The Mytilenean spokesman faced no easy task when he addressed the meeting of the Peloponnesian League in the sacred precinct of Olympian Zeus after the games were over. As usual it was important to present the action taken as just, untainted by improper self-interest, and unavoidable. To this end he spoke of the ominous encroachment of the Athenians on the autonomy of

[57] 3.7.   [58] Gomme, HCT II, 259.   [59] Ibid.

their allies which would inevitably lead to the enslavement of Mytilene unless she chose an opportune moment to rebel. Naturally he said nothing of the ambition of his city to dominate the island of Lesbos by force, speaking only of its need and determination to secure its freedom and autonomy, just what Sparta and her allies professed to be fighting for. This was an important, if tendentious, argument, but after it was made he could turn to the more persuasive portion of his speech. He emphasized that the timing of the rebellion was ideal not only for Mytilene but for Sparta and the allies. Athens was ripe for the taking and the strategy both obvious and unbeatable: "There never has been such an opportunity before, for the Athenians have been ruined by the plague and the expenditure of money. Part of their fleet is sailing around your coast, and the rest is lined up against us. It is therefore not likely that they will have any ships to spare if you make a second attack on them this summer both by land and sea. Either they will not resist you, or they will withdraw their fleet from both our territories." [60]

The final argument of the Mytileneans was even more telling: whether or not you approve of our rebellion you cannot afford to let us be defeated once it has begun. Don't think we are asking you to become involved in a distant quarrel that does not concern you. Your own victory in this war depends on your support of us:

This war will not be decided in Attica, as some people think, but in those places from which Athens gets its support. For her revenues come from her allies, and they will be still greater if we are conquered. No one else will rebel and our wealth will be added to hers, for we will be treated worse than those who were enslaved earlier. But if you come to our aid with vigor, you will enroll among your allies a state that has a great navy, which you need most of all, you will defeat the Athenians more easily by drawing their allies away from them (for every one will proceed more boldly after you have assisted us), and you will escape the charge which you now have of not helping those who rebel from Athens. If, however, you show yourselves openly to be liberators you will more surely have victory.[61]

[60] 3.13.3–4.　　　　　[61] 3.13.5–7.

The striking accuracy of the Mytileneans' forecast of the future course of the war and their description of the strategy needed to defeat Athens, unlike their estimate of the Athenian capacity to fight, need not mean that the arguments come from Thucydides and hindsight. The course of the war to that point should have made what the Mytileneans said clear to all.

The Mytilenean speech had the intended effect on the Spartans. They led their allies in accepting the Mytileneans into the alliance on the spot and ordered them to gather as quickly as possible at the Isthmus of Corinth with the usual two-thirds of their levy for the proposed invasion of Attica. The Spartans were most enthusiastic and arrived at the point of rendezvous first. Immediately they set to work building the equipment necessary to haul their ships across the isthmus from the Corinthian to the Saronic Gulf for a joint attack on Athens by land and sea. The allies, however, proved the accuracy of Pericles' calculation that the Peloponnesian League was ill-equipped to wage any but the simplest kind of war.[62] "They collected slowly because they were in the midst of harvesting the grain and reluctant to serve."[63]

The Athenians knew that the actions of Mytilene and the willingness of the Peloponnesians to support them arose from the belief that Athens was too weak and exhausted to face the new challenge. At this point the Athenians demonstrated that same determination and toughness of spirit that had served them so well at Marathon and Salamis and that would be called upon again at even worse times later in the war. They decided to put to sea a fleet of 100 triremes, in addition to the ships then located at Lesbos and elsewhere. This fleet would circle the Peloponnese making raids as in the past and demonstrating that the Athenians were confident they could ward off the contemplated Spartan attack. Actually, this expedition strained Athenian resources to the utmost. The usual rowers were Athenians of the lowest class, the thetes, supplemented when necessary by hired rowers from the subject states. This time Athenians of the hoplite census, who normally fought as heavily armed infantrymen only, and resident aliens were pressed into service as rowers.[64] These new

[62] 1.141.4.   [63] 3.15.2.   [64] 3.16.1; Gomme, HCT II, 271.

recruits could not have been as efficient as the thetes who were well-drilled oarsmen, and their employment indicates the heavy loss of life caused by the plague.[65] If the Peloponnesians had sent a fleet to fight the Athenians at this time they might have had better luck than before, for these were not the crews commanded by Phormio. But the Athenians could take the chance, for the enemy had never challenged their excursions before and did not now. The Athenians roamed freely and "made landings on the Peloponnese wherever it seemed good to them." [66]

The Athenian demonstration was totally effective. Coming on the heels of the evident reluctance of Sparta's allies to bestir themselves, the raids on the Peloponnese convinced the Spartans that the Mytileneans had misrepresented Athenian weakness. They abandoned the attack and went home. The Athenian fleet, having accomplished its purpose, sailed home. For the moment the Mytileneans and their friends on Lesbos were left to confront the Athenians alone.

While the Spartans were still planning to attack Athens in accordance with their commitment, the Mytileneans were pushing forward to gain complete control of their island. They went against Methymna, expecting it to be betrayed by a party from within. That plan failed and so did the assault on the city which followed. The Mytileneans withdrew, passing through Antissa, Pyrrha and Eresos on their way home to reinforce their authority in those towns. An attack by Methymna on Antissa also failed, and the situation on Lesbos remained as it had been before these campaigns. Mytilene dominated the island except for Methymna. The Athenians on the island were too few to prevent the Mytileneans from moving about freely. Nor had the blockade been entirely successful, for the mercenaries for whom the Mytileneans had sent at the beginning of the rebellion had arrived. Some Athenian action was called for; Athens could

---

[65] The use of hoplite rowers also indicates the drain on the Athenian treasury, for in 430 the Athenian force had consisted of 100 ships rowed by regular oarsmen as well as 4,000 hoplites. If these hoplites were paid no more than their daily drachma to row as well as fight the saving would be 4,000 drachmae daily, or over 13 talents for a voyage of three weeks.

[66] 3.16.1–2.

not leave its friends at Methymna at the mercy of the Mytileneans when a future assault might be successful. The abandonment of the Spartan offensive and Sparta's apparent withdrawal
from the Mytilene affair gave the Athenians the opportunity to
take remedial steps. They sent 1,000 hoplites to Lesbos under
the general Paches. This army was able to build a fortified wall
around Mytilene and thus shut it in by land and sea. The blockade so established would protect Methymna from further attack
and might bring Mytilene to her knees somewhat sooner.[67]

The siege of Mytilene, which became effective just at the
onset of winter, was absolutely necessary, but it strained the
diminished Athenian financial resources beyond any expectation
Pericles may have had at the beginning of the war and forced
extraordinary measures. The hoplites who had come with Paches,
like those who had sailed around the Peloponnese, were made
to serve as rowers as well. There can be no doubt that the attempt to save money was the cause of their double duty.[68] By
the winter of 428/7 the available reserve fund seems to have
been less than 1,000 talents.[69] As Busolt puts it, if the Athenians
did not open a new source of income, if they renewed their
naval operation in only a moderate way, and even if there were
no new emergencies, "the exhaustion of the treasury could be
expected within three or four years." [70] The Lesbian rebellion
and the Spartan response proved that the Athenians would need
to use their navy frequently and heavily and also that emergencies must be expected. The financial crisis was not a few years
off; it was immediate.

The Athenians, therefore, undertook two steps that had not

[67] 3.18.

[68] Busolt, GG III:2, 1015, says "Augenscheinlich infolge des Geldman-
gels mussten die Hopliten selbst die Schiffe rudern." Gomme (HCT
II, 277) suggests that not lack of money but a shortage of men explains
the use of hoplites. In this case he is certainly wrong, for by this time
the men who had rowed the 100 ships around the Peloponnese, most of
whom were necessarily thetes and not hoplites, were again available to
row the much smaller fleet that would be necessary to bring the 1,000
soldiers to Lesbos.

[69] ATL III, 343, sets the figure at 945. Busolt (GG III:2, 1015–1016
and n. 1 on 1016), who did not have as much epigraphical evidence to
work with, arrives at a figure not much higher.

[70] Busolt, GG III: 1016.

been part of the publicly announced plan of Pericles. In the late summer of 428, at the Panathenaic games, the Athenians probably announced a reassessment of the tribute from the allies aimed at raising revenue.[71] Normally the deadline for collecting the tribute was the Dionysiac festival in the spring, but in the winter of 428/7 the Athenians needed money quickly, so they sent out a fleet of 12 ships under Lysicles and four other generals to collect the newly assessed taxes.[72] Lysicles and his colleagues may have been sent to demand a special levy, quite apart from the regular tribute, as Gomme suggests.[73] They went to several cities and finally to Caria, the most remote area of the empire, where it was always hardest to collect. There the Athenians were attacked and Lysicles and many of his soldiers killed. We do not know what part, if any, of the money collected ever got back to Athens.

A bit more money from the empire would not solve the financial problems of Athens. In the short run, especially, the collection of tribute, which would take time, was inadequate to meet the demands of the siege of Mytilene without further denuding the reserve fund by further borrowing. The Athenians, therefore, decided on a desperate measure: "Being in need of money for the siege, they themselves introduced for the first time a direct tax (eisphora) in the amount of two hundred talents." [74] There has been considerable scholarly argument as to whether Thucydides means that this was the first time ever that the Athenians imposed such a tax on themselves, but the likeliest interpretation is that it was the first time during the Peloponnesian War.[75] No one doubts that such a tax had not actually been imposed in a very long time or that it was regarded

71 AFD 3-25; ATL I, 196-199. The evidence for the date of the list for spring 427 (ATL II, List 27) is not conclusive, as the editors admit. They are right, however, that the arguments "all point in the same direction and their cumulative effect is considerable" (198). Once the date is accepted it is easy to believe in a mild rise in the tribute, for several new cities in the Hellespont appear on the list, and the quota of Clazomenae goes up.

72 3.19.   73 HCT II, 279.

74 3.19.1: Προσδεόμενοι δὲ οἱ ᾿Αθηναῖοι χρημάτων ἐς τὴν πολιορκίαν, καὶ αὐτοὶ ἐσενεγκόντες τότε πρῶτον ἐσφορὰν διακόσια τάλαντα.

75 See Appendix A.

as extraordinary and painful, especially by the propertied classes on whom the *eisphora* fell exclusively.[76] The treatment of the allies might produce rebellions that would undermine the source of Athenian power. The imposition of a direct tax might sap the enthusiasm for the war of the propertied classes who formed the bulk of support for the moderate faction. We need not wonder that Pericles never suggested these expedients in his public discussion of Athenian resources.

Such reasoning has led many scholars to suppose that both measures were the work of the war party and probably of its most famous member, Cleon,[77] but there is no reason to connect him with the introduction of the *eisphora*. No ancient author attributes it to him, Thucydides does not mention him in connection with it, and the Aristophanic references prove only that Cleon was vigorous in collecting the tax, as he was in collecting all revenues for the state, not that he originated it.[78] To be sure, Cleon had been an important politician for some years, and the policy of taxing the propertied classes was in accord with his interest in prosecuting the war. We have no evidence that his power in 428 was sufficient to push through any measure unacceptable to the moderates who held the *strategia*. He was not a general, nor is there evidence that he was even a member of the Council.[79] In fact, there was little distinction between the policies of the most aggressive Athenians and the moderates in the year 428. Both thought it necessary to continue fighting the war, and neither could afford to think of aggressive new undertakings. The men who rallied the Athenians to a major effort in the face of a threatened attack on Athens by land and sea must have been chiefly her generals, Lysicles, Nicias, and Paches, among others. They, no less than Cleon and his friends, realized that the safety of Athens depended on putting down the rebellion of Mytilene before it

[76] Thomsen, *Eisphora* (Copenhagen, 1964), 118.
[77] E.g., Gilbert, *Beiträge*, 129ff.; West, *CP* XIX (1924), 139ff.; Glotz and Cohen, *Histoire Grecque* (Paris, 1929), II, 636.
[78] For a good discussion of the question and especially of the evidence of Aristophanes see Thomsen, *Eisphora*, 168–170.
[79] W. R. Connor, *Theopompus and Fifth-Century Athens* (Cambridge, Mass., 1968), 50–51.

drained the treasury and before its contagion spread throughout the empire. That required an immediate infusion of money for the siege, and they must have initiated and approved the steps that were taken. Pericles himself might have done the same. In passing the *eisphora* these leaders were taxing themselves and members of their own class, including Cleon. The sources report no significant division among the Athenians on the vote for an *eisphora*. It was not an act of partisan politics or class warfare but one of prudent patriotism, responding to an emergency.

Late in the winter, perhaps in February of 427, Salaethus, a single Spartan, landed at Lesbos in secret and made his way to Mytilene. He informed the magistrates that the amphibious campaign planned for 428 would take place in 427. There would be an invasion of Attica, and a fleet of 40 ships under the Spartan Alcidas would aid Mytilene. Salaethus himself would stay at Mytilene and be in charge of things there.[80] Whatever the reluctance of their allies, the Spartans, at least, were eager to exploit the opportunity offered by the Lesbian revolt. The arrival of Salaethus and his news stiffened the spines of the Mytileneans and made them even less inclined to yield to Athens.[81] As the winter drew to a close the Athenians faced a greater challenge than any they had yet confronted during the war. They must put down a rebellion by a powerful member of their alliance while harried by invasion and challenged on the sea. They must do so quickly, for an extended siege like the ones at Potidaea or at Samos might exhaust their reserve and end their capacity to resist.

[80] 3.25.1; 3.16.3.   [81] 3.25.2.

6. Sicily and Corcyra

The winter of 428/7 provided the Spartans with time to lay careful plans to keep their promises to the people of Mytilene and to raise the Athenian siege of the island. The members of their alliance joined in the annual invasion of Attica, which they hoped would prevent the Athenians from sending a fleet to Lesbos. Archidamus must have been on his deathbed, for he did not lead the invasion as in the past nor did his son Agis. Instead Cleomenes, brother of the exiled King Pleistoanax, took the command in place of Pausanias, the son of Pleistoanax, presumably still a minor.[1] Alcidas the Spartan navarch, with a fleet of 42 triremes including 2 from Mytilene, was to sail to Lesbos while the Athenians were occupied by the invasion of their own land.[2] The plan was the culmination of a dream cherished by the enemies of Athens in Sparta at least since the rebellion of Thasos against Athens in 465[3] and possibly from the 470's. Spartans of a confident and warlike spirit who were hostile to Athens had long believed that the Athenians could not withstand an invasion of Attica combined with a naval expedition directed against their Aegean empire. They must have hoped that a combined attack would provoke a rebellion among the allies which would quickly spread and bring Athens to her knees. The thought of such an attack may have been in their minds when they ignored the warnings of Archidamus and voted for war in 432. They had been frustrated in the past, never being able to test their

---

[1] 3.26.2; Gomme, *HCT* II, 289. See also Meyer, *Forsch.* II, 508.
[2] 3.26.1; Gomme, *HCT* II, 288–289.   [3] 1.101.1–2.

strategy: an earthquake had prevented an invasion during the Thasian rebellion; the peace party, assisted by Corinth, had prevailed and prevented an invasion during the rebellion of Samos; the overwhelming might of the Athenian navy and the absence of an opportunity in the Aegean prevented a test of the strategy in the first years of the war; the reluctance of the allies of Sparta prevented the accomplishment of the plan in the summer of 428, after the Mytileneaeans had revolted. Now, at last, the time had come.

The invasion, which probably began early in May,[4] was long and second in its devastation only to the very long invasion of the year 430. Everything untouched by previous invasions and everything that had grown up since was cut down. The invading army expected news of the success of the Peloponnesian fleet, which they imagined had already arrived at Lesbos.[5] The success of the naval expedition depended on surprise and secrecy, for the 42 ships could not hope to fight their way through the Athenian navy; as Thucydides tells us, speed was necessary. But Alcidas moved cautiously and slowly. Starting probably at Cyllene, the Peloponnesian ships "wasted time in sailing around the Peloponnesus and proceeded in a leisurely manner on the rest of the voyage." [6] Luck was with them, for they entirely escaped the notice of the Athenians until they reached Delos, but the delay had been fatal. At nearby Icarus and Myconus they learned that Mytilene had already surrendered; nevertheless they sailed on to Erythrae on the coast of Asia Minor opposite Chios, hoping to get a clearer picture of the situation. A week after the surrender of Mytilene, the bad news could no longer be doubted. To decide what to do next the Peloponnesians held a council.

Their situation was far from bad; many opportunities for hurting Athens remained. The Peloponnesian army was still in Attica, devastating the land and engaging part of the attention of the Athenians. It would remain until its supplies gave out, perhaps as late as the beginning of June.[7] The Athenian fleet at

---

[4] Gomme, HCT II, 288.   [5] 3.26.2–4.   [6] 3.29.1.

[7] 3.26.2–4. Busolt (GG III:2, 1021), as usual, puts the date a month later.

Lesbos under Paches could not readily leave the island, recently surrendered and not yet fully pacified. Enterprise and daring might find many avenues for expression. Teutiaplus, the commander of the contingent from Elis, obviously possessed these qualities. He proposed that the Peloponnesians launch an immediate attack on Mytilene. The last thing the Athenians would suspect was an attack by sea so soon after their victory. They would, no doubt, be careless and unsuspecting, their forces scattered over the island. A sudden attack by night supported by the friends of Sparta still on the island would catch the Athenians by surprise and bring victory.[8] That suggestion was altogether too bold for Alcidas, and he rejected it.

Next came a proposal by some Ionian exiles who used the unexpected arrival of a Spartan fleet on their shores to try to enlist the Peloponnesians in their own cause, and their suggestion was supported by the Lesbians who were with the fleet and who were now exiles themselves. They wanted Alcidas to seize one of the cities of Ionia or Cyme in Aeolia. The captured city would serve as a base for a general Ionian rebellion against Athens which would be successful because the Spartan arrival was universally welcome. The successful rebellion would deprive Athens of her revenues when her treasury was on the point of exhaustion. Even if a general rising did not occur immediately and the Athenians sent a fleet to blockade the captured city Athens would still be hurt. There was reason to believe that Pissuthnes, the Persian satrap who had played a hand in the Samian rebellion of 440, would again support the enemies of Athens. At worst, therefore, the result would be a protracted blockade in which the Peloponnesians would be supported by Persia and the Athenian treasury drained.

Alcidas, of course, suspected this advice which was obviously self-serving. The exiles clearly wanted to involve Sparta deeply in the region, hoping thereby to regain their homelands. No doubt they exaggerated the readiness of Athens' allies to rebel and the likelihood of Persian aid. Still, their advice was good, and if it had been taken the chances are excellent that the Peloponnesians could have taken a town on the mainland, for the Ionians

[8] 3.30.

were completely unprepared for the arrival of a Peloponnesian fleet. Thucydides tells us that when the mainlanders saw the ships, "they did not run away but instead came closer thinking that they were Athenian. For they did not have the slightest expectation that Peloponnesian ships would approach Ionia while Athens ruled the seas." [9] A Spartan force in a captured city might safely expect at least benevolent neutrality from the Persians.

Even a siege of a few months would be costly for the Athenians. Paches understood the situation clearly. When he failed to come upon the fleeing Peloponnesians in the open sea where he might hope to destroy them in battle, he considered himself lucky that he had not discovered them in a harbor where he would have been compelled to besiege them. [10] Even if an Athenian siege were ultimately successful the Peloponnesians could escape inland and get home. They would lose only the 42 ships, a worth while sacrifice in light of the cost to Athens. By 425, in fact, Sparta was compelled to abandon her naval activities completely.

Alcidas, however, had no further taste for adventure. He rejected the Ionian proposal, his only thought being to get himself and his ships back safely to the Peloponnese as soon as possible. [11] Panicked, Alcidas began his voyage home. He had captured many prisoners on the coast of Asia Minor. Now that they were a burden hindering his flight he put most of them to death. At Ephesus, where he stopped on his way home, some Samians who lived nearby told him that was no way to free the Greeks; such actions would win no friends for Sparta and would alienate those Greeks already friendly. Alcidas yielded and freed the prisoners who were still alive, but the Spartan cause had been harmed. [12]

By this time word had reached Paches that a Peloponnesian fleet was loose in the Aegean and had landed on the coast of Asia Minor. This news struck great fear in Ionia; the cities were unfortified, for no one had imagined that a Peloponnesian fleet could penetrate so far. The whole coast was ripe for conquest, or at least for plunder. Four years of defensive warfare had worn

[9] 3.32.2.   [10] 3.33.3.   [11] 3.21.2.   [12] 3.32.

down Athenian resources to the point where the Spartans were willing to risk a naval expedition in the Aegean. A greater Peloponnesian effort coupled with better leadership at this moment might have been dangerous for Athens. In the summer of 427 most of the materials were at hand which more than twenty years later would bring Athens to her knees. Athens was short of money, part of her empire was in revolt, the undefended coastal cities of Asia Minor might be persuaded to rebel, and all this could bring Persia into the war against Athens.[13] All Sparta needed was a leader like Lysander. Instead they had Alcidas, who rejected the opportunities and fled across the open seas until Paches gave up the chase at Patmos and the fleet returned safely to the Peloponnese.[14] The Spartans, as Thucydides said on a later occasion, were the most convenient of all people for the Athenians to fight.[15]

The delay of Alcidas was fatal to the rebels of Mytilene. Help from the Peloponnese failed to come, and even Salaethus, the Spartan sent to bolster the morale of the rebels, abandoned hope. He decided the only chance was to launch an attack on the Athenian army investing the city in the hope of breaking through and obtaining food, since the city's supply was almost exhausted. For this he needed more hoplites than were ordinarily available, so he hit on a bold scheme. In the besieged city were Mytileneans of the lower classes and, apparently, enough armor to equip many of them as hoplites. He decided to provide the common people with armor for the attempted breakthrough. That decision required the approval of the oligarchic government of Mytilene, and it shows that the common people had

[13] Persian readiness to take advantage of Athenian troubles, already clear in the action of Pissuthnes during the Samian rebellion (see Kagan, *Outbreak*, 172–173), was demonstrated again in the spring of 430. On that occasion Pissuthnes involved himself in a factional dispute among the Colophonians. He supplied one faction with mercenaries and drove the pro-Athenian group out of the city. Until 427, Colophon was ruled by the Persians and their friends while the Colophonians who favored Athens were confined to Notium. In that year another quarrel broke out in Notium, and the Persians were again called in. This time the losing faction called on Paches who intervened in their favor (3.34). There is every reason to think that a Spartan landing on Ionia in 427 would have gained Persian support.

[14] 3.33.   [15] 8.96.5.

given no previous evidence of disaffection from their own government or of partiality for the Athenians.[16] On this occasion, however, once armed, they turned against the upper classes, demanding that they produce the available food and divide it among all the citizens. Otherwise, they threatened, they would turn the city over to Athens and make a separate peace which would exclude the upper classes.[17]

There is no way of knowing whether the government could have met this demand and kept the people loyal and willing to continue the fight. Probably the cupboard was bare or so near to it that a general distribution was impossible. As a result the ruling oligarchs abandoned hope of further resistance and came to terms with Paches, for they realized they would be in great danger if they were excluded from the agreement.[18] The terms agreed upon resembled unconditional surrender: the Athenian army should be admitted into the city and the Athenians should have the power "to decide in whatever way they wanted about the Mytileneans." Paches agreed to allow a delegation from Mytilene to go to Athens, there to try to arrange a permanent settlement, and not to imprison, enslave, or kill any Mytilenean until the return of that embassy. These were not great concessions, for Paches was not empowered to make a final settlement or to punish individual rebels.

Those Mytileneans who had been closest to the Spartans and most involved in gaining their support for the rebellion were naturally alarmed. The sight of an Athenian army marching into their city sent them running to the altars of the gods for sanctuary. Paches behaved with the greatest correctness and

---

[16] R. P. Legon, *Phoenix* XXII (1968), 206, is right to emphasize this point. Daniel Gillis, *AJP* XCII (1971), 44, suggests that there was concealed democratic revolutionary sentiment among the common people. He argues that the demos could have afforded hoplite armor but that "heavy arms had been prohibited for political reasons." For this there is no evidence, and the suggestion is contrary to our knowledge of Greek practice. If the people of Mytilene could afford a panoply they had one. The issuance of armor by the government to its citizens was rare, to say the least. Only the panic produced by a crisis made it possible in 427. Even then it would hardly have been possible if the government had any reason to suspect the loyalty of the common citizen.

[17] 3.27.3.   [18] 3.28.1.

consideration. He assured the suppliants that he would do them no harm and removed them to the nearby island of Tenedos for safekeeping. This was probably a kindly as well as judicious act, for they could have been in danger from political opponents and even from personal enemies.[19] At this point Paches had to interrupt his activities on Lesbos and pursue the Peloponnesian fleet under Alcidas. As we have seen, he was unable to catch it on the open sea and abandoned the chase at Patmos. When he returned he asserted control over the other Lesbian towns that had opposed Athens and captured Salaethus, who was hiding. Paches sent him to Athens, along with the pro-Spartan Mytileneans on Tenedos and "any one else who seemed to him responsible for the rebellion," probably, although Thucydides does not say so expressly, by order of a decree of the Athenian assembly.[20] After removal of all those Mytileneans suspected of disaffection from Athens, there was no longer reason to keep a large Athenian force on Lesbos, so Paches sent most of his army back home. With the rest he kept order and served as the interim governor pending a final decision in Athens.[21]

The Athenian assembly that met to consider the fate of Mytilene must be seen in the light of its particular historical moment. The Athenians were in the fourth year of a war they had been told they would win by adhering to a defensive strategy. Their strength, as they knew, lay in their reserves of money, the unquestioned superiority of their fleet, the security of their empire, and the invulnerability of their walls. They had believed a mere demonstration of their determination and the futility of attacking them would bring the Spartans to their senses. All their confidence, all optimistic expectations had now been shattered. Their money was swiftly being exhausted, and their fleet had been reduced by the shortage of men and money so it could not prevent an enemy fleet from penetrating to the heart of the empire. A daring enemy commander could have fomented a general rebellion and brought the Persian power against Athens. The plague, intensified by the crowding that resulted from the defensive strategy, had leaped over the walls and caused more deaths than an enemy army would have. That plague had raged,

[19] 3.28.   [20] 3.35.1; Gomme, *HCT* II, 297.   [21] 3.35.2.

on and off, since 430, and it might come again. Meanwhile, the enemy had suffered no serious harm nor shown any signs of losing interest in the war. The only strategy employed by Athens was plainly a failure, yet none other seemed possible. Athens had been forced completely onto the defensive and had only escaped disaster by a hair's breadth thanks to the sluggishness of the enemy commander. Next time they might not be so lucky. The display of Athenian weakness on the sea that permitted the Spartans to sail unhampered to Ionia and return unharmed would soon be well known and was likely to encourage further rebellion. The situation of Athens was perilous in the extreme, and the assembly meeting to decide the fate of Mytilene must have known it.

We get some sense of the fear and anger felt by the Athenians from their decision to put to death Salaethus, the captured Spartan, apparently without a trial. The decision of the assembly appears to have been unanimous, even though Salaethus offered to persuade the Spartans to abandon the siege of Plataea in exchange for his life.[22] The more controversial fate of Mytilene produced a debate. Thucydides chose not to report this meeting in detail nor to reproduce any of the speeches made, yet he gives enough information to reconstruct its course. The embassy from Mytilene was probably permitted to speak first, just as the Corinthians and Corcyraeans were permitted to present their views to the assembly in 433 that decided on the Corcyraean alliance. The Mytilenaean embassy, which had been composed when both factions were negotiating with Paches, must have included both oligarchs and democrats.[23]

Thucydides does not tell what the Mytilenaeans said, but some of their arguments may possibly be deduced from the Athenians' later decision about the responsibility for the rebel-

[22] 3.36.1.
[23] Legon, *Phoenix* XXII (1968), 208; Quinn, *Historia* XX (1971), 408, n. 19, denies that the phrase ποιοῦνται κοινῇ ὁμολογίαν (3.28.1) need mean that the Mytilenean *demos* was engaged in dealings with the Athenians. That, however, is certainly its obvious sense, and Quinn's own suggestion, "that there was one agreement for government and demos, not two separate ones," is strained. Legon's suggestion is convincing and I accept it.

lion. A major subject of debate among the Athenians at a second
meeting of the assembly was whether all the Mytileneans or
only the oligarchical government were guilty. Legon has plausibly suggested that the subject was introduced by the embassy
from Mytilene at the first meeting.[24] With him we may believe
that the embassy split when facing the angry Athenians; the
oligarchs tried to spread the blame as widely as possible in the
hope that the Athenians would not destroy a whole people,
while the democrats, probably represented by their more politically conscious and active leaders, must have argued that the
rebellion was inspired by the oligarchic ruling faction which
coerced the demos into obedience. "They would have asked what
punishment be confined to the real culprits, the members of the
oligarchic regime." [25]

After the ambassadors from Mytilene had had their say it was
time for the Athenians to decide. The debate centered on the
motion proposed by Cleon son of Cleaenetus, to kill all the adult
males of Mytilene and sell the women and children as slaves. We
may imagine that there were several speakers, and there may
even have been other proposals, but Thucydides tells us only of
the motion of Cleon and that the chief opposing speaker was Diodotus son of Eucrates. In this debate a split appeared between
the two factions, the moderates represented by Diodotus, following the cautious policy of Pericles, and the more aggressive
faction led by Cleon. Sparta's rejection of peace proposals in 430
had discredited the advocates of peace, and lack of men and
money had prevented any offensive actions, so there were no
important grounds for disagreement, and the moderates had remained in control. The war party, however, which had been
critical of what seemed to them the half-measures taken by Pericles and his successors since the first reinforcements had been
sent to Corcyra in 433, must have been frustrated by the unhappy results of moderation. That frustration was turned into
anger by the rebellion of Mytilene, and Thucydides tells us all

[24] Legon, *Phoenix*, XXII (1968), 208–209; Quinn, *Historia*, XX (1971),
408, does not accept this and presumes that the question of guilt was
raised by the Athenians.
[25] Legon, *Phoenix* XXII (1968), 209.

Athenians shared that anger. They were angry because the Mytilenaeans rebelled in spite of their privileged status, because the
rebellion was not a sudden aberration but had plainly been long
and carefully prepared. Most of all they were angry because the
Mytilenaean revolt had brought a Peloponesian fleet into the
Aegean and to the shores of Ionoa.[26]

Presumably Cleon used these and other arguments; we are not
told what Diodotus said in rebuttal. Cleon carried the day, and a
trireme was sent to Paches with the decision and an order to
carry out the sentence immediately. Meanwhile the Athenians
were having second thoughts. Once their fury was spent they
began to consider the unreasonableness and frightfulness of their
action, which treated the innocent and guilty alike. The ambassadors from Mytilene, among whom were probably some of the
Athenian *proxenoi*, and their supporters in Athens, Diodotus, no
doubt, and other moderates, perceived the change in sentiment.
They easily persuaded the generals, all of whom we know were
moderates,[27] to ask the prytanies to call a special meeting of the
assembly to reconsider the matter.[28] This second assembly met
on the very day after the assembly had decided the fate of
Mytilene.

Thucydides, introducing Cleon into his history for the first
time, although he had been prominent in Athenian politics for
some years, calls him "the most violent of the citizens and at that
time by far the most influential with the people." [29] This is a
rare instance of direct characterization of an individual by
Thucydides, and its harshness is uniquely applied to Cleon. The
speech that follows seems amply to justify the epithet.[30] Bully-
ing and rhetoric aside, Cleon's main points were these: The
Mytileneans must be punished severely because their rebellion
was without cause and unjust, the result of unforeseen good
fortune which turned, as usual, into wanton violence (*hybris*);

[26] 3.36.2. I consider οὐκ ἐλάχιστον here to be an example of litotes.
[27] See above, pp. 131–132.
[28] 3.36.5. For the constitutional questions, see Gomme, *HCT* II, 298.
[29] 3.36.6.
[30] For an interesting discussion of this speech see A. Andrewes,
Phoenix XVI (1962), 64–85.

justice, therefore, required swift and severe punishment. No distinction should be made between common people and oligarchs, for both took part in the rebellion. Not only justice but expediency required that the punishment be severe. Cleon believed that lenient treatment would encourage rebellion while uniformly harsh punishment would deter it. This last point is not merely an exercise in criminal theory or a rationalization for Cleon's passions. It is the central point of his argument and represents an important departure from and criticism of the Periclean policy of imperial management: "We should never have treated the Mytileneans differently from the others and then they would not have reached this point of insolence. In general, it is the nature of man to despise flattery and admire firmness." [31] The implication is that the Athenians in the past ought not to have permitted Mytilene to retain its autonomy but should have reduced it, and presumably Chios as well, to subject status. Even more plain is the following reference to what Cleon considers past errors: "Consider your allies: if you impose the same penalties upon those who rebel under constraint by the enemy and on those who rebel of their own free will, tell me who will not rebel on the smallest pretext when the reward for success is freedom and the price of failure is nothing irreparable?" [32] The reference, no doubt, was general, for even in the dark days of the First Peloponnesian War, when rebellions in the empire and especially on Euboea threatened the safety of Athens, when the decrees of Cleinias and Clearchus tightened Athenian control of the allies, when the Athenians planted colonies among the rebellious Colophonians and imposed a democratic government in place of the former constitution, when Athenian cleruchies were scattered throughout the empire, the Athenians under the leadership of Pericles never imposed so harsh a punishment. [33] The harshest treatment imposed by the Athenian, the one they inflicted on Hestiaea after the First Peloponnesian War and which Xenophon lists among the atrocities committed by Athens at Melos, Scione, Torone, and Aegina, [34] deprived the

[31] 3.39.5.   [32] 3.39.7.   [33] See Kagan, *Outbreak*, 116–119.
[34] Xen. *Hell.* 2.2.3.

victims of their lands, but not their lives as Cleon now proposed.[35] Closer in time, and probably more vivid in the minds of
Cleon's audience, was the treatment of Samos and Byzantium in
440. In spite of the serious threat the Samian rebellion posed and
the difficulty Athens had in putting it down, the Samians escaped
with both their lives and their property. They lost their walls
and ships and were compelled to accept a democratic government, but they received no garrisons or cleruchies. They even
were free of tribute, paying only a reasonable war indemnity.
Byzantium suffered hardly at all. She was permitted to return
to her condition before the revolt, paying a tribute only slightly
higher than before.[36] We can easily imagine that Cleon and his
friends were the accusers in the trial of the generals who had
taken the surrender of Potidaea but allowed its citizens to escape
without personal harm.[37]

Such lenient treatment, Cleon implied, had led to the Mytilenean rebellion. If the Athenians continue the policy of softness, misplaced pity, and clemency, "we shall risk our lives and
money against each rebellious state. If we succeed we will recover a state that has been destroyed, only then to be deprived
for the future of its revenue, which is the source of our strength.
If we fail we will add new enemies to those we have already, and
the time we should devote to fighting our present enemies we
will spend combatting our own allies." [38]

Cleon's argument was not directed merely toward the fate of
Mytilene; it was a full-scale attack on the imperial policy of
Pericles and his followers. He recommended instead a calculated
policy of terror toward imperial rebels, at least in wartime. He
proposed and carried a proposal to put the people of Scione to
death after their rebellion in 423,[39] and he sold the women and
children of Torone into slavery after he recaptured that rebellious town in 422.[40] Cleon's speech was a breach in the com-

[35] For an account of the Athenian settlement of Euboea in 446 see
Kagan, *Outbreak*, 126–127.
[36] *Ibid.*, 176–177.   [37] See above, pp. 98–99.   [38] 3.39.8.
[39] 4.122.6.
[40] 5.3.4. The captured men were sent first to Athens and were sent
home after the conclusion of peace. If Cleon had lived he probably
would have argued for harsher treatment.

mon front that had informally existed between the moderate
supporters of Pericles and his own more aggressive followers
since Athens' peace proposals of 430 had been rejected by the
Spartans. It was a signal that Cleon and his friends were no
longer willing to accept the policy and leadership of the moderates and that henceforth they would challenge both.

The debate between Cleon and Diodotus, reported by Thucydides in direct discourse, is often used, but without good reason,
as evidence for the coarsening of the Athenian spirit and the
decline in morality caused by the war.[41] Thucydides' dramatic
presentation of the debate has obscured some of his own remarks.[42] He said that Cleon and Diodotus were only two among
several speakers and that they represented the extreme positions.[43] The other speakers clearly addressed themselves to the
questions of justice and humanity, and Cleon's speech is obviously a rebuttal to such speeches. Finally, we must not forget
that the second assembly was called because the Athenians were
worried by the cruelty and injustice of their actions. Diodotus'
emphasis on expediency and his avoidance of emotional appeals
to mercy and other humane sentiments must be understood in
the light of the entire debate, much of which we do not have,
and particularly as a response to the speech of Cleon.

Cleon had implied that to favor leniency was softness at the
least and corruption and even treason at most. To argue for
humanity in the face of such an assault would be bad tactics. In
such circumstances men often try to cloak any humane reasons
they may have in a pose of toughness even greater than that of
the enemy. One is reminded of the arguments used by Dean
Acheson and Harry Truman in behalf of the Marshall Plan in
response to the charges of isolationists and Republicans that it
was the product of do-gooders sacrificing American interests to
humanitarian softness. The plan was, in fact, motivated in part
by the humane desire to feed and reconstruct a starving and
shattered continent, but its supporters defended it almost ex-

[41] E.g., John Finley, *Thucydides* (Cambridge, Mass., 1942), 177.
[42] Andrewes, *Phoenix* XVI (1962), 64–85, has pointed this out. My
understanding of the circumstances surrounding the debate owes much
to his article.
[43] 3.36.6 and 3.49.1.

clusively in terms of tough self-interest.[44] In the same way Diodotus told the Athenians to vote for his proposal, without undue regard for pity and clemency, but merely out of calculations of expediency.[45]

Diodotus' main task, after the necessary defense against the arguments of Cleon, was to defend the imperial policy laid down by Pericles and supported by himself and the other moderates. He did so vigorously and skillfully, relying on two main arguments. First, he claimed that use of the death penalty for unsuccessful rebels was not an effective deterrent for rebellion. Men rebel because they think they will be successful; no threat of punishment, therefore, can prevent them. A better policy would be "not to punish excessively free men who revolt but to guard them zealously before they rebel and anticipate them before they even think of it." [46] Gomme is right to say of such a statement that it is "sound, but easy advice to give, and difficult to follow" and to notice its similarity to the advice Pericles offered at the start of the war, "keep a firm hand on the allies." [47] This is the advice of a man who believes that the principles of the present imperial system are sound and simply require better administration. Diodotus, in fact, directly reaffirms his confidence in the present system. "Consider what your policy is now: if a city, having rebelled, realizes that it will not succeed, it may wish to reach an agreement while it is still able to pay the indemnity and the tribute in the future." [48] The Athenians must have been reminded of the surrender of the Samians and Byzantines, who had yielded before being destroyed. The Samians were still paying the war indemnity and the Byzantines their considerable assessment of tribute, both of which were contributing to the

---

[44] A. W. Gomme, *More Essays in Greek History and Literature* (Oxford, 1962), 158, has noticed a similar phenomenon. "In 1945 English newspaper correspondents in Berlin were stressing the need for food to be sent to the starving inhabitants, and assuring us that this was not from pity or kindness towards a wicked and defeated enemy, but because under-nourishment can so easily cause typhus and typhus might spread to allied troops."

[45] 3.48.1.   [46] 3.46.6.

[47] 2.13.2; Gomme's remarks are addressed to sections 4 and 6 of 3.46 on page 322 of the second volume of his *Commentary*.

[48] 3.46.2.

power of Athens; neither state had tried to renew its rebellion. Diodotus' audience might well believe that the surrender of Mytilene had been influenced by these examples of Athenian moderation.

Diodotus contrasts these happy results with the possible consequences of accepting the innovation proposed by Cleon. "What city will not make better preparations than now, and hold on to the very last when besieged, if coming to terms swiftly or at leisure has the same effect? And how will it not be harmful to us to spend money besieging an enemy who will not surrender and to be deprived of its revenue for the future, for that is the source of our strength against our enemies?" [49]

Diodotus' second argument rests on a flat contradiction of Cleon's assertion that the common people of Mytilene were as guilty for the rebellion as the oligarchs. The character of the disagreement makes it likely that the subject had been debated before, whether by Cleon and Diodotus at the first meeting or by other speakers, and probably introduced by the Mytilenaeans themselves. On Cleon's side, there is no evidence that the people resisted the rebellion until hunger impelled them. On the side of Diodotus is the fact that a rebellion by the demos brought about the capitulation and the suggestion, not denied by Cleon, that the people may have been forced to join in the rebellion. [50] The question cannot be judged simply. Thucydides' narrative does not suggest opposition to the rebellion before the Athenian blockade had taken its toll, but Cleon's remark that the common people joined the revolt, "thinking there was less risk in going with the oligarchs," [51] implies that refusal to join would have been punished.

The larger question of whether the Athenian Empire was generally popular among the lower classes is also important for Diodotus. He asserts that "now the demos in all the cities is well disposed to you and either does not rebel along with the oligarchs or, if it is compelled, is immediately hostile to those who made the revolution, so that you go to war having the

[49] 3.46.2–3.
[50] Diodotus: 3.47.2; Cleon: 3.39.6 with the analysis of Legon, *Phoenix* XXII (1968), 209–210.
[51] 3.39.6, τὸν μετὰ τῶν ὀλίγων κίνδυνον ἡγησάμενοι βεβαιότερον.

majority of the opposing city as an ally." [52] Once again we cannot be sure whether Diodotus is right; there is evidence in both directions, and the debate among modern scholars waxes.[53] The case immediately at hand, the rebellion of Mytilene, does not give unequivocal support to Diodotus. He seems to realize that the evidence in his favor is far from conclusive, but this does not trouble him unduly, for he is less interested in describing the facts than in prescribing a policy. In general, after putting down a revolt, the Athenians should blame as few men as possible. To kill the people along with the noble instigators of rebellion would play directly into the hands of the oligarchs. Future rebellions would find the common people hostile to Athens, once it was known that the same fate awaited nobles and commoners, instigators and unwitting followers, guilty and innocent. "Even if the demos were guilty you should pretend otherwise so that the only group that is still friendly to you should not become hostile." [54]

Diodotus puts forth a policy of firm but moderate and judicious treatment of the allies clothed in the language of *Realpolitik*. But though this language may have been forced on him by the circumstances of the debate, and though we may credit him with considerations of humanity as well, there is no doubt that his chief concern was political or that he believed in the effectiveness of the policy he proposed. He advocated the program of Pericles, and, up to the rebellion of Mytilene, it had worked well. For Diodotus there was no reason to believe that Mytilene was anything but an isolated case. The policy of calculated terror proposed by Cleon was not only offensive but was probably unnecessary and would likely be self-defeating. Diodotus proposed instead that the Athenians pass judgment only on those whom Paches had sent to Athens as the guilty parties, but not harm the other Mytileneans.[55]

We may more readily believe that the question was less one of humanity than of policy when we realize that the number of people arrested by Paches as "most guilty" was a little over a thousand.[56] That number is probably not less than one-tenth of

[52] 3.47.2.   [53] See above, p. 132, n. 37.   [54] 3.47.4.   [55] 3.48.
[56] 3.50.1. The number has been questioned by many scholars who have thought it impossibly large. See Busolt (*GG*, III:2, 1030 n. 2).

the entire adult male population of the rebellious towns on Lesbos.[57] Diodotus did not propose that these men should be put to death, but he must have known that would be the result. The vote was extremely close; the show of hands was almo[st] equal, but the proposal of Diodotus won. Cleon took immedi[ate] advantage of the situation to propose that the assembly vote t[he] death penalty for the "guilty" thousand, and his motion passe[d]. Thucydides does not suggest that the vote on this question w[as] close.[58] Busolt rightly compares these proceedings with the tr[ial] of the Athenian generals after the battle of Arginusae.[59] Lesbia[ns] received no proper trial, either singly or en masse. The assemb[ly] simply assumed them guilty on the basis of Paches' opinion a[nd] voted the death penalty. We do not know how Diodotus vot[ed] there is no record that he objected.

Meanwhile, however, the ship that had been dispatched aft[er] the assembly on the previous day was on its way to Lesbos carr[y]ing the order to put all the men to death. A second trireme w[as] sent off immediately to cancel the order. The first ship had [a] start of about twenty-four hours, but the Mytilenean envoys [at] Athens provided food and drink to the rowers and promis[ed] them a great reward if they got to Lesbos first. Moved by t[wo] powerful stimulants, the chance for a good deed and the ho[pe] of gain, the sailors set off at a great pace, refusing even to ma[ke] the usual stops for eating and sleeping. Fortune was with the[m] for they encountered no contrary winds. The first boat did n[ot] make good speed, for its men were in no hurry to accompli[sh] their frightful task; nevertheless, it got to Mytilene first. V[Ve] must allow Thucydides to tell the rest of the tale in his ov[n] dramatic way. "Paches had just read out the decree and w[as] about to carry out its orders when the second ship put in a[nd] prevented the destruction. By so little did Mytilene escape [the] danger." [60]

Even apart from the unprecedented execution of over [a] thousand rebels, the Athenian settlement of Lesbos was unusu[al]. As always the Athenians deprived the rebellious state of its wa[lls] and ships, but they imposed no tribute or war indemnity. Inste[ad] they turned all Lesbos, except for loyal Methymna, into [

[57] Beloch, *Bevölkerung*, 235.
[58] 3.50.1.
[59] Busolt, *GG* III:2, 1030, n. 1.
[60] 3.49.4.

Athenian cleruchy divided into three thousand lots. Three hundred of these were put aside as "sacred to the gods," which means that the income from them went into the sacred treasuries, while the remainder went to Athenian cleruchs chosen by lot. There were, of course, many other Athenian cleruchies, but this one was unusual in that the Lesbians arranged to cultivate the land themselves and to pay an annual rental of two minas to each cleruch.[61] The cleruchs actually went to Mytilene and stayed for some years, though they withdrew before 412 and possibly even before 424.[62] There is no reason to think that the Athenians interfered in the formation of the new government after the withdrawal of Paches and his troops. Since all the known enemies of Athens were gone it hardly mattered whether the new government was a democracy or an oligarchy.[63] Thus, the rebellious cities of Lesbos were left at least a limited autonomy, since no government and no tribute was imposed on them and they were permitted to work their land. On the other hand, the towns across from Lesbos on the mainland that had been dominated by Mytilene were taken over by Athens as subject allies and made to pay tribute.[64]

The reason for this unique arrangement is not entirely clear, and Thucydides does not tell us. The destruction of walls and fleet and the establishment of a cleruchy were common. The granting of limited autonomy and the absence of tribute may be seen as examples of the moderate policy of Diodotus following Periclean precedents. But why, at this moment of great financial need, did not the Athenians impose a heavy war indemnity of the kind paid by Samos in lieu of tribute? And why did the Athenians establish this extraordinary kind of cleruchy in place

[61] 3.50.2.

[62] The history of this cleruchy has provoked considerable discussion at least from the time of Boeckh and Grote in the nineteenth century. It is difficult to reconcile the evidence of Thucydides with that of Antiphon, *Murder of Herodes* 77 as well as with the fragmentary inscription *IG* I²:60 = Tod 63 = *ATL* D22. Gomme, *HCT* II, 326–332, and B. D. Meritt, *AJP* LXXV (1954), 359–368, have useful discussions, but I find the views of P. A. Brunt, *ASI*, 71–92, the most persuasive.

[63] Quinn, Historia XIII (1964), argues that it was an oligarchy, but the evidence does not permit a firm conclusion.

[64] 3.50.3; *ATL* II, 43.

of the usual sort where the natives were expelled from their land and the Athenian settlers took full possession and worked it themselves? Grote put the matter well: "It seems remarkable that the Athenians, at a time when their accumulated treasure had been exhausted, and when they were beginning to pay direct contributions from their private property, should sacrifice five thousand four hundred minae (ninety talents) annual revenue capable of being appropriated by the state, unless that sum were required to maintain the kleruchs as resident garrison for the maintenance of Lesbos." [65]

But the cleruchs stayed on the island for only a few years, so the puzzle remains. The Athenians may have thought it necessary to keep a garrison on Lesbos in the first years after the rebellion, before its security was assured. We know that even after the execution of the thousand oligarchic rebels some Mytilenaeans were so dissatisfied with the new arrangement that they went into exile and some tried to recover former possessions of Mytilene on the mainland.[66] But if the garrison was to be permanent the natives would have been removed, as, for instance, at Chalcis. The arrangement, it seems likely, was intended from the beginning to be temporary, and its value to Athens was both foreign and domestic. Besides assuring the immediate security of Lesbos and deterring further rebellion in the islands at a dangerous moment it also provided a haven for the many Athenians who had been driven from their farms into the plague-ridden city. They had been prevented from enjoying their homes in the country and deprived of the crops which gave them livelihood by the regular Spartan invasions. The invasion of the past spring had been particularly severe, and the problem of supporting these people on imported grain must have been serious. In the fifth year of the war most of the victims would have exhausted any savings they might have had and must have looked to the state treasury for help just when that treasury was very low. Emigration to the fertile fields of Lesbos offered a providential solution, but the Athenian farmers were reluctant to leave Attica. Thucydides paints a moving picture of their distress at

[65] Grote VI, 297, n. 1.   [66] 4.52.

being forced to leave their farms to go to Athens, and we may imagine that they would be even less happy to settle permanently in a foreign state.[67]

Politically, the settlement was ideal. The displaced Athenians would serve as a temporary garrison on Lesbos, supported by Lesbian labor and not draining the Athenian treasury. This relieved a pressure that was both financial and political, for a hungry mass of miserable farmers in the city might turn against the defensive war policy of the moderates and support either a renewal of pressure for an unsatisfactory peace or the more aggressive policies of Cleon and his friends. Meanwhile the three hundred lots set aside for the gods provided the treasury with a new annual income of 10 talents. When the war was over, or some change in the situation made it safe to return to Athens, the cleruchs could go home without leaving the rich lands of Mytilene untilled and without abandoning a source of income for Athens, a consideration that loomed large in the argument of Diodotus. Brunt's suggestion that such a time came in 425, after the capture of the Spartan prisoners on Sphacteria made Attica secure from invasion, is very attractive.[68]

The very fragmentary inscription that deals with the settlement of Mytilene [69] may perhaps be dated to this time. Caution is required in interpreting this inscription, but it seems to have provided that the Mytileneans were to be autonomous and that the old agreements that had governed relations between Athens and Mytilene before 428 should be in force. Most commentators agree that the decree also provided for the restoration of the land to the Mytileneans.[70] What happened to the former cleruchs is less clear; did they stay on the island on other land, or return to their homes in Attica and continue to collect their rent, or return and give up their Lesbian income? [71] The absence of any further

---

[67] 2.16.2.   [68] Brunt, *ASI*, 83.

[69] *IG* I²:60; Meritt, *AJP* XXV (1954), 359–368, and *ATL* D 22, and *IG*, date it to 427/6, but as Gomme says, "this is unwarranted" (*HCT* II, 330). Gomme's own suggestion of the date 424 is neatly disposed of by Brunt, *ASI*, 83.

[70] See Brunt, *ASI*, 82; Gomme, *HCT* II, 329–331; and Meritt, *AJP*, 361.

[71] The first view is held by Meritt, the second by Brunt, and the third by Gomme.

news of the cleruchs where we should expect to find it rules out
the first possibility. The second could not be true. In 425, Athens
took the dangerous step of sharply increasing the tribute assessment on its subjects. We cannot believe that at the same time it
would permit 2,700 of its citizens, newly restored to their homes,
to continue to receive a considerable subsidy in return for no
service instead of adding 90 talents annually to the income of the
state. The Athenian citizens would not have taken kindly to
such unwarranted privileged treatment, but, much more, the
needs of the city in the midst of a desperate war forbade it. We
should return to the long-neglected opinion of Grote that the
rent was thereafter paid into the state treasury in lieu of tribute.[72] Such a development may have been anticipated at the time
of the original settlement in 427.

Still another story connected with the rebellion of Mytilene
is of some importance, though Thucydides does not mention it.
Paches, after laying down his office, came before an Athenian
court to give the usual accounting for his generalship. A charge
was brought against him, and, when the verdict was unfavorable,
Paches drew his sword and killed himself in the open court-
room.[73] Some scholars, connecting the event with an epigram by
Agathias written a thousand years later,[74] have attributed his
action to shame at the public exposure of a private misdeed. "It
appears, that having contracted a passion for two beautiful
women at Mytilene, Hellanis and Lamaxis, he slew their hus-
bands and got possession of them by force." [75] Others attribute
it to some alleged misconduct in his execution of the duties of
his office.[76] He certainly had to make many important decisions
in his term of office without orders from the sovereign assembly
at Athens. The actions he had taken and the arrangements he
had made certainly provided, as Busolt says, "plenty of material
for attacks and accusations." [77]

Whichever story is true, the trial was surely at least partly

---

[72] Grote VI, 257, n. 1.   [73] Plut. *Nic.* 6 and *Arist.* 26.
[74] *Anth. Pal.* vii. 614.
[75] Grote VI, 258; Gomme, *HCT* II, 332, also accepts the story.
[76] Busolt, *GG* III:2, 1034, and Adcock, *CAH* V, 218.
[77] Busolt, *GG* III:2, 1034.

political.[78] Most scholars agree that Paches was a moderate. In the summer of 427 he was an outstanding, and vulnerable, representative of that policy. The victory of Cleon at the first assembly, the close vote at the second, the success of Cleon's motion to kill the thousand Mytilenean rebels, show that while Cleon and his supporters were not in command of policy, the political balance on the Pnyx was a fine one. The aggressive forces in Athens who were dissatisfied with the conduct of the war and the management of the empire may have turned to the time-honored device of using the law court as a political forum. Their success in bringing down a leading opposition figure does not mean that they had won over a clear majority of the Athenians to support of their general policies. Paches very likely gave them some grounds for an accusation, and the jury must have considered the merits of the case to some degree. The trial does show, however, that in the summer of 427, Cleon and his friends had achieved an unprecedented degree of power.

Most scholars have not understood the political situation in Athens at this time. The usual view is that the elections in the spring of 427 continued to exclude the more aggressive Athenians around Cleon from political power and influence. Beloch says: "The victory of the peace party was even more decisive than in the previous year; the opposition was almost completely excluded from the strategia." [79] Busolt tells us that "the peace party won a noteworthy success in the elections to the *strategia* of March or April 427." [80] Even West, who understands that the peace party was out of the picture, that all the generals for 427/6 believed in carrying on the war, and that none of them were oligarchs arrives at unwarranted conclusions. He sees "no real issues in the elections of this year" and concludes that "the democratic party was strong and united in the spring of 427." [81] West combated the false view that Athenian political life was

---

[78] Beloch, *Attische Politik*, 33, though I think him almost completely wrong in his understanding of Athenian politics at this time, is right to see the trial as political. We must agree that, whether or not the tale of sexual passion is true, it is "politisch sehr gleichgültig," while leaning, with Beloch, toward the less romantic version.

[79] *Attische Politik*, 31.   [80] *GG* III:2, 1018.

[81] *CP* XIX (1924), 143.

dominated by a struggle between oligarchic advocates of peace
and democratic wagers of war, but the evidence permits finer
distinctions.

The generals elected in 427 whose attitudes we can estimate
were Nicias, Laches, Nicostratus, Hipponicus, Demosthenes, and
Eurymedon. Nicias, we have argued, was pre-eminently a
moderate, and Laches and Nicostratus were closely associated
with him and his policies.[82] Hipponicus, reputedly the richest
man in Athens, was the son of Callias the Treaty Maker,
Pericles' associate, and was related to the family of Pericles in
several ways.[83] These four were all moderates, representatives of
that group which had guided Athenian policy since the beginning of the war and adhered to the plans of Pericles. Demosthenes and Eurymedon, however, were different. Demosthenes
was to prove himself the most aggressive and imaginative Athenian general in the Archidamian War, the inventor and executor
of campaigns that departed completely from the strategy of
Pericles.[84] The views of Eurymedon are less clear, but most
commentators consider him a supporter of Cleon and his policies.[85] His support of the harsh policies of the Corcyraean democrats, his frequent association and cooperation with Demosthenes,[86] and his repeated involvement in campaigns against
Sicily make that belief plausible.

Busolt believes that the election of Demosthenes and Eurymedon "had no political significance"[87] because they were
military men and not politicians. But military questions were at
issue in 427 and of great political significance.[88] The questions

[82] Busolt, GG III:2, 1018 and n. 9; 1044, n. 2.

[83] West, CP XIX (1924), 143.

[84] Beloch, Attische Politik, 31, speaks of his "tolles Draufgehen" and
"ungezügelte Kampflust." Busolt places him and Eurymedon among the
"Anhänger der kriegslustigen Demokratie."

[85] Beloch, Attische Politik, 35; Busolt, GG, III:2, 1019 and n. 2.

[86] West, CP XIX (1924), 143. They disagreed sharply, however, at
Pylos (4.3.1–3).

[87] GG III:2, 1020.

[88] The inadequacy of the political analyses of Beloch and Busolt should
be plain, for each is self-contradictory. Beloch says that the victory of
what he calls the peace party in 427 was even more decisive than in the
previous year, but in the previous year there is no evidence for any
warlike generals, and he claims none, while in 427 he admits to the

dividing Athenians politically concerned the strategy to win the war or at least bring it to an acceptable conclusion and management of the empire. Generals, even those known to be military men without political talent, were most likely to influence those decisions. The election of Demosthenes and Eurymedon in the spring of 427 may be the first evidence of a growing dissatisfaction with the policies of the moderates.[89] That dissatisfaction showed itself plainly during the debate over Mytilene and was very likely felt in the trial and condemnation of Paches. Impatience with the old strategy was growing and with it the demand for new men and new directions.

About midsummer 427, but probably before the new board of generals took over, Nicias led an attack on the little island of Minoa off the coast of Megara.[90] The island served as an Athenian lookout station and garrison. The Athenians wanted to use it as an observation point to prevent a repetition of the abor-

---

election of two. Busolt speaks of a "noteworthy success" for the "peace party," but considers the election of Cleon as *Hellenotamias* at the same time as evidence that "the popular party of the city still possessed a considerable influence," and that "the parties almost balanced each other" (3.2.1020). Since there is no evidence of influence by any opposition in the previous year, much less a condition of balance, the elections of 427 could hardly be a "noteworthy success" for the party previously in control.

[89] Some scholars believe that Cleon was elected *Hellenotamias* for 427/6, and if this were true it might be further evidence for the growth of opposition power. The suggestion originated with Busolt's restoration of Cleon's name among the *Hellenotamiae* in a list for the year 427/6 (*Hermes* XXV [1890], 640–645; the restoration is on line 17 of *CIA* IV, 179b, p. 161). Even then there was little reason to accept the restoration, for which the only evidence on the stone was that one *Hellenotamias* for that year came from the same deme as Cleon. Busolt, nevertheless, accepted the election as fact and took it as evidence that "die städtische Volkspartei noch einen massgebenden Einfluss besass" (*GG*, III:2, 1020). Beloch (*GG*² I:2, 324) and West (*CP* XIX [1924], 139) followed Busolt. Since then, however, the inscription has been attributed to the year 414/13 (*IG* I²:297 and *SEG* X:229). There is no good reason for believing that Cleon held the post of *Hellenotamias* in 427/6 or at any other time.

[90] For the date see Beloch, *Attische Politik*, 301. This is the first time Thucydides mentions Nicias, though he had been a general throughout the year and Plutarch tells us he had been a colleague of Pericles (*Nic.* 2.2).

tive naval attack on Piraeus that had been launched from the Megarian harbor. They also wanted to prevent the use of that harbor for launching piratical raids on Athenian and allied shipping. Finally, they wanted Minoa to help tighten the blockade of Megara. Nicias accomplished his task with speed and ingenuity. Within a few days he built a fort on the island and withdrew with his army, leaving an Athenian garrison behind. This small but skillfull campaign was in line with the defensive Athenian strategy. It entailed no risk, especially after the pitiful performance of the Spartan fleet under Alcidas, and achieved its end neatly.

If this success buoyed Athenian spirits they were quickly depressed by news from Plataea. During the previous winter part of the garrison of Athenians and Plataeans in the city, running out of supplies and despairing of help from Athens, tried to escape to safety; 212 succeeded.[91] After the fall of Lesbos and about the same time as the attack on Minoa the remaining defenders of Plataea surrendered to the Spartans. The nature of Plataea's fall is interesting and significant. The Spartans could easily have taken the city by storm, since it was defended by a pitiful number of starving men. The commander of the Spartan forces, however, had received orders not to take the city by force but to seek a capitulation. The Spartans calculated that "if ever a peace were concluded with Athens, and if each side agreed to restore the places conquered in the war, Sparta would not have to restore Plataea on the grounds that it had gone over of its own free will." [92] This very specious argument was, in fact, used when peace was made in 421, and by its hypocritical terms the Peloponnesians were allowed to keep Plataea and the Athenians the Megarian port of Nisaea.[93] That such a plan should occur to the Spartans in 427 shows that they realized their hopes for a quick and easy victory were too optimistic and their strategy was plainly ineffective. The plague, an unanticipated but powerful ally sent by the gods, had come and apparently gone without bringing the Athenians to their knees. The defeat of the Peloponnesian navy in the Corinthian Gulf and its disgraceful failure to assist the rebels on Lesbos had shown the vanity of

[91] 3.20–24.   [92] 3.52.2.   [93] 5.17.2.

hoping for rebellions in the Athenian Empire and the achievement of naval parity or even superiority. Though by this time a shift in the political situation in Sparta may have taken place, it is certainly too much to say, as Busolt does, that "if Sparta envisioned a peace on the basis of the *status quo ante bellum* that already means the renunciation of the original goal of the war: the destruction of the Athenian Empire." [94]

There is no evidence that the Spartans had given up their hope of total victory, a dictated peace, and the annihilation of the Athenian Empire. If they were ready for a negotiated peace of the sort Busolt describes they could have offered to open the discussions they had rudely rejected in 430. There was no reason to believe the Athenians would prove recalcitrant. Pericles, the great opponent of the negotiations of 430, was gone, and the Athenian position had not improved. The plague was gone, but it had done fearful damage and it might return to the crowded city. The Lesbian rebellion had been put down, but had further drained the shrinking Athenian treasury. If, as Busolt claims, "the failure of the Lesbian rebellion had obviously strengthened the peace party," [95] why was peace not offered? The answer is that the peace party was not in power and the Spartans were not ready for a negotiated peace. Their early reverses had taught them that a negotiated peace might some day be forced upon them. In the meantime they pursued their original goal without change.

The Spartans secured the surrender of Plataea by promising the garrison a fair trial, and, in due course, five judges arrived from Sparta. But there would be no justice, for no charges were brought against the Plataeans. Each one was merely asked if he had rendered any good service to the Spartans or their allies during the war.[96] The shocked Plataeans asked permission to make a longer speech, and it was granted. They complained of the deception by which they had been led to surrender and hinted at their fear that the Spartans had already made up their minds under the influence of the Thebans. They called up the memory of the heroism of the Plataeans during the Persian Wars, of the service they had given to all the Greeks, and of the special recognition Sparta had given them—in contrast to the

[94] *GG*, III:2, 1035, n. 4.   [95] *Ibid.*   [96] 3.52.4.

treasonous Thebans. They reminded the judges of the help they had sent to Sparta almost forty years earlier, at the time of the great Peloponnesian earthquake and the helot rebellion.[97]

These arguments, though embarrassing to the Spartans, were of no avail. The Thebans, fearing that the Spartans might soften, rose to respond. The judges then repeated the original question to the Plataeans, and each one, of course, answered "no." At least 200 Plataeans and 25 Athenians were put to death, and the women who remained in the city were sold into slavery. Theban arguments were not persuasive; as Thucydides reports, they were self-serving, distorted, sophistical, and unconvincing. Neither justice nor rhetoric explains the Spartan action but, as Thucydides makes clear, Realpolitik: "The behavior of the Spartans toward the Thebans was influenced almost entirely by concern for the Thebans, for they thought that they would be useful in the war that was just then beginning." [98] If the last words represent Spartan thinking, they were not preparing for a negotiated peace, but for a long war in which Boeotian power would be more important than a reputation for justice and decency. But even if Thucydides is responsible for pointing out that the war was in its early stages,[99] the Spartan brutality shows that no peace party was in power or had important influence. Such an atrocity could only harden feeling and make peace less likely.

The city and territory of Plataea were dealt with in two stages. For about a year it was nominally in the control of the Spartans, to whom it had been surrendered, and inhabited by some exiles from Megara and the Plataeans who were pro-

[97] 3.53–59.   [98] 3.68.4.

[99] The words τὸν πόλεμον . . . ἄρτι τότε καθιστάμενον echo others used by Thucydides to describe Athenian thinking at the outbreak of the Lesbian rebellion. The Athenians were reluctant to make an enemy of Lesbos when they were troubled by the plague καὶ τοῦ πολέμου ἄρτι καθισταμένου καὶ ἀκμάζοντος (3.3.1). Gomme (HCT II, 358), assuming that Thucydides is speaking his own mind on both occasions, takes it that these passages were written late, at least after the Peace of Nicias. He is probably right in both assumptions, but both passages seem to me somewhat ambiguous. Possibly Thucydides is paraphrasing the thinking of the Athenians in the first passage and the Spartans in the second. Thus both participants realized that the war would not end soon, but was in its early stages. That should not have been hard to believe in 427.

Theban. Evidently, real control was in the hands of Thebes, which had a powerful interest in the settlement. After this brief time the Thebans leveled the town entirely. They built a stone temple to Hera and, near her sanctuary, a large inn, constructed in part from the materials of the destroyed Plataean houses. Perhaps these pious acts were intended to enlist the help of Hera in warding off the justice of Zeus. The land of Plataea was parceled out to deserving Thebans on ten-year leases. By 421 the Thebans spoke of it as part of their own territory.[100] Plataea had been obliterated, and the Athenians had not lifted a finger.[101]

The fall of Plataea and its abandonment by the Athenians were inevitable. No reasonable man could expect Athens to send an army to relieve a city that was strategically untenable, and we have no reason to believe that any Athenian complained. Yet there was reason for embarrassment, if not shame. Not only was Plataea a faithful ally of long standing; when Plataea was first attacked in 429 she could have yielded on reasonable terms had not Athens held her to the alliance and promised help.[102] That promise, we have argued, was probably made during the temporary ascendancy of the aggressive faction that was no longer in control,[103] but the vote must have been taken by the people in the sovereign assembly and was legally and morally binding on the state. The Athenians clearly felt a responsibility to the surviving Plataeans. On the motion of Pericles' nephew Hippocrates[104] the Athenians granted the Plataeans the rare, almost unique privilege of Athenian citizenship.[105]

[100] 5.17.2.

[101] The foregoing reconstruction is based on an interpretation of Thuc. 3.68.3–5 which accepts the reading of all the manuscripts Θηβαῖοι before Μεγαρέων in 68.3. Classen and Steup delete Θηβαῖοι because of the Θηβαῖοι that follows at the end of the same paragraph, and their suggestion has won much support. I share the doubts expressed by Gomme, HCT II, 357. My own reconstruction is a development of his argument. See also Busolt, GG III:2, 1037, n. 3.

[102] 2.73.3.   [103] See above, pp. 104–105.

[104] Dem. Against Neaera 104. The decree quoted by Demosthenes identifies the mover only as Hippocrates. Busolt, GG III:2, 1038, says he was "sicherlich der Neffe des Perikles," and I agree.

[105] In addition to the Demosthenes passage cited above see Isoc. Panath. 94, Lysias XXIII, 2, and the discussion by Busolt, GG III:2, 1038, n. 2.

The importance of Plataea was chiefly symbolic and emotional, but soon after its fall the Athenians were confronted by a serious threat to their alliance with the highly strategic island of Corcyra. For some months internal strife in Corcyra had threatened to result in a break with Athens, provoke intervention by the Peloponnesians, and possibly even align Corcyra with the enemy. The trouble began with the return to Corcyra of some 250 prisoners taken by the Corinthians at the battle of Sybota in 433.[106] These free Corcyraeans, unlike the 800 slave captives who were immediately sold, the Corinthians treated with great care. Thucydides tells us that most of them were men of high rank and wealth and that the Corinthians hoped to use them one day to change Corcyra's allegiance.[107] The Corinthians bided their time and won their captives' loyalty. Probably in the winter of 428/7 or the following spring, they judged the time ripe to send them back home to subvert the policy and government of their native land.[108] The Mytilenean rebellion was under way, Plataea was under siege. The prisoners were probably sent back to foment rebellion in the Ionian Sea about the time that Alcidas sailed into the Aegean and hope was high among the Peloponnesians that a general rebellion of Athens' allies would soon take place.[109]

These men who, for whatever reason, had become agents of a

[106] 1.55.

[107] 1.55.1. Thucydides speaks of the captives as follows: ἐτύγχανον δὲ καὶ δυνάμει αὐτῶν οἱ πλείους πρῶτοι ὄντες τῆς πόλεως. This language makes it clear that these were wealthy and powerful men whose subsequent behavior shows clearly what we might otherwise expect—that they were oligarchs hostile to the democrats of Corcyra. It plainly does not allow for the interpretation of I. A. F. Bruce, *Phoenix* XXV (1971), 109, that they were merely "a sample of the hoplites or *epibatae* on the Corcyraean ships," who may even have included thetes. Thucydides makes a point of telling us just the opposite. The view of Grote, VI, 266ff., is correct. The same view has been put neatly by R. P. Legon, "Demos and Stasis, Studies in the Factional Politics of Classical Greece," Ph.D. dissertation, Ithaca, N.Y., 1966, 23: "It must be obvious that a party composed of the men of wealth and influence, which opposes the aims of the democratic faction and ultimately murders its leaders, must be oligarchic."

[108] Thucydides does not tell us when the captives were sent home. I am persuaded by the arguments of Grote, VI, 266, and Busolt, *GG* III:2, 1041 and n. 1. Gomme, *HCT* II, 359, accepts the same dating.

[109] Grote, VI, 266.

foreign power against their own government, were still regarded
back home as patriotic citizens who had lost their liberty fighting
for their homeland against Corinth. Their usefulness as agents
depended on their ability to sustain that reputation, so a "cover
story" was invented to explain their safe return. The pretense
was that they had been ransomed for the incredibly high sum of
800 talents guaranteed by the *proxenoi* of the Corcyraeans at
Corinth.[110] They were wealthy, influential men whose prestige
was particularly great because of their status as returned heroes,
and they made good use of all these advantages. They went
among the citizens trying to break off the alliance with Athens.
They said nothing of oligarchy nor did they suggest changing
sides in the war. They argued for a return to the traditional
neutrality of Corcyra.[111] This suggestion must have been popular in a state with a tradition of political isolation which seems to
have taken no part in the war since its first year;[112] the Corcyraeans decided to reconsider the alliance with Athens. This
development encouraged Corinth and alarmed Athens, and each
sent a ship carrying diplomatic envoys to try to sway the
decision.

After hearing from the Corinthians and Athenians the democratic Corcyraean assembly voted to reaffirm the defensive
alliance, but also "to be friends with the Peloponnesians as they
had in the past." [113] This was certainly "a naive and unrealistic
decision," [114] for they could hardly have expected to carry out
the terms of the alliance with Athens while friendly with the
enemies it was fighting. This is by no means the only example
of such naiveté on the part of the common people in the Greek
states,[115] but the active politicians must have realized that the
new policy was impossible and therefore transitory. The vote
was a victory for the oligarchic plotters, who must have seen it
as the first step in their plan to disengage Corcyra from Athens

[110] Gomme, *HCT* II, 359, thinks the sum impossibly high and suggests
80 as the correct figure.

[111] 3.70.2. Thucydides says nothing of their arguments, saying merely
ἔπρασσον . . . ὅπως ἀποστήσωσιν Ἀθηναίων τὴν πόλιν. I deduce their arguments from the subsequent decision made by the Corcyraean assembly.

[112] 2.25.1.   [113] 3.70.2.   [114] Bruce, *Phoenix* XXV (1971), 109.

[115] See Legon, "Demos and Stasis," *passim*.

and join Corinth. They took advantage of their success to bring
to trial Peithias, a democratic leader closely attached to Athens.[116]
The charge was that he was trying to enslave Corcyra to the
Athenians. As a criminal charge this amounted to treason, but
the trial was clearly political, for it brought into the law courts
the argument over Corcyraean foreign policy. On this occasion,
it appears, the oligarchs overplayed their hand. The ordinary
Corcyraean did not regard the advocacy of an alliance with
Athens, or even its elevation to a full offensive and defensive
alliance, as a treasonous act, and Peithias was acquitted.

The initiative now fell to Peithias. He brought a suit against
the five richest men among his accusers on the charge that they
had cut vine poles from the sacred precincts of Zeus and
Alcinous, a form of sacrilege for which the law prescribed a very
high fine. Thucydides does not tell us whether they were guilty
of the deed, but the political character of the trial must have
been plain to the jury. The verdict was guilty, but, in view of
the greatness of the fine imposed, the defendants pleaded for the
opportunity to pay in installments, taking refuge in the temples
for safety. The Corcyraean council, under the influence of
Peithias who was a member, rejected the appeal and voted to
let the law take its course.

The condition of the plotters was now desperate. The two
trials had shown that their political influence was waning and
had, in fact, contributed to its decline. Their leaders were
threatened by serious financial damage or, if they could not pay
the fine, a more unpleasant punishment. They knew, moreover,
that Peithias, triumphant and more influential than ever, would
try to use his position in the council to conclude a full offensive
and defensive alliance with Athens.[117] The attempt to bring
Corcyra over to Corinth by peaceful means had miscarried. The
plotters now resorted to assassination and terror. They broke
into a meeting of the council armed with daggers, killing
Peithias and 60 others, both council members and private citi-

---

[116] Thucydides describes him as ἐθελοπρόξενός τε τῶν Ἀθηναίων 3.70.3.
What ἐθελοπρόξενος was is not entirely clear (see Gomme, *HCT* II, 360)
but the close relationship with Athens is plain.
[117] 3.70.5–6.

zens. A few democratic associates of Peithias made their escape and reached safety aboard the Athenian trireme which was still in the harbor.[118] The ship apparently sailed immediately to Athens where the refugees could explain what had happened and urge retaliatory action.

In an atmosphere of terror the assassins called a meeting of the assembly. They had to move fast, for some reaction from Athens was certain, but even in such confused and frightening circumstances they could not move the Corcyraean people to change alliances. The plotters put the best face possible on what they had done, saying that it prevented enslavement to Athens. The most they dared propose, however, was a policy of neutrality, and even this was passed only under compulsion.[119] Their position was far from secure, and they sent an embassy to Athens to plead that the events were not against Athenian interests and to persuade the Corcyraean fugitives not to urge Athenian action. The ambassadors persuaded some of the Corcyraeans but not the Athenians, who understood the matter quite well. They arrested the ambassadors as revolutionaries and placed them and the men they had persuaded on Aegina for safe keeping.

The embassy to Athens had obviously been meant to gain time for the conspirators to tighten their very tenuous hold on Corcyra. Soon after it left, a Corinthian ship carrying ambassadors from Sparta arrived, very likely summoned by the conspirators. Encouraged by the hope of support and fearing the imminent arrival of the Athenians, they attacked the common people and defeated them in a pitched battle. Even their tactics of terror had not persuaded the people, yet they must make the island secure under their rule before the Athenians came. The democrats, though defeated in battle, had not been destroyed. Under cover of darkness they seized the acropolis and the other high places of the town, as well as the seaward harbor. The oligarchs controlled the area around the market place and the harbor facing the mainland. The next day both sought support by offering freedom to the slaves; most of these joined the demo-

---

[118] 3.70.6. The Corinthians had evidently left, perhaps when it became clear that their agents would not be successful.
[119] 3.71.1.

crats, but the oligarchs were able to hire 800 mercenaries from the mainland. Full-scale civil war reigned on Corcyra.[120]

Two days later a second battle was fought. This time the democrats, better located and more numerous, were successful, and the oligarchs saved themselves only by fleeing to the part of the city they controlled, including their own houses. When night came the democrats clearly were in control; the Corinthian ship prudently sailed away, and the mercenaries sneaked off to the mainland. Their departure was timely, for the next day Nicostratus, commander of the Athenian forces at Naupactus, sailed into the harbor with 12 ships and 500 Messenian hoplites. News of his imminent arrival probably explains the panic of the oligarchs and the quick departure of their allies. Nicostratus behaved with great moderation. He must have been instructed to insist that the defensive alliance be converted to one that was both offensive and defensive, but beyond that he must have had discretion to settle matters on the island to make it safe for Athens. The spirit of his settlement, however, was the opposite of that proposed by Cleon for Mytilene and shows that the Athenians continued to accept the moderate theory of imperial rule supported by Pericles, Diodotus, and their followers. There was no proposal to put to death all the oligarchs; only the ten men judged most responsible were to be tried, and the rest were to live together and make peace with one another.[121]

But the civil war on Corcyra had gone too far to permit such a gentle solution. The ten men selected for trial fled. The democratic faction that controlled Corcyra feared the oligarchs and wanted more security. Before they would allow Nicostratus to depart they persuaded him to leave them a guard of 5 Athenian ships, in return for 5 ships of their own manned by oligarchs— their own personal enemies. The men chosen for this service, fearing they would be sent not to Naupactus for naval service but to Athens to meet some awful fate, fled for sanctuary to the temples. Nicostratus tried to reassure them, but they would not budge. The democrats took this as evidence of their evil intentions and prepared to kill all the oligarchs, but Nicostratus intervened. By now all those tinged with oligarchical sympathies,

[120] 3.72–73.   [121] 3.75.1.

fearing for their lives, had escaped to the temple of Hera; they numbered at least 400. Afraid that so large a group might start a revolution, the democrats moved them to an island across from the temple.[122]

At this point the Peloponnesians intervened in force. Their decision to become involved on Corcyra is further evidence that the peace party lacked influence in Sparta at this time. When the 40 ships under Alcidas straggled back from the Aegean they landed at Cyllene. There they were strengthened by 13 ships from Leucas and Ambracia and by Brasidas, who once again was sent as *symboulos*. They hurried their preparations in the hope of deciding the issue favorably before the Athenian fleet could arrive in force.[123] Four or five days after the oligarchs had been put on the island the Peloponnesian fleet arrived at Corcyra. The Corcyraean democrats put out to sea with 60 ships, in bad order, with poor discipline, and contrary to the advice of the Athenians. In the ensuing battle the Peloponnesians easily defeated the Corcyraeans, though fear of the 12 Athenian ships prevented them from exploiting the victory. The Corcyraeans expected them to attack the city and took the 400 prisoners back to the temple of Hera on the mainland since the island was no longer safe. But the Peloponnesians were content to sail back to the mainland across from Corcyra with the ships they had captured. The next day, though the Corcyraeans were terribly frightened, and in spite of the advice of Brasidas, they again failed to attack the city; soon it was too late. As night fell the Peloponnesians received a signal that an Athenian fleet was coming from Leucas. This was a force of 60 ships commanded by Eurymedon son of Thucles.[124] The Peloponnesians wasted no time—they left immediately and even hauled their ships across the Leucadian isthmus to avoid being seen by the approaching Athenians.

When the Corcyraeans learned that the danger was gone they gave vent to all the rage produced by fear and civil war. Protected by the Messenian hoplites left behind by Nicostratus and by the fleet under Eurymedon, they launched a frightful attack on their domestic enemies. Political execution degenerated into

[122] 3.75.   [123] 3.69.   [124] 3.80.

wanton murder; men were killed for private revenge and for
money. No impiety or sacrilege was spared.[125] The horrors of
the civil war in Corcyra give Thucydides an opportunity to
speak in general of the evil consequences of civil strife during
wartime.[126] Thucydides pointedly remarks that Eurymedon was
present with his 60 ships for seven days while the wanton killing
was done; unlike Nicostratus he made no attempt to stop it.
There is no question that he could have done so, for his force
was five times that of Nicostratus. He could not have received
specific orders when he left Athens, for the situation on Corcyra
was too fluid and mysterious. Probably his orders were not very
different from those given Nicostratus: keep Corcyra safe for
Athens. Eurymedon, however apparently held the same views as
Cleon did and deplored the moderation which seemed to be
ineffective and to encourage revolution.[127] As a result he was
willing to see the oligarchs of Corcyra destroyed, the innocent
along with the guilty.

The appearance of Eurymedon at Corcyra meant the new
board of generals had taken office, and his actions there suggest
that the feeling for a departure from the policies of Pericles was
growing. This impression is fortified by the Athenian decision
in September to send an expedition to Sicily. Syracuse wished to
dominate the island of Sicily. We do not know just when war
began, but by 427 she had attacked the neighboring state of
Leontini. The war had quickly leaped over the narrow strait to
Italy. Soon all the Dorian cities of Sicily, except Camarina, and
Locri in Italy were allied with Syracuse, while the Chalcidian
cities of Sicily, whose people were of Ionian heritage, Camarina,
and Rhegium in Italy were allied with Leontini. When it was
clear that the Leontines were losing and that their city was in
danger they sent an embassy to Athens asking the Athenians to
honor their treaty and send help.[128] A treaty with Leontini, a
symmachia, a full offensive and defensive alliance, dated back

[125] 3.81.

[126] 3.82–84. Chapter 84 is generally rejected as spurious. For a recent
argument against its authenticity see A. Fuks, *AJP* XCII (1971), 48–55.

[127] Beloch, *Attische Politik*, 35, and Busolt, *GG* III:2, 1019, n. 2, connect him with Cleon on the basis of his actions at Corcyra.

[128] 3.86.1–2; Diod. 12.53.1–2.

perhaps to the 450s and had been renewed as recently as 433/2.[129] The Athenians could have refused as they were busy fighting their own war of survival, but they chose to honor the treaty and sent a fleet of 20 ships under Laches and Charoeades. The question is why, when their manpower was decimated by the plague and their treasury depleted, did the Athenians undertake an expedition to a place so remote and seemingly tangential to the major strategy of the war? [130]

We may safely dismiss the suggestion of Diodorus that the Athenians were convinced by the rhetorical innovations of the great sophist Gorgias who led the embassy from Leontini.[131] Thucydides speaks of three reasons. The first is formal, probably the one officially mentioned in the decree of the assembly authorizing the expedition, based on relationship with the Leontines and their allies. They really made their decision, however, "because they did not want the Peloponnese to receive grain from that region and because they were making a preliminary test to see if they could bring the affairs of Sicily under their control." [132] One of the puzzles of Thucydidean scholarship is to interpret such attributions of motive. Some scholars have thought that in this passage Thucydides is merely expressing his own personal opinion of what moved the Athenians, but more likely he is selecting among arguments that were put forward in the public debate on the request of the Leontines.[133] Some Athenians, no doubt, saw some merit in all these reasons for going to Sicily, but different political groups probably were more impressed by different arguments.

The expedition is commonly attributed entirely to the group variously called the "radicals" or "democrats" or the war party of which Cleon was a leader.[134] All the evidence, however, sug-

[129] For the date of the first treaty see Kagan, *Outbreak*, 155 and n. 3. Cf., however, *GHI*, 172–175. For the date of the renewal see *GHI*, 63 and 64.

[130] The best discussion of this problem is by H. D. Westlake, *Essays*, 101–122. My debt to his work will be apparent.

[131] 12.53. Diodorus himself discusses more practical motives in his next section.

[132] 3.86.4.   [133] Westlake, *Essays*, 106–107.

[134] Beloch, *Attische Politik*, 33, says, "Auch die Absendung einer Flotte von 20 Trieren unter Laches nach Sicilien im Herbst 427 ist ohne

gests that the expedition was generally approved and provoked little, if any, opposition. Thucydides tells of no disagreements such as those concerning the fate of Mytilene, or the treaty with Corcyra in 433, or the Sicilian expedition of 415, nor does any other author. The commanders of the expedition, moreover, were Laches, a friend of Nicias, and Charoeades, whose associations are unknown. Eurymedon, who had commanded at Corcyra and who apparently was close to Cleon, was available, as was Demosthenes, but neither was chosen. It is hard to believe that the war party was strong enough to force acceptance of the Sicilian offer over the objections of their opponents but not strong enough to secure the appointment of even one of their generals to the command. We must conclude that Nicias and other moderates supported the expedition.

We must not overlook the obvious: the Athenians went to Sicily in 427 because they were asked. The request reflected a change in the situation which might prove dangerous to Athens, and they could not easily reject it. Both sides had realized that the Peloponnesians could receive important support from Sicily.[135] If the Syracusans and their allies ever provided money and ships in any significant quantity the threat to Athenian control of the sea would be considerable. That the Peloponnesians had received no help from their Dorian cousins in Sicily may well have been due to the presence on that island of Athenian allies who first presented a threat to Syracuse and then engaged her in a war. If Syracuse were permitted to subjugate those allies she would have a free hand and might then lend support to her Corinthian metropolis and to the Peloponnesian cause in general. To forestall such a possibility was quite in line with the defensive policy of Pericles as the moderates must have understood.[136]

Athenian desire to prevent the importation of grain into the

Zweifel von Kleon's Partei veranlasst worden." Meyer's conclusion, *GdA* IV, 78–79, is much the same, though it has greater nuance.

[135] See the excellent discussion by Westlake, *Essays*, 113–116.

[136] Busolt, *GG* III:2, 1055, has seen this point. Thucydides makes no mention of this consideration, though it is inescapable from his own narrative. Justin 4.3.5 is uncharacteristically shrewd in suggesting that the danger of Syracusan aid to Sparta may have caused the Athenian intervention.

Peloponnesus was defensive and in accord with the Periclean strategy, if one believes that his strategy included plans for a blockade of the Peloponnese which, together with coastal raids, would "create disaffection in the Peloponnese by causing a shortage of food." [137] We have seen, however, that Pericles' strategy did not include such actions.[138] The interest in preventing Sicilian grain from reaching the Peloponnese was a new development reflecting new conditions. To some extent the length and severity of the Spartan devastations of Attica depended on the grain supply. If Sicily were unable to supply the Peloponnesians they might be forced to curtail their attacks on Attica. The prospect of a long war must have made the Athenian moderates anxious "to check the flow of this traffic at its source by sending military aid on a limited scale to their western allies." [139] The purpose was not, however, contrary to the spirit of the Periclean strategy, rather an extension of it. Pericles, faced by the fact of an extended war, might have taken a similar step, and the likelihood is that Nicias and his associates were willing to do so.

It is highly unlikely, however, that these men intended the fleet to serve as a first step in the subjugation of Sicily. That goal was totally out of keeping with the policy of Pericles and directly violated his warning, given more than once, to avoid any attempt to extend the empire during the war. Among the Athenians who wanted to wage the war more vigorously and aggresively were a group of reckless expansionists who never lost sight of the chance to extend the empire and the wealth and power of Athens. For some time many of them had looked to the west as a likely area for conquest.[140] Hyperbolus and men like him seem to have had grandiose plans even during the war, and Aristophanes in the *Knights* teases them about aiming even at Carthage.[141] However, he does not implicate Cleon in such wild fantasies, though the comedy is directed chiefly at him. There is no indication that Cleon at any time advocated turning

[137] Westlake, *Essays*, 107.   [138] See above, pp. 29–30.
[139] Westlake, *Essays*, 108.   [140] Busolt, *GG* III:2, 1056, nn. 2 and 3.
[141] 173–174 and 1302–1305.

the war into one of expansion for its own sake.[142] The two campaigns in which he was involved directly, Sphacteria and Amphipolis, were aimed at winning the war against Sparta, not at increasing the territory of Athens. If he, and men like Demosthenes and Eurymedon, wished to try to gain control of Sicily, as we may believe they did, their reasons were different from those of men like Hyperbolus.

The same reasons that led the moderates to undertake the expedition to Sicily also appealed to the aggressive party. They, too, wanted to prevent the delivery of grain to the Peloponnese and to prevent a Sicily dominated by Syracuse from providing help to the enemy. As men of action, impatient with half-measures, they may not have been satisfied with intervening merely to restore the earlier status quo. If Syracuse was about to take over the island, Athenian intervention followed by withdrawal would only produce the same situation again. Thus they wanted to act decisively to "bring the affairs of Sicily under their control." [143] That would imply only Athenian predominance, perhaps the establishment of a garrison and naval base on Sicily to prevent future trouble. The language of Thucydides requires nothing more. Yet Cleon and his associates may have aimed at something more—the absorption of the cities of Sicily into the Athenian Empire, either as allies contributing ships and men or as subjects contributing money. This need not contradict our previous assertion that their purpose was not the expansion of the empire but winning the war. The greatest problem facing Athens in 427 was financial, and we have seen that the steps taken to alleviate it had been inadequate. The war threatened to go on indefinitely and the treasury surely would not. If the Athenians could bring the enormous wealth of Sicily under their control the effect on the war would be enormous. The pressure on the Athenian treasury would be relieved and they would avoid the dangerous and unwelcome prospect of raising the

---

[142] In 425, Cleon urged the Athenians to demand from Sparta the return of Nisaea, Pegae, Troezen, and Achaea (4.21.3). That this is not evidence of an expansionistic general policy is argued below, pp. 234–238.

[143] 3.86.4: τὰ ἐν τῇ Σικελίᾳ πράγματα ὑποχείρια γενέσθαι.

tribute paid by the allies. A more aggressive policy of attacks on the Peloponnese would be possible and the Peloponnesian fleet could be swept from the sea. The seizure by Athens of a major resource on which the Peloponnesians themselves had relied would have a devastating effect on their morale. Possibly it might bring the Spartans around and end the war. At the very least Athens would be able to fight for as long as might be necessary. Perhaps, like Canning, Cleon and his friends wanted to bring in the new world to redress the balance of the old. This was far from a bad idea, especially when pursued in the cautious way the Athenians had chosen. They might well have thought that it was forced on them by the stubbornness of the Spartans, the failure of the Periclean strategy, and the absence of a likely alternative.

The 20 ships sailed off just in time to avoid the second outbreak of the plague and a number of earthquakes that struck central Greece.[144] Their numbers did not adequately indicate their significance. Their mission initiated a new policy for Athens. Time and the course of events had moved the radicals into a position where they could influence that policy and the moderates into one where they could not completely resist. The way was open to greater departures from the defensive strategy devised by Pericles, and those departures would be conducted by his friends as well as his enemies.

[144] 3.87.

7. Demosthenes

The commitment of the Athenians to a more active policy is fully demonstrated by the campaigns they undertook in the spring and summer of 426. In Sicily, the Aegean, Boeotia, and northwestern Greece they moved aggressively to try to gain the upper hand in the deadlocked war. Scholars have usually assumed that the elections to the *strategia* in the spring of 426 were related to the new spirit of offensive warfare and brought to power men who were hostile to the former leaders and prepared to overthrow the former policy. We are told that "the shift in public opinion expressed itself in full strength. Scarcely one of the incumbent generals was re-elected; in their place came men of the war party";[1] "the peace party suffered a defeat";[2] and "the youthful, hot-headed amateur strategists had obtained the ears of the populace."[3]

There is little reason to believe any of this. In the first place two generals, Laches and Eurymedon, were re-elected. The return of two men to the panel of generals is significant; in the years 433/2 to 425/4, for instance, we know of no case when more than two generals were re-elected.[4] Further, each general represented one of the major factions, for Laches was a moderate and Eurymedon was associated with the aggressive faction. Among the generals who were not re-elected, the two best known are Nicias and Demosthenes—one figure from each fac-

[1] Beloch, *GG*² II: 1, 324.   [2] Busolt, *GG* III: 2, 1056.
[3] West, *CP* XIX (1924), 201.   [4] See Beloch, *GG* ² II: 2, 261–264.

tion was retired.[5] Finally, all the aggressive campaigns we have mentioned were undertaken by the board of generals chosen in 427, which does not fit the hypothesis that the elections of 426 replaced a cautious, conservative board of generals with a new group of aggressive radicals. We have no evidence of a change in Athenian politics, a shift in support from one set of politicians or soldiers to another. In 426/5, as in the previous year, the *strategia* probably consisted of both moderates and radicals. The change was not one of politics but of policy; the Athenians were disillusioned with the policy of inactivity pursued in the past; some were eager and others at least willing to try something more positive and daring. The sending of a fleet to Sicily late in 427 demonstrated the strength of the new feeling, and the activities of 426 showed that it continued to grow stronger. There were no major disagreements on policy among the Athenians in 426; the only question was whether a particular plan or undertaking was likely to be successful and help bring about the commonly desired goal: the quickest victory possible.

In Sicily the Athenians did remarkably well in view of the small size of their force. In 427, Laches and Charoeades had established their base at the friendly Italian city of Rhegium, just across the strait from Messina, probably because Leontini, an inland town, could provide no naval base and was too close to Syracuse for safety.[6] Thucydides' account of this first expedition is scattered and sketchy and does no justice to its potential importance.[7] He does not describe the strategy of the Athenian generals or how their tactics were related to it. This has helped obscure the very reasonable and initially successful strategy they pursued.[8]

[5] If D. M. Lewis (*JHS* LXXXI [1961], 119), R. Sealey (*Essays*, 104), and Fornara (*Athenian Board of Generals*, 57–58) are right in thinking that Nicias was re-elected for 426/5, the argument against a victory for the war party is even stronger.

[6] 3.86.5.

[7] The account is distributed chronologically in 3.86, 88, 90, 99, 103, 115, 4.1, 24–25, 58–65, and 5.4–5. The account of Diodorus 12.54 and that of a papyrus fragment, possibly by Philistus (*FGrH* 3B, 577), add only a little to our knowledge.

[8] E. A. Freeman, *History of Sicily* III, (Oxford, 1894), 29–30, wrote: "It is perhaps vain to ask what was the plan of campaign. There was

The Athenians intended to gain complete control of the Straits of Messina in order to hinder the transportation of grain from Sicily to the Peloponnese. Thus they must gain control of Messina. That city in turn would serve as a rallying point for Greek Sicilians, especially those of Ionian stock, and for native Sicels hostile to Syracuse. With a base on Sicily, command of the sea, and the support of local troops, the Athenians might hope to defeat the Syracusans. Such victory might gain them more support and even defections from the Syracusan side. At the very least their success would frustrate Syracusan plans for the domination of Sicily and prevent Sicilian help for Sparta. If all went well it might bring Sicily under Athenian control.

Soon after their arrival at Rhegium the Athenians divided their forces into two squadrons, one under each general, presumably to explore the coast of Sicily and test the sentiment of the natives. Laches sailed along the southern coast off Camarina while Charoeades explored the eastern shore off Sicilian Megara. The task of Charoeades was the more dangerous, for he sailed in Syracusan waters. He encountered a Syracusan fleet, was wounded, and died.[9] Soon after, Laches, reinforced by 10 ships from Rhegium, launched an attack on the Liparian Islands, which lie off the north shore of Sicily at the western entrance to the Straits of Messina.[10] This attack may have been made partly to please the Rhegians who supplied one-third of the fleet,[11] but there were far better reasons. The Athenian plan required control of the sea, and particularly of the area around the straits. The Liparians were allied to Syracuse and could cause the Athenian fleet mischief; their conquest was of great importance. The Athenians and Rhegians employed the usual device of devastating the island, but the Liparians would not yield.

most likely none. They came to search out the land, to see what could be done, and to do whatever might come within their power." Westlake says the Athenian strategy was improvised on the spot, "with the object of supporting their allies and damaging their enemies wherever opportunity offered" (*Essays*, 117 and n. 53. Cf., however, H. Wentker, *Sizilien und Athen*, (Heidelberg, 1956), 113–117.

[9] *FGrH* 3B, 577, 2. Thucydides does not mention the campaign except to say that Charoeades was killed in a battle with the Syracusans (3.90.2).

[10] See Map 6.   [11] This is suggested by Busolt, *GG* III:2, 1056–57.

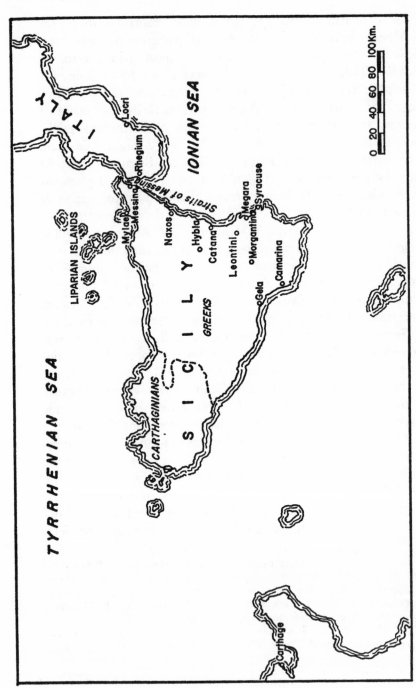

Map 5. Sicily

Since the shortage of water on the islands prevented campaigning during the dry season, the Athenians temproarily abandoned the attack. They returned to attack again the following winter, but Thucydides does not tell us whether they were successful; probably they were not.[12] After the first assault in the winter of 427/6, Laches withdrew to Rhegium. From there he moved against the Locrians, neighbors and enemies of the Rhegians, and with some success.[13] Again, this action must have pleased the Rhegians, but it was also needed to make the Athenian base secure.

The Athenian presence and activity seem to have had a great impact on Sicily, for Thucydides tells that by the summer of 426 the island was boiling with warfare.[14] With his base at Rhegium safe and the prospects on Sicily better, Laches was ready for the next step. He took Mylae, a small town west of Messina and subordinate to it, and then he took Messina itself.[15] This stunningly important victory that at one stroke gave Athens control of the straits, encouraged defections from Syracuse, and threatened her position on the island. During the summer many native Sicels who had been dominated by the Syracusans were encouraged by the Athenian successes to rebel and join forces with Athens and her allies.[16] In the winter of 426/5, Laches took advantage of their assistance to attack Inessa, a Sicel town whose acropolis was held by a Syracusan force. The town was of some importance. Located some eighty stadia inland from Catana, Inessa was one of three fortified towns that, along with Morgantina and Hybla protected Syracuse's dominion over the Sicels of southern Sicily.[17] A successful attack probably would have caused further Sicel defections from Syracuse and guaranteed the security of the Athenian allies at Leontini, Naxos, and Catana; not least, it would have presented Syracuse with a threat from both land and sea. The attack failed, and during the retreat the allies of Athens suffered some casual-

---

[12] 3.88, 115.1.

[13] FGrH 3B, 577, 2; Diod. 12.54.4; Thucydides does not mention this incident.

[14] 3.90.1.   [15] 90.2–4; Diod. 13.54.4–5.   [16] 3.103.1.

[17] For the location of Inessa see Gomme HCT II, 413; for its significance see Wentker, Sizilien und Athen, 114.

ties at the hands of the Syracusans. The failure was disappointing but not serious. Laches continued his attacks, defeating the Locrians in a battle and launching an attack against Himera together with the Sicels. The Sicels attacked from the inland direction while the Athenians came by sea, but apparently did not take Himera.[18]

Our knowledge of later events should not obscure the success Laches had achieved. He had taken Messina and control of the straits; he had prevented the Syracusan conquest of Leontini whose imminent danger had caused the Athenian expedition; he had brought over many subjects of Syracuse to the Athenian side and begun to threaten the region around Syracuse. The evidence of unhindered Athenian operations at sea together with the direct testimony of Thucydides show that the Syracusans had been totally barred from the sea by the small Athenian fleet.[19] The Syracusans clearly understood the danger presented to them by Athenian control of Messina: "They saw that the place controlled the access to Sicily and feared that the Athenians would some time use it as a base for attacking with a larger force." [20] All this remarkable success encouraged the Sicilian Greeks who were allied to the Athenians to send to Athens for even more help, for they knew that the Syracusans were preparing a fleet, and they expected a counterattack.

Thucydides does not say what arguments the Sicilian ambassadors in Athens used to press their case. His language, however, makes it plain that they did not suggest that the safety of the force already there might be threatened by an aroused Syracuse. The reasons he gives for the Athenians' decision to send help show confidence rather than alarm: they voted the ships "in part because they thought they could end the war there sooner, and partly because they wanted to give the fleet practice." [21] The Sicilians may have exaggerated the successes of Laches without indicating the extent of the difficulties still confronting him. They must have argued that the successes of the first campaign presaged the complete defeat of Syracuse; all that was needed was the dispatch of an additional force to defeat the Syracusan fleet then being built. This would end that city's power and

[18] 3.103.3 and 115.1.   [19] 3.115.3.   [20] 4.1.2.   [21] 3.115.4.

bring Sicily over to Athens. Some such arguments must have been employed, and they were successful. The Athenians voted to send 40 ships under three commanders. Pythodorus was to leave immediately with a few ships and take command from Laches. Sophocles and Eurymedon would follow with the main force later.[22] We have no reason to believe that there was any serious disagreement among the Athenians on the wisdom of sending reinforcements. The news from the Sicilian ambassadors seemed to support the high hopes cherished by the war party. Any who thought that the expedition was not worth while could comfort themselves with the thought that at least it would give the fleet some much needed practice.[23] When Pythodorus sailed westward he carried with him Athenian hopes that were probably exorbitant, but those hopes were quite reasonable on the basis of what they had been told Laches had achieved in one year with only 20 ships.

On the mainland of Greece the campaigning season seemed ready to begin in the usual way. Agis son of Archidamus called out the Peloponnesian army for the annual attack on Attica, but got only as far as the Isthmus of Corinth before a series of earthquakes compelled him to turn back.[24] Some scholars have suggested that the earthquakes were merely an excuse, that the return of King Pleistoanax from exile, probably in the winter of 427/6,[25] signaled a return to power of the peace party and the opening of negotiations with Athens.[26] The argument in favor of this hypothesis is not weighty; it rests merely on the fact of the return of Pleistoanax and on an interpretation of the passage in the *Acharnians* of Aristophanes that speaks of a demand for the restoration of Aegina.[27] We have argued that the demand fits the peace offer of 430 very well,[28] and there is no reason to invent another offer of peace on its account. Nor is there reason to connect the return of Pleistoanax with the renewal of peace

---

[22] 3.115.5–6.

[23] For a good discussion of the Athenian motives see Westlake, *Essays,* 110–112.

[24] 3.89.1.   [25] Beloch, *GG*[2] I:2, 176–177.

[26] Beloch, *GG*[2] II:2, 322–323; he is followed by Adcock, *CAH* V, 226–227, and West, *CP* XIX (1924), 204

[27] 646–654.   [28] See above, pp. 82–83

negotiations in 426. He favored peace with Athens in 446/5 and again in 421, and we may readily believe that he generally hoped for peaceful relations with the Athenians. Probably those Spartans opposed to the war welcomed his return as likely to be of use in the future, but there is no reason to think they were responsible for his restoration. Thucydides reports that the restoration was brought about by constant urgings on the part of the Delphic oracle and that the enemies of Pleistoanax accused him of bribing the oracle to accomplish his return.[29] They were probably right.

There is likewise no reason to believe that he played an important role in Spartan policy in the years soon after his return. He was the object of suspicion because of both his earlier behavior and the manner of his return. Whenever the Spartans suffered a defeat they placed the blame on Pleistoanax and his illegal restoration.[30] Another reason to believe that Pleistoanax played no important role before 421 is that in that year Thucydides singles him out as being most influential among those Spartans seeking peace and mentions him among the signers of the peace that was concluded.[31] In 423, however, when the Spartans made a truce in the hope of bringing about a lasting peace, Thucydides makes no mention of Pleistoanax, and he was not among the signers.[32] We must agree with Gomme that "his position in Sparta was too uncertain for him to take an independent line." [33]

The best reason for rejecting the notion of a Spartan peace offer in 426 is that Thucydides says nothing about it. Thucydides was very selective in what he chose to report, and there are some surprising omissions in his narrative. If, however, he left out something so important for our understanding of the war and the strategy of each side as an offer to make peace, we can have little faith in his reliability. There is no validity to the argument that "Thucydides does not think it worth while even to mention these proposals which were rejected as soon as they were made." [34] He did mention the Athenian peace offer of 430 and the Spartan peace offer of 425, although each was "rejected as

[29] 5.16.2-3.   [30] 5.16.1.   [31] 5.16.1; 19.2.   [32] 4.117; 119.2.
[33] Gomme HCT, III, 664.   [34] Adcock, CAH V, 227.

soon as it was made." We may, therefore, ignore the fiction of a Spartan offer of peace in 426.

The failure of the Peloponnesian military and naval efforts compelled the Spartans to think again about their policy. Beloch sums up the situation as it must have appeared to the Spartans: "The expectation of forcing Athens to make peace by devastating its territory had come to nothing. It was expected that the Athenian allies would rebel: but Potidaea was lost, the Lesbian rebellion remained isolated and was quickly suppressed. All attempts to meet the Athenians on their own element, the sea, had led only to humiliating defeat. Even the calculations based on an internal change in Athens were delusive. Pericles was overthrown and his opponents had carried on his policy; even his death brought no change in the situation." But it is not true that "in these circumstances in Sparta, too, they began to think of ending the war." [35] Instead the Spartans reacted as men often do when their purposes have been frustrated: instead of re-examining their policy fundamentally they intensified their determination to carry through their original plan by new means. The Spartans were no less angry than before and no less determined to achieve total victory.

Early in the summer of 426 the Spartans established one of the few colonies in their history at Heraclea in the Trachinian territory [36] in answer to a request for help from the Trachinians and from the neighboring city of Doris, the traditional mother of Sparta. Both were under attack and in danger of destruction by the nearby Oetaeans. The request must have come some months before, for the announcement of the intention to found a colony, the consultation with Delphi, the gathering of the colonists, and the preparations for their departure took time. The Spartans, however, looked beyond defense of their mother city and her friends: "The city also seemed to them to be well situated for the war against the Athenians, for a fleet could be equipped there against Euboea in such a way as to have only a short crossing, and the place would also be useful for a coastal

---

[35] GG^2 II:2, 322–323.

[36] 3.92.1. The establishment of this colony and its significance are generally given little attention. For an excellent understanding of the situation see Busolt, GG III:2, 1064–1065.

expedition to Thrace. In short, they were eager to found the colony."[37]

It is tempting to think that Brasidas was behind the Spartan decision, though Thucydides does not say so.[38] The venture accords well with the daring and imagination he displayed at other times. Whoever was responsible, the momentous decision shows us that some Spartans, like some Athenians, recognized that the original strategies had failed and that new ones were required if the war was to be won. The idea of attacking Euboea by sea was unrealistic in light of Sparta's previous encounters with the Athenian fleet. At best the new colony might serve as a base for piratical attacks on Athenian shipping for commando raids on Euboea. The idea of an attack in the direction of Thrace, however, was more promising. If the Spartans were to hurt the Athenians and reduce their capacity to fight, the empire was the obvious target. The only area of the empire that was vulnerable by land was the Thracian district. If the Spartans could bring about the defection of the cities of that region, Athenian income would be reduced and further rebellions encouraged. Beyond Thrace, moreover, lay the cities of the Hellespont, some of which could be reached by land. The opportunity of turning the Athenian flank and causing untold trouble was very real. At the same time, the plan would not be easy to accomplish nor would it be without danger. The first problem was to get an army from Sparta through central Greece and hostile Thessaly to Thrace. There the Peloponnesians would need local assistance to maintain themselves against the allies of Athens until they defected. Throughout the campaign the precious Spartan troops would be in danger of being cut off and captured or annihilated. All these considerations might deter the Spartans from undertaking the daring campaign, and in 426 they were far from ready for it. The establishment of Heraclea, however, was a necessary first step, and its accomplishment shows us again that early in 426 they were thinking not of peace but of how to win the war.[39]

[37] 3.92.4.

[38] Such is the suggestion of Busolt, GG III:2, 1064, and Gomme, HCT II, 395, among others.

[39] For a good discussion of the problems and opportunities presented by a Thracian campaign see Brunt, Phoenix XIX (1965), 273–275.

The commitment of the Spartans was serious, for they sent Spartan citizens as well as *perioeci* among the colonists and appointed three founders, including the former navarch Alcidas. They also invited other Greeks to join in the foundation, except for certain specified peoples who were regarded as unreliable.[40] They built a walled town about five miles from Thermopylae and half that distance from the sea; as Busolt says, "It dominated the gateway between central Greece and Thessaly and offered the natural and indispensable stopping point and base on the distant road to Thrace." [41] To add to its security they also built a wall across the pass of Thermopylae, and, as evidence that they intended to use the colony as a naval base against Euboea, they began to build dockyards.

The Athenians, of course, were frightened by the threat to Euboea. They must have thought the menace to Thrace too remote and unlikely to consider. Paradoxically the danger to Euboea proved unreal. The founding of a powerful Spartan colony on their borders frightened the Thessalians, who attacked it repeatedly, keeping it occupied and wearing out its citizens. Besides that, the Spartan magistrates proved, as usual, that Spartans did not know how to treat other Greeks. "They themselves ruined the operation and reduced the city to a depopulated state. They frightened most away by their harsh and sometimes unwise orders so that their neighbors defeated them more easily." [42]

The Athenians, meanwhile, were taking aggressive measures of their own. Their largest undertaking was to send a fleet of 60 ships and a force of 2,000 hoplites under the command of Nicias against the island of Melos. Nicias ravaged the land but could not compel the Melians to surrender. He sailed to Oropus, landing at night, and marched to Tanagra. There he was met by all the rest of the Athenian army which had marched overland under the command of Hipponicus and Eurymedon. They made camp and spent the next day ravaging the country. On the

---

[40] 3.92.5; Gomme *HCT* II, 395. Diodorus (12.59) says the colony consisted of 4,000 Peloponnesians and 6,000 others. Beloch (*Bevölkerung*, 512) rightly argues that these figures are impossibly large.

[41] *GG* III:2, 1065. For the location of the city see Thuc. 3.92.6, Gomme, *HCT* II, 394–398.

[42] 3.93.3.

second day the Tanagrans, reinforced by some Thebans, came out to meet them and were defeated in a pitched battle. The Athenians set up a trophy of their victory but did not try to press it further. The army of Hipponicus and Eurymedon marched back to Athens. The forces of Nicias returned to their ships, sailed along the coast ravaging some Locrian territory, and then they, too, went home.[43] Thucydides' account of this campaign is puzzling and unsatisfactory. He does not tell us whether the attack on Melos and the assault on Boeotia were both part of an original plan or improvised by Nicias from Melos. He does not make clear whether the attack on Boeotia was meant merely to do the enemy harm or if it had some larger purpose that could not be carried out. Even the motive he gives for the landing on Melos does not explain its timing. We need to examine these questions, though the evidence does not yield a confident answer.

Melos and Thera were the two Cycladic islands which were not members of the Athenian alliance at the start of the war.[44] Both were Dorian settlements, and Melos was a colony of Sparta's.[45] By 430/29, Thera had been subjected to the Athenians, paying both tribute and a war indemnity.[46] Melos, however, had maintained its independence and was formally neutral in 426.[47] Thucydides says the Athenians attacked because "the Melians, although they were islanders, did not want to be subjects nor even to join the alliance, and the Athenians wanted to bring them over."[48] The Melians, of course, had been guilty of the same sin since the foundation of the Delian League, and we may wonder why the Athenians waited so long to act, why they did not try to subdue Melos when they took Thera. The probable answer is that the capture of Melos was a far more difficult and expensive task and was not worth the strain on Athenian resources in the first part of the war.

[43] 3.91; see also Diod. 12.65.1–5.   [44] 2.9.5.   [45] 5.89; Diod. 12.65.3.
[46] Tribute: *ATL* I, 285, III, 336; indemnity: *ATL* II, 52 = D8, 11.21–25, III, 336. Thucydides does not mention the conquest of Thera.
[47] 3.91.2; 5.84.2. Although there is a great debate over the neutrality of Melos before the Athenian attack in 416 no one, not even the severest critic of Thucydides' account, Max Treu, *Historia* II (1952–1953), 253–273, doubts its neutrality in 426.
[48] 3.91.2.

In 426 a new, ambitious spirit flourished in Athens which, coupled with the pressing need for money, may explain why they tried then, but there may have been a more immediate reason. In an inscription recording financial contributions for war paid to the Spartans from various sources the Melians appear in two different places.[49] The date is not certain, and scholars have placed it anywhere from 479 to 396/5. A date between 431 and 425 has the widest appeal, Adcock's argument which places the contributions precisely in the year 427 is attractive.[50] He believes the payments were connected with the voyage of Alcidas into the Aegean in that year. He conjectures that the Spartan ships must have stopped somewhere as they sailed through the Aegean, and Melos was the likeliest place. The Spartans, of course, were short of money, yet their naval campaigns were expensive. Alcidas very likely tried to gather money wherever he went, and he seems to have received contributions from the friendly Melians both coming and going. If this suggestion is correct we can easily understand why Athenian attention was called to Melos the very next year when their hands were free. Their first concern in the Aegean would surely be to punish the Dorian "neutrals" who were helping the enemy.

The behavior of Nicias clearly indicates that the Athenians did not plan to take the island at any cost, as they did in 416. Only a siege could guarantee success, but sieges were very expensive, and the Athenian treasury could ill afford to sustain one in 426. Nicias' intentions on Melos were probably to attack the island, ravage the land, and try to force the Melians to capitulate. Should they resist, there were no plans for a siege. The Athenians would have been glad to take Melos cheaply. Barring an easy victory they would be satisfied with extending the Periclean strategy of devastation to the unfriendly island. The force with Nicias was more than was needed to commit devastation, but was necessary in case of an opportunity to assault the city.

The Athenians recognized from the first that they might fail to take Melos, and they planned for that possibility. The

[49] GHI 67, pp. 181–184.
[50] Mélanges Glotz (Paris, 1932), I, 1–6. The suggestion has won a good deal of support; see, most recently, M. Amit, Athenaeum XLVI (1968), 220.

attack on Melos was not merely a feint to cover the attack on Boeotia, the real target of the expedition.[51] Nor could Nicias have set a date in advance for the rendezvous at Tanagra with Hipponicus and Eurymedon,[52] for the Melians might have surrendered after a brief resistance, and the Athenians could not pass up such an opportunity nor predict just when it might come. More likely Hipponicus and Eurymedon were ordered to prepare their forces in Athens and wait for word from Nicias. When he saw that the island could not be taken he must have sent a messenger and prepared to land at Oropus at a fixed time to make a rendezvous with the Athenian army at Tanagra.

The purpose of the Boeotian campaign was limited to punishing the Boetians for the depradations they had been carrying on in Attica and, perhaps, to trying to deter future incursions. The failure of the Peloponnesian invasion and Athens' new aggressive spirit made 426 the first year when such an assault was possible. To press the victory further would have risked a land battle against the Theban hoplite army and might have brought a Peloponnesian army which could take the Athenian army in the rear. The Athenians would not venture a full-scale attack on Boeotia until they were sure the Spartans would not march. Such a guarantee was not available until after the capture of the Spartans on Sphacteria in 425, so the Athenian army had no thought but to return home. The fleet with Nicias stayed long enough to do what damage it could on the Locrian coast before it returned. The entire operation was a unit and only a slight departure from the original Periclean strategy. The use of a large army marching overland against Boeotia was a novelty, but was made safe by the absence of the Spartans and was used for Periclean purposes without any great risk. If Melos had been captured the empire would have been expanded in wartime, which Pericles had warned against. Still, no risk nor great expense was involved, and the campaign does not seem to have deviated from the spirit of Pericles' strategy. Both campaigns reflected attitudes of the Athenian moderates, a bit more daring, but still cautious. Nicias was appropriate as commander of the main force.

[51] As Andrewes suggests in Gomme, *HCT* IV, 156, n. 1.   [52] *Ibid.*

At the same time as the attack on Melos the Athenians sent
a squadron of 30 ships around the Peloponnese under the command of Demosthenes and Procles.[53] We are not informed of
the purpose of this expedition; no doubt the orders to the
generals were to protect and assist the allies of the Athenians
in western Greece and to do whatever damage to the enemy they
could. The 30 Athenian ships carried only the usual ten marines
each and no additional hoplites. Although they were assisted by
all the Acarnanians when they fought in Acarnanian territory
and by some Zacynthians and Cephallenians, as well as 15 ships
from Corcyra,[54] they were clearly not expected to accomplish
anything decisive. In spite of the new, active spirit in Athens the
shortage of men, and particularly money, limited the size of
campaigns.

The Athenians began by attacking Leucas. Since they outnumbered the Leucadians they were able to ravage the land at
will. The Acarnanians wanted to lay siege to the city and destroy the enemy totally. Such an accomplishment would be of
no small benefit to Athens. Leucas was strategically located
on the route to Corcyra, Italy, and Sicily, it was a loyal Corinthian colony that contributed ships to the Peloponnesian fleet and,
with the Oeniadae and Ambracia, was one of the key Peloponnesian bases on the coast of Acarnania-Epirus. Its capture would
be a great blow to the Corinthians and to the Peloponnesians in
general and would give the Athenians exclusive control of the
Ionian Sea.[55]

The Messenians from Naupactus, on the other hand, argued
against the siege of Leucas. They were eager to get help against
the neighboring Aetolians who threatened their safety. They
must have sensed in Demosthenes a capable and daring commander, and they wanted to take advantage of his presence and
that of a sizable allied force to launch an attack on Aetolia.
They promised that it would be easy to defeat the fierce but
primitive Aetolian tribesmen and bring their territory under
Athenian control. The Aetolians, to be sure, were numerous
and warlike, but they lived in scattered, unfortified villages;
they did not fight as hoplites but in light armor; some of them

[53] 3.91.1.   [54] 3.94.1.   [55] Busolt, GG III:2, 1066.

were so barbaric as to eat their meat raw. These uncivilized people could easily be subdued one by one before they could unite.[56] Demosthenes, who was in command in his first term as general, was persuaded to break off the siege. His decision has been criticized; Grote, for instance, called it a "grave imprudence" that offended the Acarnanians, "in order to attack a country of all others the most impracticable,—the interior of Aetolia." [57] The decision is questionable, and we must ask why Demosthenes made it.

In part, Thucydides tells us, Demosthenes wished to please the Messenians.[58] That was a reasonable motive, for the inhabitants of Naupactus were very important to Athens, more so than the Acarnanians. We have seen how vital was its position on the Corinthian Gulf, as when Phormio defended it. If the menace from the Aetolians was real, Demosthenes was quite right to see to the safety of Naupactus first,[59] but his bold imagination saw in the Messenian suggestion something greater than was intended. With the allies from Acarnania and Naupactus he would quickly conquer Aetolia and conscript the defeated Aetolians into his army. Then he would pass through western Locris to Cytinium in Doris.[60] From there he would enter Phocis where, presumably, the Phocians, who were old friends of the Athenians, would join him; if not they could be compelled. From there, with this large force, he could attack Boeotia from the rear.[61] No doubt he was aware that an attack on eastern Boeotia was planned by Nicias and the generals in Athens. If he could reach Boeotia's western border at the same time, the improvised pincers might bring about a great Athenian victory and drive Boeotia, Sparta's most powerful ally, out of the war. He could rely on the democratic forces in Boeotia, who had previously showed their willingness to cooperate with Athens,[62] to support a successful invasion. All this he hoped to accomplish "without Athenian forces."

[56] 3.94.2–5.   [57] VI, 296.

[58] 3.95.1, Ὁ δὲ τῶν Μεσσηνίων χάριτι πεισθείς.

[59] Max Treu, Historia V (1956), 424–425; for a shrewd criticism of Thucydides' treatment of this incident and for the career of Demosthenes in general see E. C. Woodcock, HSCP XXXIX (1928), 93–108.

[60] See Map 3.   [61] 3.95.1.   [62] See Kagan, Outbreak, 95, and n. 50.

With his whole fleet Demosthenes set out from Leucas, and at once his plans ran into trouble. The Acarnanians did not approve of his failure to besiege Leucas and refused to go with him to Aetolia; the 15 Corcyraean ships went home, unwilling to fight outside their own waters and for causes not immediately relevant to their interests. Probably in the following year a character in a comedy by Hermippus said: "May Poseidon destroy the Corcyraeans on their hollow ships because of their duplicity." [63] The loss of the greater part of his army and a third of his navy might well have deterred Demosthenes, but he went ahead. He made his base at Oeneon in Locris. The Locrians were allies of Athens, and Demosthenes counted on them heavily. They were neighbors of the Aetolians, used the same kind of armor and weapons, knew the enemy and the country. The plan was to have their entire army march inland and meet Demosthenes.[64] The campaign started propitiously; Demosthenes began his march inland, entering the territory of the tribe of Aetolians called the Apodoti. On consecutive days he took Potidania, Crocyleum, and Teichium and reached the border of the territory occupied by the tribe of Ophioneis.[65] There he stopped and sent his booty back to Eupalium in Locris for safekeeping. It is not clear why he waited. Thucydides indicates that he hoped to overawe the Ophioneis by the appearance of his victorious army. Failing that, he intended to return to Naupactus and try again.[66] This makes no sense, since there would have been no advantage in returning to Naupactus. Some scholars have suggested that the trip to Naupactus was meant to gather new forces, perhaps the long-awaited Locrians.[67] But the Locrians were to meet Demosthenes inland, and we know of no other reinforcements available at Naupactus. More likely the delay at Teichium was not part of a preconceived plan. The Locrians should have met him there or even earlier, but for unknown reasons they had not. Henderson describes the problem dramatically but plausibly: "At Teichium

---

[63] J. M. Edmunds, *The Fragments of Attic Comedy*, 304–306. The translation is my own.

[64] 3.95.3.   [65] See Map 3.   [66] 3.96.2.

[67] Classen, ed., *Thukydides* (Berlin, 1963), and Gomme *HCT* II, 405.

Demosthenes' heart misgave him badly. Still no Locrians, a treacherous river, and gloomy forests! Had he not better abandon the whole scheme, or turn it into a purely 'Aetolian project,' return to Naupactus, and threaten the Ophioneis in a later campaign?" [68] Demosthenes seems, in fact, to have been daunted by the third and most crucial defection from his forces, and therefore he hesitated. He badly needed the light-armed javelin throwers the Locrians could provide; [69] the success of his campaign and the safety of his forces might depend on them.

The Messenians, on the other hand, were not daunted. Eager for the campaign because of their private interests, they continued to urge speedy action. Victory would be easy if only Demosthenes moved quickly before the scattered Aetolians could rally their forces. Actually, the Messenian advice was already out of date. The Aetolians had noticed the preparations for the expedition and begun immediately to get ready. They had sent for help to the far borders of Aetolia, and their fellow tribesmen came to their aid in great numbers.[70] Demosthenes was unaware of this. The intelligence available to him posed a dilemma. His shortage of appropriate forces dictated caution and delay; the need to attack before the enemy could unite his forces argued for daring and speed. Demosthenes' victories up to then seemed to bear out the predictions of the Messenians that it would be easy to defeat the Aetolians if they were taken quickly and individually. With the boldness and optimism that were part of his nature he decided once again to follow the advice of the Messenians.

Demosthenes moved forward against the town of Aegitium. His luck seemed to hold and his judgment appeared to be vindicated, for he took the town easily by storm. The victory, however, was a delusion—Demosthenes had fallen into a trap. Most of the inhabitants had abandoned the town and lay in ambush in the hills overlooking it and they were reinforced by other Aetolians. When the Athenians and their allies entered the town they were surprised by an assault from above coming from several directions. The attackers, moreover, were skilled javelin throwers in light armor who could inflict serious damage and

[68] *Great War*, 146.   [69] 3.97.2.   [70] 3.96.3.

retreat easily before the heavily armed phalanx of the Athenians
could move against them. At this point the absence of the
Locrians was critical. The Athenians had to rely on their bowmen to keep the enemy off, but by another bit of bad luck the
captain of the company of archers was killed. His men scattered,
leaving the hoplites undefended and worn down by repeated
advances and retreats in heavy armor against the swifter Aetolians. At last they turned to run, and one final misfortune turned
the rout into a slaughter. The Messenian guide, Chromon, who
might have led them to safety, was also killed. The Athenians
and their allies were caught in rough, wooded, unfamiliar
country. Many of them lost their way in the forests, so the
Aetolians set fire to the woods. The losses among the allies were
heavy; the Athenians lost 120 of their 300 marines, as well as the
general Procles. Thucydides says that "these were the best men
that the city of Athens lost in this war," [71] though his meaning
is not clear, for the marines were thetes, members of the lowest
economic and social class.[72] The Athenians recovered their dead
under a truce, retreated to Naupactus, and sailed off to Athens.
Demosthenes did not sail with them, but stayed at Naupactus,
"fearing the Athenians because of what had happened." [73]

Demosthenes had good reason to fear an accounting. He had
abandoned a successful and promising campaign to undertake
one that was surely never envisioned by those who sent him. The
general who undertakes such adventures without direct orders
had better win a great victory or, like Demosthenes, stay away
from home. The boldness and even grandiosity of the plan, the
difficulties in the way of its execution, and the fact that it failed
have led historians to condemn it and its inventor. Grote says
that "the expedition against Aetolia, alienating an established ally
and provoking a new enemy, had been conceived with a degree
of rashness which nothing but the unexpected favor of fortune

[71] 3.98.4.

[72] Meyer, *Forsch.* II, 157ff., argues that the Athenians began to use
thetes as marines only in 415, but Busolt, *GG* III:2, 872, n. 3, argues
convincingly for their use earlier. Thucydides may, of course, have
meant that the men who died at Aegitium were particularly brave, but
nothing in his narrative indicates that.

[73] 3.98.5.

could have counterbalanced." [74] Beloch speaks of Demosthenes' "unbridled lust for battle and his lack of prudence." [75] Adcock even suggests that personal reasons were behind his decision to invade Aetolia, "for he had not been re-elected in the previous spring and this was perhaps the last opportunity which he would have had for distinguishing himself." [76] This last allegation is hardly plausible. If Demosthenes wanted merely to distinguish himself, he should have besieged and taken Leucas, which would have been considered a great achievement. That would have been safe, completely in accord with Athenian expectations, and carried no military risk. Success would have been a feather in his cap and failure no disgrace. We need to look beyond personal motives to understand what led Demosthenes to undertake the Aetolian campaign and to judge its wisdom.

Perhaps we can understand the matter best by analogy with another famous military disaster and its equally famous author, the Gallipoli campaign of 1915 urged by Winston Churchill. On that occasion, as in 426, a great war between powerful alliances had reached a condition of deadlock. Each side had tried its original strategy and each had failed. Unable to hit on a better idea, each had lapsed into a war of attrition. Churchill was dissatisfied with that situation and thought a better solution must be available. His thoughts seem appropriate to our problem:

Nearly all the battles which are regarded as masterpieces of the military art, from which have been derived the foundation of states and the fame of commanders, have been battles of manoeuvre in which very often the enemy has found himself defeated by some novel expedient or device, some queer, swift, unexpected thrust or strategem. In many such battles the losses of the victors have been small. There is required for the composition of a great commander not only massive common sense and reasoning power, not only imagination, but also an element of legerdemain, an original and sinister touch, which leaves the enemy puzzled as well as beaten. It is because military leaders are credited with gifts of this order which enable them to ensure victory and save slaughter that their profession is held in such high honour.[77]

[74] VI, 300.   [75] *Attische Politik*, 31.   [76] *CAH* V, 228.
[77] Winston S. Churchill, *The World Crisis II, 1915* (London, 1923), 21.

Churchill was such a leader. He conceived a plan to take Constantinople, put Turkey out of the war, and so outflank the enemy. The plan failed not because it was misconceived, but because it was carried out poorly. Had it succeeded, it might have shortened the war considerably.

Was Demosthenes also such a leader? Was the Aetolian campaign the rash, imprudent blunder its critics claim, or was it a brilliant maneuver that would have left the enemy "puzzled as well as beaten"? The answers are not to be found merely in the failure of the plan. Churchill has set down the general principles that guided him in World War I. They seem helpful in analyzing the strategy of the Archidamian War as well:

1. The Decisive theatre is the theatre where a vital decision may be obtained at any given time. The main theatre is that in which the main armies or fleets are stationed. This is not at all times the Decisive theatre.

2. If the fronts or centres of armies cannot be broken, their flanks should be turned. If these flanks rest on the seas, the manoeuvres to turn them must be amphibious and dependent on sea power.

3. The least-guarded strategic points should be selected for attack, not those most strongly guarded.

4. In any hostile combination, once it is certain that the strongest Power cannot be directly defeated itself, but cannot stand without the weakest, it is the weakest that should be attacked.

5. No offensive on land should be launched until an effective means—numbers, surprise, munitions, or mechanical devices—of carrying it through has been discovered.[78]

Let us test Demosthenes' Aetolian expedition against these principles:

1. There were no main armies in the field arrayed against each other. For Sparta the main theater was the soil of Attica; for Athens it was the territory of Sparta and its allies that they ravaged in the hope of wearing out the enemy's will to continue the war. Neither turned out to be the decisive theater.

2. There were, of course, no armies whose centers could be broken, but the main targets of each side had by 426 proven as invulnerable as the two armies entrenched across western Europe

[78] *Ibid.*, 50.

in 1915. The Aetolian campaign was amphibious, making use of superior mobility provided by sea power to land an army at a vulnerable point.

3. The western border of Boeotia was a "least-guarded strategic point."

4. The Spartans had proved that they could not be directly defeated; the Boeotians, though not the weakest of Sparta's allies, were certainly weaker than Sparta, especially on the western front. Their defeat would have made it difficult for Sparta to carry on its invasions of Attica, perhaps impossible. Athenian control of Boeotia would also have destroyed the value of the newly founded colony of Heraclea in Trachis, which could not serve as a base for an attack on the Athenian Empire in Thrace if a Peloponnesian army could not reach it. Every means available to Sparta for hurting Athens would be removed, and the Spartans would be faced with little choice but to make peace.

5. The device on which Demosthenes counted was surprise. He had every reason to think it would be effective. The Boeotians would never expect an attack from the seemingly safe west. In addition, Demosthenes knew when he improvised his attack on Aetolia that an Athenian attack on eastern Boeotia, which was already scheduled, would further distract the enemy's attention.

Demosthenes' plan was in fact brilliant, as some scholars have recognized,[79] but it was hastily conceived and sloppily executed. The main problem was haste; the plan required speed if it was to succeed, but that very speed prevented the careful preparation needed for a tricky, coordinated operation. Another problem was Demosthenes' unfamiliarity with the terrain and with the tactics of light-armed warfare. He is perhaps to be blamed for pushing ahead in the face of many uncertainties and even after things began to go wrong. But the legerdemain of which Churchill speaks is not performed by cautious generals afraid to run risks, nor are great wars frequently won without such generals. Finally, we should not forget that Demosthenes was

[79] Busolt, GG III:2, 1067, says, "Der Plan war kühn und mit weitem Blicke entworfen," and Adcock, CAH V, 228, calls it a "brilliant conception" that "reveals in Demosthenes strategic imagination and the spirit of the offensive."

risking very little, for Athens lost only 120 marines. Such a price, though regrettable, was not excessive in light of the great rewards victory would have brought. Demosthenes, moreover, was that rare soldier who could learn from his mistakes.[80] He would use what he had learned to good advantage in the future.

The failure of Demosthenes' adventure in Aetolia threatened to have serious consequences for Athens as the summer drew to a close. Some time after they learned of Demosthenes' activities the Aetolians had sent envoys to Corinth and Sparta asking them to send an army against Naupactus, which had invited the Athenian offensive and was a thorn in the Aetolian side.[81] The news of Demosthenes' defeat must have fed the aggressive spirit that had already showed itself in the establishment of Heraclea. The new colony, in fact, sent 600 men to form part of a Peloponnesian army of 3,000 under Eurylochus and two other Spartans. From Delphi they marched through Locris, bringing the Locrians over to their side by the menace of their presence and in some cases by force. The allegiance of the Locrians was guaranteed by the taking of hostages who were deposited at Cytinium in Doris. When the Peloponnesians were near Naupactus they were joined by the Aetolians. Together they ravaged the countryside and occupied the unprotected suburbs.

The failure of Demosthenes had placed Naupactus in grave danger, since the Naupactan forces were too weak to defend the walls against a large attacking army, but what Demosthenes had endangered he now worked to save. When he learned of the Peloponnesian expedition he went to Acarnania in the hope of persuading its citizens to send a force for the relief of Naupactus. We may marvel once again at his boldness, even effrontery. The Acarnanians had little reason to like or trust him, for he had abandoned their desired campaign against Leucas and gone off on what must have seemed to them a wild goose chase, with disastrous results. But his persuasive power was so great that they agreed to send with him 1,000 men on board Acarnanian ships. Demosthenes and his reinforcements arrived in time to save

[80] Thucydides (4.30.1) tells us that the lesson learned in Aetolia served Demosthenes well on Sphacteria.

[81] 3.100.1; for the time of the request see Gomme, *HCT* II, 408.

Naupactus. Eurylochus decided that he could not storm Naupactus, now properly defended, and he withdrew into Aetolia.

Eurylochus' behavior was curiously like that of Demosthenes at Leucas earlier in the summer.[82] Instead of engaging in a difficult, tedious, expensive, and possibly unsuccessful siege, he was lured by the promises of other allies to undertake a different mission. The Ambraciots, excited by the presence of a large friendly army in unfamiliar regions, wanted it used against their local enemies. They urged an assault upon Amphilochian Argos, their main enemy, and upon all of Amphilochia and Acarnania as well: "If they conquered these places they would bring the entire mainland into alliance with the Spartans." [83] This was a renewal of the plan that had failed in 429, but that campaign had been badly bungled by the Peloponnesians.[84] The hope of avoiding previous errors, the recent failure of the Athenians, and the fact that the Peloponnesian force in 426 was three times that of 429 all must have encouraged the Spartan commanders, and they agreed. They sent the Aetolians away and arranged to meet the Ambraciots near Amphilochian Argos.

The Ambracians began their part of the campaign probably in November,[85] invading Amphilochia with an army of 3,000 hoplites and taking Olpae, a fortress near the sea less than five miles from Argos.[86] The Acarnanians responded by sending troops to help protect Argos and another force to Crenae, a short distance to the southwest.[87] They knew the Spartans were entering their territory, and the contingent at Crenae was meant to intercept the army of Eurylochus coming from the south before it could join the Ambracians coming from the north. At the same time they sent a message asking for help from the Athenian fleet of 20 ships under Aristoteles son of Timocrates and Hierophon son of Antimnestus, who were making their

---

[82] The point is made by Gomme, *HCT* II, 413.   [83] 3.102.6.
[84] 2.80–82.   [85] For the date see Busolt, *GG* III:2, 1072, n. 1.
[86] 3.105.1; Diodorus (12.60.4) gives the number of troops as 1,000 and Beloch, *Bevölkerung*, 193–194, accepts that figure. We do not know enough to make an informed, independent decision, so it seems better to accept the number given by Thucydides, which appears in all the manuscripts.
[87] See map in Henderson, *Great War*, 154.

way around the Peloponnese. This fleet must have been sent from Athens in response to the news of Eurylochus' attack on Naupactus, but at the mouth of the Corinthian Gulf they were intercepted by the Acarnanians and turned northward.[88] The Ambracians also sent to Naupactus to ask Demosthenes to come and lead their armies.[89] He was now only a private citizen and, since he had not returned to render his accounts in Athens, probably in disrepute in his native city. The Acarnanians, nevertheless, wanted him to command their forces. His successful defense of Naupactus, no doubt, had raised his reputation, but the invitation is powerful testimony for the high regard the Acarnanians, no less than the Messenians, had for his military ability. The Ambracians, too, seeing the disposition of the Acarnanian forces and fearing that the Spartan army might be cut off before it could join them, sent to the city of Ambracia to ask that all the rest of the army be sent as reinforcements. These preparations guaranteed that the battle, when it came, would not be petty.

Eurylochus, meanwhile, marched through deserted Acarnania; all its troops were gathered at Crenae and Argos. On the sixth day Eurylochus attacked.[90] Marching at night, he slipped between the enemy camps and joined the Ambraciots at Olpae without being detected. The united armies then moved northward and inland and camped at a place called Metropolis. Soon after, the 20 Athenian ships arrived and blockaded the harbor of Olpae. Demosthenes also appeared, accompanied by 200 of his faithful Messenians and 60 Athenian archers. The Acarnanians withdrew from Crenae to Argos and elected Demosthenes generalissimo, with their own generals under his command.[91] He moved his army to the west and made camp between Argos and Olpae, protected by a dry river bed separating him from the Spartans. The two armies waited for five days, giving the

---

[88] Busolt, GG III:2, 1072, n. 3; Gomme HCT II, 417.   [89] 3.105.3.

[90] Thucydides does not make it clear who took the initiative. Hammond implies it was Eurylochus (BSA XXXVII [1936–1937], 135) and Henderson says it was "probably" he who crossed over (Great War, 156). It seems impossible that Demosthenes could have laid his ambush on the opposite side of the stream bed; he must have counted on the enemy taking the offensive.

[91] 3.107.2.

generals plenty of time to plan the battle.[92] Demosthenes' army was numerically inferior, but his tactical skill overcame this disadvantage. To one side of the likely field of battle, on a sunken road covered with bushes, he placed a force of 400 hoplites as well as light-armed troops. Fearing that the more numerous enemy would outflank his phalanx, he ordered these men to wait in ambush until the armies made contact. Then they were to take the enemy in the rear. This was a "queer, unexpected strategem" of the sort recommended by Churchill, and it proved to be decisive.

In the light of the battle's result the decision of Eurylochus to attack before his reinforcements came from Ambracia seems questionable.[93] We have seen, however, that allies had a way of not appearing when expected, if at all. It is not easy, moreover, to keep an army, particularly one made up of different peoples, in a condition of readiness for battle for five days, in sight of the enemy, but inactive. Eurylochus was the aggressor; it was his task to take Argos and not that of the Amphilochians and Ambracians to challenge him, and he already had numerical superiority. There is no reason to believe that additional troops would have made a difference—the battle was decided not by numbers but by tactics.

When the armies came to grips the Peloponnesian left wing, led by Eurylochus, outflanked the right wing of the Ambracians and their allies, the wing held by Demosthenes and his Messenians. As they were on the point of encircling that end of the line and beginning to roll it up, which would surely end in a classic rout, the trap set by Demosthenes sprang shut. The Acarnanians appeared from their ambush at the rear of Eurylochus and began to cut his army to pieces. Taken completely by surprise, they ran, and their panic was contagious. The Messenians under Demosthenes did the best fighting, and soon their task was merely to pursue the greater part of the enemy army

[92] I have not myself seen the region under discussion. No modern account seems to accord perfectly with the description of Thucydides. With some hesitation I follow the geography of Hammond, BSA XXXVII (1936–1937), 128ff., and his map, though I recognize the force of some of Gomme's HCT (II, 426–428) objections.

[93] Henderson, Great War, 156.

which had turned to flee. At the other end of the battle line, however, the Ambraciots, whom Thucydides calls the ablest warriors in that region, routed their opponents and chased them as far as the city of Argos. When they turned back from its walls, however, they saw that the main part of their army was in flight and were met by the victorious Acarnanians. They fought bravely, getting through to Olpae, though with many losses. As night fell and the battle ended Demosthenes commanded the field which was strewn with the bodies of the enemy including two Spartan generals, Eurylochus and Macarius.[94]

The next day Menedaïus, the Spartan general who succeeded to the command, found himself in a precarious position. He was besieged at Olpae by the enemy army on the land side and the Athenian fleet by sea. He had not expected to have the command or to face such difficult decisions; he had no idea when or if the second Ambracian army would come. He only knew that there was no way to escape, so he asked for a truce to take up the dead and discuss the safe departure of his army. Demosthenes took up his dead and planted a trophy of victory on the battle-field. He did not, however, agree to a general safe passage for the army under Menedaïus. Instead he made a secret agreement whereby he allowed Menedaïus, the contingent from Mantinea, the commanders of the other Peloponnesian troops, as well as "the most noteworthy" [95] among them to escape if they did so quickly. Menedaïus accepted, picked up his dead, and began to make secret plans for the escape.

This act of selfishness and treachery, as Thucydides calls it is understandable, if not admirable,[96] but why did Demosthenes allow the trapped Mantineans and Peloponnesian commanders

---

[94] 3.107–109.

[95] The Greek is ἀξιολογώτατοι, and its meaning is not clear. C. F. Smith translates it "the most influential men," Crawley "principal men," Classen-Steup "die angesehensten," and Romilly "principales person-nalités." Presumably these men would be nobles, though distinction might be determined in other ways. No more than a few could have been in-formed of the secret without its becoming generally known. In support of the view that not all the Peloponnesians were allowed to escape see Classen-Steup, *Thukydides*, for the opposite view see Gomme, *HCT* II, 422.

[96] 3.109.2.

and notables to escape to fight against Athens another day? Thucydides tells us that he wanted to leave the Ambracians and their mercenaries defenseless, though that hardly seems necessary, but chiefly to discredit the Spartans and the Peloponnesians by exposing their faithlessness. Such considerations of propaganda and diplomacy may have influenced Demosthenes, but military necessity pointed in the same direction. He had learned that the long delayed army from Ambracia was at last on its way, unaware that a battle had already been fought. The arrival of that force would put Demosthenes in an awkward position between two armies. He must have been glad to avoid such a predicament so cheaply.

Those of the besieged army at Olpae who were privy to the agreement began to make their escape. Pretending to gather firewood and herbs, they started to slip away from camp and their uninformed comrades. The Peloponnesian notables may have been unwilling or unable to keep the secret from their own men, for the account of Thucydides may be understood to mean that all the Peloponnesians took part in the escape.[97] But the Ambraciots and others who were excluded from the secret agreement noticed the flight of the Peloponnesians and ran to join them. The Acarnanian army became confused when the soldiers saw the entire enemy army fleeing, and they began to give chase. The generals tried to stop them, attempting to explain the tricky agreement. This would have been a difficult task at any time, but in the heart of the moment, while the entire army and not just a select portion of it seemed to be escaping, it must have been almost impossible. One soldier threw a spear at them, thinking that some treason was being perpetrated. At last the generals prevailed and the Peloponnesians were allowed to escape, though distinguishing among those in flight was not easy. The pursuing Acarnanians were free, of course, to kill all the Ambraciots they could lay hands on, and some 200 were caught and killed. The rest made their way to safety in the neighboring and friendly kingdom of Salynthius of Agraea.[98]

Meanwhile the second army from Ambracia had arrived at Idomene, a few miles north of Olpae. There were two high

[97] See Gomme, HCT II, 422–424.   [98] 3.111.

hills, the lower of which the Ambracians occupied and spent the night. Even before the Peloponnesian escape from Olpae, immediately after Demosthenes learned of the approach of the second army from Ambracia, he had sent out an advanced guard to set ambushes and to seize strategic positions.[99] These men took command of the higher hill without the knowledge of the Ambraciots below. Demosthenes was now ready to use all he had learned about mountain fighting and unorthodox tactics. Marching at night, he led one part of his army by the direct route and sent the rest through the mountains. He arrived before daybreak, making use of every natural advantage and inventing a few of his own. It was still dark, and the Ambracians were asleep. To add to the suprise Demosthenes placed the Messenians, who spoke a Dorian dialect like the Ambracians, at the front so that they might get past the outposts without raising the alarm. The ruse was so successful that the awakened Ambracians at first thought the attackers were their own men. Most of them were killed immediately, but some tried to escape through the mountains where they were caught by the rest of the army of Demosthenes. In disorder and in unfamiliar territory the fact that they were light-armed troops facing hoplites worked against them, and they were also trapped by the men who lay in ambush. Some, in panic, ran to the sea and swam toward the Athenian ships, preferring to be killed by the Athenian sailors than to die at the hands of "the barbarian and hated Amphilochians." [100]

The Ambracian disaster was almost total, very few escaping alive. Thucydides refuses to report the number killed on the grounds that in comparison with the size of the city it was too great to believe, but he does say that "this was the greatest disaster to strike a single city in an equal number of days in this war." [101] The day after the battle a herald came from the Ambraciots who had escaped to Agraea and who were ignorant of the battle at Idomene. He had come to ask for the bodies of the men who had been killed in the flight from Olpae, but when he saw the number of Ambraciot weapons lying about he was stunned. Believing that the herald came from the forces who

[99] 3.110.2.   [100] 3.112.7–8.   [101] 3.113.6.

had fought at Idomene, someone asked him how many men had been lost and why he looked surprised. " 'About two hundred,' he said. 'But these,' the same questioner said, 'are not the weapons of two hundred men, but rather of more than a thousand.' 'Then they are not the weapons of the men who fought with us in battle,' said the herald. 'They are if you fought at Idomene yesterday.' The herald answered, 'But we didn't fight yesterday; it was the day before, on the retreat.' 'Well, we certainly fought yesterday against the men who came as reinforcements from the city of Ambracia.' When the herald heard and understood that the reinforcements from the city had been destroyed he broke out in wailing and, stricken by the greatness of the disaster, he went away immediately without doing what he had come for, taking up the dead." [102]

Devastating as the defeat was for the Ambracians and for Spartan influence in that region, the victory of the Athenians was not complete. Demosthenes wanted to follow up the slaughter of the Ambraciots with an attack on their city, and Thucydides gives personal testimony that they would have taken it easily.[103] But the Acarnanians and Amphilochians were not willing because "they now feared that the Athenians would be more difficult neighbors than the Ambraciots." [104] They treated the Athenians generously, giving them a third of the booty. Three hundred panoplies, an astonishing number, were set aside for Demosthenes. With these and the glory they represented he was willing to sail home; he was shrewd enough to dedicate them to the gods and set them up in their temples, keeping none for himself in order to clear his name and increase his influence. The 20 Athenian ships returned to Naupactus, to the relief of their allies in the northwest. The Acarnanians and Amphilochians were now free to make peace with the fugitives

[102] 3.113.1–5.

[103] Thucydides says Ἀμπρακίαν μέντοι οἶδα ὅτι, εἰ ἐβουλήθησαν Ἀκαρνᾶνες καὶ Ἀμφίλοχοι Ἀθηναίοις καὶ Δημοσθένει πειθόμενοι ἐξελεῖν, αὐτοβοεὶ ἂν εἷλον (3.113.6). This passage seems to me strong evidence that Thucydides was with Demosthenes on this campaign, probably with the Athenian fleet. Otherwise it is hard to know how Thucydides can speak with such simple confidence. οἶδα, without further explanation, seems to me the word of an eyewitness and participant.

[104] 3.113.6.

who had taken refuge with Salynthius in Agraea. They allowed the Peloponnesians to return home safely and also the Ambracians, with whom they made a treaty for a hundred years. The terms were framed so as to put an end to old quarrels and to keep the region free of further involvement in the great war.

Corinth, the mother city of Ambracia, sent 300 hoplites to provide a minimal garrison for its defense, but the need for such a force shows how helpless the once powerful city had become. Its arrival, however, also shows that the Athenians had not achieved the total control of the northwest they might have hoped for. The campaign was an important success because it had prevented the Peloponnesians from gaining control of the northwest. The Athenian ships could still sail safely along the western coast of Greece and in the Ionian Sea. No more could be achieved because of the limited nature of Athens' commitment. We should remember that the Athenians contributed to the fighting no hoplites, only 20 ships, 60 archers, and a great general who was, however, a private citizen. In this way the fighting in the northwest was characteristic of the work of the entire year: marked by a more daring and aggressive spirit but limited by caution and resources. The military expenses for the year 427/6 were trifling compared with what was spent in the early years of the war. The accounts of the *logistai* show that 261 talents were borrowed from the treasuries, up, to be sure, from the 100 borrowed the year before, but only one-fifth of the amounts borrowed in the first two years of the war.[105] The war could not be won by a new strategy of activity without a solution to Athens' financial problems or some unforeseen stroke of luck.

[105] *ATL* III, 342–343.

8. Pylos and Sphacteria

As the campaigning season of 425 approached the Athenians continued to seek opportunities, as their means permitted, to damage the enemy and change the course of the war. The elections held in the spring of that year produced a board of generals representing a mixture of opinion similar to that held by the incumbent board. Sophocles, Eurymedon, and Pythodorus, all destined for the Sicilian campaign, were re-elected. The moderates elected Nicias and Nicostratus after a year's hiatus, and also probably Autocles. The radicals, however, elected Demosthenes and possibly Lamachus. We cannot guess the affiliations of Aristides, who was also elected in this year, or of Demodocus, who may have been. There is no basis for the opinion of some scholars that these elections represented a shift of political power toward the moderates.[1] Until the affair of

---

[1] For the list of generals and discussions of their political views see Beloch, *Attische Politik*, 37, 291, 302–305, and *GG*² II:1, 264; Busolt, *GG* III:2, 1084; West, *CP* XIX (1924), 208–217, and *AJP* XLV (1924), 141–160; Fornara, *Athenian Board of Generals*, 59. Beloch, followed by Busolt, believes that Lamachus and Demodocus were generals for 425/4 as well as the next year, but West denies it. Beloch (*Attische Politik*, 37) speaks of "den Umschwung der ganzen politischen Lage," and says that the election shows "wieviel die Kriegspartei . . . verloren hatte, das sie an der Regierung gewesen war." He tries to support his case by calling Demodocus and Aristides members of the faction of Nicias on no acceptable evidence, claiming Aristides because "wenigstens sein adeliger Name" seems to lead to that conclusion. But in the previous year, according to his reckoning, the war party had only two generals, Hippocrates and Eurymedon. In 425, Eurymedon was re-elected, Demosthenes was restored to office, and, according to Beloch, Lamachus joined

Pylos there is no evidence of any important divisions in Athens.

About the beginning of May the Peloponnesians, led once again by the young King Agis, invaded Attica and began their ravaging.[2] This did not deter the Athenians from sending aid to their forces in Sicily, and they dispatched Sophocles and Eurymedon with 40 ships to join Pythodorus there. They sailed thinking that things were going well for Athens on that western island and there was no need for great haste. Only a little earlier, perhaps late in April and surely too soon before the expedition sailed for it to have had the news, things had taken a turn for the worse.[3] The Syracusans and Locrians had gathered courage, put to sea with 20 ships, and recaptured Messina. At the same time the Locrians had taken advantage of the civil strife in Rhegium to attack that city, which was the Athenian base of operations and major ally in that region. Athenian success in Sicily depended on winning over as many natives as possible; an accumulation of victories would make that easier, but each defeat sapped the strength of Athens by undermining its reputation. The quick arrival of the Athenian fleet was needed to sweep the sea of the enemy and restore prestige. The Athenians might very well have sent the fleet with orders to sail directly and in haste to Sicily had they known what had happened, but they did not know.[4]

In the spring of 425, Sicily was not the only area in the west where a fleet was needed. The Athenian intervention at Corcyra in 427 had not ended the trouble on that island. When

---

them, giving a total of three radical generals. This hardly justifies a belief in a great swing in public opinion away from the war party and toward the advocates of moderation. As usual, Beloch and Busolt explain away the presence of Demosthenes by calling him a nonpolitical general, and they are joined by West (CP XIX [1924], 209) who rejects the election of Lamachus and Demodocus and considers Aristides a member of Cleon's group. His statement that "though the elections of this year resulted in an even balance between the imperialists and the moderate democrats, yet to the party of Nicias belonged the victory because it had regained so much of the ground lost in 426" is only half right. We have seen that the party of Nicias had lost no ground in 426 (see above, pp. 187–188), so it could not regain any in the next year.

[2] 4.2.1; for the date see Gomme, HCT III, 437.
[3] For the date see Gomme, ibid.   [4] 4.1.2–4.

Eurymedon sailed away, after allowing the democrats to slaughter their opponents, 500 potential victims escaped to the mainland, occupied forts in the territory controlled by the Corcyraeans, and made it a base from which they could attack the island. Over a period of time they were so successful that they brought about a famine in the city. They vainly sent to Corinth and Sparta for help and finally hired mercenaries on their own. They landed on Corcyra, burned their boats as evidence of their determination to stay until they won, and fortified Mount Istome, from which they could make raids at will and dominate the countryside.[5] Their success offered new hope to the Peloponnesians who, in the spring of 425, sent a fleet of no fewer than 60 ships to try to take the island.[6] The Athenians could not afford to let Corcyra fall into enemy hands, and to some the expedition to Sicily must have seemed of trifling importance compared to the defense of Corcyra.

Demosthenes also wanted an Athenian fleet in the west. Returned from his glorious campaign in Acarnania and general-elect for the year which would begin in midsummer 425, in the spring he was only a private citizen without a command. He was not, however, without plans and ideas. He had a scheme for landing on the coast of Messenia from which he hoped to do the enemy serious harm, and for this he, too, needed a fleet.

Each action had merit, and all three deserved to be pursued simultaneously. In the first years of the war they could have been, but in 425, Athens had not the money and perhaps not the men for all. A commitment had already been made to Sicily where much was expected; it could not be abandoned. Corcyra, of course, could not be neglected. The scheme of Demosthenes could be postponed, but he was at the height of his influence and his plan promised to cost the Athenians almost no men or money. For these reasons the Athenians sent their fleet off with orders that might otherwise seem strange. Sophocles and Eurymedon were told to sail to Sicily, "but also, as they were sailing past Corcyra, to look after the men in the city who were being attacked by the men on the mountain."[7] In addition, they were told to allow Demosthenes "to use these ships around the

---

[5] 3.85.   [6] 4.2.3.   [7] 4.2.3.

Peloponnese if he wishes." [8] The process by which these complicated orders were constructed is easily imagined. The decree
proposing the Sicilian expedition had been passed the previous
winter.[9] When news came of the arrival of the Peloponnesian
fleet at Corcyra the assembly must have amended the original
decree to deal with the new danger. Probably at the same meeting Demosthenes put forward his request as another amendment.
To the modern reader the way in which the Athenians were
compelled to make strategic decisions and conduct the war is
strange. Debates in the public assembly decided military and
naval priorities. Given the state of their information and the
limited resources available to them, the Athenians appear to have
made a reasonable decision in a difficult situation.

The fleet sailed around the Peloponnese, and off the coast of
Laconia the generals learned for the first time that a Peloponnesian fleet was at Corcyra. Sophocles and Eurymedon were
eager to get there and prevent the island from falling into enemy
hands, but Demosthenes had other ideas. Once at sea he was
free to reveal to his colleagues the details of the plan he could
not set forth in the open Athenian assembly for fear it would
reach the enemy. He meant to land at the place the Spartans
called Coryphasium, the site of Homer's Pylos, and to build a
permanent fort there. Obviously Demosthenes had noticed the
place on previous voyages and had inquired about it from his
Messenian friends who knew it well. It had every natural advantage as a permanent base where the Messenian enemies of
Sparta might be placed to ravage the land of Messenia and
Laconia and also to receive their escaped helot countrymen,
possibly even to stir up a helot rebellion. It also had great value
for the war at sea "which rested on its connection with the
spacious, secure basin, the best natural harbor on the west
coast of the peninsula." [10] Plenty of wood and stone were
available to build fortifications; the surrounding territory was
deserted, and it was about fifty miles from Sparta as the crow
flies and perhaps half again as far by the route a Spartan army
would most likely use,[11] so that the place could be made safe be-

[8] 4.2.4.   [9] 3.115.   [10] Busolt, *GG* III:2, 1087.
[11] Thucydides (4.3.2.) says it was 400 stadia from Sparta, but as

fore the occupiers faced a Spartan army. Demosthenes was quite right to think that "this place was more advantageous than any other." [12]

This plan of Demosthenes was clearly a departure from the previous Athenian strategy. Pericles may have spoken vaguely of establishing fortifications in enemy territory, but, as we have seen,[13] only as a possible response to a similar enemy action and, more important, neither he nor any of his successors did so. They had made a number of successful landings on the Peloponnese [14] but did not try to fortify them. This was a new idea of how to hurt the enemy and help win the war, and it was to prove a brilliant one. Sophocles and Eurymedon, however, were worried about the safety of Corcyra and unconvinced by the imaginative daring of Demosthenes; they thought of his scheme as a reckless diversion and told him sarcastically that "there were many deserted promontories in the Peloponnese that they could occupy if they wanted to waste the state's money." [15]

Demosthenes' plan was not rash and irresponsible, even granting the urgency of the situation at Corcyra. He did not want the Athenians to launch a lengthy campaign at Pylos but merely to put in long enough to build the fortifications, leave a small force to defend them, and then sail on to Corcyra. He believed the brief delay would be worthwhile and also that a successful landing on the Messenian coast would compel the withdrawal of the Peloponnesian fleet from Corcyra, thus achieving two purposes in the cheapest and easiest way.[16] He did not persuade his colleagues, but at that point fortune took a hand. In his entire description of the affair of Pylos and Sphacteria, Thucydides allows the element of chance an inordinate degree of importance.[17] Chance was indeed crucial in making the occupation of

---

Gomme (*HCT* III, 439) points out, that would require a march over a high and steep mountain pass. The likeliest route he calculates at nearly 600 stadia.

[12] 4.3.3.   [13] See above, p. 28.
[14] Gomme, *HCT* III, 438–439.   [15] 4.3.3.   [16] 4.8.2.
[17] F. M. Cornford, *Thucydides Mythistoricus* (London, 1907), 88ff., and Mme. de Romilly, *Thucydides and Athenian Imperialism*, tr. Philip Thody (Oxford, 1963), 173ff., have elaborated this point. Gomme (*HCT* III, 488–489), however, argues that τύχη does not necessarily imply chance or accident, but often merely contemporaneity. Even he must

Pylos possible. Demosthenes failed to persuade the generals to put in at Pylos, but a storm came up and carried them there. Once there he could not ,get them or the soldiers or their divisional officers (taxiarchs) to begin building the fortifications. Demosthenes' behavior was hardly in accord with military discipline, even in so democratic an army as the Athenian, and he must have caused considerable resentment among the generals. This must explain their refusal to do some good at Pylos when they could not go on to Corcyra.

The storm, however, continued, and the soldiers decided to do what Demosthenes asked, less, Thucydides suggests, from conviction than boredom. Gradually the spirit of the venture took hold of them, and they hurried to fortify the most vulnerable places before the Spartans could come. Within six days they completed the needed defenses. The generals left Demosthenes behind with a small force and 5 ships to defend the newly established fort and sailed on to Corcyra. Fortune and determination had permitted Demosthenes to set his plan in motion.

The Spartans were slow to react to the activity at Pylos. They were celebrating a festival, and their army was in Attica. They took the matter lightly, as was natural in view of their prior experience. The Athenians had landed on the Peloponnese before, and with much larger armies, but they had never stayed long enough to meet a large Spartan army. Even if the Athenians did intend, contrary to their previous practice, to make a permanent base, the Spartans had no doubt they could take it by force.[18] Agis and his army in Attica, on the other hand, were much more alarmed. They were short of food and troubled by unusually bad weather, but their return home after only fifteen days, the shortest invasion by far, was caused chiefly by their understanding that fortification of Pylos was a matter of grave importance.[19]

When the Spartans sent word of the Athenian fort at Pylos to

admit that the word is employed frequently, and we must add that the frequency is unique in Thucydides. It seems inescapable that Thucydides portrays the victory at Pylos and Sphacteria as the result of extraordinary luck.

[18] 4.5.

[19] Thucydides, 4.6.1. says that Agis and the Spartans hurried home, νομίζοντες . . . οἰκεῖον σφίσι τὸ περὶ τὴν Πύλον.

Agis in Attica they must also have sent a message to the fleet at Corcyra. The Spartan navarch Thrasymelidas saw the danger as quickly as Agis did and headed for home immediately. He dragged his ships across the Leucadian isthmus to escape detection, slipped past the Athenian fleet sailing north, and arrived safely at Pylos.[20] Meanwhile the army had returned from Attica, messages were sent to the Peloponnesian allies to bring their troops, and an advance guard of those Spartans who had not gone to Attica and the *perioeci* who lived closest to Pylos had been sent to attack the Athenian fort. Before the Peloponnesian fleet could close off the harbor Demosthenes sent two ships to catch Sophocles and Eurymedon and tell them he was in danger. They found the Athenian fleet at Zacynthus whence it hurried to Pylos to help Demosthenes and his men. In view of the generals' great haste to reach Corcyra scholars have wondered why they were still at Zacynthus, only some 75 miles from Pylos.[21] Thucydides' narrative does not tell us, but a reasonable explanation in accord with available evidence can be suggested. The Athenian fleet sailing north on the sixth day after the fortification began, or perhaps even the seventh, did not expect the enemy fleet to abandon Corcyra and so were not alert to intercept it on its way south. The two fleets may already have passed each other when the Athenians could have learned from a Corcyraean messenger ship of the Peloponnesian withdrawal. Sophocles and Eurymedon, unaware that they had been bypassed already, may have sailed to Zacynthus in the hope of cutting off the enemy fleet and destroying it at sea. There they waited until the message from Demosthenes made it clear they must sail for Pylos at once.[22]

[20] 4.8.1–2.

[21] The question is raised by U. von Wilamowitz-Möllendorf *SB AK. Berlin*, 1921, 306–318, and Busolt, *GG* III:2, 1089, n. 1.

[22] This reconstruction owes much to the insight of Gomme, *HCT* III, 442, and depends on his version of the time sequence. Busolt, following the order of events as they appear in Thucydides, concludes that since the departure of the Athenian fleet from Pylos at least fourteen days must have passed. He assumes that no word was sent from Sparta to the fleet at Corcyra until the army of Agis had returned, and that is a possible interpretation of the Thucydidean text, though it makes the presence of the Athenian fleet at Zacynthus inexplicable. Gomme sup-

As the Athenian ships sailed to Pylos the Spartans were planning their assault on the fort. They had little doubt that they
could take such a jerry-built structure guarded by only a few
men, but they knew that the Athenian fleet would soon arrive.
They planned to launch an immediate attack on Pylos by land
and sea and, if that should fail, to block the entrances to the
harbor and so prevent the Athenian fleet from entering.[23] They
would also land troops on the island of Sphacteria as well as on
the seaward side of the mainland, thus preventing the Athenian
fleet from making a landing or establishing a base, since the
western shore of the Pylos peninsula had no suitable harbors.
The Spartans believed that "without risking a sea battle they
could probably capture the place by siege because it had no
grain, since it had been seized with little preparation." [24] The
plan made good sense, but was not carried out. The hoplites
were landed on Sphacteria, but the Spartans did not, and in fact
could not, close off the channels.

Thucydides' account of the geography of Pylos and Sphacteria and of the campaign that depends on it is unsatisfactory
(see Map 6). It seems clear that he never saw the place himself, and the evidence he got from witnesses was not adequate
for a precise narrative.[25] No other ancient source is of any help,
so we are forced to try to reconstruct the events as best we can.
Thucydides tells us, quite correctly, that the island of Sphacteria
stretches across the entrance to the harbor of what is now called
the Bay of Navarino. He says it was deserted and wooded. He
also says that the island was 15 stadia in length, while in reality
it is 24 stadia long. But his most important error is in describing

---

plies the key, saying: "There is no great difficulty: the Peloponnesian fleet had been sent for at once (ἔπεμψαν above, contrasted in tense with
περιήγγελον), perhaps even before the departure of the Athenian fleet
from Pylos, and arrived as soon as the first hoplites from Sparta."
Gomme ignores the fact that the Spartan hoplites were already at Pylos
when the fleet arrived: παρῆν δὲ ἤδη καὶ ὁ πεζὸς στρατός, but his point is
essentially correct and permits us to understand the behavior of the
Athenian fleet.

[23] 4.8.4-5.   [24] 4.8.8.

[25] The problem has had many treatments and as many suggestions
attempting to explain the inexplicable. The more important versions are
discussed by Gomme, HCT III, 482–489.

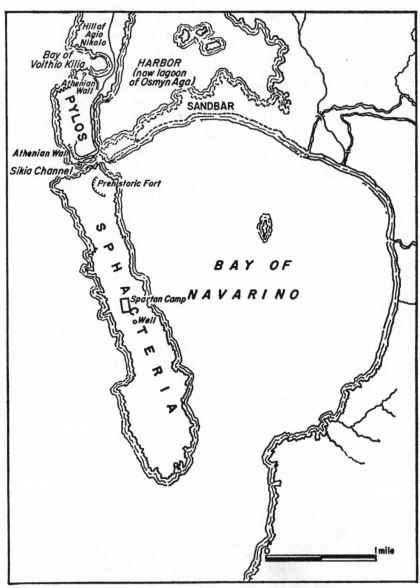

Map 6. Pylos and Sphacteria. Adapted from *The Cambridge Ancient History*, Vol. V (Cambridge, England: Cambridge University Press, 1927), by permission of the publisher.

the width of the channels at either end of Sphacteria. He says they were both narrow, the northern one, adjacent to Pylos, permitting only 2 triremes abreast to sail through, while the southern channel allowed 8 or 9.[26] That description accords quite well with the northern channel, but it is completely wrong about the southern one. As Gomme says, "The southern is not only some 1,400 yards wide, but, what is more important, about 200 feet deep, and could not have been blocked even by the whole Peloponnesian fleet." [27] The only way the Spartans could have tried to prevent the Athenians from entering the harbor would have been to offer a naval battle in the south channel with their 60 ships against the Athenian 40, which would have suited the Athenians perfectly and which there is no evidence the Spartans intended. Their plan must remain a mystery to us, but Thucydides' description indicates it must have been either misconceived or badly executed.[28] The Spartans placed 420 hoplites accompanied by their helot assistants on Sphacteria under the command of Epitadas. They must become a hostage to fortune and the Athenians unless the Athenian fleet could be kept out of the bay of Pylos, and we know that it could not.

Demosthenes, meanwhile, was making his plans to defend the fort. He beached and fenced in his 3 triremes to protect them

[26] 4.8.6. Gomme argues, contrary to the general opinion, that the Spartans did not mean to block the channels with triremes drawn up abreast, prows facing the enemy, but rather stretched out lengthwise and presumably sunk, at least in the shallow northern channel. To do so he must ignore the highly critical words τῇ μὲν δυοῖν νεοῖν διάπλουν, and his commentary does not, in fact, mention them. I think the *communis opinio* is right in this case.

[27] Gomme, *HCT* III, 443.

[28] For an excellent discussion of the topography see W. K. Pritchett, *Studies in Ancient Greek Topography*, Part I (Berkeley and Los Angeles, 1965), 6–29. He correctly points out that what Gomme has called "the very remarkable topographical errors in Thucydides' account of the Pylos and Sphacteria campaign may be reduced to one: the statement that there was room for eight or nine ships between Sphacteria and the 'other mainland.' " He persuasively refutes the theories of Grundy and Barrows (see n. 27 on p. 15 for full bibliography) and argues that the sand bar which now separates the main harbor from the lagoon of Osman-Aga existed in antiquity while the lagoon did not, for the sea has since risen. This solves many problems, but the error that remains is the chief one, and it indicates that Thucydides did not know the site.

from the enemy fleet. Thucydides emphasizes the impromptu nature of the landing at Pylos by telling us that Demosthenes, unable to procure arms in hostile and deserted country, armed the crews of his ships with wicker shields. He reports, however, that a Messenian privateer happened to arrive just at that time carrying weapons and 40 hoplites. Obviously this was no accident but had been prepared in advance by Demosthenes.[29] The crews of the 3 ships with him must have provided Demosthenes with something under 600 men, most of whom would be equipped with wicker shields, no armor, perhaps not even swords or spears. He probably had at least 90 hoplites, 10 from each of the 5 ships originally assigned to him, and the 40 Messenians. Possibly Sophocles and Eurymedon had left more hoplites behind, but Thucydides does not say so. The Athenian force defending the fort clearly was badly outnumbered and inferior in armament.

Demosthenes placed most of his troops, hoplites as well as the others, behind the fortifications facing inland. He himself, with 60 hoplites and a few archers, took on the more difficult job of defending the place on the coast that was least fortified and most vulnerable to an enemy landing. The defensive wall was probably weakest on the southwestern corner of the peninsula. Demosthenes never thought that Athenians would ever have to fear Spartan control of the sea with which they might force a landing. He knew that if the Spartans could once force a landing they would have little trouble defeating the Athenian force.[30] Accordingly he placed his hoplites at the very edge of the sea to repel any attack.

[29] 4.9.1. Gomme (*HCT* III, 445) is careful to translate οἳ ἔτυχον παραγενόμενοι as "had just arrived," but he was compelled to admit that "it remains notable that Thucydides does not say that an immediate message had been sent to Naupactus to send Messenians."

[30] 4.9.2–4. Gomme asks, "why had Demosthenes never imagined that he would be so much weaker at sea, when the main Athenian fleet had left in a hurry for Sicily?" The answer lies in an understanding of the expectations held by the Athenian fleet. They imagined they would go to Corcyra where they would find and defeat the enemy fleet. If it happened that the Peloponnesians left Corcyra before that could be accomplished the Athenians assumed they would intercept them and destroy them at sea. In either event there was no reason to expect that a Peloponnesian fleet would dominate the waters around Pylos.

The Spartans attacked just where Demosthenes had expected, urged forward by the conspicuous courage of Brasidas, who was overcome by his wounds and lost his shield.[31] His efforts and those of the other Spartans, though spirited, were unavailing. Demosthenes told his troops in his speech before the battle that "it is impossible to force a landing from ships against an enemy on shore if he stands his ground and does not give way through fear." [32] The Athenians stood firm, and the Spartans, who could use only part of their fleet at one time in the narrow waters, were forced to withdraw after two days of fighting.

The Spartans had pulled back to prepare another assault, but they never had a chance to mount it. On the third day after the first attack on the Athenians at Pylos, Sophocles and Eurymedon arrived from Zacynthus with a fleet that had grown to 50 triremes by the addition of some Chian ships and some from Naupactus.[33] Since the Spartan occupation of Sphacteria and the mainland gave them no place to anchor they withdrew briefly to the small desert island of Prote, some distance to the north. The next day they returned to Pylos fully ready for battle. The Athenians probably hoped the Spartan fleet would come out and fight in the open sea; if not the Athenians would fight their way into the harbor. As it turned out they were required to do neither, for the Spartans did not come out and offer battle, nor could they block the entrances. Instead they waited inside the harbor, preparing their ships for combat there. The battle that followed was a great victory for the Athenian navy and a disaster for the Spartans whose courage was spent mainly in wading into the surf after defeated and empty triremes and preventing the Athenians from towing them away. When the fighting was over the Athenians set up a trophy of victory and sailed freely around the Spartan hoplites, who were cut off and imprisoned on the island.[34]

The stunning effect and importance of this naval victory cannot be exaggerated. The Spartans sent their magistrates [35] to view the results of the disaster and to recommend a course

[31] 4.12.1.   [32] 4.10.5.
[33] The MSS give the figure of forty, but most editors emend it to fifty as our other information requires. See Gomme, HCT III, 450.
[34] 4.13–14.   [35] τὰ τέλη, presumably the ephors.

of action. When they saw that their men could not be rescued they decided immediately to ask for a truce at Pylos during which they would send envoys to Athens to negotiate a general peace and recover the men on Sphacteria. Men of the twentieth century, accustomed to casualty lists that run into the millions, may marvel that so tough a military state as Sparta should be willing to make peace merely to recover 420 prisoners. But this number represented fully one-tenth of the Spartan army,[36] and at least 180 of them were Spartiates from the best families. In a state that practiced a strict code of eugenics, killing imperfect infants, whose separation of men from women during the most fertile years guaranteed effective birth control, whose code of honor demanded of its soldiers death rather than dishonor, and whose leading caste married only its own members, we may readily understand that concern for the safety of even 180 Spartiates was not merely sentimental but extremely practical.

The truce agreed upon was very much in Athens' favor. The Athenians were to continue their blockade of the island, but they were not to attack it or the men on it, and they were to allow the delivery of food and drink. In return the Spartans promised not to attack the Athenian fort at Pylos nor to send any ships secretly to the island. Most striking was the clause whereby the Spartans promised to deliver to the Athenians as hostage not only all the ships then at Pylos but all other warships in Laconia, a total of 60. Meanwhile the Spartan envoys would be carried to Athens on an Athenian trireme and the truce would last until their return. At that time the Athenians were to return the Spartan ships in the same condition they received them. The agreement, however, contained a clause providing that the truce would come to an immediate end if either party violated any of its terms. If the negotiations proved unsuccessful, however, the Athenians could easily claim a violation and keep possession of the Spartan navy, but the Spartans agreed to terms nonetheless.[37]

This turn of events for Athens was fortunate; no one could have predicted that a landing at Pylos would produce a foolish Spartan reaction and therefore have such great consequences,

[36] Busolt, *GG* III:2, 1095.   [37] 4.16.

but Thucydides certainly overestimates the role played by luck
in this campaign. A storm happened to come up just in time to
force the Athenian fleet to put in at Pylos in accordance with
the plan of Demosthenes; the Spartans happened to be celebrating a festival that prevented their coming immediately to destroy
the fort; a couple of Messenian boats carrying hoplites and
weapons happened to come along just in time to enable the
Athenians at Pylos to resist the Spartan attack.[38] On the contrary, the entire campaign was conceived and executed by
Demosthenes with a keen eye for the special opportunities
offered by Pylos and Sphacteria. Success depended to some
degree on luck, as it always does, but intelligence and good
planning were present and vital. Demosthenes could not have
expected the Spartans to occupy Sphacteria and run the risk of
encirclement. If the Athenians could occupy Pylos and damage
and embarrass the Spartans by launching raids from it and receiving escaped helots that would be enough. Yet one might
imagine that the Spartans would find the Athenian occupation
of a permanent base in Messenia unendurable. Initiative and daring provoke the enemy to make mistakes; he is much less likely
to err if he is not challenged and the initiative is left to him. A
proper military judgment must give credit for the victory to
the general who devised and executed the plan that forced the
enemy to make his mistake and then to seek peace on such unfavorable terms.

The ambassadors arrived in Athens and offered their terms
of peace to the assembly in a speech, reported by Thucydides,
that was conciliatory, tactful, and long. The Spartans recognized
that the Athenians had the upper hand but reminded them
politely that this was not the result of a basic change in the
balance of power. The Athenian success might not last, and they
would be wise to make peace while the advantage persisted. In
exchange for the prisoners on Sphacteria the Spartans offered to
make peace and an offensive and defensive alliance with Athens.
No mention was made of any territorial adjustment.[39] Such a

---

[38] In each of these passages Thucydides uses τυγχάνω: 4.3.1, κατὰ τύχην;
4.5.1, ἔτυχον ἄγοντες; 4.9.1, ἔτυχον παραγενόμενοι.
[39] 4.17.20.

peace would have left Athens in control of Aegina, Minoa, and with a foothold in the northwest; in return she would abandon Plataea. Gomme commented on the tactful nature of the Spartan speech that "they had need of tact, for they have in fact nothing but a sermon to offer, no *quid pro quo* at all." [40]

Yet the general opinion of modern scholars is that the Athenians should have accepted the Spartan offer. "Athens had it in her power to conclude an advantageous peace." [41] "The future offered a shining prospect if a moderate peace were granted to Sparta." [42] Acceptance of the Spartan offer "would have achieved what Pericles had envisioned as the attainable goal of the war: the maintenance and security of what they possessed." [43] The scholars' reaction is not surprising, for it is almost certainly the view of Thucydides, and he does a masterly job of conveying it. [44] Most scholars, moreover, believe that Pericles would have accepted the Spartan terms, and, since they judge his aims and strategy favorably, think that Athens should have made peace in 425. "The logical conclusion of the Periclean strategy would be to make peace now, without insisting on the possession of those places which Pericles had surrendered because Athens was not strong enough to hold them." [45]

It is questionable, however, whether the Periclean goal had been attained when the Spartans came to ask for peace in 425. The aims of Pericles were largely psychological. He did not hope to render the Spartans incapable of making war on Athens but to make them unwilling to do so. [46] That depended on convincing the Spartans that they had not the power to defeat Athens, but the tenor of their speech shows just the opposite.

---

[40] Gomme, *HCT* III, 454.

[41] Beloch, *GG*[2] II: 1, 327.

[42] Meyer, *GdA*, 103.

[43] Busolt, *GG* III:2, 1096.

[44] Most students of Thucydides who deal with the question believe that he favored accepting the Spartan offer. See E. Meyer, *Forsch.* II, 346; John Finley, *Thucydides*, 195; J. de Romilly, *Athenian Imperialism*, 172. Gomme ⟨*HCT* III, 459–460⟩, responding to de Romilly, claims that we cannot know the opinion of Thucydides, but the arguments of Woodhead (*Mnemosyne*, XIII (1960), 310–313) seem to refute him conclusively.

[45] Adcock, *CAH* V, 234; see also Busolt, *GG* III:2, 1096, and Meyer, *Forsch.* II, 346.

[46] See above, pp. 35–36.

They believed the Athenian ascendancy was the result of an error which could be reversed at any time.[47] "This misfortune we have suffered came not from our want of power or because, having grown great, we became arrogant. On the contrary, though our resources remained the same we miscalculated, to which error all men are equally liable." [48] From the Periclean point of view the Spartans had learned nothing useful. A peace made with an enemy holding such opinions certainly raises the questions Beloch asks about the peace Pericles hoped for when the war began: "What guarantee would such a peace give that Sparta would not begin the war again at an opportune time? Was that a goal that would have been worth such a vast sacrifice? And would Athens, and especially, would its allies then be again in a position and be willing to make these sacrifices a second time?" [49]

The Athenians must have considered these questions, though Thucydides does not report any of the speeches that followed the Spartan proposal. The Spartan ambassadors, remembering that the Athenians had asked for peace earlier in the war, thought they would gladly accept the offer.[50] Perhaps this confidence explains why they were willing to entrust their fleet to the Athenians during the truce. Spartan confidence was natural, for, excepting what seemed to them the aberrant and accidental misfortune at Pylos, the Athenians had done them and their allies little damage after six years of war, they had lost a great portion of their population in the plague, their land had been ravaged and their homes destroyed, their treasury was approaching exhaustion, and no hope of victory was in sight. Why should they not seize the chance for peace? Spartan understanding of the state of opinion in Athens, however, was faulty, for since 430 the plague had come and gone, and the Athenians, enured to suffering, had survived. Instead of being eager for peace at any price, they had become more determined and aggressive. The campaigns in Sicily, Boeotia, and the northwest,

---

[47] 4.17.4, εὐτυχίαν τὴν παροῦσαν. . . . τὰ παρόντα ἀδοκήτως εὐτυχῆσαι; 4.18.3, ὥστε οὐκ εἰκὸς ὑμᾶς διὰ τὴν παροῦσαν νῦν ῥώμην πόλεώς τε καὶ τῶν προσγεγενημένων καὶ τὸ τῆς τύχης οἴεσθαι αἰεὶ μεθ' ὑμῶν ἔσεσθαι.
[48] 4.18.2.   [49] Beloch, *Attische Politik*, 23.   [50] 4.21.1.

while not decisive victories, had raised Athenian hopes of doing
enough damage to the enemy to bring a satisfactory peace. The
news of the success at Pylos must have raised such hopes higher,
but the terms offered by Sparta could not be attractive to the
Athenians of 425.

As Thucydides says, the Athenians knew that as long as the
men on Sphacteria were under their control they could have
peace whenever they wanted it, "but they grasped for more." [51]
His implication is that greed, ambition, and the extension of
empire were the Athenian motives, [52] but we need not believe
that. The Athenians were quite right to want more than merely
the promise of Spartan good will in the future and an alliance
which depended on the continuation of that good will. Once
the Spartans received their hostages back there was nothing to
stop them from resuming the war with power, morale, and
determination unimpaired. Even if the envoys and the men who
sent them were sincere in their offer of peace and friendship
these men might not continue in power. The volatility of Spartan internal politics had helped bring on the war; the advocates
of war had been strong enough to reject a peace offer from
Athens in 430; why should the war spirit not take command
again as soon as it was safe? Any reasonable Athenian would
have wanted a firmer guarantee than was offered.

Cleon led the opposition to the Spartan proposal. Thucydides
introduces him again, as if not previously mentioned, calling
him a "popular leader (demagogos) at that time who was most
influential with the masses," [53] and Cleon's view carried the
Athenian assembly. He made a counterproposal that the Spartans on Sphacteria should surrender and be brought to Athens.
Then the Spartans should hand over Nisaea and Pegae, the ports

[51] 4.21.2.
[52] The words τοῦ δὲ πλέονος ὠρέγοντο are parallel to those used by the
Spartans to describe imprudent men who try to push their luck too far.
Such men αἰεὶ γὰρ τοῦ πλέονος ἐλπίδι ὀρέγονται. . . . 4.17.4. For an excellent analysis of the bias in Thucydides' language in this section see
Woodhead, Mnemosyne XIII (1960), 312.
[53] 4.21.3. I think Woodhead (ibid., 311) is right in saying, "We are
again told he was πιθανώτατος with the πλῆθος, and this lends to the
description δημαγωγός a sinister flavour, even if the word was not as
yet the 'smear word' it later became."

of Megara, and also Troezen and Achaea, since all these places had not been taken from Athens in war but had been given up "by a previous agreement because of a misfortune, at a time when they were rather more eager for a treaty." [54] Only then would the Athenians give back the prisoners and agree to a lasting peace.

These conditions were, of course, unacceptable to the Spartans, but rather than reject them they asked for the appointment of a commission with which they could negotiate further in private. Cleon violently denounced the proposal, saying that the Spartans must have improper intentions to request a private hearing with only a few men. If they had something decent to say, let them say it before the open assembly. The Spartans, of course, could hardly discuss the possible betrayal of their allies in public, particularly in the bargaining stage, so they gave up and went home.[55] Cleon has been denounced for breaking off the negotiations in this way. Even Grote, Cleon's warmest defender, calls his action "decidedly mischievous." [56] Scholars generally feel that nothing would have been lost and much might have been gained by private negotiation.

But what could be negotiated? A frequent suggestion is that the Spartans might have been willing to give up Megara, or at least its harbors, "certainly not by a formal surrender on the part of the Spartans but merely by abandonment." [57] Such a suggestion is quite unrealistic. Sparta could abandon the northwest and ignore Corinth's demands in regard to Corcyra and Potidaea, but to abandon Megara would place the power of Athens on the isthmus, open the Peloponnese to possible invasion, and cut Sparta off from Boeotia and central Greece. Sparta's credibility as leader of its alliance and protector of its allies would be destroyed. Corinth, Thebes, and Megara would resist. To keep such a commitment to Athens, Sparta would have to abandon major allies, and even, under the terms of the *symmachia*, fight alongside Athens against them. This was inconceivable, as the period after the Peace of Nicias would show.

Grote, who argues it would have been wise to negotiate,

[54] 4.21.3.   [55] 4.22.   [56] Grote, VI, 332.
[57] Busolt, *GG* III:2, 1099. Grote, VI, 332, makes the same suggestion.

nevertheless notices these difficulties and offers a second reason
for continuing discussions: "Even if such acquisition had been
found impracticable, still, the Athenians would have been able
to effect some arrangement which would have widened the
breach, and destroyed the confidence, between Sparta and her
allies; a point of great moment for them to accomplish." [58] But
if not the cession of Megara to Athens, what other meaningful
"arrangement" was possible? Grote can think of none nor do the
other supporters of this view, for Sparta could make no useful
concessions.

If nothing could be gained by secret neotiation, however,
something could be lost. Delay might be useful to the Spartans;
though unlikely, some unforeseen reversal of fortune might
allow the men on Sphacteria to escape. Also if the Athenians
meant to reduce the island by blockade, the coming of winter
would make this impossible and the trapped men could escape.[59]
Each day the truce permitted food to be brought to Sphacteria
was another day the island could hold out. Though Thucydides
gives no hint of it, there was disagreement among the Athenians,
and Cleon's view was supported by the majority.[60] Some Athenians spoke in favor of accepting the peace offer, or at least in
favor of the secret negotiation in committee. The usual assumption, though supported by no direct evidence, is that Nicias was
one of them, which seems reasonable in light of his later policies.

Let us suppose that Athenians had voted to negotiate by
commission in secret. Given the political situation in Athens,
Nicias and his friends would have been elected to it. Such a
commission, eager for peace, sincere in their desire for friendship with Sparta, and ready to believe in its good faith, might
have made a proposal very attractive to the Athenians including,
perhaps, an alliance, promises of eternal friendship, the restoration of Plataea, and even the abandonment of Megara. In return
the Spartans might ask only the freeing of the men on Sphacteria
and the evacuation of Pylos, an offer hard to reject. The Spartans would sign the peace and the treaty of alliance and the

[58] Grote, VI, 332.   [59] 4.27.1.
[60] The account comes from Philochorus preserved in a scholion to
Aristophanes' *Peace*, 665. See *FGrH* 328, Fr. 128.

Athenians would restore the prisoners. Then the trouble would start. The Spartans might tell the Boeotians to yield Plataea, but they would certainly refuse. They might abandon Megara, but the Megarians, Corinthians, and Boeotians would band together against Athens. The Athenians would call on the Spartans to honor the alliance, and the Spartans would surely refuse. The ensuing bitterness would soon lead to hostility and war, with the Spartan capacity to wage it undiminished. We have described no fantasy but a rough approximation of what really happened after the Peace of Nicias. Cleon and the Athenians who supported him had reason to be suspicious of and to reject secret negotiations with Sparta.[61]

The unreported debate marks an important turning point in Athenian politics. Between the Spartan rejection of Athenian peace offers in 430 and the affair at Pylos, Athens was for the most part united in waging the war as vigorously as possible to force the Spartans to seek peace. Disagreements as to the nature of that peace were buried in the common effort. The victory at Pylos and the resulting Spartan peace mission changed all that. Before this event, to talk of making peace with Sparta was plainly treason; afterward it was a course patriotic men could advocate with a clear conscience. The Periclean war aims, the restoration of the prewar situation, the preservation of the empire, and the end of the Spartan crusade against it, all seemed to be within easy reach. Some Athenians might argue that such a peace was insufficiently secure and that Pericles himself would have asked greater guarantees,[62] but prudent men could argue that it was wise to trust Sparta and pave the way for a lasting peace. Nicias probably held such views in 425; there is no doubt that he did in 421.[63]

[61] Even scholars holding a different view concede grounds for suspicion. See Grote, *History* VI, 330; Busolt, *GG* III:2, 1098.

[62] See above, pp. 232–233. Eduard Meyer, who believes Pericles would have accepted the peace, is sufficiently uncomfortable with that opinion to concede that "he might have held on to, *e.g.*, Megara or Troezen, if the chance came, if somehow in these towns the Athenian party came into complete control and annihilated their opponents" (*Forsch.* II, 345–346).

[63] Plutarch (*Nicias* 7.2) says Cleon opposed the Spartan peace offer because he saw Nicias cooperating enthusiastically with the Spartans:

Cleon, however, had very different aims. His demands make deliberate reference to the state of affairs that existed *before* the Thirty Years' Peace of 445, when Athens controlled Megara, Boeotia, and other parts of central Greece, as well as a number of coastal cities of the Peloponnesus. The Athenians had been compelled to abandon these territories in a treaty they had signed because of certain "misfortunes." [64] Now, in 425, Cleon implied, the Athenians must insist on a return to an earlier situation when peace did not depend on the condition of Spartan politics or on Spartan good will but was guaranteed by the Athenian possession of strategic defensive locations. Possibly, as is often suggested, Cleon aimed at unlimited Athenian expansion, certainly on the Greek mainland and perhaps elsewhere. Aristophanes puts into the mouth of the Paphlagonian slave who represents Cleon in the *Knights* the determination to let the Athenian demos rule over all the Greeks, [65] but, as usual, it is hard to know if this is meant to reproduce a position really taken by Cleon or is mere comic exaggeration. Thucydides never accuses Cleon of such aims, though he specifically attributes far-reaching imperial aims to Alcibiades. [66] Plans for imperial expansion are not necessary to explain Cleon's firm rejection of Spartan peace offers in 425. As Woodhead says, Cleon's aim "was total victory," in his view, "the first yelps of Spartan anguish were only the beginning, and not the end, of the affair. Stalingrad, El Alamein, Midway Island, Sphacteria, are in Churchill's phrase 'hinges of fate,' and the fullest profit should on any commonsense view be reaped from them. Peace after Pylos would have solved no problems, and Sparta would have lived to fight again another day—unless, of course, the Spartans were publicly so humiliated that the old dualism could not be restored, and the negotiations so handled that they were a victory in themselves." [67]

When the Spartan ambassadors returned to Pylos the truce

προθύμως ὁρῶν συμπράττοντα τοῖς Λακεδαιμονίοις. This would be strong evidence for the views expressed here if we could be sure that this was not merely a Plutarchian inference but came from a reliable source.

[64] The word is ξυμφοραί, and is the same word used by the Spartan ambassadors to describe their defeat at Pylos.

[65] 797, ἵνα γ' Ἑλλήνων ἄρξῃ πάντων.   [66] 6.15.2; 6.90.2.

[67] *Mnemosyne*, XIII (1960), 311.

was at an end, but the Athenians, alleging violations by Sparta, refused to return the ships they held in hostage. Henceforth the Spartans must fight on land alone, which may not have been too great a misfortune in view of the use they had made of their navy heretofore. The Athenians were committed to capturing the men on Sphacteria, and they sent an additional 20 ships to enforce the blockade meant to starve them into surrender. The Spartans renewed their assaults on Pylos and tried to discover a way to save their men.[68] The Athenians expected quick success, for Sphacteria was a desert island containing no food and only brackish water, and the Athenian fleet had complete control of all approaches to it. The Spartans, however, displayed surprising ingenuity, offering rewards to free men and freedom to any helots who would run the blockade with food and drink for the prisoners. Many, especially helots, were willing to risk the danger and took advantage of wind and darkness to land on the island. Some went in little boats that they were willing to wreck on the harborless seaward shore and others as underwater divers. They were successful enough to keep the men on Sphacteria alive long after the time expected.

The Athenians now found themselves in an increasingly uncomfortable position. They were troubled by a shortage of food and water. Over 14,000 men depended on a single small spring on the Pylian acropolis and what little water they could find on the beach.[69] They were uncomfortably cramped into a small space, and their morale was low because of the unexpected duration of the siege. More serious than this discomfort was the growing fear that the onset of the winter season would force them to lift the blockade, since it would prevent the regular arrival of supply ships on which they depended for food. As time passed and the Spartans sent no more embassies the fear grew that the Spartans were confident of recovering their men, that Athens might emerge from the situation without either a great strategic advantage or a negotiated peace. The result inevitably was the feeling that a mistake had been made and that Cleon, who had urged rejection of the peace offer, was to blame.

When messengers arrived at the Athenian assembly to report

[68] 4.23.   [69] 4.26.2; Gomme, *HCT* III, 466.

the alarming state of affairs at Pylos, both Cleon and his policy came under fire. Thucydides describes this assembly in great detail in one of the most remarkable sections of his history. In spite of the dramatic nature of the debate he reports no speeches in direct discourse. Instead he gives brief accounts of what was said, filling them out with statements of what the speakers had in mind when they spoke. His description of this important assembly deserves careful examination. When the messengers told the Athenians the bad news from Pylos, Cleon accused them of not telling the truth, "knowing that their suspicion was directed against him because he had prevented the treaty." [70] The messengers invited the Athenians to appoint a commission to test the truth of their report; the Athenians complied and elected Cleon as one of the commissioners. Cleon, however, protested against the sending of a commission, arguing that it was a waste of time which might lose the great opportunity. He urged instead that if they believed the bad news was true they should send an additional force to assault the island and capture the men in that way.[71] He did this, "knowing that," if he went to Pylos, "he would be forced to say the same thing as had the men he had slandered, or, if he said the opposite, be exposed as a liar." Besides, "he saw that the Athenians were now rather more eager to make an expedition." [72] Then he turned and pointed a censorious finger at his enemy Nicias and said that it would be quite easy, if the generals were men, to take an adequate force to Pylos and capture the men on the island. "He would do so himself, if he were in command." [73]

Now, Thucydides says, the Athenians asked Cleon why he didn't sail off, if the job were so easy. Nicias, seeing the mood of the crowd and "noticing Cleon's taunt," [74] said that the generals would be glad for him to take any force he liked and try. At first Cleon was ready to accept, "thinking that the offer was only a ploy," but then he drew back, saying that Nicias and not he was general, "when he realized that the offer to relinquish

[70] 4.27.3.
[71] 4.27.4–5; this is my understanding of εἰ δὲ δοκεῖ αὐτοῖς ἀληθῆ εἶναι τὰ ἀγγελλόμενα, πλεῖν ἐπὶ τοὺς ἄνδρας. Gomme's comment (HCT III, 468) seems to support it.
[72] 4.27.4.   [73] 4.27.5.   [74] 4.28.1: ὁρῶν αὐτὸν ἐπιτιμῶντα.

the command was genuine." [75] But Nicias continued to urge him to make the campaign, offering to resign his own command and calling the Athenian people to witness his action. Cleon continued to try to evade, but the Athenians, "as is the way with the crowd," [76] kept telling Nicias to give up the command and Cleon to take it. At last, Cleon, "not having any way to escape the consequences of his own proposal," agreed to lead the expedition. Denying fear of the Spartans, he proposed to sail without any Athenian reinforcements, taking with him only a body of Lemnian and Imbrian troops who were in Athens, some peltasts from Aenos, and 400 archers from elsewhere. With these men and those already at Pylos, he promised that within twenty days he would "either bring back the Spartans alive or kill them on the spot!" [77]

This lighthearted promise provoked a burst of laughter from the audience, but the "sensible men" (sophrones) among them concluded that one of two good things must result: "Either they would be rid of Cleon, which they considered more likely, or, if that judgment were confounded, he would put the Spartans in their hands." [78] Such is Thucydides' account, unique in character and style [79] and bristling with difficulties. For what purpose was the Athenian assembly called together, or, if the debate took place at a regular meeting, on what question did it center? How could Nicias offer the command to Cleon on behalf of all the generals, for the strategia had no generalissimo, and we are told of no consultation among the generals? How could Nicias offer to resign his command, when we are not told it had been given him? Why were the Lemnians and Imbrians and the peltasts from Aenos so conveniently at Athens at just the right time? Thucydides' account does not give clear or certain answers, but we must try to reconstruct the events, keeping these questions in mind.

The meeting probably was called to discuss a request by Demosthenes for reinforcements with which to attack Sphac-

---

[75] 4.28.2: γνοὺς δὲ τῷ ὄντι παραδωσείοντα.

[76] 4.28.3: οἷον ὄχλος φιλεῖ ποιεῖν. [77] 4.28.4. [78] 28.5.

[79] Mme. de Romilly (Thucydide III, xiii) perceptively points out that "Le récit, habituellement si sobre, prend ici des allures de comédie: hablerie, improvisation, impudence, tout s'y trouve."

teria.[80] When Cleon sailed he already knew of Demosthenes' plan to attack the island; the kind of light-armed troops needed for the campaign were already assembled at Athens when the debate took place, and Demosthenes had begun to make preparations for the assault, sending to the allies in the vicinity for additional troops.[81] With the messengers who came from Pylos no doubt came also a request from Demosthenes for the specially selected troops he needed to capture Sphacteria and the men on it.[82] We cannot be sure whether the request was made formally by Demosthenes to the assembly or privately to Cleon who then proposed it. Cleon was certainly in close communication with Demosthenes.[83] He did not necessarily have any secret information not available to the generals and council, but he probably had received more details of Demosthenes' plans and needs.[84]

Cleon, of course, was the natural man for Demosthenes to choose as his advocate. He had a special interest—he was most responsible for rejecting the Spartan peace offer and would be in serious trouble if the men on Sphacteria were allowed to escape. He was also an effective politician, supporter of the aggressive policy, and of a temperament to seize on the prospects of success in Demosthenes' bold plan. Nicias was a natural opponent. He was a political, and perhaps a personal, enemy of Cleon. If we have judged his attitude rightly he now favored a negotiated peace, and he knew that the capture of the Spartans would inflame the aggressive spirits in Athens and make such a peace impossible. He may have been eager to delay an attack as long as possible in the hope of negotiating a peace before it was too late. Nicias was a careful man, and his caution was proverbial.[85] Since he had none of Demosthenes' experience in

[80] Busolt, GG III:2, 1101, n. 2.   [81] 4.29.2; 28.4; 30.3.

[82] Grote, VI, 339, and Busolt, GG III:2, 1101, n. 2, take it for granted that Demosthenes is the subject of the verb ᾐτήσατο in the following sentence of 4.30.4: Κλέων δὲ ἐκείνῳ τε προπέμψας ἄγγελον ὡς ἥξων καὶ ἔχων στρατιὰν ἣν ᾐτήσατο, ἀφικνεῖται ἐς Πύλον. If they are right the case for Demosthenes' request is unquestionable, but it seems more likely that Cleon is the subject.

[83] 4.29.1; 30.4.   [84] See Gomme, HCT III, 471.

[85] Plut. Nic. 2.4–8.

fighting on rugged terrain with light-armed troops and was not on the spot to judge the prospects of success, his cautious disposition may have led him honestly to fear the dangers of forcing a landing on an island held by hoplites. In either case we may believe that he opposed the request for reinforcements to attack the island and supported the suggestion that a commission be sent to investigate conditions at Pylos.

Cleon had questioned the veracity of the messengers' doleful report in part, no doubt, because his optimistic spirit interpreted the prospects of Demosthenes' plan more hopefully and he wanted to lift the spirits of the Athenians so they would be willing to support the new expedition. He thus fell into the trap that allowed his opponents to suggest an investigatory committee which would cause an unwelcome delay and, incidentally, get Cleon himself safely out of town where he could not influence the assembly. Cleon must have seen the danger after he was selected as a commissioner, argued against the delay, and accused Nicias and the other generals of unmanliness. At this point, unless we are to believe that Thucydides uses uncharacteristic and indefensibly loose terminology in speaking of Nicias' "command against Pylos," [86] we must imagine that the assembly had already decided to send the expedition and appointed Nicias as its commander. Nicias could not resign a command he had not been granted, even if his intention was only rhetorical. Once again, Cleon was taken by surprise; he never could have anticipated that Nicias would be so irresponsible as to offer the command of an Athenian force to a man without important military experience. Cleon's aim had been to goad Nicias into taking his force to Demosthenes without delay and joining him in the attack, so he naturally recoiled when Nicias offered him the command. Nicias, seeing his opponent's embar-

---

[86] τῆς ἐπὶ Πύλῳ ἀρχῆς 4.28.3. Gomme, without saying so, makes exactly such an assumption: "We have not been told that Nikias had any command at Pylos. We must suppose that the words mean only that if reinforcements were to be sent, Nikias, as strategos, would have good claim to their command; and probably that reinforcements had been officially requested" (*HCT* III, 468). But the words clearly do not mean that, and if Thucydides meant to convey the message Gomme thinks, he failed to do so.

rassment, repeated the offer in the hope of discrediting Cleon totally, and the crowd soon took up the game, some in earnest, others from hostility to Cleon, and still others for the fun of it. Nicias, of course, had not the power to make the offer on his own behalf, much less on behalf of the other generals, but when the assembly took up his cry, the Athenians clearly would accept the suggestion. Cleon could not back down, but he could take heart at the thought that the military part would be in the hands of Demosthenes, who was well suited to the task. Cleon at the head of the reinforcements, instead of Nicias or another opponent of the plan, would help the chances for success. Such is our reconstruction of the debate.

Cleon's promise to succeed within twenty days and without the use of any Athenian hoplites was neither bravado nor foolishness. Demosthenes had obviously decided that experienced light-armed troops with special skills were needed to carry out his plan, and the Athenians had made them ready even before the assembly met. Given that the plan of Demosthenes was to attack at once, that the necessary forces were at hand, and that a quick decision was inevitable, Cleon knew he would succeed in twenty days or not at all.[87] The attitude Thucydides attributes to the *sophrones* seems hard to understand or excuse. That patriotic Athenians could have agreed to give the command of the Athenian expedition, control of hopes for victory, and responsibility for the lives of allied soldiers and Athenian sailors to a man they believed to be foolish and incompetent is surprising. If Thucydides reports their views rightly, we have an idea of the degree to which the new course of events had aggravated old political hostilities and of the potentially dangerous division among Athenians which had been created.

Cleon had been in close touch with Demosthenes, and, once he had been granted the command and the troops he requested, he immediately named him as his colleague and sent word ahead that help was on the way.[88] At Pylos, Demosthenes had long hesitated to attack the heavily wooded island on which an unknown number of Spartan hoplites were concealed. At this point, again, fortune favored the bold. A contingent of Athenian

[87] Busolt, *GG* III:2, 1105.   [88] 4.29.1; 30.4.

soldiers, prevented by the cramped conditions at Pylos from preparing a hot meal there, landed on Sphacteria. Their intention was only to cook and eat a meal there, protected by pickets, and then to sail off. One of them accidentally started a forest fire, and before long most of the woods had been burnt off. Now Demosthenes could see that the Spartans were more numerous than he had thought, which helps explain his request for reinforcements. He also saw places to make a safe landing that had been obscured before, and he realized that one of the great tactical advantages of the enemy had been removed by the fire. When Cleon arrived with the fresh special troops, Demosthenes was ready to put to use the valuable lessons he had learned in Aetolia.[89]

Cleon's appearance seems to have removed Sophocles and Eurymedon from the picture. He and Demosthenes, agreed on goals and tactics, were in full control. Their first step was to send a herald to the Spartans offering them gentle treatment if if they would surrender and remain in Athenian custody while a lasting peace was negotiated. The Spartans refused, and Demosthenes put his plan into action. On the second day after the refusal he put 800 hoplites on board a few ships which set off under cover of darkness and landed just before dawn on both the seaward side of the island and the side facing inward toward the harbor.[90] Now that the woods concealing the Spartans had been removed, Demosthenes knew that most of their troops were near the center of the island guarding the water supply, and another force was near the northern tip of the island opposite Pylos, leaving only 30 hoplites to man the guardpost nearest the point of landing, somewhere at the southern end of the island.[91] After watching the Athenians sail by harmlessly for so many days, the Spartans were not prepared for a landing. They were caught still in bed and swiftly wiped out. It was a repetition of the battle of Idomene.[92] The Athenians established a beachhead and landed the rest of their forces at dawn. Some men were left to guard the fort at Pylos, but all the rest, hoplites, peltasts, archers, even most of the barely armed rowers from the fleet, disembarked on

---

[89] 4.29–30.   [90] 4.30.1.   [91] 4.31; Gomme, HCT III, 473.
[92] See above, p. 215.

the island to swell the Athenian numbers and increase their impression on the enemy. Almost 8,000 rowers, 800 hoplites, the same number of archers, and over 2,000 light-armed troops must have faced the 420 Spartans.[93]

Demosthenes divided his troops into companies of 200 and had them seize all the high places on the island, so that wherever the Spartans fought they would find an enemy in their rear or on their flanks. The key to the strategy was the use of light-armed troops, for they "were the most difficult to fight, since they fought at a distance with arrows, javelins, stones and slings. It was not possible to attack them, for even as they fled they held the advantage, and when their pursuers turned, they were on them again. Such was the plan with which Demosthenes first conceived the landing, and in practice that is how he arranged his forces." [94] At first the Spartans lined up facing the Athenian hoplites, but since they were assailed by the missiles of the light-armed troops from the side and the rear, and since the Athenian hoplites did not advance, they were unable to make contact. The light-armed troops forced them to wear themselves out in fruitless charges which had to be abandoned when the peltasts, archers, and slingers retreated to the high ground and rough terrain.

After a while the light-armed troops realized that the enemy had suffered more casualties and was getting tired, so they became more bold. They launched a major assault against the Spartan hoplites, charging with a shout and hurling every sort of missile as they came. The shouting itself disconcerted the Spartans, for they were not used to such barbaric sounds in battle, and it prevented them from hearing the orders of their officers. At last, confused and desperate, they closed ranks and retreated to the northern end of the island where most of them joined with the garrison there behind the fortification. There, free from harassment from behind and on the flank, they were able to repulse a frontal attack and maintain a defense.[95]

At that moment the Messenian general Comon[96] came to Cleon and Demosthenes with a plan. He asked for a contingent

---

[93] 4.32.1–2; Gomme, *HCT* III, 474.   [94] 4.32.4.   [95] 4.33–35.
[96] Paus. 4.26.2.

of archers and light-armed troops and proposed to find a path around the precipitous shore of the island whereby he might take the Spartans from the rear. Since the approach was so difficult, the Spartans had not thought it necessary to waste any of their badly outnumbered troops in guarding the rear, so they were stunned by the appearance of Comon and his troops. Once again they were surrounded and outnumbered, by now they were weak from exertion and lack of food, and they had no place to run. Complete destruction was imminent.[97]

Cleon and Demosthenes realized that live prisoners would be far more valuable than Spartan corpses, so they called a halt and sent a herald to offer the opportunity of surrender. The Spartans accepted the offer and a truce to decide what to do. Epitadas was dead, and his second in command, Hippagretas, was thought to be, so Styphon, third in succession, represented the Spartans in the conversations with Cleon and Demosthenes. He refused to take the responsibility for a decision, so a herald was sent to bring the official word from Sparta. The Spartan authorities tried to avoid responsibility, saying "The Lacedaemonians order you to decide your own fate yourselves, but to do nothing dishonorable." [98] The Spartans surrendered. Of the 420 who had come to the island, 128 were dead; the remaining 292, among them 120 Spartiates, were taken prisoner to Athens within the twenty days that Cleon had promised. The Athenian casualties were few. "The promise of Cleon, mad as it was," Thucydides says, "was fulfilled." [99]

[97] 4.36.   [98] 4.38.3.

[99] 4.39.3: that this passage and Thucydides' treatment of Cleon's role at Pylos reveals the historian's bias has been recognized since the time of Grote VI, 348–351. Delbrück (*Strategie*, 188ff.) has tried to support Thucydides' view that the battle at Sphacteria was won through luck and Spartan mistakes. His view is adopted and summarized by Steup in his commentary to 4.28.5: "Bedenkt man aber, dass Kleons glänzender Waffenerfolg lediglich eine Folge der mangelhaften Wachsamkeit der Besatzung von Sphacteria gewesen ist, und dass diese Besatzung bei geschickter Führung und gehöriger Wachsamkeit den Athenern einen ganz anderen Widerstand hätte leisten können, so wird man Kleons bestimmte Verheissung, die Spartaner in zwanzig Tagen entweder gefangen nach Athen zu bringen oder an Ort und Stelle zu töten, nicht anders als unsinnig nennen können." This view is rejected by so staunch a defender of Thucydides as Eduard Meyer, *Forsch.* II, 333ff. and *GdA*

Psychologically and strategically, the great victory fashioned by Cleon and Demosthenes was very important. "In the eyes of the Greeks it was the most unexpected event in the war," for no one could believe that the Spartans could be brought to surrender.[100] The Athenians sent a garrison to man the fort at Pylos, and the Naupactian Messenians also sent a force, which used Pylos as a base for launching raids. The helots began to desert, and the Spartans grew uneasy at the prospect of increased revolutionary activity within the Peloponnese. The Athenians, moreover, held a trump card in the Spartan hostages, threatening to kill them if the Spartans again invaded Attica. All this was totally new and frightening to the Spartans. Although anxious to keep their condition secret from the Athenians, they sent repeated embassies to Athens to negotiate for the return of Pylos and the prisoners, but the Athenians continued to raise their demands beyond what the Spartans were willing to grant.[101]

The events at Pylos completely changed the outlook of the war. Athens was free of the threat of invasion, free to move anywhere at sea without danger from the enemy fleet, which Athens held, and free, therefore, to extort further funds from the allies to replenish the almost exhausted treasury. The situation had also been reversed in another way. Heretofore the Spartans had been doing damage to the Athenians without appreciably suffering in return. Now the Athenians could inflict continuing harm on their enemies, on land and by sea, fearing no retaliation. The Athenians showered their gratitude on the hero of the hour, Cleon, for Demosthenes seems to have stayed behind at Pylos to see to its security.[102] The assembly voted Cleon the highest honors in the state, meals at the state expense

---

IV, 106, n. 1, where he says, "Kleons Versprechen war in der Tat keine κουφολογία, sondern der Plan durchaus sachemäss; aber er stammt nicht von ihm, sondern von Demosthenes. Auch die Ausführung ist das Werk des letzteren; aber Kleon hat sie ermöglicht." Busolt holds very much the same opinion, though he thinks the promise "war nur ein nicht ganz vorsichtiges," since bad weather might delay or prevent the attack (GG III:2, 1105–1106). Soften the statement as we may, we must agree with Gomme that "Thucydides' bias is once more clear" (HCT III, 478).

[100] 4.40.   [101] 4.41.   [102] Busolt, GG III:2, 1109 and n. 5.

in the Prytaneum, and front seats at the theater.[103] Meyer goes too far in calling him "for the moment, indeed, the regent of Athens, the successor of Pericles," [104] but since the death of Pericles no Athenian politician had achieved so much power.

Cleon seized the opportunity to make Athens financially able to carry on the war for the victory he believed necessary. Triumphantly he brought his prisoners home about the second week in August.[105] About two months later, in the third prytany of 425/4, September–October 425, a certain Thudippus proposed a decree, which was approved by the assembly, ordering a new assessment of the tribute levied on the allies of Athens and setting up the machinery to carry it out.[106] Although no positive evidence attaches Cleon's name to this action, and neither Thucydides nor Aristophanes connects him with it,[107] the overwhelming majority of scholars are right to believe that he and his supporters were behind the new assessment.[108] The attitude it expresses toward the empire accords perfectly with his views

[103] Aristoph. *Knights* 280, 702, 709, 766, 1404.   [104] *GdA* IV, 107.

[105] I follow the chronology of Gomme, *HCT* III, 478.

[106] *IG* i² 63 = *GHI*, 69. Meiggs and Lewis provide a bibliography and a good discussion of the major disputed points. I find their interpretations and arguments persuasive. Meritt and Wade-Gery, *AJP* LVII (1936), 377–394, employ a chronology that places the affair at Pylos and Sphacteria one month later and brings the victory into much closer temporal proximity with the decree. Meiggs and Lewis (*GHI*, 194–196), however, support Gomme's dates convincingly. For a different chronology see M. F. McGregor *TAPA* LXVI (1935), 146–164.

[107] These points are emphasized by Gomme, *HCT* III, 500–502, who concludes from them that Cleon had nothing to do with the decree. Neither author mentions the decree at all, and in Thucydides' case, at least, as Gomme admits, this is "the strangest of all omissions in Thucydides." Thucydides' failure to connect Cleon with the decree, therefore, is only part of the mystery of his larger failure to mention the decree and ought not to be used as negative evidence. That Aristophanes should have omitted to use the decree against a man known for squeezing the allies is surprising, but only one of many unsolved riddles arising from the great comic poet. For a good response to Gomme's arguments see Woodhead, *Mnemosyne* XIII (1960), 301–302.

[108] Among those arguing in favor of Cleon's predominant role in the reassessment decree are: Beloch (*Attische Politik*, 40 and *GG²* II, 1, 330–331); Eduard Meyer (*GdA* IV, 107–108); Busolt (*GG* III:2, 1117); Adcock (*CAH* V, 236); Bengtson (*GG*, 226); Woodhead (*Mnemosyne* XIII [1960], 301–302); and Meiggs and Lewis (*GHI*, 196–197).

in the debate about Lesbos.[109] His connection with it is supported by the references in the comic poets to Cleon's connection with finance.[110] Most telling is his unquestioned ascendancy
during the period of the decree's passage. From midsummer 425
at least until the spring of 424, when he was elected general,
Cleon was supreme in Athens. No bill to which he objected was
likely to have passed through the assembly. Also, 425 was not a
Great Panathenaic year, when reassessments normally took
place, and the bill was introduced too late in the year to permit
representatives from the allied cities to come to Athens until
winter. As Meiggs and Lewis say, "Some special explanation is
required," [111] and it is fair to assume that this important measure,
fully in accord with Cleon's views, passed at the height of his
influence, was supported and sponsored by him.

The purpose of the reassessment, of course, was to raise more
money with which to fight the war, and a clause in the decree
provided that the assessors "shall not assess a smaller tribute for
any city than it was previously paying, unless owing to the
poverty of the territory they cannot pay more." [112] At the bottom of the list of cities and their assessments the inscription gives
a total figure. Since the first letter of that figure is missing,
scholars have disagreed whether the total was 960 talents or
1,460. The accumulation of evidence now makes it clear that
the higher figure is correct, so that the assessment of 425 more
than trebled earlier assessments. This high total was reached not
only by raising the contributions from almost every city paying
tribute, but also by listing cities that had not paid for years, and
even some that had never paid at all. "In the thirties the number
of cities recorded in the annual lists of *aparchai* never exceeded
175. In 425 not less than 380 and possibly more than 400 were
assessed." [113]

Clearly the Athenians meant to undertake a thorough and ra-

109 See above, pp. 156–159.
110 For Cleon's special role in financial matters see Busolt, *GG* III:2,
993. Aristophanes' *Knights*, especially, has several references to this interest of Cleon's; see lines 312, 774, 925, and 1071.
111 *GHI*, 194.
112 11.21–22, translated by Meiggs and Lewis (*GHI*, 193).
113 *GHI*, 194.

tional reorganization of their empire. The prosperity of the allied states had increased enormously since the assessment of Aristides so that their contribution to Athens represented a much smaller proportion of their wealth and income.[114] Considerable inflation caused by a rise in prices made the real value of the payments far smaller than they had been a half-century earlier,[115] yet Athens collected no more in 425 than she had in 477. The decree of Thudippus also provided for the tough and efficient collection of the revenue, very much in the spirit of Cleon. It is "perhaps the strongest decree that has survived from the fifth century. The executive is threatened with penalties at every turn, in a manner reminiscent of, but more intensive than, the Coinage decree and the decree of Kleinias." [116] Cleon and his supporters also wanted to abolish the anomalies in the empire which could produce trouble. Melos, which had never paid tribute, was now assessed at 15 talents, a sign that the Athenians meant to bring the island under their control. The Carian cities, which had been allowed to fall away, were restored to the list. These attempts to increase Athenian revenue might be difficult to enforce, but they reflect Cleon's determination to restore the empire to its full size, to govern it with a tight reign, and to draw from it the greatest revenue possible. The condition of Athens made some such steps necessary, and Cleon's great victory had made them possible.

We have no reason to believe that the raising of the tribute aroused any political opposition within Athens. Since the rejection of Sparta's peace offers made it clear that the war must go on, more money was vital. Cleon's success, moreover, had humiliated Nicias and his followers and made talk of peace impossible. The only way to regain influence was through success in war, and Nicias tried to recover his position with a victory to balance that of his opponent. Immediately after Cleon's success at Pylos, Nicias, along with two unnamed generals, took command of an expedition against the territory of Corinth. They led

[114] Busolt, *GG* III:2, 1117.
[115] Busolt, *GG* III:2, 1117; A. French, *The Growth of the Athenian Economy* (London, 1964), 168.
[116] *GHI*, 196–197.

a very large force, consisting of 80 ships, 2,000 Athenian hoplites, and 200 cavalry; in addition there were soldiers from Miletus, Andros, and Carystos.[117]

The Athenians landed on the beach near the village of Solygeia located on a hill bearing the same name, a little more than a mile from the town, six or seven miles from Corinth, and about three miles from the isthmus.[118] The Athenians counted on their usual advantage as a sea power to make a fast, surprise attack in an unexpected place. However, the Corinthians had been warned by Argives, though we have no information as to where the informers learned of the Athenian plan.[119] Unsure where the Athenians would land, the Corinthians posted their forces at the isthmus. From there they could move northward to protect Crommyon on the Megarian border, if that were the target, or southward to defend the port of Cenchreae if it were attacked. The Athenian ships eluded the watch by landing unexpectedly at night at Solygeia, still further to the southeast of Corinth.[120] Thucydides once again does not state the purpose of the invasion. Some scholars have thought that Nicias, trying to emulate the success of Cleon, intended to fortify and garrison a base in Corinthian territory to harass the Corinthians and Megarians as the Spartans were being harassed from Pylos.[121] But Gomme points out that to hold Solygeia the Athenians would have had to build walls a mile and one-half to the sea and leave a considerable force of men to hold them.[122] Solygeia was not

[117] 4.42.1.

[118] 4.42.2; for a good discussion of the geography see Gomme, *HCT* III, 493. See Map 7.

[119] The Argives were neutral, traditionally hostile to Sparta, and had a democratic constitution, so that it might be thought they would not favor the enemies of Athens. Cleon appears to have tried even to bring Argos over to the Athenian camp (Aristoph. *Knights*, 465). We know, however, that an aristocratic faction in Argos was willing to bring in the Spartans if they could gain power (see Kagan, *CP* LVII [1962], 209–218), and it may have been one of its members who betrayed the expedition.

[120] 4.42.

[121] Busolt, *GG* III:2, 1114; Adcock (*CAH* V, 236–237, and *CR* LXI [1947], 6) believes that after Pylos the policy of ἐπιτειχισμός "dominates Athenian strategy."

[122] *HCT* III, 494.

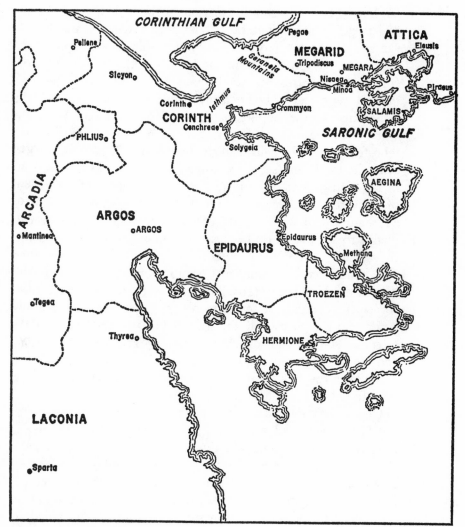

Map 7. Northeast Peloponnesus

worth such an investment, and there is no evidence that this was part of the Athenian plan.

When the Corinthians learned that the Athenians had landed and where, they hurried to meet them, but with only half of their army. The other half was left at Cenchreae in case the landing at Solygeia should turn out to be a feint to cover the real target which might be Crommyon.[123] Once again the advantage of the sea power was considerable. Nicias apparently did not move directly from the beach up the hill to Solygeia, for the Corinthians got to the village first and held the high ground with part of the army while the rest attacked the Athenians. In the hoplite battle that followed the Athenians were victorious, losing fewer than 50 to the 212 Corinthians who fell. The Athenians held the field and picked up their dead after the battle and set up a trophy. Still, Corinthian possession of the high ground, their prudence, and the threat of the arrival of reinforcements prevented the Athenians from accomplishing anything worth while. The Corinthian army at Cenchreae was unable to see the battle because of a mountain in between, but they could see the dust it raised. They, as well as the older men who had stayed in the city of Corinth, came rushing up to help. Nicias, thinking the approaching men were Peloponnesian reinforcements, quickly returned to his ships, carrying the spoils of battle and the corpses of the slain Athenians, and sailed to the safety of some islands off shore. Characteristically, the cautious and pious Nicias sent heralds to ask the Corinthians for a truce to recover the bodies of two fallen Athenians which had not been found in the rush to get back to the ships. [124]

On the very same day the Athenians sailed for Crommyon, as the Corinthians had earlier expected they would. This might suggest that the landing at Solygeia had been a decoy to draw the Corinthian forces away from Crommyon and make a landing possible, but Nicias made little use of the opportunity so gained. He made no attempt to take the town, but was content to ravage the territory and spend the night. The next day he sailed to Epidaurus where he landed briefly before moving on to Methana, a peninsula between Epidaurus and Troezen. Here he

[123] 4.42.4.   [124] 4.43–44.

walled off the narrow neck of the peninsula and left a garrison which afterward raided the territory of Troezen, Halieis, and Epidaurus, all within easy reach.[125] The planting of a fort at Methana must have been the major purpose of the campaign and the raid on Corinthian territory merely a side show intended to do whatever damage to that enemy state possible. The fort at Methana, on the other hand, might have important results. If Troezen and Halieis could be persuaded to come over to Athens, Epidaurus would be threatened. If Epidaurus could be taken, it might be possible to bring Argos from neutrality to the Athenian side. We know that Cleon was currently negotiating with the Argives to this end.[126] Such, very likely, were the hopes that inspired Nicias' expedition.

About the same time as the expedition of Nicias, the fleet under Sophocles and Eurymedon sailed from Pylos to Corcyra. There they found that the democratic friends of Athens in the city were still under attack from the oligarchs on Mount Istome. The Athenians joined their allies in an attack on the mountain stronghold and captured it. The defeated oligarchs, certain of their fate if they fell into the hands of their countrymen, agreed to surrender, but only to the Athenians and if they were sent to Athens to have their fate decided. The Athenians accordingly offered them a truce and protective custody on the island of Ptychia nearby, on condition that if anyone tried to escape, the truce would be considered broken for all. The leaders of the democratic faction, however, wanted nothing less than the blood of their enemies. They resorted to trickery, sending friends of the oligarchs to the island to say that the Athenians were planning to turn the prisoners over to the democrats and urging them to escape. Such a ruse should have been transparent, but the attitude of the Athenian generals lent it plausibility. Sophocles and Eurymedon could not themselves take the prisoners to Athens, for they were under pressure to sail to Sicily as quickly as possible. But, if someone else delivered them, the generals would lose credit for their capture. Sophocles and Eurymedon obviously did not conceal their concern, and the captive Corcyraeans feared the worst. A few tried to escape and

[125] 4.45.   [126] See above, p. 252, n. 119.

were captured. The truce was broken and the prisoners turned over to their bloodthirsty compatriots. Those who were not killed with the greatest cruelty committed suicide; their women were sold into slavery. Sophocles and Eurymedon permitted these terrible atrocities. "In this way," says Thucydides, "the Corcyraeans from the mountain were destroyed by the demos, and the party strife which had lasted so long ended in such a manner, at least in so far as this war is concerned, for there were no longer any oligarchs left worth mentioning." [127] Sophocles and Eurymedon could now sail to Sicily, free of the fear that someone would steal their glory.

The speed and ease with which the Athenians settled affairs at Corcyra shows that the triple mission the fleet had been assigned was neither foolish nor impossible. Demosthenes could have been left to fortify Pylos with little delay, and he would have required no help if the Peloponnesian fleet had not slipped by Sophocles and Eurymedon. Had they performed their task successfully they might have met the Spartan fleet on the open sea and destroyed it. Then they could have gone on to Corcyra and dealt with the situation quickly, as they did. At last they could have gone on to Sicily, having lost little time. The long delay that wasted most of the summer was caused by their unfortunate failure to cut off the enemy fleet. The Athenian campaign in Sicily would pay a heavy price for that failure.

As the fighting season drew to a close the Athenians won another victory in the northwest. The garrison at Naupactus joined the Acarnanians in an attack on the city of Anactorium which was defended by 500 Corinthian troops.[128] The city fell by treachery, so often the way with Greek sieges. The Corinthians were expelled and the place colonized by Acarnanians.[129] The loss of Anactorium was keenly felt by the Corinthians,[130] for communication with Apollonia was made more difficult and their waning prestige in an important region was further reduced.

The growing power and authority of Athens manifested itself in the Aegean as well. Some time late in the summer or in the autumn of 425, the Chians, the last of Athens' important "au-

[127] 4.49.6.   [128] 4.42.3.   [129] 4.49.   [130] 5.30.2.

tonomous" allies in the Aegean, built a defensive wall on their island. The Athenians, suspecting that the Chians planned rebellion, ordered them to tear it down. Perhaps these suspicions were unfounded, but it is hard to know what other purpose the wall could have had at a time when the Athenian fleet was fully capable of defending the Aegean against any possible enemy. The Chians, of course, had no choice. They received a promise from Athens that no punishment would follow and destroyed the wall. After the victory at Pylos no island could think of defying the Athenians.[131]

All during the war, of course, both sides negotiated with barbarian powers for assistance, and the most important of these was Persia. We are not well informed about these discussions, but occasionally we get a glimpse. Aristophanes' *Acharnians* contains a hilarious scene in which a messenger from the Great King is brought onto the stage in Athens,[132] which shows the Athenians had been in touch with Persia, probably from the beginning of the war.[133] The Spartans had tried at least as hard to gain Persian support. We know that they, too, began wooing the Persians at the start of the war, and a Spartan embassy to the Persian court had been intercepted by the Athenians in 430.[134] In the winter of 425/4 another envoy was intercepted by the Athenians, and his capture gives us some insight into the state of Persian negotiations with Sparta. The captive this time was a Persian on his way from the Great King to Sparta. He carried a message in the Persian language which, when translated, yielded the following message: "In regard to the Spartans the King did not know what they wanted. Though many envoys had come to him, they did not say the same things. If they wanted to say anything that was clear they should send men to him in the company of the Persian messenger." [135] Possibly, as Gomme suggests,[136] the Spartans' lack of clarity came from their reluctance to abandon the Asiatic Greeks to Persia, surely a minimum demand, while they were claiming to fight for Greek freedom. It

[131] 4.51.   [132] Aristoph. *Acharn.* 65ff.   [133] 2.7.1.
[134] 2.7.1; 67.1–2.
[135] 4.50.2. For a discussion of Athenian relations with Persia during the war see A. Andrewes, *Historia* X (1961), 1–18.
[136] Gomme, *HCT* III, 499.

may also have reflected shifts in factional politics in Sparta otherwise unknown to us. In either case, the Persian answer offered
the harried Spartans no comfort or hope for help against Athens.

The Athenians tried to take advantage of their vigilance and
good fortune by sending some envoys back to the Great King
with the intercepted messenger. When they reached Ephesus,
however, they learned that King Artaxerxes had died, and they
judged it a poor time to pursue negotiations.[137]

The events of 425 had changed the course of the war entirely.
The stalemate had been broken, and Athens held the advantage
everywhere. Her financial problems had been solved by the new
imperial assessment. The capture of the enemy fleet ended the
threat on the sea and any prospect of revolt in the maritime por-
tions of the empire. The northwest was almost totally free of
enemies. There was no immediate threat of Persian intervention,
and the Athenian campaign on Sicily guaranteed that the
Greeks in the west would help their Dorian cousins in the
Peloponnese. Finally, and most important, the prisoners taken
at Sphacteria were safely in Athens, where their presence guaranteed that Attica would not be invaded. Athens did not seem
likely to lose the war and could hope that she might win it decisively. All Athenians had reasons to be pleased, and all were
eager to press on to victory. The question was how to proceed,
and the answer depended on what kind of victory was wanted.
Those who wanted a negotiated peace in which Sparta would
recognize the integrity of the Athenian Empire and make an
alliance with Athens to prove it would prefer a cautious, safe,
and sure strategy. They would wish to continue to avoid major
land battles, hold their fortified places on the Peloponnese, even
take more of them when possible, and use them to harass, discourage, and wear down the enemy—to continue the original
policy of Pericles.

Cleon and men of like opinions might well reject those aims
and strategy as inadequate. They might point out that such a
peace could not be secure since it rested ultimately on Spartan
promises and good will. The events of 435 to 431 had shown
that Sparta's good will was not reliable, and seven years of war

[137] 4.50.3; Diod. 12.64.1.

had not increased the supply. Even if the Spartans who offered peace in 425 were honest, they could be replaced by a hostile faction at any time. Something tangible, a secure defense against renewal of the war was needed, and that something was control of Megara and the neutralization of Boeotia. Sparta might even promise these concessions to Athens in negotiation, but she could not deliver them. The only satisfactory peace was one which gave Athens control of Megara and a friendly Boeotia. To make peace at a time when the enemy was weak and demoralized and when the Athenian power was at its height would be foolish. The proper strategy was to move against Megara, Boeotia, and any other appropriate places. Then the time might be ripe to negotiate a peace that would be really lasting. Such must have been the reasoning of Cleon and his friends. We need not be surprised that the Athenians followed their advice.

9. Megara and Delium

Cleon's great success at Sphacteria led to his election as general in the spring of 424,[1] which with the re-election of Demosthenes and Lamachus has led some scholars to think that the elections were a victory for the "democratic war party." [2] This view is strengthened by the belief that Hippocrates, the nephew of Pericles, also elected in 424, was a member of the same faction. But Nicias, too, was re-elected, and with him his associates Nicostratus and Autocles. In addition we know of two other generals for 424/3, Eucles and Thucydides the historian. We know nothing of the political position of Eucles, and no evidence associates him with Cleon or his views. Thucydides, of course, was hostile to Cleon and should be ranked among his opponents. Among the nine known generals, five were re-elected, of whom three were opposed to Cleon, and four new ones elected, two for him, one against, and one unknown. The *strategia* was not significantly changed in its balance. The Athenians embarked upon the most daring campaigns of the war in 424 not because of a change in the alignment of generals but because the successes of the previous year had convinced most Athenians that a more aggressive strategy was both necessary and promising.

[1] Aristoph. *Clouds*, 581ff. Cleon's election is accepted by Busolt, Beloch, and most scholars, but Gomme (*HCT* III, 505–506) has raised some questions about the reference. For a pointed and satisfactory response see Fornara, *Athenian Board of Generals*, 61.

[2] Busolt, *GG* III:2, 1125. West, *CP* XIX (1924), 219, says, "All along the line Cleon's henchmen were preferred to his opponents."

Nicias himself, along with Nicostratus and Autocles, led the first Athenian expedition of the campaign of 424. In the early part of May he led an Athenian force of 60 ships, 2,000 hoplites, and some cavalry, as well as some Milesians and other allies in an attack on Cythera.[3] The plan was to seize it, place a garrison on it, and use it as a base for raiding the Peloponnese, since it lay just off the southeastern tip of Laconia (see Map 2). This was not in accord with the original Athenian strategy which included raiding enemy territory, ravaging the land, even taking cities, but not taking permanent possession and planting garrisons. Instead, the new strategy was to place bases on the periphery of the Peloponnese, such as the ones at Pylos and Methana, from which the Athenians could damage, harass, discourage, and demoralize the enemy in the hope of bringing him to his knees. After the failure of peace negotiations in 425, Nicias had no choice but to participate in this strategy if he wanted to maintain office and influence. It was, moreover, only an extension of the strategy of Pericles, one which he might have supported in the circumstances, and one which might, in fact, lead the Spartans to make concessions that the Athenians would accept. It did not run great risks, making use of Athenian superiority at sea, and omitting the confrontation of great hoplite armies that Pericles had wanted to avoid. We need not doubt that Nicias led the attack on Cythera gladly.

The island was very important to both sides. It served the Spartans as an entrepôt for the trade with Egypt that must have brought them grain and other items and as a base for deterring piracy and for defending the Peloponnesian coast. In the hands of Athens it could cut off that trade, serve as a springboard for raids on the Peloponnese, and as another stopping place on the route to the west that included Pylos, Zacynthus, Naupactus, and Corcyra.[4] In view of Cythera's importance we may wonder why the Athenians had not moved to take it earlier. Busolt has suggested that the disaster of Sphacteria had so frightened the Spartans that they removed the garrison and magistrate they regularly sent to the island in order to defend the homeland,

[3] 4.53.1; for the date see Gomme, *HCT* III, 507.
[4] 4.53.3; Gomme, *HCT* III, 510.

that the Athenians knew this, and attacked as a result.[5] The suggestion rests on Thucydides' failure to mention any Spartans in the battle which followed, but his omissions are many and hard to explain. Since he states plainly that the Spartans sent out the special magistrate called *Kytherodikes* and a garrison annually and that the Spartans "kept a careful watch over the place," [6] his failure to mention any withdrawal is even more striking.[7] We must believe that the garrison was still on the island when the Athenians attacked and explain their decision more simply as a result of their new, more aggressive strategy.

Nicias' plan was to divide his forces and make a two-part attack to confuse the enemy. With 10 ships and a small number of Milesian hoplites he landed at the seacoast town of Scandeia, while the main force landed on the northern shore of the island and marched toward the inland city of Cythera.[8] His force did not waste time with the usual ravaging but seized Scandeia immedately. The main force likewise did not delay but marched straight toward the city of Cythera where they found the enemy prepared. After a pitched battle the Cytheraeans and, presumably, their Spartan garrison fled to the upper town. Probably soon after this some of the Cytheraeans learned in private conversations with Nicias that they would be treated gently if they surrendered, but that if they resisted they would be expelled from their island. The Spartans probably were not included in these conversations. The Cytheraeans surrendered, leaving their fate to the discretion of the Athenians, except that the death penalty was expressly excluded. Nicias offered very generous terms. The natives were permitted to stay on their island and keep their land at the cost of a tribute payment of 4 talents annually; the only other change was that an Athenian garrison

[5] Busolt, *GG* III:2, 1126.   [6] 4.53.2: πολλὴν ἐπιμέλειαν ἐποιοῦντο.

[7] See Gomme, *HCT* III, 510.

[8] 4.54.1–2. The MSS give the number of Milesians as 2,000, which all agree is too large. Stahl suggested 500 and Classen 200 as the correct number, but there is no way of knowing. The text provided by the MSS also describes both Scandeia and the city of Cythera as being ἐπὶ θαλάσσῃ, but this is impossible since the descriptions are meant to make some geographical distinction. Some editors have suggested deleting the second ἐπὶ θαλάσσῃ, the one describing Cythera. I accept the emendation of Stahl which replaces it with ἀπὸ θαλάσσης.

replaced a Spartan one. The Cytheraeans were *perioikoi* of the Spartans, and we cannot be sure how unpleasant they found this new arrangement.[9]

The fall of Cythera struck the Spartans almost as hard as the loss of Pylos and the men on Sphacteria. The blow was all the more demoralizing because of the cumulative effect of a series of unexpected losses close to home. No sooner had the Athenians secured their control of Cythera than they launched raids on the coastal towns of Asine and Helus, among others.[10] The Spartans responded by sending garrisons to various places in the Peloponnese and by organizing for the first time a corps of 400 cavalry as well as a troop of archers. But the recent misfortunes had shaken their nerve. Thucydides vividly describes their state of mind:

They were very much on guard for fear that there would be a revolution against the established order, for the disaster they had suffered on the island was great and unexpected, Pylos and Cythera were captured, and from every direction a war rose up around them which was swift and defied precaution. . . . In military affairs they now became more timid than ever before since they were involved in a naval contest, outside their normal conception of preparation for war, and in this unaccustomed area they fought against the Athenians, to whom the omission of an enterprise was always a loss in respect to what they had expected to achieve. At the same time, the misfortunes that had struck them in such numbers unexpectedly and in such a short time caused great terror, and they were afraid that another calamity might again strike them sometime like the one on the island. For this reason they were less daring in going into battle, and they thought that whatever they undertook would turn

[9] They fought on the side of Athens in the Sicilian campaign (7.57.6), although the Peace of Nicias provided that the Athenians must restore the island to Sparta (5.18.7).

[10] 4.54.4. Gomme, *HCT* III, 510, says that Cythera was no suitable base for a raid on the Messenian town of Asine and that Thucydides may have been referring to another Asine mentioned by Strabo in connection with Gytheion on the Gulf of Laconia. "If this is correct," says Gomme, "and Thucydides meant this place, he should have distinguished it." More likely Thucydides meant the well known Asine in Messenia. The Athenians may have deliberately undertaken raids at unlikely and unexpected places to increase the Spartan confusion and alarm.

out badly because they had no self-confidence as a result of having little previous experience with misfortune.[11]

The immediate result was that the protective garrisons the Spartans had sent did little good. They generally refused to resist the invading Athenians, and on the one occasion when a garrison did offer battle it did so against light-armed troops and retreated when faced by hoplites. The Athenians next attacked Thyrea in Cynuria, the area which had long been a bone of contention between Sparta and Argos and which the Spartans had given to the Aeginetans whom the Athenians had expelled from their home island at the beginning of the war.[12] The question again arises as to why the Athenians chose this moment to attack, and once again part of the answer lies in the new aggressive spirit. The Athenians probably had learned of the fort the Aeginetans were building near the sea and that they decided to destroy it before it was completed. Some of the Spartan garrison troops were helping the Aeginetans in their task, and when the Athenians sailed up, they all retreated to the upper town, a little over a mile from the sea. The Aeginetans had wanted to make a stand in the partly built fort, but could not as the Spartans refused. A determined effort might have prevented the landing, but the Spartans' morale was not up to it. Even after their withdrawal the Spartan troops seem to have played little part in the ensuing battle, though their commander Tantalus fought alongside the Aeginetans. The Athenians landed unopposed and marched straight to Thyrea. They took the city and burned it, carrying off whatever valuables remained. Many of the Aeginetan defenders were killed; the rest were taken prisoner and with them the wounded Tantalus. All these, together with some Cytheraeans who had been thought dangerous and removed from their island, were sent to Athens. The Cytheraeans were scattered among the Aegean islands for safekeeping. Tantalus was imprisoned with the men from Sphacteria. All the Aeginetans were put to death "because they had always been enemies in the past."[13] As Gomme put it, "The 'customs of war' were becoming grimmer, as the fighting progressed."[14]

[11] 4.55.   [12] 4.56.   [13] 4.57.5.
[14] HCT III, 513. Diodorus (12.65.9) says that the men in Thyrea were taken off to Athens as slaves and kept prisoner there, while Plutarch

The Athenian success around the Peloponnese was not matched in Sicily. Since they had captured Messina in the spring of 425 the Syracusans and Locrians had held the initiative. When they learned that the large Athenian fleet under Sophocles and Eurymedon was delayed in the blockade of Sphacteria they were encouraged to take to the sea, reduce Rhegium by a combined land and sea attack, and so drive the Athenians from the straits (see Map 5). Deprived of a base on either side of the narrows, the Athenians would have no convenient harbor for their fleet and could play no large part in Sicilian affairs.[15] The Athenians were able to save Rhegium, but not to dominate the sea. Factional politics, which seem to have played no smaller part in the Greek cities of Sicily than in the rest of the Greek world, now appeared on the scene and forced the Athenians to weaken an already tenuous position. A report reached them that a pro-Syracusan faction was about to betray Camarina to the enemy. Camarina was the one Dorian city in Sicily that was allied to Athens. The Athenians could not afford to let it fall; they sailed to its rescue and were successful.[16] The cost, however, was to leave their friends near the straits undefended. With the Athenians away the Messenians attacked the neighboring town of Naxos, an ally of Athens as well as the next best base for their fleet on Sicily after Messina.[17] The first impact of the attack successfully shut the Naxians into their city. But the native barbarian Sicels who were their allies came to help and enabled the Naxians to break the encirclement and inflict a heavy defeat on the Messenians, killing more than a thousand men. The Athenian force under Sophocles and Eurymedon might have changed the tide, but it was busy blockading the harbor at Pylos. The weakened condition of Messina, nevertheless, invited an attack, and the Athenians returned from Camarina, together with the Leontines and other allies, and tried to recover the city. They were not strong enough to take the place by siege or storm, however, and withdrew to Rhegium, their goal unac-

---

(*Nic.* 6.7) seems to indicate also that the Aeginetans were not killed. It appears that there was a contrary tradition, but there is no reason here to prefer it to Thucydides.

[15] 4.24.   [16] 4.25.7; 3.86.2. Freeman, *History of Sicily* III, 41.
[17] Busolt, *GG* III:2, 1129.

complished and their prestige tarnished. The Athenians fought no more that year, but left the Sicilian Greeks to fight among one another without interference.[18]

At the end of the summer of 425, Sophocles and Eurymedon finally arrived at Sicily, but too late.[19] Their allies had become war-weary and, according to Timaeus, Eurymedon found it necessary to urge on the Sicilians,[20] who must have lost confidence in the will and capacity of Athens to fight for their interests while fighting for their own on the Greek mainland. We need not wonder that by the fighting season of 424 there was considerable peace sentiment on the island.

The first step toward general peace was made by Gela and Camarina. The two cities were natural friends, for the men of Gela had helped found Camarina. Camarina, however, was an old and implacable enemy of Syracuse, Gela's ally, and hatred for Syracuse, proving stronger than friendship for Gela, had placed the Camarinaeans among the enemies of Gela.[21] We have seen that in the previous year, some in Camarina were ready to change sides. Although the arrival of an Athenian force had prevented their success, the failure of Athens to take effective action in Sicily must have strengthened their hand as time passed. When Gela, worn out by the struggle, invited Camarina to make a separate peace the offer was accepted with enthusiasm.[22]

The two states would find it hard to remain safely at peace while a general war still raged on the island, so they invited the other cities to send representatives to Gela to try to arrive at a common agreement. The Sicilian cities complied, sending ambassadors who apparently had full powers to a diplomatic conference of a sort rare in Greek history.[23] The discussion began typically enough with squabbling over the selfish interests of each state. Hermocrates of Syracuse intervened, claiming to

[18] 4.25.   [19] 4.48.6.   [20] FGrH 566 F22.
[21] Freeman, *History of Sicily* III, 46–47.
[22] Thucydides (4.58) does not make it clear who made the request, but Timaeus (F 22) does, and there is no reason to doubt him. On this point see Westlake, *Essays*, 176.
[23] 4.58; Timaeus F22; for a discussion of the nature of the congress and the powers of the representatives see Freeman, *History of Sicily* III, 47–48 and 634–636.

speak in the interests not of his own city but of all Sicily. He urged that the Sicilians offer concessions in the name of compromise and peace. He spoke of the evil designs of Athens and her great power, a common threat. He advocated the noble idea that the Greeks of Sicily should ignore the racial differences between Dorian and Ionian that divided them and made them easy prey for outsiders. Instead he put forward a notion, new so far as we know, of a nation of Greek Sicily, of a lasting peace for all the Greek cities, of Sicily for the Sicilians. "We are, generally speaking, neighbors, and together we inhabit a single land surrounded by the sea and are called by one name, Siceliots. We shall go to war, I imagine, when the situation arises, and we shall make peace again by employing common discussions among ourselves. But if we are wise, when foreigners attack us we shall always act together to repel them, for if any of us is harmed individually we are all endangered. And we shall never again call in strangers as allies or mediators. If we do these things we shall not deprive Sicily, at the present time, of two advantages: to be rid of the Athenians and of our civil war. As for the future, we will live among ourselves in a free country and less exposed than now to dangers from outside." [24]

Hermocrates' speech has been called a Sicilian Monroe Doctrine, sincere and unselfish, for the common good,[25] but there is some reason for doubt. The Monroe Doctrine itself was hardly without special advantage to the state which promulgated it. As the most powerful nation in the western hemisphere the United States stood to gain most from the removal of outside influence, even if she had no designs on the territory of her weaker neigh-

---

[24] 4.64.3–5. Thucydides was certainly not present at the Congress of Gela and, as Gomme says, "This is one of the speeches which scholars feel *must* have been entirely composed by Thucydides out of his own head" (*HCT* III, 520). Freeman, however, presents very good arguments in *History of Sicily*, Appendix VI, 631–636, for believing that Thucydides has given us a reasonably accurate version of the ideas Hermocrates put forth in the speech. He employs the motto "Credo quia impossibile." "It is the very unexpectedness of the position taken by Hermokrates which is the strongest ground for believing it to be genuine" (p. 632).

[25] Freeman, *History of Sicily* III, 52; Westlake (*Essays*, 178–179) also defends Hermocrates' sincerity.

bors. Syracuse would benefit in the same way if the weaker Greek cities of Sicily agreed not to call in the powerful states of the Greek mainland. In 424, moreover, Syracuse and its leading position in Sicily were most in danger from Athens. Hermocrates' later behavior raises doubts of his sincerity. In 415 he urged the Syracusans to invite help against the Athenian invasion of 415 not only from the Greek cities of Corinth and Sparta, but even from Carthage, and he also urged the Siciliots to join in the war the Peloponnesians were waging against Athens even after the Athenians had been driven from Sicily.[26]

In 424, however, the weary Siciliots at Gela were won by the eloquence of Hermocrates, backed by the Syracusan evidence of good faith in ceding Morgantina to Camarina, and agreed to a peace on the basis of the status quo.[27] The Athenians, of course, were still near by with a considerable fleet. Their allies informed them of their decision to join in the peace and invited Athens to be included. At this point the Athenian generals had little choice. They lacked a base in Sicily, the allies they had come to help no longer were willing to fight, and their own force was inadequate to conquer Sicily. They agreed to be included in the peace and sailed for home. There is no reason, however, to believe that the peace was forced on unwilling Athenian generals.[28] If the outcome seemed unsatisfactory they could have refused to agree to it, and if agreement seemed desirable but likely to be unpopular in Athens they could have lingered abroad as Demosthenes had done after his defeat in Aetolia. But the generals had left Athens in the winter of 426/5, when the purpose of the expedition had been to protect the allies of Athens, prevent Syracuse from controlling all of Sicily, and, perhaps, study the prospects for further gains. The Congress of Gela, they might well believe, accomplished all these purposes, and they were probably not reluctant to go home.

On their arrival they were brought to trial on the charge that when they could have subjugated Sicily they accepted bribes to withdraw.[29] Such a charge was often leveled at unsuccessful commanders, or even those whose success had not

---

[26] 6.34.2; 8.26.1.   [27] 4.65.1.   [28] *Pace* Beloch, *GG*² II: 1, 336.
[29] 4.65.3.

been as complete as expected. The great Cimon himself almost forty years earlier had been charged with taking bribes not to invade Macedonia, though that was not part of his mission.[30] The generals may have accepted some presents from friends in Sicily,[31] but there is no evidence of bribery. The Athenians, nevertheless, convicted them all; Sophocles and Pythodorus were exiled and Eurymedon fined. Thucydides explains the condemnations as follows: "In this way, because of the good fortune they enjoyed at this time, they expected that nothing would go against them but that they could achieve equally what was easy and more difficult whether their power was adequate or insufficient. The cause of this was their implausible success in most undertakings which gave them the strength of hope." [32]

The Athenians of 424, after the victories at Pylos and Sphacteria, Methana and Cythera, had greater expectations than before and may have felt an unrealistic optimism. The formal charge certainly seems unjustified, and the conviction of the generals may have resulted from unreasonable expectations, but the Athenian people had some reason to be displeased with the generals. Athenians who had never gone to Sicily might have thought the commanders did very badly. The first expedition under Laches and Charoeades with only 20 ships had prevented a Syracusan victory, taken Messina, gained support from Sicilian Greeks and native Sicels, and created enough enthusiasm among the islanders that they sent a mission to Athens requesting more help. The Athenians could have believed that 40 more ships might bring the war to a quick end,[33] having received little news from Sicily between the arrival of that embassy and the return of the generals after the Congress of Gela.[34] These generals returned with the news that the war had been concluded on the

---

[30] Plut. *Cim.* 14.

[31] Busolt, *GG* III:2, 1133, does not believe the generals were bribed but says of their decision to accept the peace: "Geschenke mögen immerhin diesen Entschluss erleichert haben." Westlake, *Essays*, 120–121, likewise rejects bribery, conceding, however, that "possibly they had imprudently accepted presents from their Siceliot allies."

[32] 4.65.4.   [33] 3.115.4.

[34] Laches, relieved by Pythodorus in the winter of 426/5, would have reported much the same situation.

basis of "Sicily for the Sicilians," a slogan put forward by a leading aristocratic politician from Syracuse. The Athenians had
been informed, not consulted, by their allies and told of the
peace and that their services were no longer needed. Hermocrates might speak of "Sicily for the Sicilians," but the Athenians
had reason to believe that the slogan might be a cloak for "Sicily
for the Syracusans," and to fear in the future a Sicily united
under a Dorian state friendly to the enemy. The Athenians,
unaware of factional squabbles in allied cities and other problems,
might well believe that a Sicily almost conquered by an expedition of 20 ships had been lost by one of 60.

Sophocles, Eurymedon, and Pythodorus had, in fact, shown
little initiative and accomplished little. They had been delayed
at Pylos, and they arrived in Sicily too late to do much, but it
is important to emphasize, as Thucydides does not, that the people might blame the delay on them. Because the Spartan fleet
from Corcyra slipped by them and threatened Demosthenes at
Pylos they were forced to come back and engage in the long
blockade that took up most of the summer. Had they been more
vigilant, or fortunate, they could have arrived in Sicily soon
enough to make a great difference. Any people might decide to
dismiss its officers in such circumstances. The Athenians sometimes took stronger action, punishing failure with exiles and
fines. Such unfortunate action can deprive the state of the services of useful men, although Eurymedon, like Pericles, returned
to service and office after his disgrace. In this case the Athenian
action seems not to have been unreasonable but excessive. Those
who see in it the foolishness characteristic of democracy should
remember that Admiral Byng, who was executed, according to
Voltaire, "pour encourager les autres," was condemned in a
monarchy.

During the same summer, probably in July,[35] civil strife in
Megara offered Athens the opportunity to gain control of the
southern entrance to Attica and end the threat of invasion from
the Peloponnese. At the outbreak of the war Megara and Athens
were violently hostile toward each other. The war brought
terrible suffering to Megara. Each year the Athenians invaded

[35] Busolt, *GG* III:2, 1137.

and ravaged their territory.[36] Before the outbreak of hostilities the Megarian Decree kept the Megarians from the harbors of Athens and her allies, and afterward Athenian control of the sea must have cut off most Megarian trade by sea. The Athenian capture of Minoa in 427, which made it impossible for a boat to slip out of the port of Nisaea into the Saronic Gulf, pulled the noose still tighter. Almost certainly in the same year factional conflict led the Megarians to expel a group of extreme oligarchs.[37] The new democratic regime in Megara did not inspire confidence in Sparta or in her Peloponnesian allies, most of whom had oligarchic governments and were suspicious of states that shared the constitution and the dangerous democratic ideas of Athens. The Spartans showed their sympathy by settling the Megarian exiles at Plataea after the Plataeans had been removed. Perhaps about the same time the Peloponnesians placed a garrison of their own at Nisaea to watch the Megarians.[38] A year later the oligarchic exiles left Plataea, and probably then seized Pegae, the western port of Megara on the Gulf of Corinth. From there they added to Megara's problems by closing off the last remaining access to the sea and by conducting additional raids (see Map 7).[39]

By 424, Megara's situation was desperate. Her land was regularly devastated and she could get food and other needs only overland from the Peloponnese by way of Corinth. As a democratic state, however, she was disliked and suspected by the allies on whom she depended, and her freedom of action was limited by the exiles in Pegae and the Peloponnesian garrison at Nisaea. We need not wonder, therefore, that the Megarians decided to reduce their burdens by recalling their exiles. This would end the raids and the exclusion from Pegae, and it might lead to better relations with the Peloponnesians. The friends of the

[36] 2.31; 4.66.1.

[37] Thucydides first mentions these exiles in 3.68.3 when he tells that the Spartans settled them in Plataea. It is only in 4.66.1, however, that he mentions that they were exiled by the πλῆθος. When these exiles returned they killed the democrats and established a narrow oligarchy, 4.74.3–4. For a discussion of the date of this first *stasis* see Ernst Meyer, *PW* XV, 190–191, and R. P. Legon, *Phoenix*, XXII (1968), 214–215. My reliance on Legon's fundamental article will be evident.

[38] 4.66.4.   [39] 4.66.1.

exiles who were still in the city urged such action. The leaders of the democratic faction realized that the return of the oligarchs would mean disaster for them. They knew, moreover, that the common people were more concerned with alleviating their own sufferings than with preserving democracy. The democratic constitution did not have deep roots, for Megara appears to have been oligarchic for most of its history.[40] In fear the democrats turned to treason and to Athens.

They approached the Athenian generals Hippocrates and Demosthenes and offered to surrender Megara to them. The plan was to proceed in two stages: first the Athenians should gain control of the long walls connecting Megara to Nisaea and so prevent the Peloponnesian garrison from bringing help to the city. Then the democrats would try to hand over Megara.[41] Alliance with Athens would have solved most of Megara's problems. The Athenian invasions would cease, as would the naval embargo and blockade. The oligarchic exiles at Pegae could be put down with the aid of the Athenians, and both it and Nisaea would again be open for import and export, permitting Megara to regain her prosperity. Nor would association with Athens leave the Megarid open to attack from the Peloponnese. The border between Megara and Attica lay on a plain, and was impossible to defend. The southern boundary, however, touching Corinth, was protected by the Geraneia range. Properly manned and fortified, this ridge could keep the Peloponnesians out of the Megarid.

In light of these many advantages we may wonder why the leaders of the democratic faction in a democratic state needed to resort to secrecy and treason. Why could they not merely propose a shift of alliances in the open assembly? The answer tells us something important about Greek politics and foreign

[40] The evidence for the constitution of Megara is not good. I deduce the oligarchic nature of Megara's constitution most of the time from its comfortable membership in the Peloponnesian League down to the First Peloponnesian War and the absence of any reference to democracy in Megara before 427. Mantinea and Elis, to be sure, were democracies and members of the league, but they both had trouble with Sparta, in part on that account. For references to other discussions of this point see Legon, *Phoenix* XXII (1968), 212.

[41] 4.66.4.

policy. As between many Greek neighboring states a great mutual hatred existed between the Megarians and the Athenians. In the sixth century the two states had fought over possession of Salamis, and the Athenian victory certainly caused great resentment in Megara.[42] The marriage of convenience between the two states in the First Peloponnesian War ended when the Megarians slaughtered the Athenian garrison.[43] The years between the wars were marked by boundary disputes, accusations of sacrilegious murder, and, of course, the Megarian Decree.[44] The punishment inflicted by Athens during the war could hardly have made the Megarians more friendly. The proposal of an alliance with a bitterly hated enemy, however advantageous, was too cynical for the people of Megara to accept. Active politicians, whether democratic or oligarchic, may have been capable of vertiginous shifts in policy, ready to betray the independence and autonomy of their state in the interests of a faction or even in the interests of an ideal of government, but the common people were not. Legon states it well: "To the *demos* Megara was a sovereign state whose freedom was jeopardized by Athens. Any concession to the Athenians would have diminished Megara and exalted her enemy, and no Megarian patriot could allow this to happen." [45] The democratic leaders, therefore, had no choice but to call for Athenian action.

The Athenian plan for taking Nisaea was complicated and dangerous. Hippocrates sailed by night from Minoa with 600 hoplites, landed, and took cover in a trench near the walls. At the same time Demosthenes came overland by way of Eleusis with some light-armed Plataeans and Athenian hoplites from the frontier garrisons and set up an ambush at Enyalius, a bit closer to Nisaea.[46] All depended on surprise and secrecy; Demosthenes' troops were chosen because they were close at hand so that no time would be wasted in collecting them and no rumor could get out. The attempts at security were successful, for Thucydides tells us that "throughout the night no one knew what was happening except the men whose business it was to

[42] Arist. *Ath. Pol.* 17.2.   [43] 1.114.1.   [44] Plut. *Per.* 30.
[45] *Phoenix* XXII (1968), 221.
[46] 4.67.1–2; Gomme, *HCT* III, 529–530. See Map 1.

know." [47] At the same time the Megarians were preparing for their part in the three-pronged attack on the walls. Long in advance they laid the groundwork. Each night they received permission from the commander of the Peloponnesian garrison at Nisaea to open the gates long enough for them to wheel out a small boat on a cart. Their purpose, they said, was to slip by the Athenian fort on Minoa and perform acts of piracy against Athenian shipping. Before dawn they would return and bring their little boat back through the gates. On the night agreed the opening of the gate would permit the hidden Athenians to enter the walls.

The plan was risky, dependent on careful planning, the utmost secrecy, and precise coordination; any slip would mean failure. The Athenians, as in the previous campaigns of Demosthenes, were risking few of their own forces. If the plan was discovered those few could escape by sea or run safely home. The most imaginative schemes of Demosthenes characteristically promised great returns for a very small investment. On the night in question all went perfectly. The Megarian traitors had the gate opened to permit the boat to pass through and killed the guards. The Athenians under Hippocrates, right on time, ran from their ditch and kept the gate open. This gave Demosthenes and his force time to enter the walls; the Plataeans rushed in to fight off the late-arriving Peloponnesian reinforcements and shield the arrival of the Athenian hoplites. By daybreak the Athenians commanded the long walls. The entire plan was completed when a force of 4,000 Athenian hoplites and 600 cavalry, which had made a night march from Eleusis, arrived at the prearranged time to make the Athenian position secure and the conquest of Megara possible. [48]

Even though the Spartan garrison was routed and a large Athenian army at hand, the Megarian democrats knew the patriotism of their fellow citizens and their hatred for Athens too well to make a public appeal for a change of alliances. Instead they planned to urge the Megarians to march out of their gates and attack the Athenian army. They, themselves, would be marked so that the Athenians would know them and spare them

[47] 4.67.2; Gomme HCT III, 530.   [48] 4.67–68.

in battle; the others, presumably, would be slaughtered unless they surrendered. This was bitter medicine for all but the most determined and frightened men and was probably the reason one of the conspirators betrayed the plot to their enemies, men of oligarchic leanings, the friends of the exiles at Pegae. They did not immediately reveal the plot to the populace, fearing a riot or civil war. The Athenians were outside the wall with a large army and would take advantage of confusion to take the city by storm. Delay would give the Spartans and their allies time to bring up an army to confront the Athenians.[49] The enemies of the conspiracy, therefore, argued against marching out to a pitched battle and threatened to fight anyone trying to do so. Their argument was sound enough to win support, and the gates remained shut.[50] A critical part of the grand plan had gone wrong. Had the Megarian democrats maintained security or acted more quickly, the city would have fallen into Athenian hands swiftly and easily, before the Spartans could send an army. The Athenians still dominated the situation and were easily able to force the Peloponnesian garrison at Nisaea to surrender and pay a ransom. The Spartan commander and any other Spartans in the garrison were surrendered to the discretion of the Athenians. They were probably sent to Athens to join the other prisoners.[51]

The Athenians believed that the capture of the long walls and Nisaea would soon compel the surrender of Megara, too, but they reckoned without fortune and Brasidas. He was near Corinth and Sicyon, gathering an army for a different purpose when he heard what was happening at the gateway to the Peloponnese. He quickly sent word to Boeotia, asking that an army be sent to meet him at the little Megarian village of Tripodiscus. With his army of 2,700 Corinthian hoplites, 400 from Phlius, 700 from Sicyon, and perhaps a few hundred of his own troops,[52] he set out, hoping to save Nisaea. When he learned that it was too late, he left his army on its way to Nisaea and took 300 troops to the city of Megara. He meant the enemy to think that his purpose was to recapture Nisaea, a secondary

[49] Legon, *Phoenix* XXII (1968), 218, n. 25.   [50] 4.68.
[51] 4.69; Gomme, *HCT* III, 531.   [52] Gomme, *HCT* III, 532.

goal, as his chief concern was to prevent the fall of Megara. He must have feared treason within the city and wanted to place an army there to prevent its betrayal.

The Megarians, however, were unwilling to admit him. The democrats had good reason to believe that the entry of the Spartans would mean the return of the exiles, the restoration of oligarchy, and disaster for themselves. The friends of the exiles feared that the arrival of the Spartans would touch off a civil war and give the Athenian army the chance to take the city. Both sides preferred to await the result of the battle they were sure would occur between the Athenian and Peloponnesian armies. The victory would decide the future of Megara. Megara, therefore, a member of the Peloponnesian League, and under attack by a hated enemy, refused admission to an allied army sent to rescue the city.[53]

Meanwhile, the Boeotians were on their way. Even before receiving the summons from Brasidas they had resolved to come to Megara's aid, for they understood that Athenian possession of the Megarid would bar communication with the Peloponnese and leave the Athenians free to attack them.[54] When Brasidas' message came, their entire army was already at Plataea. Heartened by the news of Sparta's involvement, they sent 2,200 hoplites and 600 cavalry to Brasidas and sent the rest of the army home. The military situation was now changed drastically. No more than 5,000 Athenian hoplites faced 6,000 of the enemy. The original plan, depending on speed and surprise, had been to pit the considerable Athenian army against the Megarians alone and had counted on treason to open the gates and avoid a siege. Having no reason to suspect that an army would be gathering in the vicinity, the Athenians must have counted on having some days before Peloponnesian reinforcements came. The facts were surprising and discouraging. To take Megara now would require a pitched battle of the kind Pericles had excluded from his strategy and few Athenians sought. The Athenian generals were content to take up a defensive position before Nisaea and wait.

Brasidas, however, did not attack. He took up a strong de-

[53] 4.71.   [54] 4.72.1; Gomme, *HCT* III, 532.

fensive position and waited for the Athenians to take the initiative. Thucydides tells us that he thought he had a double advantage: if the Athenians attacked he held a superior position from which to fight; if they refused he would have achieved his purpose, the defense of Megara without a battle.[55] These calculations were reasonable, yet Brasidas' behavior is surprising. Here seemed to be the moment the Spartans had hoped for since the start of the war: a Peloponnesian army facing the Athenians with prospect of a pitched battle between hoplite phalanxes. Why, then, did this boldest of Spartan generals hold back? Some scholars have suggested that his restraint is evidence of Sparta's continued lack of self-confidence after its recent defeats,[56] and they blame him for not making an attack whose success "would have made a moral impression on both sides that should not be underestimated." [57] It is hard, however, to believe that the daring Brasidas who, both before and after the affair at Megara showed incomparable enterprise, was lacking in confidence. The explanation of Thucydides is perfectly sound. Additionally, the Athenian army was arrayed just outside a fortified place. If Brasidas had attacked it and gained the advantage the Athenians could have taken refuge in Nisaea and suffered few losses. On the other hand, the Athenians might win, which would be disastrous for Sparta. Even if the Spartans won after a long and hard battle, serious losses of men might prevent Brasidas from undertaking the expedition for which he had gathered an army originally, which held greater strategic importance even than the prospect of annihilating thousands of Athenian hoplites.

Brasidas' expectations were fulfilled. After the armies had spent some time drawn up in battle array, the Athenians withdrew into Nisaea. Brasidas returned to seek admission to Megara, and this time he was successful. The Athenian retreat had left the field to Brasidas and turned the tide within the city. The Athenian army went back to Attica, leaving a garrison to

[55] 4.73.1–3.
[56] Wilhelm Vischer, *Kleine Schriften* I (Leipzig, 1877), 77. He is followed by Busolt, *GG* III:2, 1139.
[57] Busolt, *GG* III:2, 1139, n. 1.

hold Nisaea. The Peloponnesian army was dissolved, and Brasidas was free to resume his original undertaking. The Athenians may have lost a great opportunity by leaving so soon. Gomme suggests that if they had remained in force at Nisaea, "they probably would have worn down the patience of the Peloponnesians; and if not that, they would have delayed decisively Brasidas' march into Thrace." [58] But as Gomme himself points out, the Athenians did not yet know of Brasidas' plans, and Demosthenes and Hippocrates had ambitious plans of their own that required troops and time for preparation.

In Megara, a revolution was inevitable. The democrats, exposed as traitors, fled the city as best they could, while the oligarchic exiles were restored. They swore an oath "not to remember past injuries but to plan for what was best for the city," [59] but they had vengeance in their hearts. They gained office and abused the democratic process to obtain the condemnation of such of their enemies who were still in the city. They then established a very narrow oligarchy. [60] Henceforth Megara was a loyal ally of Sparta and an even more bitter enemy of Athens.

After their return from Megara, probably about the beginning of August, [61] the Athenians began to prepare for the greatest and most intricate compaign yet conceived during the war. [62] The plan and origins of the campaign bear a striking resemblance to those at Megara, and the two campaigns may have been planned at the same time and be seen as complementary. [63] A successful attack on Megara would have guaranteed that no help would reach Boeotia from the Peloponnese, it would have discouraged

---

[58] HCT III, 535–536.   [59] 4.74.2.   [60] 4.74.3–4.
[61] Gomme, HCT III, 558.

[62] About the same time the Athenians sent a considerable force under three generals into the Aegean and Pontic regions to collect the newly assessed tribute. They quickly found trouble, for Anaea, opposite Samos, had previously been in the hands of exiles who caused trouble for the Samians in much the same way as Pylos did for the Spartans (3.19.2; 32.2; 4.75.1), and now exiles from Mytilene were fortifying Antandros, across from Lesbos, for the same purpose (4.52; 75.1). The Athenian generals gathered an allied army locally and defeated the men of Antandros, but the exiles at Anaea continued to flourish (4.75).

[63] Adcock, CAH V, 239, sees the attacks on Megara and Boeotia in 424 as two parts of a single scheme.

dissident forces within the Boeotian cities, and in every way it would have made the Boeotian enterprise easier. The fact that Megara had not fallen, however, did not deter Demosthenes and Hippocrates from attempting to remove Boeotia from the war.

At the heart of the scheme were negotiations between the Athenian generals and factional leaders in several towns who wanted to introduce democracy on the Athenian model into their cities and were willing to resort to treason.[64] Thucydides does not say whether they or the Athenians intitated the plot, but it is likely that Demosthenes and Hippocrates, eager to break the stalemate in the war and guarantee the security of Athens, tried to discover and make use of a "fifth column" of discontented democrats in oligarchic cities as the key to a new strategy. Such expectations were not farfetched. During the first Peloponnesian War democratic parties that resisted the domination of Thebes over the other Boeotian towns supported Athens and were placed in power after the Athenian victory at Oenophyta in 457.[65] Though they were overthrown after the victory of the oligarchs over the Athenians at Coronea in 447, these democratic factions remained alive, and the long years of the Archidamian War made them eager to cooperate with Athens again. There was every reason to trust them and to count on their support.

The plan was for treason to put Siphae, the port of Thespis, into Athenian hands, while Chaeronea, at the extreme western edge of Boeotia, bordering Phocis, would be betrayed.[66] At the same time the Athenians were to occupy the sanctuary of Apollo at Delium, just across the Athenian border, on the eastern shore of Boeotia.[67] As at Megara, the success of the plan depended on perfect timing to guarantee simultaneous attacks and prevent the Boeotians from massing their forces against the main Athenian army at Delium. It also depended on secrecy, for if word got out the delivery of Siphae and Chaeronea could be prevented. If the plan were successful, however, and the affair at Megara had

---

[64] 4.76.2.

[65] 1.108.1–3; 113; Diod. 11.81–3; Gomme, *HCT* I, 317–318; Walker, *CAH* V, 82, 469.

[66] See Map 1.   [67] 4.76.1–4.

shown that such a complicated scheme depending on secrecy and perfect timing could work, the results would be well worth the risk. At best the shock of the loss of three strongholds at once might weaken Theban resolve, encourage the dissident forces in Boeotia, and produce democratic, antifederalist rebellions which could make Athens the master of Boeotia as she had been from 457 to 447. Failing this, Athens would have three fortresses on the borders of Boeotia from which plundering expeditions could go forth and to which exiles could escape. In that case, as Thucydides makes clear, "the situation would not last long, but after a time, when the Athenians had come to the aid of the rebels and the forces of the enemy were scattered, they could settle matters to their own advantage." [68] In this second, less optimistic form the plan was an extension of the strategy of establishing permanent fortified bases in enemy territory that was working so well in Laconia. The Spartans would be prevented from sending help to their northern allies because they were fully occupied with their own troubles. The Boeotians would find themselves alone, jabbed at from three directions and unable to mass their troops against any one of them. The pressure might eventually make them crack.

The undertaking, however, was much bigger than the one against Megara, and this caused serious problems. The Athenians would need a considerable army for the main blow against Delium and another for the landing at Siphae. Athens had enough troops to do both jobs, but committing them would not leave enough reserve for an emergency and would expose more Athenian soldiers to danger than they were willing to risk. They counted, therefore, on Demosthenes' demonstrated ability to recruit useful troops from the allies in the northwest. Though reasonable, this meant a much longer lag between conception of the scheme and the moment of attack than in the assault on Megara. That gave the Boeotian and other foreign conspirators more time to let the secret out, but the risk was unavoidable.

The two generals agreed on the time to attack. Hippocrates stayed in Athens to prepare his army while Demosthenes sailed for Naupactus with 40 ships. There he found that the friendly

[68] 4.76.5.

Acarnanians had forced the people of Oeniadae, formerly hostile, to join the Athenian alliance and the expedition. He then turned to raising a levy in Acarnania, but was forced to fight against Salynthius and his Agraeans. After defeating them he waited for the moment fixed for the attack on Siphae.[69] Some three months passed between the departure of Demosthenes from Athens and his appearance at Siphae.[70] The delay is hard to explain, for he did not need that long in the northwest, nor does Thucydides indicate that the attack was postponed. The long wait was probably due to the need of the Boeotian deomcrats to prepare their coup. They apparently initiated the idea of betraying their cities to Athens and proposed it to Demosthenes and Hippocrates.[71] They also must have fixed the date of the attack to suit their own needs, and the date they set required more delay than was needed by Demosthenes for recruiting troops and settling affairs in Acarnania.

At last, early in November, Demosthenes and his army appeared on their ships in the harbor at Siphae, but everything had gone wrong. A Phocian member of the conspiracy had revealed the plot to the Spartans who had told the Boeotians. Armies were sent to occupy both Chaeronea and Siphae, and the rebels dared not move. If the timing of the double attack had been properly coordinated some of the occupying troops might have been drawn off by Hippocrates' attack on Delium, but this, too, misfired. Demosthenes arrived before Hippocrates, and the Boeotians were free to concentrate on him. Which of the generals was in error is not clear, but it did not matter much. The main failure was in secrecy. Once the Boeotians had prevented the rising at Siphae and controlled the shore where Demosthenes was to disembark, he could not force his way onto the land, as he had pointed out to his men at Pylos.[72] He could do nothing but look on helplessly and sail off.

Hippocrates marched to Delium with an army that was large by Athenian standards: about 7,000 hoplites, and a great mass of others, well over 10,000, metics and foreign allies as well as Athenians, who were largely unarmed and were meant only to

[69] 4.77.   [70] 4.89.1; Gomme, HCT III, 558.   [71] Diod. 12.69.1–2.
[72] 4.89; 10.5.

help build a fortification at Delium quickly.[73] The movement of so large an army of hoplites into enemy territory was not in complete violation of the Periclean principle of avoiding hoplite battles. The main purpose of the expedition was to establish a fort at Delium. The function of the army, we may suppose, was merely to overawe a challenging Boeotian army, which would be small because the main Boeotian force would be distracted by Demosthenes at Siphae and the rising at Charonea. When the fort was secure only a small garrison would be needed to hold it and exploit its possibilities. The main army could return home without danger; Demosthenes and Hippocrates never intended to risk it in battle against an army of comparable size.

The march to Delium took two days. Three more were required to complete the fort. Hippocrates had been at Delium for three days, completed his mission, and seen nothing of the Boeotian army. He must have assumed that all was going well in the west and prepared to bring his army back home. Had the Boeotians been expected to try to hinder the retreat with any considerable force the plan could have provided for a return by sea. Had Hippocrates thought that the Boeotians would try to intercept his army he might have moved quickly to Oropus in the opposite direction and so avoid a battle.[74] Hippocrates, however, knew neither that the other two-thirds of the plan had failed nor what the Boeotians were doing. He sent the bulk of his army home on the direct route to the south, the hoplites stopping about a mile away to wait for Hippocrates who was completing his final dispositions at Delium.[75]

Hippocrates could not know that the Boeotians, informed of the Athenian plan and free to deploy their troops where they would, were gathering at Tanagra, just a few miles from Delium. The Boeotians had 7,000 hoplites, the same number as the Athenians, but in addition they had 10,000 light-armed troops, who were armed and ready for battle, 1,000 cavalry, and 500

[73] 4.94.1; 90.1.
[74] See discussions of Gomme, HCT III, 558–560, and the fine topographical study of Pritchett, who persuasively argues that the site of the battle was a plateau near the modern village of Dilesi and that it suits the description of Thucydides quite well.
[75] 4.90.

peltasts.[76] In spite of Boeotian superiority and the Athenian success in building a fort in their territory, nine of the Boeotarchs, who were the magistrates of the federal league of Boeotia, wanted to avoid battle. They knew that the Athenians, on their way home, were almost in Athenian territory on the borders of Oropus.[77] Their view was shortsighted, for the right strategy was not to permit the fort at Delium to stand, and not to lose the rare opportunity to catch an outnumbered Athenian army in the field. Their attitude reflects the common Greek reluctance to accept the casualties that result from a hoplite battle. Perhaps it may also show that only Thebes among the Boeotian cities was ardent in pursuit of victory, for the two Boeotarchs who argued for staying and fighting were both Thebans.[78]

The more determined and persuasive of these was Pagondas son of Aeolidas, the commander of the army, probably the aristocratic subject of an ode by Pindar, and if so, a man over sixty.[79] He realized that the Athenians were in a vulnerable position and that an unexampled opportunity must not be lost. He persuaded the Boeotians to stand and fight. They marched forward to a position where a ridge separated the two armies.[80] Pagondas arranged his troops with ingenuity and originality. On either flank he placed cavalry and light-armed troops to counteract any turning movement by the Athenians. Their role was vital, for in the hoplite phalanx he placed the Theban contingent on the right to the extraordinary depth of twenty-five compared to the usual eight, leaving the hoplites from the other cities to line up at varying depths. This is the first recorded employment of the very deep wing in a hoplite phalanx, a tactic which would be used with devastating effect by Epaminondas of Thebes and Philip and Alexander of Macedon in the next century. The Boeotian right wing would almost surely defeat the enemy's left. On the other hand, the enemy, arrayed at the usual depth of eight, would have a longer line, since the number of hoplites was equal, and could threaten a flanking movement. Success for the Boeotians would depend on a quick victory for the Thebans on the right, leading to a rout. At the same time

---

[76] 4.93.3.   [77] 4.91.1.   [78] 4.91.1.   [79] Gomme, *HCT* III, 560.
[80] 4.93.1.

the cavalry and light-armed men on the left flank must prevent the Athenians from turning that flank and starting a rout there.

Hippocrates willingly accepted battle. We cannot be sure that escape was still possible when he first heard of the approach of the Boeotian army, but he appears not to have thought of it. In his exhortation to his troops he does not suggest that the battle is unavoidable but says rather that it is a great opportunity. "If we win, the Peloponnesians, deprived of the Boeotian cavalry, will never again invade your country; in a single battle you not only gain this land but also guarantee the freedom of your own." [81] This was the rationale for the entire Boeotian campaign: to drive Boeotia from the war, remove it permanently as a threat to Athens, and deprive the Peloponnesians of the ally they needed to make war on Athens. In spite of the failure of the three-pronged attack, and the size of the Boeotian army must have shown Hippocrates that it had failed, a victory in battle might accomplish everything that had been desired. A man of Hippocrates' views and spirit could not let the chance slip by.

Hippocrates had only reached the center of his line with his speech that must be repeated several times to reach all the troops, when the Boeotian army appeared at the top of the ridge. He was on lower ground, and therefore at a disadvantage, 300 of his cavalry had been left to guard Delium and join in the fighting if the battle moved that way,[82] and he had few light-armed troops, yet Hippocrates neither withdrew nor waited, but ordered his men to attack on the run.[83] Hippocrates has been criticized for this maneuver,[84] but his thinking is easy to understand. When he saw the enemy order he realized at once that he could outflank the phalanx on his right, and he wanted to exploit that opportunity before it was closed off. He must have noticed, too, that the ravines on either side of the battlefield hampered the activities of the cavalry and light-armed troops on the flanks where he was inferior.[85] He could not, of course, see that the Thebans on the right were unusually deep. Even so, his

[81] 4.95.2.   [82] 4.93.2.   [83] 4.96.1.

[84] Henderson, Great War, 235, says "This order was perhaps unwise."
[85] Pritchett, Studies in Ancient Greek Topography, II (Berkeley and Los Angeles, 1969), 35.

decision, which was both swift and daring, was also shrewd, and it almost was crowned with success.[86]

The Athenians on the right quickly broke the Boeotian left held by the Thespians, Tanagrians, and Orchomenians and produced a rout. Meanwhile the Thebans at the opposite end of the field were not doing so well. They had superior weight and the advantage of higher ground, but the tough Athenians opposite them gave ground slowly, step by step, and would not break and run.[87] This was a moment of great peril for the Boeotians and hope for the Athenians. If nothing intervened the Athenian right would roll up the Boeotian line before the Thebans on their right could do the same to the Athenians. The Thebans would be caught in a pincers and the Boeotian army routed and perhaps destroyed. At this point Pagondas displayed great presence of mind and a touch of tactical genius that turned the tide. He sent two cavalry squadrons from the right wing around behind the hill, out of sight of the Athenians, to assist the beleaguered left. They appeared behind the victorious Athenians and threw them into a panic, for they thought a completely new army had arrived to take them in the rear. This broke the momentum of the Athenian charge and gave the Thebans time to break the Athenians opposite them and turn them to rout. The Athenian army was now a mob; some fled toward Delium and the sea, some toward Oropus, some directly south toward Mount Parnes. Their flight was hampered by the pursuit of the Boeotian cavalry as well as some Locrian horse that had come up just as the rout began. Only the fall of night prevented even a greater slaughter. The next day those who had been able to get to Delium or Oropus were ferried home by sea.[88] No doubt they bitterly thought that the ships might have been sent a day or two earlier. When the Athenians were finally permitted to take up their dead after long and complicated negotiations they found they had lost, in addition to many light-armed troops and

[86] The usual explanation for the Athenian action is that Hippocrates was forced to fight by the charging Boeotians (Busolt, *GG* III:2, 1148, and Henderson, *Great War*, 235). But this does not explain why he did not stand where he was to meet the charge or retreat to reduce its impact, but ordered a charge himself.

[87] 4.96.1–5.   [88] 4.96.2–8.

noncombatants, almost a thousand hoplites, among them the general Hippocrates, the heaviest losses by far in the Archidamian War.[89]

The victorious Boeotians were determined to remove the Athenian fortress at Delium. They sent to the region of the Malic Gulf for slingers and javelin throwers and to Corinth for an additional 2,000 hoplites. They also got help from the men who had formed the Peloponnesian garrison at Nisaea and from the Megarian oligarchs. The problem of taking a fortress by storm was still so great in the fifth century that ingenuity was required. The Boeotians and their allies constructed a kind of enormous flame thrower with which they set fire to the walls and drove the defenders off. In this way Delium was taken; an unknown number of the garrison, probably only a few, were killed, and 200 were captured. The rest made their way to the sea and the Athenian ships that took them home. The attempt to drive Boeotia from the war came to nothing and at a heavy cost.[90]

The battle of Delium was especially famous in antiquity, perhaps because Socrates fought bravely in it as a hoplite and Alcibiades with the cavalry.[91] It deserves attention because of the strategic and tactical brilliance displayed by Pagondas, the courage of Hippocrates and his Athenian hoplites, and its strategic and psychological importance for the course of the war. The failure to knock Boeotia out of the war left the Spartan coalition intact and encouraged its members to hold out against Athens after victory had seemed impossible and defeat imminent. On the other hand, the disastrous end of the campaign and the death of Hippocrates badly hurt the aggressive faction in Athens and raised the influence of those favoring a negotiated peace.

In light of the failure of the Boeotian campaign and the serious consequences that followed scholars have condemned it as "radically unsound." [92] Some critics have been influenced by the idea

---

[89] 4.101.2.   [90] 4.100.

[91] For references see Gomme, HCT III, 567–568. See also Busolt, GG, III:2, 1149, n. 3.

[92] Henderson, Great War, 231; Beloch, GG² II:1, 334, condemns it as "zu kompliziert" and lacking in "der nötigen Präzision."

that the Periclean strategy of defense was the only correct one.[93] Others regard the strategy and tactics of Napoleon as expounded by Clausewitz, the strategy of direct assault, as the only correct one and view complicated schemes and maneuvers with contempt. "The co-operation of armies acting from different bases of supply has been condemned again and again by Napoleon. Simplicity, he declares, is the keynote of success in warlike operations." [94] To the first complaint we have suggested that the Periclean strategy had already failed; by 424 it was a thing of the past. To the latter we must point out that the Napoleonic-Clausewitzian strategy is no good to an army inferior in numbers and morale to its enemy. Danton during the French Revolution could demand "audace, toujours l'audace"—he had the largest and most spirited army in Europe. When the French army relied on such advice in 1914 it produced not victory but near suicide. If they wanted to win the war, the Athenians were right to try to remove Boeotia as an enemy. Given their inferiority in hoplites, cavalry, and light-armed troops, they were right to rely on surprise and the strategy of divide and conquer. Nor can they be blamed for risking too much. The plan as originally conceived risked little. Demosthenes would not land at Siphae unless the revolutions had made it safe to do so. There was no intention to fight at Delium or anywhere with a great army. If something had gone wrong in that area the road back home was secure. The combination of the failure of secrecy, confusion in timing, and the decision of Hippocrates not to retreat produced the disaster. Even then it took a brilliant tactical maneuver by Pagondas to defeat the Athenians. The Boeotian campaign, probably devised by Demosthenes, was both sound and imaginative. With a bit of luck it might have produced an important victory, but in 424 luck was running against Athens.

In mid-August, while the Athenians were preparing their attack on Boeotia, Brasidas took an army northward toward Thrace to threaten the only part of the Athenian Empire acces-

[93] Bengtson, GG, 227, calls the defeat at Delium "ein Zeichen für die Richtigkeit des perikleischen Kriegsplanes!"
[94] Henderson, Great War, 231.

sible to the Spartans.[95] This army, consisting of 700 helots armed as hoplites and 1,000 mercenary hoplites from the Peloponnese,[96] happened to be gathering near Corinth when the Athenians attacked Megara and thus enabled Brasidas to save that city.[97] The Spartans had anticipated a northward expedition at least since 426 when they established the colony at Heraclea. By 424 their situation was desperate. The Athenian harassment of the Peloponnese from Pylos and Cythera was becoming unbearable, and the Spartans were ready to seize on almost any plan to divert the enemy.[98] They were glad to be rid of 700 bold and able-bodied helots at a time when the Athenian presence at Pylos made the idea of escape or revolution most appealing to the subjugated population. The only Spartiate in the army was its commander; the Spartans were clearly unwilling to risk much. Yet they would have liked to gain control of the Athenian allies in the Thraceward region. These did not, to be sure, contribute much to the Athenian treasury and were not very important, except for Amphipolis, which, as Brunt has pointed out, "was of the greatest value to Athens, both for its mining revenues and timber and for its strategic situation commanding the passage of the Strymon; control of Amphipolis would open the route to the rich subject allies of Athens to the east and even imperil Athens' grain supply through the Hellespont or Bosporus."[99]

In light of the importance of this region, its relative vulnerability, and the opportunities it presented, we may wonder why the Spartans had not tried to attack it earlier in the war. In part, the answer lies in the traditional conservative caution of the Spartans, their unwillingness to send any considerable army far from the Peloponnese. Beyond that, however, the undertaking was dangerous. Between Heraclea and Thrace lay Thessaly, formally allied to Athens, a flat land and difficult for a hoplite army to march through safely if threatened by the splendid Thessalian cavalry. There was also the problem of supply. Normally the Spartans had no friends in northern Greece who could be relied on to supply their troops, nor could they be

---

[95] 4.78.1; for the date see Busolt, *GG* III:2, 1141 and n. 3.   [96] 4.80.5.
[97] 4.70.1.   [98] 4.80.1.
[99] *Phoenix* XIX (1965), 274, based on 4.108.1 and 105.1.

supplied by sea while Athens ruled the waves. Brasidas, optimistic, daring, and energetic, was eager to make the attempt.[100] We may guess that the establishment of Heraclea in 426 as a base for such a campaign was his idea.

Before 424, however, the undertaking was imposible. Then the Bottiaeans and Chalcidians, who had been in revolt from Athens since 432, and Perdiccas, the treacherous king of the Macedonians, sometimes at peace or allied with Athens but at heart always its enemy,[101] invited the Spartans to send an army to Thrace, each for his own reasons. The rebels were frightened by the recent successes of Athens and believed that soon an army would come to put them down. They were secretly supported by the Athenian subjects in the region who were still ostensibly the allies of Athens. Brasidas could expect good will if he ever got to Thrace. Perdiccas, though formerly at peace with Athens, also feared her new power. Besides, he had a private quarrel with Arrhabaeus, the king of the Lyncestians, and wanted to enlist the Peloponnesian army in his cause.[102]

All this, coupled with the troubles facing Sparta in 424, enabled Brasidas to persuade his government to send his expedition to the north. This was a most dangerous undertaking, one on which the Spartans would risk none of their own troops. Its audacity is comparable to the Aetolian and Boeotian campaigns of Demosthenes and equally the product of an unusually daring and imaginative military mind. If Brasidas failed, as well he might, he would be condemned as a reckless fool. Small wonder that the Athenians did not expect the expedition and did little to prevent it.

Brasidas needed all his personal and diplomatic talents to get his army through Thessaly. The common people of Thessaly were friendly to Athens, and no Greeks wanted a foreign army to march through their territory. As Thucydides says, "If Thessaly had not been ruled by a narrow oligarchy (*dynasteia*), as is usual in that country, rather than a constitutional government Brasidas would never have gotten through."[103] From

[100] 4.81.1.   [101] Brunt, *Phoenix* XIX (1965), 274.   [102] 4.79.
[103] 4.78.3; I accept Hude's reading of ἐγχωρίῳ in place of the MSS' τὸ ἐγχώριον. For a discussion of the difficulties see Gomme, *HCT* III, 542–543.

Heraclea, however, he sent a messenger to friends at the important Thessalian city of Pharsalus. They arranged for him to be met south of Thessaly proper by men of the region, some of whom were closely connected with either Perdiccas or the Chalcidians. These men were to guide him through their country and use their influence to guarantee his safety.

Even then the course was not easy. Brasidas, his army, and their guides were stopped in Thessaly by men of a different faction, presumably advocates of "constitutional government of their usual kind." The expedition might have foundered at its beginning, but for a combination of smooth talk and trickery. The guides professed merely to be showing hospitality to unexpected strangers (in the form of 1,700 hoplites!), while Brasidas pointed out that there was no quarrel between Thessaly and Sparta, inviting, by implication, the Thessalians to walk through Laconia sometime. He promised that he would go no further without permission, pointing out that he could not do so since they barred the way, and requesting politely that they cease doing so. This confused the Thessalians; they had, moreover, been taken unaware, were surely outnumbered, and needed time to organize resistance. They had little choice but to back off. No sooner were they out of the way than Brasidas raced off to the safety of Pharsalus by forced march without any stops. From there his Thessalian escort was able to take him the rest of the way to Dium, a Macedonian town at the edge of the southern slope of Mount Olympus, in the territory of Perdiccas.[104]

When news reached the Athenians that Brasidas had arrived in the north, they took action to safeguard their interests in that area. They declared Perdiccas an enemy and "established a stricter watch over their allies there."[105] This may have been when Thucydides and Eucles were sent out to safeguard Amphipolis and Eion.[106] Brasidas' troubles were not over when he reached Macedonia. Perdiccas had called the Peloponnesians to his country in large part to use them against his fellow Macedonians, the Lyncestians. Brasidas, of course, had come for other purposes, and was not eager to waste either time or men

[104] 4.78.   [105] 4.82.   [106] Gomme, HCT III, 550.

on such an escapade. But he did not wish to alienate Perdiccas, who was helping to support his army and could be difficult. When the joint Peloponnesian and Macedonian armies arrived at the pass leading to Lyncus in northwestern Macedonia the disagreement came out into the open.

When Arrhabaeus heard that a Peloponnesian army was on the scene, he offered to submit the quarrel with Perdiccas to arbitration by Brasidas. The Spartan general was glad to discuss the matter, for while Perdiccas was suing for Spartan help, he had indicated that he would bring many peoples in his general territory into the Spartan alliance. Besides, the Chalcidians did not want Perdiccas' problems solved, fearing he would lose interest in their quarrel with Athens, perhaps even leave the entire cost of the Peloponnesian army in their hands. For these reasons, too, Brasidas wanted a free hand to deal with the Lyncestians. Perdiccas faced a test of who would control the expedition, and he tried to exercise the authority he thought belonged to him for paying half the costs. Brasidas would not be bluffed; he quarreled with Perdiccas, ignored his objections, and held the meeting with Arrhabaeus. As a result he withdrew without a battle. The disgruntled Perdiccas responded by reducing his support of the army to one-third instead of one-half; some of his demands must have been met, and he had not the courage to defy the fierce Spartan further. Brasidas had passed his second test.[107]

Late in August the Peloponnesian army appeared before the town of Acanthus, on the northeastern finger stretching southward into the Aegean from the Chalcidic peninsula.[108] Brasidas may have chosen it for his first assault because it could provide a base on the Strymonian Gulf for the attack on Amphipolis that was his main goal, but he may have learned of internal strife that might make the town vulnerable.[109] There was a factional split between some who worked with the Chalcidians and

[107] 4.83; Gomme, *HCT* III, 550–551.

[108] 4.84.1; for the date see Gomme, *HCT* III, 551; for the location see Map 8.

[109] Gomme (*HCT* III, 551) makes the first suggestion and points out that Thucydides, as so often, does not explain the strategic or political reasons for the action.

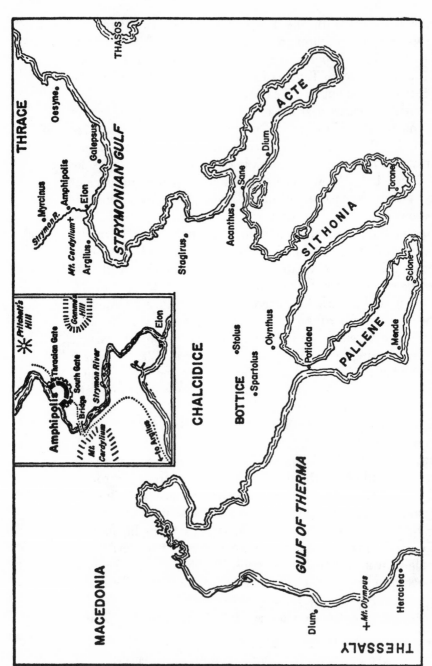

Map 8. The Chalcidic Peninsula and Amphipolis. Adapted from *The Cambridge Ancient History*, Vol. V (Cambridge, England: Cambridge University Press, 1927), by permission of the publisher.

wanted to invite the Peloponnesians in and the demos. The situation resembled the one the Athenians had faced at Megara earlier in the year, but in reverse. Brasidas, however, made no attempt to take the place by storm or by treachery. Instead he resorted to a technique rare among generals and almost unique among Spartans: rhetorical skill.[110]

He asked to be permitted into the city alone and unattended and there to make his case, leaving the Acanthians to decide. His tact and demeanor must have been persuasive, but Thucydides says that common people admitted him because they feared for the grape harvest that had not yet been gathered. Brasidas employed a combination of gentle words and threats in his speech to the Acanthians. He emphasized Sparta's role as liberator of the Greeks. He promised to leave the city autonomous and avoid involvement in factional disputes. He argued that the Acanthians should not fear Athenian retaliation if they should change sides, claiming that the Peloponnesians could protect them and exaggerating the significance of the Athenian reluctance to fight at Megara. Finally, he threatened to destroy the crops, just ready for harvest.[111] After considerable debate and by secret ballot the Acanthians voted to revolt from Athens and admit the Peloponnesians "because of the seductive words of Brasidas and fear for their crops." [112] The revolt of Acanthus induced the nearby Andrian colony of Stagirus to join in the rebellion.[113] Brasidas had achieved a crucial first success, and his campaign was gaining momentum.

Early in December, Brasidas set out from the Chalcidice on a campaign against Amphipolis, the Athenian colony that was the main target of his expedition to the north.[114] The city was important to the Athenians as a source for the timber that enabled them to rule the sea. Although it did not pay tribute, it produced

---

[110] Thucydides says with delicious irony or condescension, it is not clear which, that Brasidas "was not an incompetent speaker, though a Spartan" (4.84.2).

[111] 4.85–87.   [112] 4.88.1.   [113] 4.88.2.

[114] 4.102.1; for the date see Busolt, GG III:2, 1151 and n. 5. For the argument as to whether Amphipolis was a colony see Kagan, *Outbreak*, 187, n. 24. To that note I would now add R. E. Bauman, "A Message for Amphipolis," *A Class* XI (1968), 174–175.

significant revenue perhaps from silver mines near by and from tolls collected on the bridge over the River Strymon on which Amphipolis sat. Its exemption from tribute was probably due to the position it occupied as the main Athenian stronghold east of the Chalcidic peninsula. If it fell, the road to the Hellespont and control of the lifeline of Athens was open to the Spartans.[115] Its capture by the Spartans, moreover, might well have led to a general rebellion in the entire area.

Such an important city, of course, was well located and well fortified.[116] Lying on a sharp bend in the river, it was defended by water in three directions. A bridge across the river gave access to the city from the west, which, when there was danger, must be carefully guarded. If an enemy made his way across the river he would meet a wall facing west that surrounded the hill on which Amphipolis was built. To the east the city was protected by another wall which, in effect, turned it into an island. A small fleet could easily defend it from attack from the west.[117] Amphipolis, however, had serious weaknesses that might make it particularly vulnerable to a siege. Its citizenry included only a few Athenians, consisting chiefly of what Thucydides calls "a mixed multitude," [118] among them some settlers from nearby Argilus. The people of Argilus viewed Amphipolis with great secret hostility,[119] and the Argilians within Amphipolis were not trustworthy. In case of an attack and siege Amphipolis would be endangered from within as well as without.

We may be sure that Brasidas knew all this, for he was advised by Macedonians, Chalcidians, and Argilians. His plan of attack employed every advantage offered by nature and by these political facts. He planned his march so as to arrive at Bormiscus at dusk.[120] He stopped only for a meal and then marched through the dark and snowy night to Argilus where he was happily received by the people whom Thucydides considers the most enthusiastic plotters against Amphipolis. Argilus immediately

[115] On the importance of Amphipolis see 4.108.1–3 and Kagan, Outbreak, 186–188.
[116] See map in Gomme, HCT III, 654.
[117] For the topography of Amphipolis see Pritchett, Studies, 31–45.
[118] 4.106.1.   [119] 4.103.3.4.   [120] 4.103.1; see Map 8.

declared its rebellion from the Athenian alliance, and, still before dawn, Brasidas and his army were led to the bridge over the Strymon. Control of that bridge was crucial to the success of the attack. Their arrival in a snow storm at night caught the guards at the bridge completely by surprise, and even within that small body of troops some were traitors. The Peloponnesians easily gained control of the bridge and all the land outside the city walls.[121]

Brasidas' unorthodox tactics threw the entire city into confusion. The Amphipolitans were stunned by his arrival. Many prisoners were captured outside the walls, and within them the old suspicions between different kinds of settlers broke out furiously. Brasidas himself appears to have underestimated the shocking effect of his coup, for Thucydides reports, without attribution or comment, the opinion that if Brasidas had attacked the city immediately instead of pillaging the countryside he could have taken Amphipolis.[122] His delay is quite understandable, for to storm a fortified place with such a small army was a fearsome thing, sure to produce casualties and likely to produce failure. The usual way to take a walled town was by treachery, and Brasidas counted on that. But the Amphipolitans soon recovered their courage and were able to prevent any traitors from opening the gates. Brasidas, seeing that his first plan had failed, made camp and waited. His position was like the one in which Demosthenes and Hippocrates had found themselves after taking Nisaea and breaking into the long walls to Megara. Had he depended on force of arms, he, like them, would almost certainly have failed.

In Amphipolis, Eucles, the Athenian commander of the garrison, immediately sent word by a semaphore system of some kind,[123] to Thucydides, son of Olorus, the historian of the Peloponnesian War, who was in command of the Athenian fleet in the Thraceward region, asking him to bring help to the threatened city. Thucydides was not at Eion, less than three miles away near the mouth of the Strymon, but at Thasos, about a

---

[121] 4.103.4–5.   [122] 4.104.2.
[123] See Gomme, *HCT* III, 579, and Bauman, *A Class*, IX (1968), 177–179.

half-day's sail away.[124] The Amphipolitans had clearly counted on his being on guard at Eion whence his fleet could come to the rescue almost immediately.[125] Scholars have tried to explain why Thucydides was at Thasos and not Eion, but he himself offers no explanation.[126] He may have been trying to gather troops to help reinforce Amphipolis, though we have no evidence for such a purpose. Perhaps, as seems more likely, his trip had nothing to do with Amphipolis, and he was completely surprised, like Eucles and the others. In any case, his delay in arriving was critically important.

Brasidas certainly placed great weight on the impending arrival of Thucydides and the fleet, fearing not only its material influence, but its psychological impact. He knew that Thucydides had considerable influence in the region, and so did the men of Amphipolis. If the popular party saw Thucydides arrive with his ships they would be encouraged and expect his personal influence to bring additional help from the neighborhood, which would guarantee their continued resistance and end the Peloponnesians' hope that the city would be betrayed.[127] Thucydides tells us that these fears moved Brasidas to haste and led him to offer moderate terms of surrender to the Amphipolitans. Brasidas, of course, had offered moderate terms at Acanthus, as was fully in accord with his general strategy; Brasidas wanted Amphipolis and would have offered almost any terms to get it, regardless of Thucydides and his fleet. His fear of the arrival of Thucydides gives an important clue to Brasidas' own estimate of his situation. As R. A. Bauman has put it: "To Brasidas the decisive event would be Thucydides' arrival. And in the context Brasidas expected it to happen, in other words he thought that the town could and would hold out. In short, he believed that he could not take Amphipolis by assault *at all*, and that he

---

[124] 4.104.5. .

[125] 4.108.1. Delbrück, *Strategie*, 185–186, has tried to argue that Eion could not be a naval base because it had no harbor. He offered no evidence for this hypothesis which, in any case, seems to be contradicted by 4.108.1. For further contrary arguments see Busolt, *GG* III:2, 1156, n. 2, and Westlake, *Essays*, 135.

[126] For a discussion of some of the explanations see Gomme, *HCT* III, 585–588, and Westlake, *Essays*, 135–136.

[127] 4.105.1.

could not even do so on terms unless these were accepted before Thucydides arrived." [128]

Eucles and the Amphipolitans, of course, did not know what was in Brasidas' mind. He was a famous soldier and a dangerous opponent full of stratagems, as they had already learned to their sorrow. They knew that Thucydides had only a few ships, which might have been important in defending the city if the enemy had not already crossed the river and taken the bridge, but which would be of little value otherwise. His recruiting abilities would be of no use in the immediate crisis. An assault with or without tricks or treachery was imminent. Though attacks on walled towns were rarely successful, they sometimes worked, and if anyone could bring it off Brasidas was that man. If the city were taken the results for the citizens would be grim. The settlers who had come from Athens might expect slavery, possibly death; the others would lose their home and lands and be sent off to wander and to starve. These considerations are important for understanding the response of the Amphipolitans to the very much gentler conditions offered by Brasidas.

His proposal was that any resident of Amphipolis, whether of Athenian origin or other, could either remain where he was in full possession of his property and with equal rights, or could leave freely within five days, taking his property with him.[129] The price, though Thucydides takes it for granted and does not mention it, was that Amphipolis must change from the Athenian to the Spartan alliance. Thucydides says, "compared to what they had feared the proclamation seemed just," [130] and it had a powerful effect on the Amphipolitans' will to resist. The resolution shown by Eucles and the majority that had prevented treason and sent for help with the evident intention of defending their city evaporated with the news of Brasidas' offer.[131] The

---

[128] A Class XI (1968) 171, n. 9. I am much indebted to this article, particularly for its revealing focus on the internal situation in Amphipolis. I cannot, however, agree with its conclusion that the culpability of Thucydides in the loss of Amphipolis is proved.

[129] 4.105.2.   [130] 4.106.1.

[131] Bauman, A Class XI (1968) 175, speaks of a new factor that changed the situation, arguing, however, "that this new factor is not to be found in the reasonableness of the terms, for this aspect was apparent as soon as the proclamation was made, and yet it still needed anxious

non-Athenian portion of the population, we may imagine, cared more for their safety and property than for the alliance with Athens. The Athenians in the city could not fully trust their fellow Amphipolitans. Resolution gave way to doubt, and the friends of Brasidas in the city used the growing doubt well. Though Thucydides does not report the very important speeches during the debate,[132] his account shows that Eucles, as might be expected, argued against capitulation. At first, apparently, few dared to oppose him, but gradually the sentiment in favor of accepting Brasidas' terms found expression; then Brasidas' collaborators found it safe to justify them quite openly, and at last the city gave way and accepted the terms.[133]

Not many hours after Brasidas had entered the city, on the evening of the day he had arrived at the bridge over the Strymon, Thucydides arrived at Eion with his 7 ships. He had come remarkably quickly, traveling almost fifty miles in about twelve hours, assuming that he received word to come to Amphipolis by signal about dawn.[134] What message did he receive? We know too little about the capacities of Greek signaling systems, but surely they could transmit "bridge fallen, enemy here." [135] Such a message would explain the reaction of Thucydides as he himself reports it: "He wanted especially to arrive in time

debate, lasting some hours, before either the Athenians or the rest were persuaded." He then supports his argument by pointing out that the people of Torone and the garrison at Lecythus did not surrender in similar situations. None of this is persuasive. Even if the terms of Brasidas seemed guaranteed to cause capitulation, the people were not convinced of it. For one thing, acceptance depended on faith in the honesty of Brasidas, something not to be conceded lightly, especially by the Athenian citizens of Amphipolis. Secondly, even a man who conceded the generosity and honesty of the terms might prefer to hold out and might need to be convinced that this was impossible—which was not, in fact, true. We need not, therefore, wonder that there was a debate. Neither Torone nor Lecythus, moreover, consisted of suspicious "mixed multitudes," and each had the benefit of the mistake of Amphipolis.

[132] See the critical remarks of Bauman (*A Class* XI (1968), 173) on Thucydides' omission of the details of this discussion.

[133] 4.106.1–2.

[134] 106.3–4, 104.5; Gomme, *HCT* III, 579. As Gomme points out the message must have gone by signal, since a messenger would have taken twelve hours to reach Thucydides at Thasos.

[135] As suggested by Bauman, *A Class*, 179.

to save Amphipolis before it gave in, but if that were impossible to be early enough to save Eion." [136] Even without a hint about treachery in the message he received, Thucydides would have known, as Brasidas knew, that Amphipolis was a divided city that might yield when an enemy army appeared at its gates. He was too late to save Amphipolis, but he did prevent the capture of Eion. We have no reason to doubt that his swift response saved Eion or that without it Brasidas would have taken the town at dawn, for the next day the Spartans sailed down the river, only to be repulsed by Thucydides.[137]

The Athenians valued Amphipolis and were very frightened by its capitulation to the Spartans. They held Thucydides responsible for the loss, brought him to trial, and sent him into an exile that lasted the twenty years until the end of the war.[138] The ancient biographers of Thucydides report that Cleon was his accuser and that the charge was *prodosia*.[139] Though these sources are notoriously unreliable, we have no reason to doubt either assertion. *Prodosia*, like peculation, was a charge often leveled against unsuccessful generals. Cleon, of course, was the leading politician in Athens, a famous prosecutor, and the likeliest candidate to introduce such a charge.[140] Historians have long puzzled over the justice of the court's decision, and the problem is compounded because our only useful account is by Thucydides.[141] That account is quite puzzling. Thucydides never directly confronts or denies the justice of the sentence passed on him, but confines himself to a narrative description of the events. This has led some scholars to marvel at his objectivity and lack of self-justification,[142] but a more careful investigation shows that the bare narrative is a most effective defense.[143] The

[136] 104.5.   [137] 4.107.1–2.   [138] 5.26.5.

[139] Marcellinus, *Life of Thucydides* A 23; B 46; Anonymous, *Life of Thucydides*, 3; see Busolt, *GG* III:2, 625, n. 1.

[140] See Gomme, *HCT* III, 585. Thucydides' notorious mistreatment of Cleon in his history makes the case even more plausible.

[141] Diod. 12.68.1–3 is of no value whatever.

[142] G. B. Grundy, *Thucydides* I², 1948, 30; Meyer, *Forsch.* II, 343, says he tells the story "ohne auch nur ein Wort zu seiner Vertheidigung zu verlieren."

[143] Adcock, *CAH* V, 244, speaks of "the apologia which underlines this part of the narrative," without further explanation. Westlake (*Essays*, 123–137), however, has shown in detail how Thucydides has

proof is that we can so easily convert it into a direct answer to the charge that Thucydides was to blame for the fall of Amphipolis: "The emergency arose," he might say, "when Brasidas made a surprise attack on the bridge over the Strymon. The guard at the bridge was small, partly disloyal, and unprepared, so Brasidas took it easily. Responsibility for guarding the bridge belonged to Eucles, the commander of the city. The city was unprepared, but managed to rally in time to prevent immediate treason and send to me for help. I was at Thasos at the time, and set out immediately to relieve Amphipolis if I could, but to save Eion at least. I made amazingly good time because I knew the danger of treason would be great and that my arrival would turn the tide in our favor. If Eucles could have held on one more day we would have thwarted Brasidas, but he did not. My quickness and foresight saved Eion."

Thucydides' implicit defense of his actions did not convince an Athenian jury, although it has had much more success among modern historians.[144] If the defense he offered in court was essentially the same as the one in his history we can understand why he was convicted, for he gives no answer to the key question, why he was at Thasos instead of at Eion. Elaborate explanations have been provided by modern historians,[145] but the evidence is not provided by Thucydides. Just as it is wrong to argue that the historian's silence on this point is evidence of his guilt,[146] so it is wrong to use it as a license to invent evidence of his innocence.[147]

---

put forward a most effective defense of his action by his choice and omission of evidence. Bauman, *A Class* XI (1968), assumes that the Thucydidean account is an apologia.

[144] For the fullest and most vigorous defense of Thucydides see Delbrück, *Strategie*, 178–188. He is followed by Meyer, *GdA* IV, 120, n. 1. Finley's judgment (*Thucydides*, 200) is typical: "It was for this failure—a failure which, given the forces then and previously at his command, would seem to have been unavoidable—that Thucydides was exiled. Like the generals who had been punished for accepting peace in Sicily, he seems to have been a victim of the people's exorbitant hopes. Indeed, after Delium, there must have been a still greater demand for scapegoats."

[145] For an account of these see Westlake, *Essays*, 135ff.

[146] As does W. Oncken, cited by Busolt, *GG* III:2, 1154, n. 4.

[147] As do Steup, *Thuk.* I, xii–xiii, Busolt, *GG* III:2, 1154–1155, and Delbrück, *Strategie*, 178–188.

We must assume that Thucydides was at Thasos on some legitimate mission,[148] but that does not acquit him of the charge of failing to anticipate the expedition of Brasidas and of being at the wrong place at the wrong time. The error does not seem to be deserving of so severe a penalty, particularly when we consider Brasidas' daring and unusual tactics and the fact that Eucles, who allowed the bridge to be captured and the Amphipolitans to surrender, seems not to have been brought to trial or condemned.[149] If the irrational demos was seeking scapegoats for the failure of its overly ambitious plans and its negligence in failing to provide for the defense of the northeast, why did it condemn only Thucydides and spare Eucles? We know no reason why the Athenian jury would make any distinctions between them on political or any other grounds. The Athenians, in fact, seem to have been rather discriminating in their punishment of generals. Demosthenes was not condemned, in spite of his failures. Even when the court condemned Pythodorus, Sophocles, and Eurymedon for their failure in Sicily, it distinguished among them as to their degree of guilt. The former two were exiled, but Eurymedon was only fined. The Athenian juries may have based their decisions on the facts of the case, among other considerations. The only facts we have are provided by the defendant; if we had all the evidence the jury did, we might decide as they did.

As A. W. Gomme, certainly no enemy of the great historian, says:

It is clear . . . that Brasidas' sudden march, after some two months or more of quiet in winter quarters, took both Eucles and Thucydides by surprise. It was this which was decisive; and responsible commanders should not allow themselves to be surprised by the enemy. Thucydides, I feel, was conscious not only of his failure, but of his partial responsibility; it is noteworthy that after Kleon's death and the peace, no one, as far as we know, not Nikias nor Demosthenes nor Alkibiades, tried to get his banishment ended;

[148] Unlike W. Schmid in W. Schmid-O. Stählin, *Geschichte der Griechischen Literatur* (Munich, 1948), V: 2, 12, who imputes the motive of concern for his own gold mines.

[149] Thucydides tells us nothing of the fate of Eucles, nor is he mentioned elsewhere. The silence of all the sources gives us no reason to believe that he was attacked when he got home.

and the bitterness with which he pursues Kleon in the narrative of the second Amphipolis campaign reflects this. He had failed and Kleon (probably) had mercilessly abused him and got him banished; what would Kleon himself accomplish, with a larger, a prepared force, on the same ground, against the same opponent? [150]

The fall of Amphipolis, as the Athenians had feared, encouraged rebellions in the rest of the Thracian area. The moderation of Brasidas, his winning ways, his misrepresentation of Athenian timidity at Megara, and his recent successes all led factions in the several cities to send secret messengers to ask him to come and bring their cities over to Sparta.[151] Immediately after the capture of Amphipolis, Myrcinus, just up the Strymon, then Galepsus and Oesyne on the Aegean coast defected to Brasidas.[152] Most of the cities of the Acte peninsula came next, though Sane and Dium held out; men in Torone, on the Sithonia peninsula, were ready to betray it to Sparta, but it also had an Athenian garrison to prevent treachery, so Brasidas was compelled to take it by assault.[153] The citizens of the Chalcidic towns had reason to hope for a major Spartan commitment in the area and a low estimate of Athenian strength, but they were deluded in both respects. After the fall of Amphipolis, though it was winter and the notice short, the Athenians sent garrisons to strengthen their hold on the Thracian district; probably one of these garrisons fought at Torone.[154] The Athenians were determined to recover their losses, and the next years would show they had the means to do so.[155] The rebellious towns would pay a heavy price for underestimating the will and power of Athens.

The Greek cities of Thrace erred also in their expectations of major Spartan support. Brasidas, of course, sent to Sparta after his victory at Amphipolis to ask for reinforcements, while he began to build ships in the Strymon. He, at least, intended a major campaign aiming at a decisive victory in the war. He may have hoped to use his reinforcements and the forces he could gather in Thrace, both military and naval, to march eastward,

[150] HCT III, 587.   [151] 4.108.1–5.   [152] 4.107.3.
[153] Acte: 4.109; Torone: 110–116.   [154] 4.108.6.
[155] Westlake (Essays, 141–142) points out that almost all of the cities lost had been recaptured by 421.

gain control of the Hellespont, cut Athens off from her main grain supply, and bring her to her knees. If this were his plan, as the Athenians clearly feared,[156] it was bold and daring in the manner of Demosthenes and had at least some chance of success. The Spartan government at home, however, refused to send the troops requested, and Thucydides offers two reasons why: "The Spartans did not grant his request because of jealousy toward him by the leading men and also because they preferred to recover the men from the island and put an end to the war." [157] We need not doubt that personal jealousy, probably on the part of the kings toward an unusually successful subject and perhaps among others as well, played some part in the Spartan decision. A real difference of opinion on policy was critical, however. Ever since the capture of the Spartans on Sphacteria a faction favoring negotiated peace had been dominant at Sparta. The Spartans had sent mission after mission offering terms, only to be rejected by the ebullient Athenians. The victories of Brasidas were not seen as an invitation to greater risks and efforts to achieve total victory, but as a chance for the negotiated peace they had vainly sought. They had reason to hope that the Athenian defeat at Delium would have a sobering effect, and the capture of Amphipolis and other towns gave the Spartans something to trade for the prisoners, Pylos, and Cythera.

Perhaps Corinth and other allies might deplore the Spartan conservatism, but, with Brunt, "it is not hard to sympathize with the Spartan government in its failure to support Brasidas." [158] Perdiccas of Macedon paid part of the support for the army, and even though he was quick to effect a reconciliation with Brasidas after the fall of Amphipolis,[159] he was a tricky and unreliable ally and might become a dangerous enemy. To get another Spartan army through Thessaly to Brasidas might not be easy, especially if Peridiccas proved treacherous. The Spartans were also reluctant to send an army of any size away from home while there were enemy forces at Pylos and Cythera and while a helot rebellion was more threatening than usual. The Spartans were wise to reject the remote and slight possibility of total

[156] 4.108.1.   [157] 4.108.7.   [158] *Phoenix* XIX (1965), 276.
[159] 4.107.3.

victory in favor of a more likely immediate and not unacceptable peace.

The Athenians, of course, were not compelled to make peace. The losses in Thrace could be recovered in time, the increased tribute provided the resources to keep fighting, they continued to rule the sea, and they still held the captured Spartans as hostages against invasion. But the recent defeats inevitably had a psychological effect. The zealous advocates of aggressive warfare were discredited; the chances of total victory seemed remote. In these circumstances the advocates of peace gained influence and the Athenians became receptive to Spartan overtures. They had begun the year inflated by hopes of a complete triumph but ended it in a chastened mood, ready for compromise.

10. The Coming of Peace

In early spring 423, the Spartans and the Athenians agreed to a one-year truce in the hope and expectation of using the time to negotiate a more lasting peace.[1] It was about the same time as the election of the generals for 423/2, and though we can be sure of only two names on the list, Nicias and Nicostratus, we may believe that the friends of peace were well represented.[2] The truce shows evidence of considerable negotiation, and discussion must have occurred over a period of time to produce the final document. The initiative probably came, as usual since 425, from Sparta; there followed discussions between the Spartan and Athenian negotiators, and the resulting draft was "brought to Athens to be put before the ekklesia by Spartan and allied delegates who had been given power to conclude a truce on these terms."[3] The first two clauses, promising free access to the sanctuary at Delphi and the punishment of unnamed criminals who had robbed sacred treasuries, are plainly Peloponnesian

[1] 4.117.1.

[2] Nicias and Nicostratus are attested by 4.129.2 and are universally accepted. Westlake (*Essays*, 145ff.) argues that Sophocles the poet was elected general for this year. I do not find the suggestion convincing, though it is accepted by Sealey, *Essays*, 110. Fornara (*Athenian Board of Generals*, 61–62) argues that Cleon was elected, on the basis of Thucydides (5.1–2). His reading of a difficult passage is far too strict, and there is no good reason to believe that Cleon was general in 423/2.

[3] Gomme, *HCT* III, 598; Gomme here essentially follows the views set forth by A. Kirchhoff (*Thukydides und sein Urkundenmaterial*, (Berlin, 1895), 3–27), and I think they are fundamentally right. Julius Steup (*Thukydideische Studien*) in the appendix to the fourth volume of Classen-Steup, *Thuk.*, 306–310, also makes some useful points.

concessions to specific Athenian complaints. Delphi was in territory controlled by the allies of the Peloponnesians, and we must imagine that, contrary to custom, Athenian pilgrims had been barred from the sacred places. Thucydides does not tell us what was behind the second clause, but here, too, the language makes it clear that the Athenians had some particular grievance.[4] Still another concession to Athens restricted Peloponnesian activity at sea to commercial vessels of limited tonnage; no warship was to put to sea.[5] The clause forbidding either side to receive deserters, on the other hand, plainly favored the Spartans, who were eager to stop the escape of their helots to Pylos.[6]

The territorial provisions of the truce were based on the principle *uti possidetis*. Athens was to keep Pylos and Cythera, but its garrisons were to stay within narrow limits at Pylos and to have no contact with the Peloponnese from Cythera. The same provisions were made for the Athenian garrison at Nisaea and on the islands of Minoa and Atalante.[7] Athenian presence at Troezen in the eastern Peloponnese was sanctioned according to agreements already made with the Troezenians. Thucydides did not previously mention any accord with Troezen, and we must assume that it fell under Athenian control as a result of the threat posed by the Athenian fort at Methana.[8]

The remainder of the truce was calculated to establish favorable conditions for negotiating a lasting peace. Heralds and envoys from both sides were to have safe conduct on land and sea. Any disputes would be settled by arbitration. The final clause eloquently expressed the seriousness of the Spartans and their

[4] 4.118.1–4; Gomme, *HCT* III, 596–598.   [5] 4.118.5.   [6] 4.118.7.

[7] 4.118.4; The text as we have it does not mention Atalante by name, speaking only of τὴν νῆσον, ἥνπερ ἔλαβον οἱ Ἀθηναῖοι. It is possible that the reference here is only to Minoa, but I think Steup's suggestion that there is a lacuna which should be filled with Atalante is plausible and attractive (See Classen-Steup, *Thuk.*, IV, 230). Gomme, *HCT* III, 600, following Herbst, thinks the reference is to Methana.

[8] 4.45.2; Halieis probably made an alliance with Athens at the same time: *IG* i² 87 = Bengtson, *Staatsverträge* II, 103–105 #184. Cf., however, W. E. Thompson, *Klio* LIII (1971) 119ff., who questions the date of the treaty. The Athenians may also have made a treaty with King Darius II of Persia about this time. See Bengtson, *Staatsverträge* II, 183, 101–103. If they did its only effect was to calm their fears of Persian intervention on the side of Sparta.

determination to make peace on any reasonable terms: "These things seem to be good to the Spartans and their allies, but if anything seems fairer or more just to you than these proposals, come to Sparta and tell us. Neither the Spartans nor the allies will reject any just proposal you make. Only let those who come have full powers, just as you required of us. And the truce will last a year." [9] The decree of the Athenian assembly accepting the truce was moved by Laches and passed on the fourteenth day of the month Elaphebolion, perhaps March 24, and required the generals and prytanies to call an assembly specifically to begin discussions of terms for the final peace. [10] Athens' signers were Nicias, Nicostratus, and Autocles, all friends of a negotiated peace. It was not thought necessary, or perhaps possible, to obtain the signature of a leading figure in the other camp. [11] The Spartans ratified the agreement on the twelfth day of their month Gerastius, perhaps the same day. [12] While the Athenians were understood to sign on behalf of all their allies, the Spartan alliance granted greater autonomy to its members, so that ambassadors from Corinth, Sicyon, Megara, and Epidaurus signed for their respective states. [13] The truce ushered in high hopes that a lasting peace would be achieved and that the end of the war was at hand.

Reaction to the first clause of the truce showed that such hopes might be premature. The Boeotians, buoyed up by their

[9] 4.118.8–10.

[10] 4.118.11–14; Gomme, HCT III, 701, proposes the equivalent date in our calendar.

[11] Gomme, HCT III, 605, argues that the fact that these men signed the truce tells us nothing of their party affiliation. "The strategoi who 'signed' this agreement were ordered to do so by the ekklesia, and were so ordered, because, as likely as not, they were the only strategoi present." But the generals for 424/3 included Demosthenes, Cleon, and Lamachus, and we have no reason to believe that any of them was away in March 423. Of the remaining three generals for that year Thucydides was in exile and Hippocrates dead; we do not know about Eucles. It is at least interesting that the three men generally supposed to favor peace signed the treaty and the three generally supposed to oppose it did not. The fact is that we do not know how signers of treaties were chosen, and there is no warrant for the supposition that they were ordered to do so willy-nilly.

[12] 4.119.1; Gomme, HCT III, 604.   [13] 4.119.2.

victory at Delium, and the Phocians, nursing their old grudges, refused to agree to the cessation of fighting. Athenian access to Delphi by land depended on permission they were unlikely to grant. The Spartans could not compel their acquiescence any more than they could make them accept the truce; they could only try to persuade their allies. Nor would peace terms satisfactory to both the Athenians and Sparta's allies be easy to find. The Corinthians and Megarians might be willing to negotiate, but neither would gladly permit the Athenians to keep what they had taken, yet Athens was unlikely to give up its gains by negotiation. By far the greatest barrier to peace, however, was Sparta's inability to control the willful genius who commanded her armies in Thrace.

Just about the time the truce was being concluded, and before word could reach Thrace, the town of Scione on the southern coast of Pallene revolted from Athens. Immediately on hearing of the rebellion Brasidas crossed over by boat to exploit the new opportunity. At Scione he delivered his customary speech, adding special praise for the citizens who had bravely joined the cause of freedom without compulsion, even though they were almost islanders and so exposed to Athenian vengeance. "If things turned out as he hoped he would regard them, in truth, as most loyal friends of Sparta and hold them in honor generally." [14] This speech unified the Scionians, even those who had not favored the rebellion. Their enthusiasm was so great that they took the unprecedented public gesture of granting Brasidas a golden crown as "liberator of Hellas." Privately, he was treated like a victorious athlete, and the Greeks knew no better treatment.[15] After temporarily leaving a small force in Scione, he returned with a larger force, for he hoped to use the town as a base for attacks on Mende and Potidaea on the same peninsula before the Athenians learned what was happening. The Athenians, perhaps distracted by truce negotiations, perhaps not yet recovered from the shock of their recent defeats, had not taken adequate steps to defend their possessions in Thrace. Brasidas was eager to accomplish what he could before reinforcements arrived.

[14] 4.120.3.   [15] 4.121.1.

We may imagine his chagrin and disappointment when he learned from the team of Athenaeus the Spartan and Aristonymus the Athenian that a truce had been concluded. He was compelled to give up his plans and take his army back to Torone. There he was formally told of the agreement, and his Thracian allies had no choice but to accept it. When Aristonymus learned that Scione had revolted after the truce was signed, he excluded the town from the agreement. Brasidas heatedly said the rebellion had come before the truce. He knew better, of course, but after his impassioned speech to the citizens of Scione and the unique reception they had given him he could hardly abandon them immediately to the vengeance of Athens. He may also have wanted a pretext for sowing discord in the hope of regaining a free hand in Thrace. This act shows how much Brasidas was willing to risk for his policy. He assured the Spartans that legality was on their side, that the rebellion had preceded the truce, and the Spartans believed him, claiming control of Scione, though they were willing to arbitrate the dispute. Brasidas' deception would soon be known at Sparta; if his plans went wrong he could expect an unfriendly reception on his return. Other Spartans, even kings, had been condemned to exile or death, but Brasidas was ready to run the risk in the hope that he could achieve such success as to guarantee a welcome when he returned.

The Athenians, of course, were furious. They knew they were right and would not hear of arbitration. Not only was Scione an Athenian ally that had rebelled, but one that was located on the sea, as good as an island. If such states thought it safe to revolt and were left unpunished and protected by Sparta, no part of the empire was safe. In such a mood the Athenians passed Cleon's proposal to send an expedition to Scione, to destroy it, and to put the citizens to death.[16] Cleon had given the same advice in regard to the fate of the rebels on Lesbos, but this time it was accepted. In part this can be explained by the angry mood of the Athenians, enraged by the rebellion and its support by Brasidas at the very moment when they expected peace to permit a consolidation of their possessions in the

[16] 4.122.

Thracian area. But the Athenians had been angry about the Lesbian rebellion, too. Perhaps by this time the moderate imperial policy of Pericles and Diodotus had been discredited by the unprovoked defections of Amphipolis, Acanthus, Torone, and other towns in the northeast. The Athenians seem to have been willing to try Cleon's policy of deterrence through terror.

Their willingness must have increased with the rebellion of Mende soon after, which obviously happened during the time of truce, yet Brasidas accepted the rebels. He offered as excuse some unconvincing alleged Athenian violations. The truth is that he was unwilling to accept the truce and was determined to push forward his conquests. His action at Scione had encouraged the Mendaean rebels. Thucydides makes it clear that they were a small minority of the citizens, who seized power and then coerced the others into making the rebellion. This intensified the anger of the Athenians, who immediately prepared a force to move against both cities. Brasidas, expecting the onslaught, removed the women and children to safety and sent a garrison of 500 Peloponnesian hoplites and 300 Chalcidian peltasts, the whole force to be under Polydamidas.[17]

At this point, when Brasidas and all his limited force were so badly needed in the Chalcidice, his reliance on Perdiccas cost him dearly. The Macedonian king, still partial paymaster of the Peloponnesian forces, compelled Brasidas, probably by threatening to withhold supplies,[18] to turn away from the vital theater of operations and march with him against Arrhabaeus of Lyncus. They soon met the Lyncestians in a pitched battle and scored a decisive victory, driving the enemy back into the hills. Then they waited a few days for the arrival of some Illyrian mercenaries hired by Perdiccas. Once again the antagonistic goals of the two generals caused disagreement. Perdiccas wanted to pursue the Lyncestians and destroy their villages, while Brasidas was impatient to get back to Pallene and save its cities from the impending Athenian attack.[19] While they argued news came that the Illyrians had proven treacherous and gone over to Arrhabaeus. These barbarian mercenaries were fierce and dangerous fighters, and the news of their approach persuaded

[17] 4.123.   [18] Gomme, HCT III, 612.   [19] 4.124.

Perdiccas to retreat, as Brasidas had wanted. The quarrel had prevented the two generals from concerting a plan of withdrawal. But during the night panic struck the Macedonian army which turned and ran in undisciplined flight; Perdiccas had no choice but to follow his army without informing Brasidas, who was camped some distance away. The coming of morning found Brasidas in a most uncomfortable position. The Macedonians were gone, and Arrhabaeus and the Illyrians were about to attack. By his rhetorical skill in heartening his troops, his personal bravery, his keen and professional sense of military detail, and by superb tactical genius he was able to effect a withdrawal against a vastly superior force in enemy territory.[20]

The sudden withdrawal of the Macedonians and the failure of communication put an end, morally if not legally, to the alliance between Perdiccas and the Spartans. The Spartan soldiers were angry at being deserted; they slaughtered the Macedonians' oxen wherever they came upon them and took off any booty they could find. Henceforth Perdiccas considered Brasidas a hated enemy, which, as Thucydides points out, was inconsistent with his feelings toward the Athenians. Rational interest gave way to personal hatred and, perhaps, fear. "Departing from his necessary interests, he sought how he could most quickly make peace with the Athenians and get rid of Brasidas." [21]

The Athenians, meanwhile, had sent an expedition to Pallene consisting of 40 Athenian ships and 10 from Chios, 1,000 Athenian hoplites, 600 archers, 1,000 Thracian mercenaries, and some peltasts from the Athenian allies in the region.[22] The commanders Nicias and Niceratus aimed only at rebellious Scione and Mende; Torone, which had revolted earlier, was under Spartan control according to the truce. The two generals wanted a negotiated settlement and would not reduce its chances for success by violating the terms of the truce, whatever Brasidas had done. Nor should we wonder that these advocates of peace should lead a campaign against a Spartan army. Brasidas' violations had angered the Athenians, played into the hands of Cleon and those who sought a total victory, and threatened the chances of peace. If Nicias and his friends were not to be com-

[20] 4.125–128.2.   [21] 4.128.5.   [22] 4.129.2.

pletely discredited they had to recover the rebellious towns and restore the conditions under which the truce had been made. Nor could they trust the campaign to anyone else if it was to pursue the limited goals they had in mind and not become an uncontrolled provocation for more fighting.

The size of their force is a further indication of their limited goals; indeed it was too small to guarantee the success of the mission if Brasidas and his army were on or near Pallene when it arrived. Compared with the 4,000 hoplites Pericles had taken to Epidaurus, or the 2,000 hoplites Nicias had taken to Melos, or the 7,000 Hippocrates had taken to Delium, the Athenian force under Nicias and Niceratus does not seem very large. To be sure, the defeat at Delium had been costly in men and probably discouraged risking too many Athenians; it was preferable to hire Thracian mercenaries who were less reliable but expendable. Money, in spite of the increased tribute, was still a problem; by the summer of 423 the reserve fund appears to have shrunk to 596 talents.[23] Still, a stronger effort, though difficult, would have been possible, and we may believe that the decision to use only a moderate force was the result of policy as well as a shortage of means.

When the Athenians arrived at Potidaea, their base of operations on Pallene, Brasidas had not yet returned from the north. Mende was defended only by the natives, 300 men from Scione, and 700 Peloponnesians under Polydamidas. They took up a strong position on a hill outside the city and easily withstood the Athenian attack on the first day; the Athenians barely escaped defeat and destruction.[24] On the second day Nicias took advantage of Athenian naval superiority to sail round to the south of Mende and ravage the suburbs in that area. On the next day he continued his depredations as far as the borders of Scione, while Nicostratus invested Mende from the north. The Athenians had no better plan than to besiege the town, but there is no reason to believe that they would have taken it before the return of Brasidas had its citizens been unified in opposition. However, the rebellion at Mende had been fomented by a few oligarchs against the will of a majority and depended on Spartan

[23] *ATL* III, 344.   [24] 4.129.

support. The appearance of an Athenian army had shaken their control of the town. Nicias' first day of ravaging had been unopposed because Mende was torn by civil strife; it had been serious enough that the 300 Scioneans went home during the second night. The situation was difficult, but a Peloponnesian army under a Spartan commander was still in the town. Brasidas, who could have handled the problem, was far away. Polydamidas was far more typical of the Spartan abroad.

On the third day after the Athenian arrival Polydamidas gathered his troops in the part of the city facing north to launch an attack against the army of Nicostratus. As he was making the usual hortatory speech, some of the Mendaean democrats spoke up in protest, refusing to go out and fight. This was the moment for the magic tongue of Brasidas, for words of cheer, encouragement, and persuasion. Instead Polydamidas shouted at the offender and laid violent hands on him. This caused the other Mendaeans to take up arms, attack the Peloponnesians and their own oligarchs, and open the gates to the Athenians. Polydamidas and his forces turned and ran, for they were taken completely by surprise and feared the Mendaean action had been prearranged with the Athenians, which was not true. The Athenians burst into the city, somewhat confused, thinking at first that the Mendaeans were enemies. They began to plunder, as was legitimate in a city taken by storm, and only with difficulty did Nicias and Niceratus prevent them from killing the citizens. Many Peloponnesians were killed on the spot, while others took refuge on the acropolis where they were fenced in and watched by guards. The Athenians restored the Mendaean democracy and ordered trials to deal with the oligarchs.[25] Mende was restored to the Athenian alliance.

The Athenians then turned to Scione. The defenders took up a position on a hill outside the city to prevent the Athenians from coming up to the walls of Scione and building a siege wall. The Athenians attacked and took the hill. While they were working on the surrounding wall, however, the Peloponnesian troops locked up in Mende escaped and made their way into Scione.[26] Helped by these reinforcements, the people of Scione

[25] 4.130.   [26] 4.131.

and their Peloponnesian allies were able to hold out for the entire summer. At the end of that summer the Athenians finally completed their wall around Scione. The forces under Nicias and Niceratus were clearly inadequate to take the place by storm, and the harsh decree proposed by Cleon guaranteed that Scione could not be talked into surrender. This was not the only time in Athenian history that a policy invented by one man and supported by his friends would be executed by others who did not approve of it. Nicias did not send for reinforcements or conceive a stratagem to take the town by trickery; instead he withdrew his army, leaving only a garrison behind.[27]

While the Athenian army was still at Scione, however, Athens gained an important diplomatic victory reaping the reward of the feud between Brasidas and Perdiccas. Perdiccas sent a herald to Nicias and Niceratus, and an offensive and defensive alliance was formed between Athens and Macedon.[28] The alliance was immediately useful. While the Athenian army was still at Scione the Spartans decided to send some reinforcements to Brasidas under Ischagoras, Ameinias, and Aristeus. But Perdiccas, urged by Nicias to give some token of his new commitment to Athens, used his considerable influence in Thessaly to such good effect that the Spartans did not even try to get their army through.[29] This must have brought great relief to the Athenian friends of peace, for the army would not only have threatened further

[27] 4.133.4.

[28] 4.132.1; I believe this is the treaty inscribed on *IG* i² 71 = Bengtson, *Staatsverträge* no. 186, II, 109ff. In my *Outbreak*, 261, I accepted the arguments of the authors of *ATL* placing this inscription before the war, in the 430s. I now believe that Gomme, *HCT* III, 621, and Bengtson, *Staatsverträge*, 113, are right to prefer the dating chosen by earlier scholars, i.e., 423/2. Bengtson succinctly gives the reasons for choosing the later date: "einmal spricht die Verbindung von Perdikkas II. und Arrhabaios mehr für ein späteres Datum als ca. 435 (so auch A. W. Gomme), zum anderen ist das Monopol der Athener auf das makedonische Ruderholz (κωπέας, Z. 22–23) im Kriege verständlich, nicht aber im Frieden." In addition to the alliance the treaty decreed peace and friendship between Perdiccas and Arrhabaeus, and that Perdiccas was to sell timber for oars to Athens only. Now that the Athenians had cleared the seas of Peloponnesian ships, they were taking measures to see that no more would be built or manned.

[29] 4.132.1–2.

the Athenian position in the Thracian district, but the increased intensity of the fighting would almost certainly have shattered any chance of negotiating a lasting peace.

That the Spartans should have sent reinforcements to Brasidas during a period of truce and after having refused to do so earlier raises questions about the always cloudy political situation in Sparta. The Spartans may have accepted Brasidas' story that Scione had fallen before the truce, that Sparta was therefore in the right, and that Athens was wrong to attack it.[30] Even so, Brasidas' support of the revolt of Mende clearly violated the truce and should have been repudiated if Sparta wanted to show good faith and get on with the negotiations. The Spartan refusal to chastise or repudiate their general and the decision to reinforce him did not necessarily result from a shift in power in favor of a war faction and of Brasidas; part of the mission of Ischagoras and the others, in fact, seems to have been to keep a close watch on him and make an independent evaluation of the situation.[31] Even the peace faction wanted to preserve the Spartan position in Thrace and particularly not to risk the loss of Amphipolis. If Brasidas were defeated and the Chalcidian cities recovered by Athens there was every reason to believe that Amphipolis would fall, too, sooner or later. Without Amphipolis, Sparta would have nothing to trade for the men from Sphacteria, for Pylos, or for Cythera; Athens would no longer have reason to make peace. Like their opposite numbers in Athens the Spartan friends of peace were in the awkward position of intensifying the war in order to make peace possible.

Though the Spartan army was barred, the Thessalians allowed Ischagoras and his two colleagues to go through to meet Brasidas and carry out their orders. As Busolt says, "His mission was not benevolent toward Brasidas." [32] Later, in 421, Ischagoras was a signer of the peace and the accompanying alliance with Athens. He was also one of the envoys who, after the peace, ordered the Spartan commander to surrender Amphipolis to Athens and the Spartan allies in the region to carry out the terms of the treaty.[33]

---

[30] Such is the view of Gomme, *HCT* III, 622.

[31] 4.132.3: ἐπιδεῖν πεμψάντων Λακεδαιμονίων τὰ πράγματα.

[32] *GG* III:2, 1170.   [33] 5.19.2; 21.1; 24.1.

He may well have been one of those Spartans opposed to Brasidas and his policies.[34] He brought with him men to serve as governors of the cities in the region allied to Sparta, Clearidas for Amphipolis, and Cleonymus for Torone. Contrary to Spartan custom, these men were still young enough for military service, no doubt because vigorous leadership was thought necessary to rule and defend towns that must certainly face Athenian attacks soon.[35] They had another qualification: they owed their posts and allegiance entirely to the Spartan government, not to Brasidas, and could be expected to follow orders. Their appointment was a blow to Brasidas and his policy in still another way. Brasidas had promised freedom and autonomy to Amphipolis, Torone, Acanthus, and the other cities he had won, but placing Spartan *archontes* in them was a clear breach of those promises and would damage the reputation of Brasidas and make future defections from Athens unlikely. These were both results very much desired by those Spartans eager for a peace negotiated as soon as possible.[36]

Without reinforcements or encouragement, Brasidas accomplished nothing for the rest of the year. In February or early

[34] This discussion and what follows on the mission of Ischagoras and his colleagues owe much to the fine analysis of Gomme, *HCT* III, 623–624. My conclusions, however, are quite different from his. This, I believe, is because he did not consider the possibility that the friends of peace had just as much reason to send an army to Thrace as did the supporters of a more dangerous policy. He naturally assumed, therefore, that only men who supported Brasidas and his policy would send reinforcements to him.

[35] See the important discussion of Grote, VI, 449–450.

[36] I accept the reading αὐτῶν after τῶν ἡβώντων in 4.132.3 which is given by all the MSS and reject Stahl's emendation αὐτῷ, though it is accepted by Steup and Hude, and favored, with reservations, by Gomme. They find it attractive because it supplies a singular subject for καθίστησιν a few lines down and avoids a pleonasm. I see no difficulty in assuming that Ischagoras is meant to be the subject of that verb and am not troubled by the pleonasm which is not unique. On the other hand, I find it impossible to believe that Brasidas willingly broke his own promises, as would be necessary if we accepted αὐτῷ. Like Gomme, *HCT* III, 624, I do not think that Brasidas was a saint, but I do think he was "a moderately honest man." Much more important, I think he was no fool but an unusually shrewd soldier-diplomat-politician who would have realized that so blatant a breach of his promises would mean disaster for his policy.

March he attempted to surprise Potidaea by a rare assault at night, but without success.[37] As spring approached, and with it the expiration of the truce, the situation was more confused than it had been a year earlier. Outside of the Thracian region there had been no fighting, but the activities of Brasidas had bred anger and suspicion and prevented any progress toward a lasting peace. Negotiations continued, but in both states, Athens especially, those who doubted that peace was possible in the present circumstances grew in strength.

The Athenian elections in the spring of 422 returned Cleon to the *strategia* for 422/1.[38] Although we do not know the names of any of his colleagues, we should not assume that all friends of peace were swept from office because, though the truce expired late in March or early in April, it was continued, at least de facto, until after the Pythian games toward the beginning of August.[39] We must imagine that the men in Athens and Sparta who favored peace were able to prevail on their fellow citizens to avoid hostilities and continue negotiations.

After the Pythian games, however, the Athenians lost patience. By now the Spartans must know the truth about Scione, and, in any case, they knew that Brasidas had violated the truce on several other occasions. Yet they not only failed to disown and punish him, but had even sent an army of reinforcement and Spartan governors to rule some of the rebellious cities. The Spartans must have seemed to lack not only the power but also the will to carry out the terms of the truce. It was easy to believe that the armistice had been made in bad faith in order to win time for Brasidas to gain even more successes, cause further rebellions, and thus to make possible greater demands in the bargaining for peace. Most Athenians must have seen that their vital interests required an expedition to recover the rebellious cities and especially Amphipolis. We should not be surprised, therefore, that Cleon persuaded them to vote an expedition of 30 ships, 1,200 Athenians hoplites, 300 cavalry, and a larger force of excellent Lemnians and Imbrians for that purpose.[40]

Even more surprising, Cleon was willing to take command of

[37] 4.135.   [38] See the discussion of Beloch, *Attische Politik*, 306–307.
[39] 5.1; For the textual difficulty see Gomme, *HCT* III, 629.   [40] 5.2.1.

the expedition, though he was inexperienced in military tactics and command and had to face an enemy general acknowledged to be an outstanding soldier.[41] The professionalism of Greek commanders of hoplite phalanxes should not be exaggerated. The tactics were generally well known and depended less on military experience than is true in modern wars. Still, skill and experience were important, and the Athenians were not likely to entrust such an important army and campaign to a single amateur and unskilled general, though we should remember that Athenians gave Cleon most of the credit for winning the incredible victory on Sphacteria. We should expect, at least, that they would send an experienced soldier with him as a colleague, such as he had in Demosthenes on Sphacteria.

Thucydides mentions no colleague, though it is almost impossible that Cleon had none. If we examine only the campaigns in the Thracian district throughout the war, we find that none was commanded by a single general. In 432, Archestratus sailed against Potidaea accompanied by four other generals.[42] In 430, Hagnon and Cleopompus were sent to put an end to the siege and take the city.[43] In the winter of 430/29 we hear of three generals operating in the region.[44] In 423, Nicias and Niceratus were sent out to restore the Athenian position threatened by Brasidas.[45] We cannot believe that the Athenians deliberately made an exception in this case and entrusted the command of so many of their men to only one general, who was inexperienced and suspected by many of his fellow citizens. Nor can we believe that Thucydides' failure to mention his colleague or colleagues is an accidental omission. The campaign ended in disaster which has ever since been blamed on the only man we know to be connected with it; that could not have been unintended.

The force under Cleon and his anonymous associates, even if we accept Busolt's figure of 2,000 to 3,000 for the Lemnian and Imbrian contingents,[46] was not strong enough to guarantee suc-

---

[41] Grote, in fact, is so embarrassed by this thought that he suggests that Cleon did not want the command, but was forced to take it by the reluctance of Nicias, as in the Pylos affair (VI, 461). This is supported by no evidence and does not seem justified.

[42] 1.57.6. Callias soon brought reinforcements, 1.61.   [43] 2.58.

[44] 2.70.   [45] 4.129.2.   [46] *GG* III:2, 1175.

cess. Busolt calculates that in addition to the men doing garrison duty in Scione and Torone, Brasidas had about the same number, as well as the incalculable advantage of defending walled towns.[47] We cannot be certain whether the number of troops was limited by financial considerations, a reluctance to endanger too many Athenians, or the efforts of Cleon's opponents to reduce the size of the campaign. Athens must have counted on help from Perdiccas and from some of its allies in Thrace proper.[48] Brasidas was cut off and could expect no more help from Sparta. Perdiccas would no longer supply him with money or provisions. The Spartan breach of faith at Torone and Amphipolis and Brasidas' failure to save Mende or take Potidaea might have undermined his position still further. With reasonable luck Cleon might hope to win another important victory and remove Spartan influence from the Thracian district. That would give the Athenians favoring peace a much stronger bargaining position or, as Cleon hoped, it would encourage the Athenians to resume the offensive in the Peloponnese and central Greece on the way to a peace based on victory.

The first part of Cleon's campaign in the north, though insignificant in the account of Thucydides, achieved important and remarkable successes. The obvious tactic would have been to attack Scione at once, since it was the most annoying defector and was already under siege. Brasidas probably expected the attack there; he was inexplicably away from Torone, his main base in the Chalcidice, when Cleon launched a surprise assault on that city. The Athenians touched at Scione only to pick up additional soldiers from the garrison there, and, perhaps, as a feint to mislead Brasidas. From there Cleon sailed across to the little port of Cophus, just south of Torone, where he learned what he must have hoped to hear: Brasidas was away and the forces left in the city were no match for the Athenians.

To make the city more defensible and better able to last through a siege Brasidas had built a new wall around it which also encompassed the suburbs, giving the inhabitants more room and some safe land to farm.[49] Cleon brought up his main army against this new wall and drew the Spartan governor Pasitelidas

[47] *Ibid.*   [48] 5.6.2.   [49] 5.2.

and his garrison out of the city to defend the outer fortification. He seems to have taken no thought for the defense of the inner city which was vulnerable to an attack by sea—which the Athenians had planned in concert with the inland assault on the wall. While Cleon was engaging the Peloponnesian force there the ships, necessarily under the command of one of Cleon's unnamed colleagues, sailed against the undefended city. When Pasitelidas saw what was happening he realized that a trap had been set and that he had stepped into it. Even without the diversion the Athenians were already pressing him hard,[50] and the sight of the ships sailing to Torone completed his discomfort. He was afraid that the men on the ships would take the city and that he would find himself trapped between the old wall around Torone and the new wall surrounding the suburbs, with Athenians attacking him from both directions.[51] He therefore abandoned the outer wall and ran to Torone, but he found the Athenian fleet had arrived first and taken the city. Meanwhile the forces under Cleon, now unopposed, got through the wall and pursued him closely. The old wall around Torone had been breached when the new wall was built, and through this opening the Peloponnesians ran, followed by the Athenians who broke into the city, too, without further difficulty. The battle was soon over; some defenders were killed on the spot, others, including Pasitelidas, were captured. Pursuing his hard policy toward rebels, though in a somewhat moderated form, Cleon sent the 700 adult males to Athens as prisoners. The women and children were sold as slaves. Cleon set up two trophies of victory, one at the harbor and the other at the new wall; [52] the

[50] 5.3.1. Gomme takes ἐβιάζοντο to mean that the Athenians were already forcing their way through the defenders of the wall and points out that such a forcing of a defended wall was very rare among the Greeks. He is led to suggest that perhaps the wall was not yet finished or badly built, though Thucydides does not say so. It seems to me that Gomme gives too much force to ἐβιάζοντο. It need not mean "they were being overcome," as he implies, but merely, "they were hard pressed," as Crawley and Smith each render it.

[51] This is how I interpret the words δείσας ὁ Πασιτελίδας μὴ αἵ τε νῆες φθάσωσι λαβοῦσαι ἐρῆμον τὴν πόλιν καὶ τοῦ τειχίσματος ἁλισκομένου ἐγκαταληφθῇ, 5.3.1.

[52] 5.3.

duplication of monuments was amply justified by the importance of the victory and the brilliance of the strategy. Soon after
the fall of the city Brasidas arrived with a relieving army; he
was less than four miles from the city when it fell.[53]

The details of the capture of Torone have rarely been given
much attention so its strategic interest and the light it sheds on
the generalship of Cleon and Brasidas have not been appreci-
ated.[54] Gomme's excellent evaluation of the campaign is useful:
"The victory was decisive and the strategy—the decision to
leave Skione to the slow siege and to attempt to carry Torone
by storm—both intelligent and bold; the action was as brilliant
as that of Brasidas at Amphipolis. Pasitelidas seems to have been
no more competent than Eukles (we are not even told that he
was hindered by discontent within the city); and Brasidas must
bear at least as much blame for the defeat as Thucydides bears
for Amphipolis, for Kleon was already near at hand." [55]

After placing a garrison in Torone, Cleon sailed to Eion to
establish a base for the attack on Amphipolis.[56] Brasidas must
have hurried there immediately to prevent the most important
Spartan prize from falling into Athenian hands.[57] Once again
Cleon took advantage of his sea power and the limited mobility

[53] 5.3.3.

[54] Honorable exceptions are Woodhead, *Mnemosyne* XIII (1960),
304, B. Baldwin, *PACA*, 211–212, and, especially, Gomme, *HCT* III, 631–
632.

[55] 3.632. After all this, Gomme, always reluctant to stray from Thucydides' own interpretations, says, nevertheless, that "Brasidas' reputation is scarcely tarnished, and Kleon's not at all whitened," presumably
because "the loss of Torone was not so important for the Peloponnesians
as that of Amphipolis had been for Athens."

[56] 5.3.6.

[57] Thucydides' account of the campaigns around Amphipolis and of
the battle itself is unsatisfactory in many ways. At this point the chronology is not so clear as we should wish. As Thucydides tells the story
Cleon first established a base at Eion, then attacked Stagirus and Galepsus, then sent for help to Perdiccas and to the Thracian king Polles.
Only then does Thucydides tell us that Brasidas took up a position on a
hill outside Amphipolis to keep watch on Cleon's movements (5.6.1–3).
Immediately on hearing of Cleon's arrival at Eion, Brasidas must have
gone to Amphipolis; probably he waited there before taking up his
position on the hill. We cannot doubt that Brasidas had reached Amphipolis before Cleon attacked Stagirus.

of the Peloponnesians to attack weak points and win back lost ground. Thucydides tells us that his attack on Stagirus in the Chalcidice failed, but he was successful in storming Galepsus.[58]

Thucydides tells us no more, but the evidence of the inscriptions indicates strongly that Cleon's activities in Thrace were very successful. The assessment list of the Athenian Empire for the year 422/1 includes the names of many cities in the region that must have been recovered by Athens, and there is every reason to think this was the accomplishment of Cleon.[59] At the same time, in the realm of diplomacy, he was doing everything possible to bring Perdiccas and his Macedonians as well as the Thracian Polles, king of the Odomantians, to the side of Athens. Pinned down all this time by the threat to Amphipolis, Brasidas could do nothing to prevent these losses or the encirclement that threatened his position. As Woodhead has put it, "The war in fact came to be focussed on Amphipolis: the net was skilfully laid and tightened round Brasidas until the moment came for the *coup de grâce*, and political strategy was allied to generalship in the field in bringing this about." [60]

Cleon planned to wait at Eion until the arrival of his Macedonian and Thracian allies permitted him to encircle Brasidas, to lock him up in Amphipolis, and reduce the place by storm or siege.[61] To fight a battle would be more dangerous, but also quicker and cheaper; the numerical superiority Cleon expected to achieve when his barbarian allies came made the risk acceptable. When Cleon and his army returned to Eion after his several attacks on rebellious cities and settled there to wait for his

[58] 5.6.1.
[59] The list is A10, II, 44 in *ATL*. The fundamental study is by West and Meritt in *AJA* XXIX (1925), 54–69. See also *ATL* III, 347–348; Adcock, *CAH* V, 248. Some have resisted giving Cleon credit for this achievement, either by denying that the assessment was realistic and that Athens necessarily controlled all the cities listed, or by giving Nicias credit for their capture. These arguments are satisfactorily answered by Woodhead, *Mnemosyne* XIII (1960), 304–306.
[60] *Mnemosyne* XIII (1960), 305.
[61] I follow the topographical description of Pritchett, *Studies*, 30–45, and benefit from his account of the battle; other useful accounts are those of Woodhead, 306–310, Baldwin, *A Class* XI (1968), 211–214, and Gomme, *HCT* III, 635–637, and Ἑλληνικά (Thessalonike) XIII (1954), 1–10.

allies, Brasidas must have realized that an attack on Amphipolis impended, and probably then he moved his army to the hill called Cerdylium to the southwest of the city in the territory of the Argilians, leaving Clearidas in charge of Amphipolis.[62] From there he had a good view in all directions and could watch Cleon's every move.

Now Thucydides' narrative becomes very puzzling. He says that Brasidas had taken up his position expecting Cleon to attack with only his own army, in contempt for the small number of men under Brasidas.[63] But Brasidas announced to his troops that their numbers were approximately equal to the enemy, and Cleon could not have been grossly deceived in this matter.[64] If Brasidas expected Cleon to misjudge the situation so badly, however, he was disappointed, for Cleon continued to wait for his reinforcements. Here again the account of Thucydides presents difficulties. After a short period of waiting Cleon marched his army northwest from Eion to a strong position on a hill northeast of Amphipolis,[65] but the purpose of this maneuver is far from clear.

Thucydides tells us that it was not inspired by a military purpose but by the grumbling of the Athenian troops, who were annoyed at the inactivity and distrusted the leadership of their general, contrasting his incompetence and cowardice with the experience and boldness of Brasidas.[66] That the Athenian soldiers should have had this opinion of Cleon is surprising.

---

[62] 5.6.3. Gomme, *HCT* III, 636, suggests two possible locations for this hill, one southwest of the city, closer to Eion, and 172 meters high, about 60 higher than the hill of Amphipolis; the other is further west, 3–4 kilometers from the bridge, 312 meters high. J. Papastavrou, *Amphipolis, Klio*, Beiheft XXXVII (1936), prefers the latter. W. K. Pritchett (*Studies* I, 39) argues for Hill 339, between Ano Kerdylion and Kato Kerdylion. I cannot tell whether this is the same as Papastavrou's, but if not, it is close to it. See Map 8.

[63] 5.6.3.

[64] 5.8.2–4. This is forcefully put by Baldwin, who says, "It is at this point that the Thucydidean account begins to strain credulity" (*PACA*, 212).

[65] Pritchett, *Studies*, 41–43.

[66] 5.7.1–2. The word μαλακία may mean "softness," "weakness," or "lack of energy," but here, where it is contrasted with τόλμα, I agree with Gomme, *HCT* III, 637, that it must mean "cowardice."

Cowardice and lack of daring are not qualities indicated by Thucydides' earlier accounts of Cleon. Everywhere he shows a spirit which is, if anything, too bold and optimistic. His support of Demosthenes' plan to take Sphacteria was the boldest idea put forward, his promise to do so within twenty days brought laughter to the Athenian assembly because of its optimism and raised the not unwelcome prospect of his failure and demise in the minds of those Athenians whom Thucydides calls "the sensible men." Cleon had urged the present expedition to track down Brasidas and recover Amphipolis. Brasidas, if we are to believe Thucydides, did not consider Cleon cowardly or reluctant to fight, but expected him to be rash enough to attack without waiting for his allies to come and make such an attack safe. Nor is it easy to understand the grounds for the opinion that Cleon was incompetent. Since his first appearance as a general in 425 his record of achievement had been amazing. He had carried out his promise at Sphacteria. The very men who are alleged to have doubted him were with him at Torone where his strategy was masterful and successful. They had been with him when he stormed Galepsus and recovered the other towns in the region. It is hard to understand the basis for the feelings Thucydides describes and hard to deny the truth of Gomme's observation that "the whole sentence shows the strongest bias against Kleon, a hatred and contempt for him." [67]

[67] *HCT* III, 637. Gomme goes on to say, "Yet there is also no reason to suppose that Kleon did possess any military skill, and every reason to think that his confidence, which had hitherto carried him almost from one success to another, arose from nothing but an overweening arrogance." One would think that the winning of such victories as the ones at Sphacteria, Torone, and Galepus would provide some reason for supposing Cleon had military skill and justify any growth in his confidence. Gomme, as ever reluctant to disagree with a Thucydidean judgment, was sensible enough to feel uncomfortable with his argument and felt compelled to support it with the following, which concludes the quotation above, "for Thucydides' picture of him agrees in all essentials with that of Aristophanes." It is hardly impressive to support the testimony of one enemy of Cleon in prose with that of another in verse. See the very pertinent remarks of Woodhead, *Mnemosyne* XII (1960), 292–293. Such an argument should not have survived the demolition by Grote more than a century ago. He points out the absurdity of taking seriously the portraits of public figures painted by the comic

If we reject the first motive proposed by Thucydides, the rest of his account makes it clear that Cleon's plan was to wait until the Thracians came, encircle the city, and then take it by storm.[68] A general expecting to lay siege to a town will naturally need a good picture of its size, shape, the height and strength of its walls, the disposition of the forces and population in it, and the lie of the land outside it. That requires a reconnaissance expedition of exactly the kind Thucydides describes Cleon as making: "He came and established his army on a strong hill in front of Amphipolis and himself examined the marshy portion of the Strymon and how the city was situated in respect to Thrace." [69] The wait for the Thracians, though not long, may have made the soldiers restless, and Cleon thought they needed something to do, but such a march would have been necessary in any case. He did not expect to fight, but he had to take a sizable force with him to deter an attack when he got close to the city.

When Cleon reached his observation post on the hill he saw no one on the wall of Amphipolis and no one coming out of the gates to attack him. Thucydides tells us that Cleon then thought he had made a mistake not to take siege equipment with him, for he thought it was undefended and he could take it with the force he had at hand.[70] Though Thucydides often tells us what was in the minds of generals during battles, in this case we must wonder how good his information was. Cleon, of course, died in the battle and could not be a direct source, and the Athenian soldiers who might have informed Thucydides almost two decades later were not likely to be unbiased, even if they were privy to Cleon's private thoughts.[71] We cannot know what Cleon thought, but we have no reason to believe that he under-

poets of Athens. How accurate would our picture of Socrates be if it depended on his portrayal in the *Clouds?* What would we think of Pericles if we believed Aristophanes, Eupolis, and the others? "No other public man, of any age or nation has been condemned upon such evidence. No man thinks of judging Sir Robert Walpole, or Mr. Fox, or Mirabeau, from the numerous lampoons put into circulation against them: no man will take the measure of a political Englishman from *Punch*, or a Frenchman from the *Charivari*" (Grote VI, 482).

[68] 5.7.3: ἀλλ' ὡς κύκλῳ περιστὰς βίᾳ αἱρήσων τὴν πόλιν. [69] 5.7.4.
[70] 5.7.5.   [71] Woodhead, *Mnemosyne* XXI (1960), 308.

estimated the Peloponnesian force and so foolishly endangered his army. Even when Brasidas, who must have begun to move his army to Amphipolis when he saw Cleon marching north from Eion, united his force with the troops of Clearidas in the city he did not dare make an attack, thinking his force inferior in quality if not in numbers.[72] Cleon had every reason to believe that, having completed his reconnaissance, he could withdraw safely to Eion.

Brasidas, however, was desperately anxious to prevent such a withdrawal. His position grew weaker and more dangerous each day. No help was to be expected from Sparta; the Macedonians had deserted him; money and provisions were in short supply. The Athenians, on the other hand, were equal in number and superior in quality. They were commanded by a bold and successful general who had shown extraordinary skill in besieging and storming fortified towns. The arrival of the Thracians would complete their encirclement of his forces. Time was on their side, and Brasidas could not afford to lose the chance of attacking the Athenian army in the field, whatever the danger. He left the main body of troops under the command of Clearidas, selecting 150 men for himself. "He planned to make an immediate attack before the Athenians could get away, thinking that he would not again find them so isolated if their reinforcements should arrive." [73]

Brasidas' plan seems to have been something like this: after arriving in the city he ostentatiously made the sacrifices that precede battle and gathered with the forces of Clearidas near the northernmost, or Thracian gate of the city. He would threaten to attack Cleon from that gate and force him to move southward, past the eastern wall of Amphipolis, toward Eion.[74] As the Athenian army filed past the city, down from the heights so that it could no longer observe movements within, Brasidas would place his picked men at the southern gate. There he could wait for a favorable moment to make a sudden and unexpected attack, for the Athenians would think the danger was past when they had safely gotten by the Thracian gate. The surprised Athenians would be forced to engage and would probably con-

[72] 5.8.1.   [73] 5.8.4.   [74] See Map 8.

centrate all their attention on their attackers, not knowing how many they were and assuming that the whole army had moved from the northern to the southern gates to make the attack. While the Athenians were occupied by Brasidas, Clearidas could then come out of the Thracian gate, take the Athenians in the flank, and rout them.[75]

To be sure, the plan contained an element of risk. If the Athenians were alert and kept their heads, they might destroy the small attacking force under Brasidas before Clearidas could come to its rescue. But speed and surprise were in Brasidas' favor, and he had no satisfactory alternative. In the circumstances it was a brilliant device, and it worked to perfection. Cleon appears to have gone forward to conduct his reconnaissance ahead of the main body of his army, somewhere to the north or northeast.[76] Word was brought to him that the whole army was visible in the city, most of it massed at the Thracian gate. Since the bulk of his army must have been south of that position, he judged it wise and safe to order a withdrawal to Eion, for he had never planned to fight a pitched battle without reinforcements. This was a sensible response, and, as Thucydides tells us, the march south to Eion and the left turn for the army it required was "the only way possible." [77] Success depended on two things: an accurate judgment of the time available for the withdrawal and the proper use of military techniques to guarantee the safety of the maneuver.

As Thucydides tells the story Cleon, judging that there was time to get away, gave orders to signal the retreat and at the same time passed the word verbally. It appears that some complicated maneuver by the left wing was involved to guarantee the safety of the retreating column.[78] This movement took some time, however, and Cleon, thinking things were going too slowly, himself posted at the most dangerous position on the

---

[75] The foregoing reconstruction fits the topography of Pritchett, but does not conflict with that of Gomme in any important way, the main difference being the placing of the gates.

[76] Gomme, *HCT* III, 646.   [77] 5.10.3–4.

[78] Romilly, ed., *Thucydide*, III, 187, says, "Une chose est sûre, c'est que ὑπάγειν designe une manoeuvre précise, permettant une retraite organisée."

right wing, wheeled it around to march left, leaving its un-
shielded right side exposed to attack. Apparently this movement,
or the failure to coordinate it with the movement of the left,
caused confusion and a breach of order.[79] Brasidas, who had
allowed the Athenian left wing to go by, took this as a signal to
attack. He burst from the southern gates on the run and struck
the Athenian center which was taken wholly by surprise. The
Athenians, "amazed by his daring and terrified by their own
disorder, turned and ran." [80]

At just the right moment Clearidas came out from the
Thracian gate, catching the Athenians on the flank and throw-
ing them into further confusion. The men on the left wing, instead of rallying to the aid of their comrades, fled to Eion. The
right wing, where Cleon was in command, stood its ground
bravely. Thucydides tells us that Cleon, since he had never intended to stand and fight, "fled immediately," and was killed by
the spear of a Myrcinian peltast. His men, however, stood their
ground and fought bravely; they were not routed until attacked
by javelin throwers and cavalry. The Athenian cavalry, apparently, had been left at Eion, since no battle had been intended
or expected. About 600 Athenians, including their commander
Cleon, were killed. The rest escaped to Eion. Of the Spartans
only 7 men fell; among them, however, was Brasidas who died
soon after his first assault. He was carried from the field still
breathing and lived long enough to learn he had won his last
battle.[81]

The picture that emerges from Thucydides' narrative is that
Brasidas was heroic and brilliant while Cleon was cowardly and
incompetent. The historian's report of the grumbling of the
Athenian soldiers, the story of the battle, emphasis on Cleon's
error and flight, closes the case. Yet modern scholars have wondered. The Athenians certainly made some mistake, but what it
was Thucydides does not make clear. Perhaps Cleon misjudged
the time available for a safe withdrawal; he may have ordered
the right to wheel too early; he may have been insufficiently

[79] Pritchett explains αὐτὸς ἐπιστρέψας τὸ δεξιόν, 5.10.4, as being intransi-
tive and meaning "to do the epistrophe, a quarter-turn." I do not understand the significance of this version.
[80] 5.10.6.   [81] 5.10.6–12.

acquainted with the proper techniques for conducting a withdrawal in the face of an enemy,[82] or he may have been inexperienced in giving military signals and caused confusion in that way.[83] All of these explanations are possible, though none is certain, and Cleon may have been surprised by an extremely clever stratagem and could not recover from the initial disadvantage. None of these explanations would be evidence of general incompetence, especially in light of the great ability he had already displayed at Torone, and Galepsus. At worst they would show that a talented amateur soldier had made a mistake caused by inexperience; at best that a good general had been beaten by a brilliant one. The truth is somewhere between those positions.

Though Thucydides does not openly accuse Cleon of cowardice, he reports such a charge on the lips of Athenian soldiers before the battle, and it is implicit in his account of Cleon's death: "As for Cleon, since from the first he had not intended to stand and fight, he fled immediately and was overtaken by a Myrcinian peltast and was killed." [84] Modern scholars have used this passage as a basis for saying that Cleon was "stabbed in the back as he fled," [85] or "as better soldiers have done, he ran away, and was killed." [86] Busolt was right to see "a cutting irony" in the account of Thucydides, but it is not justified. Cleon, as Gomme pointed out, did not run off with the left wing, "but stayed in the rear, as Greek commanders did when an army was in retreat; for he was killed by one of Klearidas' force." [87] He was killed by a peltast, moreover, and so "by a javelin, i.e., something thrown from a safe distance, and, for all that we know, he was struck in the chest." [88] As the Spartans had said in respect to their men at Sphacteria, "It would be quite a shaft that could distinguish the brave."

Thucydides, to be sure, contrasts the flight of Cleon with

[82] The suggestion adopted by Gomme, HCT III, 647–648, and Hellenika, XIII (1954), 6–7, is a combination of the second and third of these possibilities.

[83] Such is the view of J. K. Anderson, JHS LXXXV (1965), 1–4.

[84] 5.10.9.

[85] J. G. Frazer on Pausanias 1.29.13, cited by Gomme, HCT III, 652.

[86] Adcock, CAH V, 248.   [87] Gomme, Hellenika XIII (1954), 7.

[88] Ibid.

the behavior of his soldiers on the right wing, who stood their ground and resisted until their position became impossible. But, since the plan was not to stand and fight, Cleon was right to flee and the hoplites of the right wing wrong to make a stand if there were any way to avoid it. We cannot know what was possible from the account of Thucydides, but even his staunch defender, Gomme, admits that "with the evidence of Thucydides' bias before us, and considering the uncertainty of any report of this kind from the middle of a confused battle which ended in a humiliating defeat, I would not be certain that he was, on this occasion, sufficiently awake to his own principles of work, 1.22.3." [89] An ancient tradition clearly shows Cleon fighting bravely at Amphipolis. [90] Pausanias tells us that in the Cerameicus in Athens, where the state's honored war dead were buried, Nicias' name was excluded from the stone commemorating those who died fighting in Sicily because he surrendered to the enemy, while his colleague Demosthenes made a truce for his men but not for himself and tried to commit suicide. Nicias, therefore, was excluded as "a voluntary prisoner and an unworthy soldier." On the other hand, the Athenians placed the name of Cleon at the head of those who fought at Amphipolis. [91] We should not doubt his courage any more than his countrymen did.

The main result of the battle of Amphipolis was the deaths of the two whom Thucydides referred to as "the men on each side most opposed to peace." [92] Brasidas, even in death, received extraordinary honors from those who admired and followed him alive. The people of Amphipolis gave him a solemn funeral, buried him publicly within the city in a spot facing the *agora*,

[89] Gomme, *HCT* III, 652.

[90] Diod. 12.74.2. While his account of the battle itself is worthless, there was no good reason why Diodorus, or his probable source Ephorus, neither of whom is particularly friendly to demagogues, democrats, or Cleon, should have abandoned the account of Thucydides to invent Cleon's bravery. Most likely, they are merely reporting an alternate account, although Diodorus is fond of describing heroic deaths of generals. As Baldwin (*PACA*, 214) points out, moreover, there is support for the idea of a pro-Cleon tradition in psuedo-Demosthenes, *Second Speech against Boeotus*, 25, where Cleon is spoken of as a great general because of Pylos.

[91] Paus. 1.29.11–13.   [92] 5.16.1.

built him a monument and fenced it in, adopted him as founder of the city in place of the Athenian Hagnon, and worshiped him as a hero, a man become a god, instituting athletic contests and annual sacrifices in his honor.[93] The devotion to an individual Spartan signaled by these honors helps explain why conservative Spartans were suspicious of the plans and purposes of their great general. Since he received extraordinary honors while alive, we can understand the basis for Thucydides' statement that Brasidas opposed peace "because of the success and honor he got in the war." [94] It would be wrong, however, to emphasize personal motives alone. We need not doubt that Brasidas sincerely believed that the best interests of Sparta required the destruction of the Athenian Empire and the restoration of Spartan supremacy, unquestioned in the Hellenic world and respected by barbarian kings. He must have been a Spartan of the sort who had wanted to pursue the war against Persia after Plataea and Mycale, who regretted acquiescence in the growth of the Delian League and its conversion into an empire, who opposed the peace of 445 and exiled King Pleistoanax for his part in it, and who supported Sthenelaidas against King Archidamus on the vote for war. We know that during the war Brasidas was the strongest voice in Sparta for daring and aggressive campaigning. His plan of ignoring the truce in the hope of forcing Sparta to keep fighting for victory, moreover, was working. Even as he died reinforcements had been sent from Sparta. Nine hundred Peloponnesian hoplites under three Spartan commanders were on their way to Thrace. At Heraclea in Trachis they were stopped by Thessalian opposition, but their dispatch shows that the supporters of war had regained strength.[95] Had Brasidas lived we may be sure that the war in the north, at least, would have continued. His death was a serious blow to the men of his persuasion and deprived Sparta of its ablest general, but what the Spartans needed more than anything in 422/1 was peace, and the death of Brasidas removed an important barrier to it.

Thucydides' final words on Cleon make a fitting conclusion to the damning portrait he had already painted—Cleon opposed

[93] 5.11.1.   [94] 5.16.1.   [95] 5.12.1–2.

peace because its coming would make the exposure of his evil
deeds more likely and his slanders less capable of belief.[96] Such
motives would be treated as incredible if they were suggested by
Diodorus instead of Thucydides, yet they are very similar to the
motives Diodorus attributes to Pericles for starting the war,
which are generally and rightly dismissed as absurd.[97] Grote
long ago presented the most powerful reasons for rejecting this
judgment of Thucydides'[98] and we should reject it, too. We
have no reason to doubt that, like Brasidas, Cleon pursued an
aggressive policy out of sincere conviction that it was best for
his city. We need not question the judgment of the ancient
writers that his vulgar style lowered the tone of Athenian political life, nor approve the harshness of his policy toward rebellious allies. We must, however, recognize that in the formation and conduct of Athenian foreign policy Cleon represented
a broad spectrum of opinion and that he always carried his
policy forward energetically and bravely. We have argued that
he was right to urge rejection of the Spartan peace offers in and
after 425, to insist on the support of Demosthenes at Sphacteria,
and to propose an expedition to Thrace after the expiration of
the truce in 422. Whether or not those judgments are correct
we must understand that in each case Cleon represented a considerable number of Athenians, and he spoke for them honestly
and directly, without deception or deviousness. Though he is
often referred to as the first of the Athenian demagogues, he
did not flatter the masses but addressed them in the severe,
challenging, realistic language sometimes used by Pericles.[99]
Moreover, he put his own life on the line, serving on the expeditions he recommended and dying on the last one. Whatever
Thucydides' "sensible men" might think, Athens was not better
off after his death. The views he represented did not disappear
but were put forward by other and worse men, some of whom
lacked his capacity, some his patriotism, others his honesty, still
others his courage. Thucydides is right, however, when he says
that Cleon's death, like that of Brasidas, cleared the way for
peace. For the moment there was no one in Athens with the

[96] 5.16.1.   [97] See Gomme, *HCT* III, 660–661.   [98] VI, 480–489.
[99] *Ibid.*, 483–484.

stature to oppose the movement for peace powerfully led by Nicias.

Brasidas' death stopped the reinforcing expedition to Thrace. Its chief commander Ramphias judged that the time was no longer ripe: the Athenians no longer threatened Amphipolis, he did not feel capable of carrying out Brasidas' plans without his inspired leadership, and the Thessalians still proved stubborn. Even more important, however, was the general's knowledge of sentiment in Sparta: "They went back chiefly because they knew, when they set out, that the Spartans were more inclined toward peace." [100]

In spite of the victory at Amphipolis, Ramphias understood the feelings of his countrymen correctly. That victory changed little; every day Sparta's need for peace grew greater. Most Spartans had given up hope of achieving total victory and their grandiose original war aims, the destruction of the Athenian Empire and the liberation of the Greeks. As early as 427 they had recognized that a negotiated peace might be necessary,[101] and since the capture of their men at Sphacteria they had sought it repeatedly. The original strategy had failed: repeated invasions of Attica had neither forced the Athenian army to come out and fight nor had they, in spite of the unforeseen disaster of the plague, broken the Athenian spirit and will to resist. The Spartans, moreover, could no longer invade and ravage Attic soil for fear that their men held prisoner in Athens would be killed. The Peloponnesian navy had proven useless and no longer existed. Rebellions in the Athenian Empire had failed because they were not supported effectively by the Peloponnesians. Brasidas' new, more daring strategy, though more successful than anyone expected, could accomplish little without a much greater commitment of men than Sparta was willing to make, and even if it were willing there was no way to send reinforcements while Athens ruled the sea and Perdiccas and his Thessalian friends were hostile.

[100] 5.13.2; Gomme, *HCT* III, 657, suggests that they may have thought as follows: "Brasidas had to be helped against Cleon, but there is now no need for that, and they will *prefer* that we return."

[101] 3.52.2; see above, p. 171.

To these reasons for discouragement were added causes for
alarm. The Peloponnese continued to be open to assaults from
the Athenian bases at Pylos and Cythera, and these frightening
attacks would resume if the war continued. Because these bases
existed as places of refuge, the helots were deserting, and the
fear grew in Sparta of another great helot rebellion incited and
supported by those who had escaped.[102] No less menacing was
the fact that Sparta's Thirty Years' Treaty with Argos was on
the point of expiring. The Argives, who had prospered during
the war,[103] were eager to take advantage of Sparta's troubles
and insisted on the restoration to them of Cynuria as a condition
for renewing the treaty.[104] Before his death Cleon had negotiated with the Argive democracy,[105] and if the war continued
the Spartans would surely find themselves faced with an Argive-
Athenian coalition which they could not have combated.[106]
They also feared with good reason, that in such an event several
members of the Spartan alliance would go over to Argos.

The Mantineans were the most likely to defect from the Spartan alliance and join with Argos. Their moderate democratic
constitution accorded well with the Argive democracy. The
war had no meaning for Mantinea but was a drain on her manpower and a nuisance; the Mantineans probably were among the
allies of Sparta who voted against the motion to go to war.[107]
In spite of an agreement made by Sparta's allies at the start of
the war that each state's territory should be secure,[108] the Mantineans had taken advantage of Sparta's preoccupation to extend
their frontier westward into the territory of the Parrhasians and
to build a fort on the border of Laconia.[109] In the winter of
423/2, during the truce, Mantinea fought a battle against its old
enemy and neighbor Tegea, probably because the Tegeans were
troubled by the growth in Mantinean power.[110] The battle
ended in a draw and checked expansion of Mantinea, but its
people must have been aware that a Sparta free of distractions
would try to undo what Mantinea had accomplished and pun-

[102] 5.14.3.   [103] 5.28.   [104] 5.14.4.
[105] Aristoph. *Knights* 465–466.   [106] 5.14.4.
[107] Busolt, *GG* III:2, 1187.   [108] 5.31.5; Busolt, *GG* III:2, 857, n. 2.
[109] 5.33.1; Gomme, *HCT* IV, 31–34.
[110] 4.134; Busolt, *GG* III:2, 1187–1188.

ish them for a breach of the agreement. If Argos joined in the war against Sparta, Mantinea could be counted on to go along.

The Spartans were also on bad terms with Elis. Some time before the war the Eleans had gained control of the town of Lepreum and forced it to pay tax of a talent to Zeus at Olympia, whose sanctuary they controlled.[111] Until the war the Lepreates paid regularly, but they used the war as an excuse to stop. The Eleans resorted to force and the Lepreates turned to Sparta for help. The Spartans said they would arbitrate the dispute, but the Eleans, knowing the Spartan suspicion of them and their recently unified state with its moderate democratic constitution, did not expect justice, rejected arbitration, and attacked the land of Lepreum. Sparta now decided that Lepreum was independent and Elis the aggressor and sent a garrison to aid Lepreum. The Eleans regarded this act as a breach of the agreement guaranteeing the integrity of each state's territory.[112] If Argos broke off the peace with Sparta, and especially if Mantinea joined her, Elis was more than likely to do the same.

Finally, some of the leading Spartans had pressing private reasons for wanting peace as soon as possible. A number of the prisoners taken at Sphacteria were from the leading families and relatives of the most influential Spartans.[113] They had been imprisoned for more than three years, and their friends at home were eager to bring them back. Perhaps the most important advocate of peace was King Pleistoanax. Although his entire career suggests he was sincerely in favor of peace, the limitation of Spartan activity to the Peloponnese, and friendship with Athens, Thucydides tells us he also had personal reasons for wishing to end the war. His enemies had never forgiven him for failing to invade and destroy Attica in the First Peloponnesian War when it seemed easy to do so. He had been accused of misfeasance on that occasion, fined, and ultimately exiled.[114] He had been brought back in the twentieth year of his exile, but even then

---

[111] 5.31.2; Busolt suggests that the tax was for admission to the Olympic games (GG III:2, 1188), thus payable every four years. Thucydides does not make that clear and it is possible, though perhaps less likely, that the payment was annual.

[112] 5.31.   [113] 5.15.1; see Gomme, HCT III, 659.

[114] Plut. Per. 22.

his enemies accused him of bribing the Delphic Oracle to bring about his restoration. Thereafter, whenever the Spartans suffered a defeat or misfortune they blamed Pleistoanax and his illegal restoration. He believed that if peace were concluded there would be no disasters, the prisoners would be returned, and his enemies would stop their attacks, and so, as Thucydides says, "he was very eager for a treaty." [115] Because of their discouragement, their fears, and these personal reasons, the Spartans pressed hard for peace.

From a coldly objective point of view the Athenians seem to have had less reason to be eager for a negotiated peace. Their territory had not been ravaged for over three years, and they continued to hold the prisoners who guaranteed that immunity. Though the attack on Amphipolis had failed, the Spartans were unable to send reinforcements. The financial condition of Athens at this time is much debated. Most scholars, simply subtracting the amount borrowed from the sacred treasuries during the war from the reserve fund available before the war, omitting the special emergency reserve of 1,000 talents, conclude that the treasury was all but exhausted and that the Athenians had no choice but to make peace.[116] If they are right it is truly amazing that Thucydides, who makes so much of the critical role of money in waging war and takes such pains to describe the precise condition of Athenian finances in 431, does not mention the lack of money as a motive for making peace ten years later.[117]

[115] 5.17.1.

[116] Eduard Meyer (*Forsch.* II, 127–130) estimates that in 421 the Athenians had a disposable reserve of only 700 talents. *ATL* gives the figure for the reserve in the summer of 422 as 444; its authors say, "In this year the treasury was almost depleted, the sum still available being considerably less than was required for one year of war, and the balance growing progressively smaller" (III, 344, n. 94).

[117] Gomme (*HCT* II, 433–434) has suggested that the problem of determining the amount the Athenians had in reserve in any year is more complicated. He imagines that each year, after a large sum "had been put aside for maintenance of ships and arsenals, training of crews, and routine exercises, and perhaps for building new ships, the rest was automatically handed over to the tamiai of Athena to be placed in her treasury." Thus annual income and reserve would be placed in the same treasuries and the records we have of "loans" would include pay-

Whether the amount in the treasury was less than 500 talents, or 700, or a higher figure, the reserve was shrinking. The war could not go on indefinitely without exhausting the treasury. On the other hand, the lowest figure would have enabled the Athenians to hold out for another year. As a result of the increased tribute Athens' annual income at the time of the peace was somewhere between 1,500 and 2,000 talents,[118] which would allow a considerable war effort without dipping too deeply into reserves. A calculation of the average depletion of the treasury in the last six years of the war yields a figure just over 83 talents.[119] At the same rate of expenditure, accepting the lowest figure for the reserve, the Athenians might expect to keep fighting for five years more. Even if we assume the highest depletion in those years as typical the Athenians could have fought three more years. While financial considerations were important, in 421 they were not yet critical, and we need not be too surprised at Thucydides' failure to mention them.

---

ments from the annual income as well as from the reserve. He suggests that the *eisphora*, too, may first have been placed in the treasuries before being expended. He concludes: "If this is right, it is important that we cannot simply subtract the total sum borrowed from Athena and the Other Gods from the 5,000 tal. in the reserve in 431. . . , and say that only so much was left at the end of the ten years' war, because some money will have been paid in every year, and perhaps considerable sums after the reassessment of tribute in 425." He estimates that Athens must have had not much less than 1,400 talents in reserve at the Peace of Nicias (*HCT* III, 687–689).

There is no direct evidence to support Gomme's theory and certainly little support for his high figure for the Athenian reserve in 421, though we cannot be sure he is wrong. Perhaps Meyer's figure of 700 talents is closer to the truth than either extreme.

[118] *ATL* III, 344–345.

[119] The figures are taken from the estimates in *ATL*, III, 342–344:

Year	Reserve	Depletion
428	945	–
427	835	110
426	835	–
425	674	161
424	654	20
423	596	58
422	444	152
		501

501 divided by 6 yields 83.5 as the average annual depletion.

The Athenians could, therefore, have continued the war, but most of them did not want to. The failures in Megara and Boeotia and the rebellions in Thrace dimmed the hopes they had conceived after Pylos. Their losses at Delium, in particular, showed the high cost of waging an aggressive war. Even more important was their fear that if the war went on there might be more rebellions in the empire. The response to Brasidas' invasion of Thrace might be a harbinger of the future. The increase in the tribute made possible by the great victory at Pylos and the resulting humiliation of Sparta had certainly caused resentment. Allied fear of Athens had been reduced by her recent defeats, and resentment might produce further uprisings.[120] Such were the fears of the Athenians, but they were exaggerated. In fact, there was little danger of revolt in the islands or on Asia Minor as long as Athens ruled the seas unchallenged. Even the risings in the Chalcidice had been checked and were no longer likely to spread. For the Athenians, however, the fear was a reality, and it helped move them toward peace.

The political situation in Athens also favored peace. The supporters of a continued war were, of course, in disrepute because of their recent failures. Even more important in their loss of influence was their loss of leadership. Hippocrates had died at Delium, and Cleon, their most influential voice in the *ecclesia*, at Amphipolis. Demosthenes survived, but he seems not to have been as effective in Athens as he was in the field. This left the way clear for Nicias to exert his considerable influence with little effective resistance. Thucydides, as usual, emphasizes Nicias' private motives for seeking peace. He had been the most successful Athenian general of his time, according to Thucydides, and he wanted to keep his record clean, to give himself and his countrymen a rest from the labors of war, but also "to hand down a name to posterity as a man who had never done harm to his city." He therefore wanted to avoid taking further chances, a course possible only in peacetime.[121] We may be inclined to emphasize less personal motives. Nicias had fought bravely and well when called upon. He was cautious by nature, but he had not wavered from Pericles' policy of fighting with

[120] 5.14.1–2.   [121] 5.16.1.

determination and restraint. We have no evidence that he sought peace before the victory at Pylos made a Periclean peace seem possible. After that he saw no further reason to fight and consistently sought to persuade the Athenians to make peace out of conviction that such a course was best for Athens; a discussion of other motives is interesting but of secondary importance.

Discouragement with the progress of the war, financial problems, the removal of the leaders of the war party, all help explain a movement toward peace, yet we still may wonder why the Athenians, after so many sacrifices, should have been willing to make peace at the very moment when their prospects were brighter than at any time since Pylos. All they need do was wait for Argos to break off her treaty with Sparta and join with her in a renewed effort. A coalition of Argos, Mantinea, Elis, and perhaps others could be left to engage the Spartans in the Peloponnese. The Athenians could launch simultaneous attacks from Pylos and Cythera and try to stir up the helots. This would completely occupy the Peloponnesians, leaving Athens free to use all its forces against Megara. There was at least a good chance that the Peloponnesian League might collapse, destroying Sparta's power and leaving Athens free to deal with an isolated Boeotia. Even if these happy results were not achieved Sparta was bound to be badly weakened and forced to make a peace more favorable to Athens.

These rational calculations do not reckon with the fatigue, the simple war weariness, felt by the Athenians in 421. They had suffered heavy losses in battle and in the plague, they had wasted treasure long in the accumulation, and they had seen their homes in the country destroyed, their olive trees and grape vines cut down. Plutarch indicates that the men of property and the farmers were most receptive to the peace,[122] something we might have inferred from general probability and from the evidence of Aristophanes. Dicaeopolis in the *Acharnians*, produced at the Lenaean Dionysia early in 425, must be regarded as typical of the Attic farmer, crowded into Athens against his will, eager for peace and return to his farm, and only somewhat

[122] *Nic.* 8.4.

exaggerated for comic effect. He sits on the Pnyx on assembly day at the beginning of the play; having arrived early, he complains of the tardiness of the city folk who tarry in the *agora* below:

> But as for making Peace
> They do not care one jot. O City! City!
> But I am always first of all to come,
> And here I take my seat; then, all alone,
> I pass the time complaining, yawning, stretching,
> I fidget, write, twitch hairs out, do my sums,
> Gaze fondly country-wards, longing for Peace,
> Loathing the town, sick for my village-home,
> Which never cried, *Come, buy my charcoal*, or
> *My vinegar, my oil, my* anything;
> But freely gave us all; no *buy*-word there.
> So here I'm waiting, thoroughly prepared
> To riot, wrangle, interrupt the speakers
> Whene'er they speak of anything but Peace.[123]

By the winter of 422/1, Athenian farmers might return to look at their farms, but were not secure enough to rebuild their houses and, even if they had replanted their trees and vines, most of these could not yet bear fruit. We are told that while peace talks were going on, men "longed for the old undefiled life without war," hearing with pleasure the line from a chorus in the *Erechtheus* of Euripides: "Let my spear lie unused for the spider to cover with webs," [124] and gladly recalling the saying that "in peace sleepers are awakened not by the trumpet but by the cock." [125] Aristophanes' *Peace*, produced at the great Dionysia in Athens in the spring of 421, just before the peace was finally approved, is full of the same kind of longing, now expressed joyously at the prospect of an end to the war. Trygaeus, a later version of Dicaeopolis, sings a paean to Peace:

> Think of all the thousand pleasures,
> Comrades, which to Peace we owe,
> All the life of ease and comfort
> Which she gave us long ago;

[123] Aristophanes, *Acharnians*, trans. B. B. Rogers (London, 1910), 26–39.
[124] Cited in Plut. *Nic.* 9.5.   [125] *Ibid.*

Figs and olives, wine and myrtles,
Luscious fruits preserved and dried,
Banks of fragrant violets, blowing
By the crystal fountain's side;
Scenes for which our hearts are yearning,
Joys that we have missed so long,—
—Comrades, here is Peace returning,
Greet her back with dance and song! [126]

Trygaeus also looks forward to the opportunity to worship at the sacred places in the country from which the Athenians had been driven at the beginning of the war [127] and the opportunity once again to celebrate religious festivals and games.[128] As Ehrenberg says, "Peace is realized in what seemed to the poet, and to the majority of the people, its most important aspect: as the necessary condition for the farmer's tranquil work and for the religious obligations and festivals which were part of the normal life of Greece." [129] The entire play "is a lively illustration of the feelings at Athens at this time, soberly described by Thucydides," [130] and the mood it depicts helps us understand the Athenian decision in favor of peace in 421.

In spite of the growing sentiment for it, peace was still not easy to attain. Though negotiations must have begun soon after the battle of Amphipolis, in the winter of 422/1,[131] discussions continued into the following spring. The main figure, not only in negotiating with the Spartans but also in convincing the Athenians, was Nicias.[132] He made good use of the great popularity he had won by his military successes and his reputation for piety, fortified by his lavish expenditure for religious observations and other public services,[133] to bring more bellicose Athenians around to his view. He also had a special relationship with the Spartans which made him the ideal negotiator. Though not their proxenos (that post was held by Alcibiades) [134] he had shown

[126] Aristophanes, Peace, trans. B. B. Rogers (London, 1866), 571–581.
[127] 2.16.2.   [128] Peace 887–908.
[129] Victor Ehrenberg, The People of Aristophanes (Oxford, 1951), 56.
[130] Gomme, HCT III, 658.
[131] 5.14.1; Plut. Nic. 9.5; Busolt, GG III:2, 1190.
[132] 5.43.2; Plut. Nic. 9; Alc. 14.   [133] Plut. Nic. 3.
[134] Plut. Alc. 14.

special kindnesses to their prisoners and so earned the confidence and affection of the Spartans [135] who might well believe they had found a new Cimon, for he had been an advocate of peace and friendship since 425.

In Athens, however, Nicias' arguments were still unavailing, and the Spartans turned to a dangerous expedient in a desperate gamble to obtain peace. Toward the beginning of spring "there was a preliminary flourish of preparation on the part of the Spartans" as though for the building of a permanent fort in Attica, so that the Athenians might be more inclined to listen to reason.[136] Though this might have been a bluff that could be withdrawn if the Athenians held fast, it was risky. The Athenians in fear and anger might have killed the prisoners at once and put an end to the chance for peace. We cannot know whether the action was seriously intended and ordered by the friends of war who had gained influence because of Spartan exasperation with Athenian delay or a dangerous attempt undertaken by the desperate supporters of peace. If it was a bluff, however, it worked. Agreement was reached to make peace on the general principle of *status quo ante bellum*, with the necessary exceptions that Thebes was to keep Plataea and Athens would keep Nisaea and the former Corinthian territories of Sollium and Anactorium.[137]

The peace was to last for fifty years. It provided for free access to common shrines, for the independence of the temple of Apollo at Delphi, and for the resolution of disputes by peaceful means.[138] The territorial provisions included the restoration of the Athenian border fort of Panactum that had been betrayed to the Boeotians in 422.[139] Sparta also promised to restore Amphipolis to Athens, though its citizens and those of other cities were free to depart unhindered and take their property with them. The idea, no doubt, was to prevent future civil strife which

---

[135] Plut. *Nic.* 9.   [136] 5.17.2.

[137] 5.17.2; 30.2 Plataea and Nisaea are not mentioned in the treaty. They were omitted, no doubt, on the specious grounds that they had yielded by agreement and were not taken by force. Thucydides does not even mention Sollium and Anactorium in this context. See the discussion of Gomme, *HCT* III, 666.

[138] 5.18.1–4.   [139] 5.3.5.

would endanger the peace.[140] The Spartans also abandoned Torone, Scione, and such other towns as the Athenians had recaptured or were still besieging. For the men of Scione this meant death, since the Athenian assembly had already decreed their fate.[141] The other rebellious Thracian cities were divided into two categories, those states that the Athenians had recovered and those still independent at the time of the peace: Argilus, Stagirus, Acanthus, Stolus, Olynthus, and Spartolus. Amphipolis and the cities of the first class were simply restored to their former condition under Athenian control. The other cities, however, presented a source of great embarrassment to the Spartans who had encouraged their revolts in the name of Greek freedom. As a way of saving face for Sparta the Athenians made a concession, allowing these cities to pay only the Aristidean tribute, not one in accord with the increased assessment of 425. The Athenians promised, moreover, not to attack them in the future as long as they paid their tribute. They were to be neutrals, belonging to neither alliance, but the Athenians were permitted to use peaceful persuasion to try to win them back.[142] Gomme has understood these clauses well: this was "a difficult arrangement to carry out, and not clearly expressed; . . . doubtless because Sparta, to save face, wished to insert something on behalf of those she had so gallantly liberated, but was not prepared to insist on anything precise, and in fact left them in the lurch. They had been allies of Sparta; they were now to be allies of neither—one can see the compromise." The provision allowing Athens to use peaceful persuasion was clearly dangerous and unclear, "but Sparta was anxious to get out of Thrace, and was ready to give her late allies away." [143]

Athens, however, yielded a great deal in her effort for peace, for she conceded a degree of independence to the Chalcidian states not in keeping with her policies in the rest of the empire. Strictly speaking, she accepted a diminution of that empire, which ran counter to the policy of Pericles.[144] She agreed to

[140] 5.18.5; Gomme, HCT III, 668.   [141] 5.18.7.
[142] 5.18.5.   [143] III. 670.
[144] There is some controversy about the meaning of the next clause, dealing with the Thracian towns of Mecyberna, Sane, and Singos (5.18.6).

restore the bases on the periphery of the Peloponnesus that were
giving Sparta so much trouble: Coryphasium, the Spartan name
for Pylos, Cythera, and Methana. Athens also agreed to give
back the island of Atalante and Pteleum, a place not previously
mentioned by Thucydides but perhaps a town on the coast of
Achaea.[145] The clause providing for the exchange of prisoners
deprived Athens of her last hold on Sparta, for she gave up the
men from Sphacteria,[146] but there could be no peace otherwise.

The treaty prescribed the form of the oaths to be taken, the
number of persons in each city to swear them, provided that
they should be renewed each year,[147] and ordered that stelae
bearing copies of the treaty be set up in Athens, Sparta, and at
Olympia, Delphi, and the Isthmus of Corinth, sites of the major
Panhellenic festivals.[148] The final clause made clear that the
peace was one Athens and Sparta imposed on their allies: "If
either side forgets anything, about anything whatsoever, it shall
be in accordance with the oath for both sides, employing just
discussions, to make a change wherever it seems good to both
sides, the Athenians and the Spartans." [149]

The treaty was ratified immediately after the City Dionysia,
"at the end of winter and the beginning of spring," as Thucydides says, only a few days more than ten years after the first
invasion of Attica, perhaps about March 12, 421.[150] There can
be little doubt that the occasion was one of great joy to most
Athenians and Spartans, indeed to most Greeks. In Athens, Plutarch tells us, "it was the opinion of most men that it was mani-
festly a release from evils, and Nicias was in every mouth as a
man dear to the gods, on whom, because of his piety, the divine

---

The authors of *ATL* (III, 90) believe that it gives these towns independence from Athens on the same basis as Olynthus and Acanthus,
while Gomme, *HCT* III, 672–674, thinks it guarantees them security
against Olynthus and Acanthus. Gomme's arguments seem too specu-
lative, and my understanding of καθάπερ 'Ολύνθιοι καὶ 'Ακάνθιοι supports
the views expressed in *ATL*. If they are right, this clause represents still
another Athenian concession to obtain peace. For the suggestion that
Sane should be corrected to Gale, see A. B. West, *AJP* LVIII (1937),
166–173.

[145] 5.18.7; Gomme, *HCT* III, 674.   [146] 5.18.7.   [147] 5.18.9.
[148] 5.18.10.   [149] 5.18.11.
[150] 5.20.1; the estimate of the date is by Gomme, *HCT* III, 711–713.

forces had bestowed the honor of giving his name to the greatest and most beautiful of blessings." [151] It has always been called the Peace of Nicias, and to him, more than any other man, belongs the responsibility for it.

The historian must evaluate the results of the war and judge the character of the peace that followed. On the first question most scholars believe that the Archidamian War resulted in defeat for Sparta and victory for Athens. Eduard Meyer argues that Nicias and his collaborators "deserve the highest recognition for the extraordinary diplomatic skill they showed. In spite of all the defeats of the last years, Athens had achieved what Pericles had set forth as the aim of the war. . . . Athens, in spite of all the mistakes of Cleon and his supporters, had come out of the war the victor; the future of Greece once again lay in her hands." [152] Adcock's judgment is much the same: "If the war was an attack on the Empire of Athens, the Peace acknowledged its failure. . . . Athens had secured by the war what Pericles set out to attain, the vindication of Athenian power." [153] The sober and magisterial Busolt is of the same opinion:

The Spartans, contrary to their often proclaimed purpose of the war, the freeing of the Greeks and the destruction of the Athenian Empire, had not achieved it; much more, they had really recognized the possessions of the Athenians and abandoned the cities that had rebelled trusting in their assurances, some conditionally, others unconditionally. They had even left Nisaea in Athenian hands, although the members of the Peloponnesian League had been guaranteed that they would emerge from the Athenian war with what they had when they entered it. Besides the Megarians, the Boeotians, Corinthians and Eleans wanted nothing to do with the treaty. Sparta's authority was deeply shattered; the Peloponnesian League threatened to fall to pieces. The Spartans found themselves compelled to seek a union with Athens. For the Spartans the ten years' war ended with a decisive political defeat.[154]

Beloch is one of the very few who believe that the peace was not advantageous to Athens, that it produced an unfavorable balance of power, that Athens would need many peaceful years

[151] *Nic.* 9.6.   [152] *GdA* IV, 132–133.   [153] *CAH* V, 251–252.
[154] *GG* III:2, 1197.

"to restore the old equality; but the only security it had that there would be such a respite was a piece of paper, or what came to the same thing, an inscription on a block of marble," that Athens was foolish to make peace when circumstances were most favorable for war.[155] But even he concedes that "the program that Pericles put forth at the beginning of the war had been carried out victoriously." [156]

In spite of this formidable consensus, and in spite of our belief that Sparta had not achieved her purposes and was in serious danger even within the Peloponnese, we cannot agree that the Athenians had achieved anything remotely worth the expenditure of blood and money the war had required. The aim of the Athenians when they went to war was not merely to maintain the status quo but, far more important, to show the Spartans that they could not coerce Athens, that the Athenians were invulnerable, that the empire was a permanent reality and Athens its master, that in the future grievances and differences must be settled by discussion and negotiation, not by threats and force. That aim had not been achieved. To begin with, the status quo had not been restored. Even if the Spartans were willing to try to restore Amphipolis and Panactum, it was far from clear that they could do so. Each was held by a people very hostile to Athens and by no means subservient to Sparta. Plataea, the old and faithful friend of Athens, her comrade in arms at Marathon and loyal ally ever since, was lost. The loss of Amphipolis was compensated by the gain of Nisaea, a place of more strategic, if not sentimental, importance. But Pericles would surely have been appalled by the settlement made with the rebellious cities of Chalcidice. The Athenians had permitted Sparta to intervene in the relations between Athens and her subject allies. Their condition in the future, even the amount of tribute they would pay, was fixed not by Athenians, but by a provision in a treaty between Athens and Sparta. The provision whereby the Spartans implied they might in the future avert their eyes if the Athenians wanted to force these allies into their former condition did not palliate the breach of principle for which Pericles fought the war: the legitimacy, integrity, and independence of the Athenian Empire. This settlement was contrary to what the Corinthians claimed was their understanding of the meaning of the Thirty Years' Peace of 445, the right of each side to deal with its allies as it wished.[157] Argilus, Stagirus, Acanthus, and the Chalcidian towns were still allies of Athens, but Athens was no longer free to do with them as she pleased, but was limited by a treaty with Sparta.

Even more important than these details, however, was the way the peace had been achieved. Though Sparta, as Pericles had expected, initiated the negotiations and had been trying for peace since 425, she did not do so from the conviction that Athens was invulnerable, that the empire was a permanent fact of life. The main forces moving Sparta to peace were either the result of accident or external circumstances: the desire to recover the prisoners and the expiration of the Argive alliance. The Spartans were in temporary difficulty. There was no evidence, however, that the faction that had favored the war was either destroyed or permanently discredited, that after restoring order in the Peloponnese, the Spartans would not seek revenge for the disgrace and damage they had suffered at Athenian hands. The peace gave them time to recover, left them capable of revenge, and unconvinced of their inability to win the war. As Thucydides tells the story the Athenians were *forced* to make peace, at last, by a military threat. That was certainly not the kind of peace Pericles had expected to make. The Archidamian War, we must conclude, brought no useful result to either side: it did not destroy the Athenian Empire, bring freedom to the Greeks, or put an end to Sparta's fear of Athenian power, nor did it bring to Athens the security for which Pericles risked a war. The expenditure of lives, suffering, and money was in vain.

The Peace of Nicias reflected the conditions which produced it. It resembled the Thirty Years' Peace that ended the First Peloponnesian War in that it was a negotiated peace concluding a war that neither side had been able to win. But there the resemblance ends. The territorial provisions in the treaty of 445 reflected reality.[158] The treaty of 421 did not, for it rested on

[157] 1.40.5.   [158] *Outbreak*, 129–130.

implausible Spartan promises to restore Amphipolis and Panactum to Athens and did not even mention Nisaea, Sollium, and Anactorium, certain to embitter Megara and Corinth and so threaten the peace. The earlier treaty was agreed to by an Athens firmly under the control of Pericles, a leader sincerely committed to observing both its letter and spirit, while the Spartans had reason honestly to be satisfied with its terms. The Athens of 421 lacked stable leadership; her policy had shifted many times in recent years, and the enemies of the peace were overcome because of the temporary absence of influential leaders. The internal situation in Sparta is less clear, but many influential Spartans were dissatisfied with the peace. The annual election of ephors could bring enemies of peace to power, so precarious was the Spartan devotion to it, and even the ephors who made the peace were less than zealous in their commitment to carry out all its provisions.[159] Perhaps the most important difference between the treaty of 445 and that of 421 is that Sparta's allies seem to have accepted the former without objection, but Boeotia, Corinth, Elis, Megara, and the Thracian allies refused to accept the latter.[160] In addition, Argos in 421 was bound to neither alliance, ambitious to regain her long lost hegemony in the Peloponnese, and eager to exploit the divisions in the Greek world in her own interest. All these difficulties made the prospects for peace dubious from the start.

These problems were far from the minds of most Athenians when, weary of war, they laughed at Aristophanes' *Peace* at the Great Dionysia in 421. Brasidas and Cleon, the mortar and pestle of war, are dead, and the god of war himself is forced to leave the stage. Trygaeus and the chorus of Athenian farmers are now free to draw the goddess of peace, *Eirene*, from the pit where she has been buried for ten years. Trygaeus and the god Hermes who is helping him may notice that the Boeotians, Megarians, and Argives, and an Athenian like the bellicose Lamachus are not pulling,[161] but the chorus of Athenian farmers has no time for such thoughts. They sing:

> Come then, heart and soul, my comrades,
> > haste to win this great salvation,

[159] 5.35–36.   [160] 5.17.2; 35.3.   [161] 466, 473–477, 481–483.

Now or never, now if ever,
                come, the whole Hellenic nation!
Throw away your ranks and squadrons,
                throw your scarlet plagues away,
Lo, at length the day is dawning,
                Lamachus-detesting day!
O be thou our guide and leader,
                managing, presiding o'er us,
For I think I shan't give over
                in this noble task before us,
Till with levers, cranes and pulleys
                once again to light we haul
Peace, the Goddess best and greatest,
                vineyard-lovingest of all.[162]

Though the Athenians were able to drag peace onto the scene in 421, her visit was not likely to be long.

[162] Aristophanes, *Peace*, trans. B. B. Rogers, 301–308.

Conclusions

The end of the Archidamian War disappointed both sides, which is not surprising in light of the inadequate and ill-conceived strategy with which each entered the war. Thucydides implies and many have believed that the Spartans' flaw was their lack of daring.[1] In the face of the growth of Athenian empire and power, "the Spartans, perceiving what was happening, did little to prevent it and remained quiet for most of the time, for even before this they were not quick to go to war unless they were compelled."[2] He also says that "the Spartans were the most convenient people of all for the Athenians to fight against. . . . For there were very great differences between them in character, the Athenians being quick, the Spartans slow, the Athenians enterprising, the Spartans fearful."[3]

It is hard to think, however, how a more daring policy would have helped. The Spartans might have planted a permanent fort in Attica at the outbreak of the war. That would have annoyed the Athenians and made their lives somewhat more difficult in the years 431 to 425. After 425, Athens' holding of the hostages from Sphacteria would have forced the withdrawal of the garrison and the dismantling of such a fort. Whatever advantage they might gain would not be worth the risk of placing a significant number of men far from home or the cost to main-

---

[1] Brunt, *Phoenix* XIX (1965), 278, says, "Thucydides is highly critical of Spartan lack of enterprise. It is plain from later passages in his work that if he did not invent the Corinthian character sketch in 1.70, he concurred in it."

[2] 1.118.2. [3] 8.96.5.

tain them. To build such a fort, moreover, required a "margin of superiority and the willingness not to reduce it by commitments elsewhere, however urgent might be representations of allies, whose immediate interests might make them support diversionary operations. What was needed, then, was a considerable organized effort, the readiness to provide supplies and some finance, a great and assured military superiority in the field, and some degree of self-confidence and resolute leadership aimed at a result that would be only slowly achieved." [4] All this would in no way guarantee an Athenian surrender.

They might have done better by sea. More skillful and daring admirals might have saved Mytilene and encouraged rebellion elsewhere in the Athenian Empire; they might have destroyed Phormio's little fleet and dominated the Corinthian Gulf; they might have gained control of Corcyra. Their failure to do all this was not from lack of trying but from inability. Pericles knew that a strictly land power could not be converted into a naval power overnight and rightly counted on Spartan naval inexperience. The Spartans cannot be blamed for lack of enterprise in an area of operations where inexperience naturally made them timid. As Brunt says,

His condemnation of Sparta seems . . . too severe. Their fault in 432 lay not in too long deferring an attack on Athens but in overestimating their chances of success. But the estimate they made, that devastation of Attica would give them the victory and that Athens could make no equally effective reply, was at least based on the experience of the past, though belied in the event. When the annual invasions failed and were actually abandoned, there was nothing left for Sparta to do except to embark on the perilous northern adventure. This they did in the very year after Pylos. It was more successful than might reasonably have been predicted, and if the Spartans preferred to "take profits" rather than gamble further, they were not necessarily wrong. . . . Their prestige and authority in the Peloponnese was broken for the time. Events showed that they retained the solid military power needed to restore it.[5]

[4] Adcock, *CR* LXI (1947), 4.   [5] Brunt, *Phoenix* XIX (1965), 278.

No conceivable strategy could guarantee victory to the Spartans against an enemy such as Athens. Great errors of judgment, a failure of will, or some unforeseen natural disaster might bring Athens to her knees, but no military plan could be devised to do it. If the Athenians were prepared to put up with the inconvenience of war and to make sacrifices as long as necessary they could not be defeated by a power such as Sparta, even aided by her allies. The Spartans in a moment of fear and anger had voted to go to war relying on the experience of past wars as a guide to victory, but that experience was no longer relevant. Some Spartans must have known that but depended on the psychological exhaustion of the Athenians after a period of being shut up in their walls, watching their lands devastated and their homes destroyed. Thucydides tells us that most Greeks thought Athens could not hold out for more than three years.[6] Their error was common, perhaps the most frequent and serious in the history of war. They thought that punishment and devastation would bring the enemy to the ground, that he would find the suffering unbearable and accept even an unsatisfactory peace. The truth is that such tactics often stiffen the spine of an enemy, make him angry, sometimes beyond reason and self-interest, and more determined than ever to resist until the end. The Spartans should have taken the advice of Archidamus and delayed before entering a war they were ill-equipped to fight. Having made the mistake of going to war, they should have seized the opportunity offered them by fortune—the great plague at Athens—and made peace on favorable terms in 430. When they rejected that chance they had no further possibility of winning the war, barring egregious Athenian errors or natural disasters.

The Athenians also entered the war with a strategy that could not guarantee nor was likely to produce victory. Pericles did not expect to disable the enemy, to render him physically incapable of resistance. Instead, he also counted on the early psychological exhaustion of the Peloponnesians. His plan of avoiding major battles and even eschewing the fortification of and placing permanent garrisons at strong points around the Pelopon-

[6] 7.28.3.

nese would not bring victory if the Spartans were willing to put up with minor raids and with the annual trouble of making an expedition into Attica. In fact, the Spartans were not exhausted but infuriated by their frustrating attempts to bring Athens down. They refused to see that they could not win and so refused to make the reasonable peace Pericles sought. Pericles never envisaged a war of ten years; neither he nor Athens was ready for it. He was over sixty years old when the war broke out [7] and believed that his own leadership was crucial for the successful operation of his strategy. He could not count on ten more years of active political life.

Pericles' financial plans were also inadequate for a war of ten years. Gomme has estimated that Athens had as much as 1,400 talents in reserve when the war ended and draws the following conclusions: "This would be justification enough for Perikles' confidence that, financially, Athens could hold out: he was right not to act as though the war would last longer than ten years; and even after the disasters of the last three years, they had foiled the Peloponnesian attack, and their empire, the object of that attack, was, in the main, still held. Athens had won, and won without exhausting the financial reserve which had been accumulated for this very purpose of being spent in the defence of the empire." [8] Even if Gomme's high figure for the reserve is accepted, though it is two or three times as high as others, his conclusions do not follow. We have already argued that the peace did not represent a victory for Athens such as Pericles had envisaged. We must also reject the assertion that his financial preparations had proven adequate for a war of ten years. The financial means for carrying on the war so long were provided by the institution of the *eisphora* and an increase in the tribute, both measures not planned for by Pericles and never mentioned at the beginning of the war. The *eisphora* was always

[7] *IG* ii 2318.9–11 shows he was choregus for Aeschylus' *Persians* in 472 which gives 490 as the latest possible date of his birth, though he is unlikely to have performed this liturgy at the tender age of 18. He is not likely to have been chosen as prosecutor of Cimon in 463 if he were not at least 30. That would move his birthdate at least to 493 making him not less than 62 in 431.

[8] *HCT* III, 689.

unpopular with the propertied classes and might have shaken Pericles' control of Athens had he tried to institute it. It was introduced as an emergency measure when the treasury was close to exhaustion and even then was acceptable only because there was no alternative. The Spartans had turned down a peace offer in 430. After that the war must continue whatever the cost. The great increase of the tribute, which was even more important to the Athenian treasury, was something Pericles could not have counted on. In normal times it would have provoked rebellion, but was made possible in 425 by the amazing Athenian victory at Sphacteria, the precipitous decline of Sparta's influence, and the sudden enormous growth of Athenian prestige. No ally dared rebel at that moment, and the tribute could be raised to produce the necessary revenue. This was the result of a strategy employed by Pericles' more aggressive successors. In the judgment of De Sanctis: "If the plan of war did not change, if the Athenians did not try those bold strokes which Pericles wanted to avoid at all costs, it does not appear in any way that the conflict could have been concluded victoriously, and it was to be presumed, without taking account of the unforeseeable things which always have a noteworthy importance in wars, especially when the contenders are roughly equal in strength, that both, after a few years, would have emerged from the conflict drained and impoverished by means of a compromise peace which would not at all have the effect of strengthening the Athenian dominion over her empire, as Pericles had promised." Though De Sanctis knows the Peace of Nicias was no victory for Athens, he believes that it was more favorable to the Athenians than we have suggested. But whatever security Athens had in 421 was "owed above all to the abandonment of the plan of war that Pericles had advised." [9]

Such a conclusion runs directly counter to the judgment made by Thucydides himself that Pericles had excellent grounds before the war "for his personal forecast that Athens would win through quite easily in the war against the Peloponnesians alone." [10] A historian arriving at such a conclusion is necessarily uncomfortable, and most scholars have understandably avoided

[9] De Sanctis, *Pericle*, 253ff.   [10] 2.65.13.

doing so. One way, of course, is to conclude that Pericles was right and that his strategy worked. Most scholars hold this view, but we have been compelled to reject it. Another escape is to argue that the words of Thucydides in this passage do not mean what they seem to. Although the problem of understanding the ambiguities of Thucydidean language will always be great, this particular statement seems clear enough so that we must put aside that possibility.[11]

Finally, some scholars have argued that Pericles' strategy is not the one we have described and that most historians have attributed to him.[12] Gomme, for instance, could not help notic-

[11] My own translation is very close to that of C. Forster Smith. Crawley translated it as follows: "So superfluously abundant were the resources from which the genius of Pericles foresaw an easy triumph in the war over the unaided forces of the Peloponnesians." Mme. de Romilly renders it as follows: "Tant étaient fondées les prévisions personnelles de Périclès, lorsqu'il disait qu'il serait tout à fait aisé pour eux de prendre le dessus dans la guerre les opposant aux seuls Péloponnésiens." I accept the Oxford text by Henry Stuart Jones revised by John Enoch Powell which reads: τοσοῦτον τῷ Περικλεῖ ἐπερίσσευσε τότε ἀφ' ὧν αὐτὸς προέγνω καὶ πάνυ ἂν ῥᾳδίως περιγενέσθαι τὴν πόλιν Πελοποννησίων αὐτῶν τῷ πολέμῳ. Classen deleted τὴν πόλιν and replaced αὐτός with αὐτούς and Steup accepted the substitution on the grounds that still another emphasis on the personal role of Pericles is unsuitable. Gomme, HCT II, 198, saw some difficulties in simply reading αὐτούς "in this emphatic position," and in deleting τὴν πόλιν. He prefers to keep τὴν πόλιν and to bracket αὐτός. He believes that "if we keep in this section, there is in my view only one way to translate it—he saw that he himself, i.e., Athens if guided by him and no other, would defeat the enemy." He regards the reading as barely possible and so rejects it. So should we if we accepted his translation which makes Pericles seem incredibly arrogant, but there is no reason to do so. Mme. de Romilly, who reads the same text as we do, puts the matter well: "Classen a voulu corriger αὐτός en αὐτούς (en ne gardant pas les mots τὴν πόλιν). A. W. Gomme préférait le supprimer et ne le garde qu'en lui donnant la valeur, assez étrange, de 'il voyait que lui-même, c'est-à-dire, Athènes sous sa direction à lui seul'.—Αὐτός a, à notre avis, une valeur plus simple et excéllente. Dans ce passage destiné à montrer combien, malgré les apparences, les prévisions faites par Périclès se revélèrent sûres, le mot αὐτός rappelle qu'il avait formé ces prévisions seul, à la différence de tous" (Thucydide II, 101–102).

[12] Among those scholars who have said that his strategy was wholly or chiefly defensive are Eduard Meyer, Forsch. II, 342; Grote, VI, 122–123; Beloch, GG² II:1, 300; Finley, Thucydides, 141; Grundy, Thucydides, 320, 331; Westlake, Essays, 84ff.; Miltner, "Perikles," PW XIX,

ing that several important passages, he noted four, "show, to a greater or smaller degree, a discrepancy with the narrative of those events," [13] and two of these come from Thucydides' encomium of Pericles and his accurate foresight in 2.65. Thucydides says that Pericles' strategy was right but that his successors "did the opposite of what he advised," but except for the Sicilian expedition of 415–413 he does not say which actions he thought were contrary to that strategy. As Gomme says, "It is a pity that Thucydides was not more precise." [14] Gomme himself would include the campaign that resulted in the battle of Delium, Demosthenes' campaigns in Acarnania and Aetolia during the Archidamian War, and Alcibiades' campaigns in the Peloponnese as well as the Sicilian expedition in the list of departures from the Periclean policy. However, he considers all the other actions, including the taking of Pylos and Cythera, to be in accord with Pericles' policy and thinks that the few departures are "far from justifying the wholesale condemnation of Perikles' successors." He believes, in fact, that "by and large, in spite of Aetolia and Delion, his strategy continued to prevail." To resolve this, to him, intolerable contradiction between the facts narrated by Thucydides and the judgment he makes of them, Gomme resorts to the time-honored device of seeking an explanation in different layers of composition. "There is a discrepancy between II. 65. 6–10 and the narrative of the events to which they should refer; the comment or summing-up, and the narrative were not *thought* at the same time, nor written." [15] But the campaigns of Demosthenes in Aetolia and Acarnania and the great undertaking in Boeotia which culminated in the disaster at Delium are not so lightly brushed off. Nor, we have already argued, were the fortification of Pylos or the seizure of Cythera part of the Periclean plan. If they were, we must repeat the question, why did he not undertake these actions, easy as they were and important as they proved, during the years when he dominated Athenian policy? The successors of Pericles certainly did

---

781; Adcock, *CAH* V, 195–196; Henderson, *Great War*, 62; Busolt, *GG* III:2, 901–902; De Sanctis, *Storia dei Greci*, II, 268; Delbrück, *Strategie*, *passim*.

[13] *More Essays*, 92.   [14] *Ibid.*, 93.   [15] *Ibid.*, 95.

turn against his policy, and with a vengeance. The problem that remains, and the one that prompted Gomme's discomfort, is that the truly Periclean policy was a failure and that Athens was saved because it was abandoned, while Thucydides tells us quite the opposite.

This problem must have led a number of scholars to suggest that Pericles actually had two different strategies. Wade-Gery seems to have invented this approach, putting it forward in capsule form in the first edition of the *Oxford Classical Dictionary*:

The present writer believes that Pericles (having planned an offensive war) lost his striking power, first because Potidaea revolted, next because of the Plague. Forced to the defensive, he left that as his testament. T. was reluctant to face the fact of this failure, and accepted the testament, siding with the defeatist officer class against the revived offensive of Cleon. This is why Pericles' huge effort against Epidaurus is recorded as a minor futility; why Phormion's first campaign in Acarnania is left timeless; why we hear nothing of the purpose of the Megara decree; why, when that nearly bore fruit at last, T. suggests that the capture of Megara was of no great moment.[16]

In its favor, this theory recognizes that the strategic legacy of Pericles was thoroughly defensive and that the account of Thucydides presents many problems. Its main thesis, however, faces insurmountable obstacles. The first is that Thucydides tells us nothing about the dual strategy. We have remarked on the often inexplicable omissions of Thucydides, but if he knew that Pericles originally had one strategy and then was compelled to change to another by events he describes and that he deliberately failed to tell us about it, he was guilty not of omission but the most serious kind of distortion. If Thucydides really did what is here suggested it would in our view be a unique instance and one very damaging, not to the quality of his judgment but to his reputation for honesty. It does no good to say that "the very fact that we can reconstruct Periclean strategy in the war from Thucydides alone ought to show that he did not wholly mis-

[16] 904; this interpretation, with reservations and variations, is accepted by Mortimer H. Chambers, *HSCP* LXII (1957), 79ff., and Raphael Sealey, *Essays*, 75ff., particularly 94–99.

understand the movements."[17] We can often reconstruct the truth about the Duke of Marlborough and William III from Macaulay's very tendentious account in the *History of England* alone, but that does not mean that the account is not seriously distorted.

An even more serious barrier to the acceptance of this theory is the fact, which we must emphasize again, that Pericles did not take any aggressive action in the first year of the war when his resources were close to their peak and the plague had not yet struck. The rebellion and stubborn resistance of Potidaea is no answer. It did not occupy many men and ships before the expedition of 430. The drain on the treasury was never great enough to prevent actions like the fortification of Pylos or the capture of Cythera; it had not been particularly large by the spring of 431. If the extended siege had any effect on the strategy of Pericles, it should have moved him to take aggressive action as soon as possible so as to gain a victory before his money gave out. We have suggested that this was one of his motives in sending Hagnon to Potidaea in 430. In short, there is no evidence for an offensive strategy where we might expect to find it, and the actual course of events discredits the idea that there ever was such a strategy.[18] The same objections apply even more intensely to the argument of B. X. de Wet that a close examination of Thucydides' account reveals that the strategy of Pericles was essentially offensive, the only defensive portion of which applied to the territory around Athens itself. There is no reason to tarry long over this view, either.[19] We are thrown back, then,

[17] Chambers, *HSCP* LXII (1957), 86.

[18] The reasons for cherishing this view are never stated by Wade-Gery in his article, but as they are suggested by Chambers we can see their antecedents in Wade-Gery's old opinion that even after 445 Pericles pursued an aggressive, expansionist policy in both east and west (see Wade-Gery, *Essays*, 239–270). We have argued at some length elsewhere that Pericles' policy after 445 was not expansionist. See Kagan, *Outbreak*, 154–192.

[19] *AClass.*, XII (1969), 103–119. Few of de Wet's arguments carry any weight. The least impressive, perhaps, is the one which urges us to take ἡσυχάζοντας in 2.65.7 to "refer to the particular requirements of the strategy around Athens itself, but because it occurs in a general statement of Periclean policy, it has been misunderstood to refer to his

on the conclusion that Pericles began the war with a strategy that was essentially defensive, one calculated to show the influential men of Sparta the futility of a war against Athens. He expected that they would sue for peace on the basis of *status quo ante bellum* but this time he expected a lasting peace, resting on thorough Spartan recognition of Athenian invincibility. The first year brought signs of trouble. The Spartans showed no sign of yielding, and Potidaea held out stubbornly, draining the Athenian treasury beyond expectations and dangerously cutting Pericles' margin for error. The next year the plague almost brought disaster. Even before it struck, Pericles had decided to increase the pressure with a major attack on Epidaurus. This does not indicate a change of policy, but merely an intensification of the same strategy in an effort to speed the education of the Peloponnesians. We cannot completely exclude the possibility that Pericles intended to take and hold Epidaurus, which would have represented a shift to the kind of strategy later employed by Demosthenes and Cleon. If there was any change in Periclean strategy, this was it, but on balance, the evidence seems to be against it.[20] The attack on Potidaea by Hagnon and his large army was not a departure from the same strategy but a desperate attempt to put an end to the drain on Athenian funds. When Pericles died he "left the defensive war as his testament."[21]

Pericles may not have adhered to the same strategy as the war wore on and discredited his expectations. He was an intelligent and resourceful leader, and there is no reason to doubt that he would soon have seen what was necessary and done it. His error, though serious, is, as we have said, very common. He expected the enemy to see reason when punished and when the futility of further fighting was demonstrated. In our own time the failure of strategies based on aerial bombardment, superior firepower, and naval supremacy have shown that the enemy does not suffer

---

strategy in general" (117). The advice "to remain quiet" certainly does occur in a general summation of Periclean strategy, and it is not limited or modified in any way. We have no right to do so without clear evidence, and de Wet supplies none.

[20] See above, pp. 73–77.   [21] Chambers, *HSCP* LXII (1957), 86.

psychological collapse, but often becomes more determined to persist as punishment increases. This is particularly true when policy makers are not remote aristocratic professional diplomats but citizens of a state where public opinion is a force and where passion and hatred of the enemy often obliterate rational considerations of self-interest. Sparta and Athens were pre-eminently such states. Our century has seen very small powers hold out beyond prudence against vastly superior enemies; in the war between Athens and Sparta, when the two sides were roughly equal, stubborn resistance and sacrifice were even more likely.

When it became clear that the quick peace Pericles sought was impossible—and that was certainly clear after the Spartans rejected peace terms in 430—there was no alternative to a more offensive policy. From 430 to 425 men like Nicias reluctantly moved away from the Periclean program, retaining his desire for a negotiated peace without victory while extending the offensive possibilities. This was an unwise compromise, for the basis for a reliable peace of friendly coexistence was removed by the extension and intensification of the war and by the hatreds it engendered. Demosthenes and Cleon saw the picture more clearly. The only conclusion of the war that would leave Athens secure required either that Spartan power be broken and incapable of menacing Athens, or that the Athenians acquire control of such strategic areas as to make them invulnerable. The first plan was unrealistic, for Spartan military power was too great to encourage the risk of a major battle on land, and that power could not be shattered without such a battle as the Theban victory at Leuctra in 371. The daring and tactical skill of Cleon and Demosthenes, aided by a bit of luck, brought Athens Pylos, the prisoners from Sphacteria, and a respite from attacks from the Peloponnese. Cleon's tough imperial policy of raising the tribute, daring but necessary, made it possible to contemplate offensive actions again. The Spartans were so distracted by raids from Pylos and Cythera and by the escape of helots which gave rise to fears of another great helot rebellion that Cleon and Demosthenes were free to pursue the second of the two routes to victory and safety for Athens. Cleon was quite right to argue against the Spartan peace offer of 425. As Gomme has put it, "The Spartan offer was an empty one: they had been badly defeated and were in a corner; they *ask* for peace; and all they have to offer is a promise of friendship. . . . [The Athenians] refused an empty and, almost certainly, a vain offer; they had obeyed the good military maxim to follow up a victory, to press the enemy hard." [22]

The keys to Athenian invulnerability were Megara and Boeotia. The attack on Megara was well conceived, well executed, and failed only because of extremely bad luck. The democratic fifth columnists in the town just failed to bring off their part of the coup; that would not have been fatal had it not been for the totally unforeseeable accident that Brasidas was nearby gathering his army for the Thracian expedition. Had he not been close enough to defend the city it might have fallen to the Athenians and guaranteed against further attacks from the Peloponnese. The plan to take Boeotia out of the war was more difficult and dangerous. It failed, perhaps because it was too complicated and relied on secrecy for too long a period, certainly because of errors in execution. We need not believe that it was foredoomed. If all the rest of the scheme had failed and only the fort at Delium had been erected without the great defeat that followed, the threat to the Boeotians would have been enough to hinder their incursions into Attica. We must resist the attractions of the *fait accompli*. Both parts of the plan might have succeeded well enough to guarantee immunity for Athens. The attacks from Pylos and Cythera, in the new circumstances, could hardly fail to wear Sparta down and discourage her enough to make peace on Athenian terms. These were goals well worth the risks that Cleon and Demosthenes took. After Pericles' plan had failed they were right and Nicias was wrong.

We may well believe that Pericles would have agreed with them; more than once he had changed strategies to meet new circumstances. His political talents and the steadiness of policy would have made it much easier to succeed in the new strategy. Even so, we must doubt whether Pericles would have embarked upon the war if he had suspected that it would last for ten years and cost so much in men and money. He might have swallowed

[22] *Essays*, 105–106, 107.

his pride, withdrawn the Megarian Decree, and negotiated other differences in the hope of preserving peace through a difficult moment. It is always hard, however, for a proud and able leader of a proud and powerful state, even for so talented a man as Pericles, to see the future clearly and to draw back in the face of a challenge to its pride and power.

Appendix A: Pericles
and Athenian Income

❦

Pericles did not count on increasing Athenian income by asking for the levy of a special direct tax, the *eisphora*, or by raising the assessments of the allies. He made no mention of such plans in his speech to the Athenian people on the eve of the war (2.13), which seems reasonable as his purpose was to encourage the Athenians and win support for his policy. The fact is, however, that the *eisphora* could not have played any part in his thinking. Possibly there never had been an *eisphora*, and it was introduced into Athens for the first time in 428 after the death of Pericles. The words of Thucydides certainly imply that: ἐσενεγκόντες τότε πρῶτον ἐσφορὰν διακόσια τάλαντα. Rudi Thomsen (*Eisphora* [Copenhagen, 1964], 145–146) suggests that Thucydides means to say that in 428 the Athenians levied for the first time an *eisphora* of 200 talents. Earlier G. H. Stevenson (*JHS* XLIV [1924], 1ff.) implied that Thucydides meant "for the first time since the founding of the Delian League," and A. W. Gomme (*HCT* II, 278) suggests "for the first time during the war." The difficulty arises from a reference to *eisphora* in the Callias Decrees, generally dated to 434 (*GHI* 58), in the lines: [ἐς ἄλλ]ο δὲ μεδὲν χρῆσ[θ]α[ι τοῖς χρέμασιν ἐὰμ μὲ τ]ὲν ἄδειαν φσεφ[ίσεται] ὁ δῆμος καθάπερ ἐ[ὰμ φσεφίσεται περὶ ἐσφ]ορᾶς. If the restoration is correct there is a strong implication that the Athenians had employed an *eisphora* some time before 434 and that it was by that time so extraordinary that the

363

assembly had to pass a special vote of immunity before it could be spent. Mattingly's attempt to date the decrees to 422/1 (*BCH* XCII [1968], 450–485; see also Fornara, *GRBS* XI [1970], 185–196) would remove this difficulty, but most epigraphers continue to place it in 434. Probably it is best to assume that Gomme (supported by Meiggs and Lewis, p. 161) is right in thinking that Thucydides meant that the *eisphora* of 428 was the first one levied during the Peloponnesian War. In any case, no one believes that an *eisphora* had been levied since 478, not even during the stresses of the First Peloponnesian War, so its introduction at the urging of Pericles would be shocking and unwelcome to the propertied classes (Busolt, *GG* III:2, 878). The amount collected in 428, moreover, presumably as much as the traffic could bear, would not have significantly altered the financial problem faced by Pericles. It would therefore have been foolish for him to think of undermining his support in Athens by insisting on an unpopular tax which would do him little good.

It should also be clear that he could not have planned to raise the allied tribute. He had strong memories of the rebellions Athens had been forced to suppress in the 450s and 440s. The rebellion in Euboea of 446 had forced him to make peace with Sparta. The rebellion of Samos had provoked one in Byzantium and threatened to cause others. It had brought the Persians into the Aegean and almost caused the Peloponnesians to break the peace. He knew that he had almost been faced with the deadly coalition of rebellious allies, the Great King and the Peloponnesian League (see Kagan, *Outbreak*, 173). Nor could he forget that the defection of Potidaea in 433 had followed shortly after her assessment had been raised (*ibid.*, 274–275). Pericles could not have planned to raise money in that way. The best evidence, of course, is that he made no use of either expedient in the years he guided Athenian policy.

Appendix B: Pericles' Last Speech

❦

2.60.7; this last speech of Pericles is one of those whose authenticity is most commonly doubted. De Sanctis, *Pericle*, 263, for instance, says, "Il discorso é anche qui degno di Tucidide e di Pericle, ma non é tale che Pericle possa per davvero averlo pronunciato davanti all'assemblea. Esso mostra traccie palesi delle ulteriori esperienze della guerra e delle impressioni lasciarono in Tucidide." The view of Eduard Meyer (*Forsch.* II, 389ff.) has been most influential. He argues that Pericles could not have given the speech Thucydides reports at the time he reports it. He may have said some such things, but if so, it must have been at a previous meeting, when the proposal to send an embassy to Sparta was being debated. Thucydides, says Meyer, addresses the speech we have to a later generation, the one which in 404 and shortly after blamed Pericles and Athenian imperialism for Athens' disaster. "Es ist Thukydides selbst, der zu uns spricht; kaum wirt noch die Fiction aufrecht erhalten, dass der Fall Athens nur hypothetisch ist und die Wörte 26 Jahre vorher gesprochen sein sollen. Aber mit vollem recht sind sie dem Perikles in dem mund gelegt . . . , Thukydides darf ihn so sprechen lassen, weil diese gedanken die nothwendige Consequenz der Auffassung des Perikles sind, weil sie seine Denkweise durchaus entsprechen, mit einem Worte nicht weil er so beredet hat, sondern weil er so geredet haben würde—ὡς ἂν ἐδόκει ἐμοὶ τὰ δέοντα μάλιστ' εἰπεῖν—nämlich wenn er die ganze Situation, d.h. hier die

Entwickelung bis zum Jahre 404, hätte übersehen können."
Meyer is followed in these opinions by E. Schwartz, *Thukydides*, and, with greater nuance, by Mme de Romilly, *Thucydides*, 147–155. Meyer's interpretation is characteristic of the
genre in that it totally ignores the second part of Thucydides'
crucial statement on the nature of the speeches—ἐχομένῳ ὅτι
ἐγγύτατα τῆς ξυμπάσης γνώμης τῶν ἀληθῶς λεχθέντων, οὕτως
εἴρηται. That clause seems to me to rule out the possibility that
Thucydides moved speeches around from one place to another
and, *a fortiori*, that he invented speeches. The problem of the
speeches is tricky, but we must set limits to the realm of interpretation if we are to credit Thucydides with the intention of
telling the truth. It seems to me that we must believe that
Pericles did call a meeting of the assembly after the Athenian
peace embassy had been rejected and that Pericles said things
much like what is reported. The role of Thucydides is to be
found in the organization of the speech and the choice of some
of the language. He may even introduce, I believe, a subject
closely related to the speech in order to clarify the reader's understanding of something important. I agree with Gomme's views,
for instance, on 2.60.5–6: "I find these two sections, however,
perhaps the most artificial thing in all Thucydides' speeches, the
farthest removed from actuality, and, therefore, apparently, devised by Thucydides himself, not 'as Perikles would have said τὰ
τότε δέοντα' " (*HCT* II, 167). I also agree, however, with his
cautious conclusion about these passages which deal in an ab-
tract way with the qualities necessary for a statesman. "Yet we
may be misled in this. The Athenians, just as this time, certainly
had a passion for generalization in rhetoric such as we find it
difficult to appreciate, as can be seen most easily in Euripides,
nearly as well in Antiphon, and, in his own way, in the 'Old
Oligarch.' The antithetical style is its suitable vehicle." The
most important aspect of Thucydides' role is not in the possibility
of free invention, which I exclude, but in his choice of which
speeches to report from among the many available. This gives
him freedom to achieve his purpose which, I agree with Meyer,
is to speak to posterity and convey lasting truths. We should
understand Thucydides much better if we knew, for instance,

why he reports this last speech of Pericles but not, as Meyer points out, a previous one which he must have given during the debate on the peace embassy, and why, for that matter, he does not report the speeches of the opposition. It will not do to say, as Meyer does, that these speeches were historically irrelevant because nothing came of them. The same is true of the speech he does report, for Pericles was condemned anyway. Thucydides, moreover, reports in full the speech of the Spartan ambassadors who seek peace in 425 (4.17–21), even though they were equally fruitless. It would be valuable to know why Thucydides gives us one and not the others, but that is the subject of a different book. Pericles' last speech, though it speaks to future generations like all the rest of Thucydides, is examined here for its place in the events of 430 and for its effect on the listeners of that time.

Bibliography

Adcock, F. E. "Alcidas ἀργυρολόγος," *Melanges Gustave Glotz* I, 1–6. Paris, 1932.
——. "The Archidamian War, B.C. 431–421," *CAH* V (1940), 193–253.
——. "ΕΠΙΤΕΙΧΙΣΜΟΣ in the Archidamian War, *CR* LXI (1947), 2–7.
Amit, M. "The Melian Dialogue and History," *Athenaeum* XLVI (1968), 216–235.
Anderson, J. K. "Cleon's Orders at Amphipolis," *JHS* LXXXV (1965), 1–4.
Andrewes, A. "Thucydides and the Persians," *Historia* X (1961), 1–18.
——. "The Mytilene Debate: Thucydides 3.36–49," *Phoenix* XVI (1962), 64–85.
Aristophanes. *Acharnians*, ed. and tr. B. B. Rogers. London, 1910.
——. *Peace*, ed. and tr. B. B. Rogers. London, 1866.
Badian, E., ed. *Ancient Societies and Institutions, Studies Presented to Victor Ehrenberg on his 75th birthday*. Oxford, 1966.
Baldwin, B. "Cleon's Strategy at Amphipolis," *AClass* XI (1968), 211–214.
Bauman, R. E. "A Message from Amphipolis," *AClass* XI (1968), 170–181.
Beaumont, R. L. "Corinth, Ambracia, Apollonia," *JHS* LXXII (1952), 62–73.
Beloch, K. J. *Die Attische Politik seit Perikles*. Leipzig, 1884.
——. *Die Bevölkerung der griechisch-römischen Welt*. Leipzig, 1886.
——. "Griechische Aufgebote," *Klio* V (1905), 341–374; VI (1906), 34–78.

———. *Griechische Geschichte.* 2d ed. Strassburg, Berlin, and Leipzig, 1912–1927.

Bengtson, H. *Die Staatsverträge der griechisch-römischen Welt von 700 bis 338 v. Chr.* II. Munich and Berlin, 1962.

Bengtson, H. *Griechische Geschichte.* 3d ed. Munich, 1965.

Béquignon, Y. and E. Will. "Observations sur le décret de 425 relatif à la taxation du tribut (IG I²63)," *Revue archeologique* XXXV (1950), 5–34.

Boeckh, A. *Die Staatshaushaltung der Athener.* 3d ed. Berlin, 1886.

Bradeen, D. W. "The Popularity of the Athenian Empire," *Historia* IX (1960), 257–269.

Bruce, I. A. F. "The Corcyraean Civil War of 427 B.C.," *Phoenix* XXV (1971), 108–117.

Brunt, P. A. "Spartan Policy and Strategy in the Archidamian War," *Phoenix* XIX (1965), 255–280.

———. "Athenian Settlements Abroad in the Fifth Century B.C.," *ASI,* 71–92.

Busolt, G. "Nachtrag zu C.I.A. IV 179B.," *Hermes* XXV (1890), 640–645.

———. *Griechische Geschichte.* 3 vols. Gotha, 1893–1904.

Cavaignac, E. "L'augmentation du tribut des alliés d'Athènes en 425, *REG* XLVIII (1935), 245–249.

Cawkwell, G. L. "Anthemocritus and the Megarians and the Decree of Charinus," *REG* LXXXII (1969), 327–335.

Chambers, M. H. "Thucydides and Pericles," *HSCP* LXII (1957), 79–92.

Cohen, R. "Quelques mots sur Nicias," *Melanges Gustave Glotz.* I, 227–239. Paris, 1932.

Connor, W. R. "Charinus' Megarian Decree," *AJP* LXXXIII (1962), 225–246.

———. *Theopompus and Fifth Century Athens.* Cambridge, Mass., 1968.

———. "Charinus' Decree Again," *REG* LXXXIII (1970), 305–308.

———. *The New Politicians of Fifth Century Athens,* Princeton, 1971.

Cornford, F. M. *Thucydides Mythistoricus.* London, 1907, reprinted, 1965.

Delbrück, H. *Die Strategie des Perikles.* Berlin, 1890.

———. *Geschichte der Kriegskunst.* I, *Das Altertum.* Berlin, 1920, reprinted 1964.

De Sanctis, G. "La τάξις φόρου del 425 a.C.," *Rivista di Filologia* XIII (1935), 52–60.

——. *Pericle*. Milan and Messina, 1944.

——. *Storia dei Greci*. 2 vols. Florence, 1963.

Dittenberger, W. *Sylloge Inscriptionum Graecarum*. 4 vols. 4th ed. Leipzig, 1915, reprinted Hildesheim, 1960.

Dover, K. J. "ΔΕΚΑΤΟΣ ΑΥΤΟΣ," *JHS*, LXXX (1960), 61–77.

Duncker, M. W. *Geschichte des Altertums*. 9 vols. Leipzig, 1878–1886.

Eberhardt, W. "Der Melierdialog und die inschriften ATL A9 (IG 1² 63 +) und IG 1² 97 +," *Historia* VIII (1959), 284–314.

Eddy, S. K. "Athens' Peacetime Navy in the Age of Perikles," *GRBS* IX (1968), 141–155.

Edmonds, J. M. *The Fragments of Attic Comedy*. Leiden, 1957–1961.

Ehrenberg, V. "Pericles and His Colleagues between 441 and 429 B.C.," *AJP* LXVI (1945), 113–134.

——. *The People of Aristophanes*. Oxford, 1951.

Finley, J. H. *Thucydides*. Cambridge, Mass., 1942.

Flashar, Hellmut. "Der Epitaphios des Perikles," *Sitzungberichte der Heidelberger Akademie der Wissenschaften*. Heidelberg, 1969.

Fornara, C. "The Date of the Callias Decrees," *GRBS* XI (1970), 185–196.

——. *The Athenian Board of Generals*. Wiesbaden, 1971.

Forrest, W. G. "Aristophanes' Acharnians," *Phoenix* XVII (1963), 1–12.

Freeman, E. A. *A History of Sicily*. 4 vols. Oxford, 1891–1894.

French, A. *The Growth of the Athenian Economy*. London, 1964.

——. "The Tribute of the Allies," *Historia* XXI (1972), 1–20.

Fuks, A. "Thucydides and the Stasis in Corcyra: Thuc., III, 82–3 versus [Thuc.], III, 84," *AJP* XCII (1971), 48–55.

Gauthier, P. "Les clérouques de Lesbos et la colonisation athénienne au Vᵉ siècle," *REG* LXXIX (1966), 64–88.

Gilbert, G. *Beiträge zur innern geschichte Athens im zeitalter des peloponnesischen Krieges*. Leipzig, 1877.

Gillis, D. "The Revolt at Mytilene," *AJP* XCII (1971), 38–47.

Glotz, G. and Robert Cohen. *Histoire grecque*. II, Paris, 1929.

Gomme, A. W. "The Athenian Hoplite Force in 431 B.C.," *CQ* XXI (1927), 142–150.

——. *A Historical Commentary on Thucydides*. I–III. Oxford, 1950–1956.

——. "Four Passages in Thucydides," *JHS* LXXI (1951), 70–80.

——. "Thucydides ii 13, 3," *Historia* II (1953), 1–21.

——. "Thucydides and Cleon, The Second Battle of Amphipolis," Ἑλληνικά XIII (1954), 1–10.

——. *More Essays in Greek History and Literature.* Oxford, 1962.

——. A. Andrewes, and K. J. Dover. *A Historical Commentary on Thucydides.* IV. Oxford, 1970.

Grote, G. *A History of Greece.* 4th ed. London, 1872.

Grundy, G. B. *The Topography of the Battle of Plataea.* London, 1894.

——. *Thucydides and the History of His Age.* 2d ed. Oxford, 1948.

Hammond, N. G. L. "The Campaigns in Amphilochia During the Archidamian War," *BSA* XXXVII (1936–1937), 128–140.

——. "The Main Road from Boeotia to the Peloponnese through the Northern Megarid," *BSA* XLIX (1954), 103–122.

——. *A History of Greece to 322 B.C.* Oxford, 1959.

Henderson, B. W. *The Great War between Athens and Sparta.* London, 1927.

Herbst, W. *Der Abfall Mytilenes.* Cologne, 1861.

Hignett, C. *A History of the Athenian Constitution.* Oxford, 1952.

Hiller von Gaertringen, F. *Inscriptiones Graecae.* I, *editio minor, Inscriptiones Atticae Euclidis anno anteriores.* Berlin, 1924.

Jacoby, F. *Die Fragmente der griechischen Historiker.* 3 vols.: I–II, Berlin, 1923–1930; III, Leyden, 1940.

Jones, A. H. M. *Athenian Democracy.* Oxford, 1957.

Kagan, D. "Argive Politics and Policy after the Peace of Nicias," *CP*, LVII (1962), 209–218.

——. *The Outbreak of the Peloponnesian War.* Ithaca, 1969.

Kahrstedt, U. *Untersuchungen zur Magistratur in Athens.* Berlin, 1936.

Kirchhoff, A. *Thukydides und sein Urkundenmaterial.* Berlin, 1895.

Kirchner, J. E. *Prosopographia Attica.* 2 vols. Berlin, 1901, reprinted 1966.

Lange, E. "Thukydides und die Parteien," *Philologus* LII (1894), 616–651.

Legon, R. P. "Demos and Stasis: Studies in the Factional Politics of Classical Greece." Unpublished Ph.D. dissertation, Cornell University, Ithaca, N.Y., 1966.

——. "Megara and Mytilene," *Phoenix* XXII (1968), 200–225.

Lewis, D. M. "Double Representation in the *Strategia*," *JHS* LXXXI (1961), 118–123.

Mattingly, H. B. "Athenian Finance in the Peloponnesian War," *BCH* XCII (1968), 460–485.

McGregor, M. F. "Kleon, Nikias and the Trebling of the Tribute," *TAPA* LXVI (1935), 146–164.

Meiggs, R. *The Athenian Empire*. Oxford, 1972.

——, and D. Lewis. *A Selection of Greek Historical Inscriptions to the End of the Fifth Century* B.C. Oxford, 1969.

Meritt, B. D. *Athenian Financial Documents*. Ann Arbor, 1932.

——. "Athenian Covenant with Mytilene," *AJP* LXXV (1954), 359–368.

——. "The Chronology of the Peloponnesian War," *Proceedings of the American Philosophical Society*, CXV (1971), 97–124.

—— and M. F. McGregor. "The Athenian Quota-List of 421/0 B.C.," *Phoenix* XXI (1967), 85–91.

—— and H. T. Wade-Gery. "Pylos and the Assessment of Tribute," *AJP* LVII (1936), 377–394.

——, H. T. Wade-Gery, and M. F. McGregor. *The Athenian Tribute Lists*. 4 vols.: I, Cambridge, Mass., 1939; II–IV, Princeton, 1949–1953.

—— and A. B. West. *The Athenian Assessment of 425* B.C. Ann Arbor, 1934.

Meyer, E. *Forschungen zur alten Geschichte*. II, Halle, 1899.

——. *Geschichte des Altertums*. 5th ed., reprinted in 1954 and 1956, Basel.

Milchoefer, A. *Karten von Attika*. Heft VII–VIII, Berlin, 1895.

Miltner, F. "Perikles," *PW*, XIX (1937), 748–790.

Papastavrou, J. *Amphipolis, Klio*. Beiheft XXXVI, Berlin, 1936.

Pflugk-Hartung, J. von. *Perikles als Feldherr*. Stuttgart, 1884.

Pritchett, W. K. *Studies in Ancient Greek Topography*. 2 vols., Berkeley and Los Angeles, 1965 and 1969.

Quinn, T. J. "Thucydides and the Unpopularity of the Athenian Empire," *Historia* XIII (1964), 257–266.

——. "Political Groups in Lesbos during the Peloponnesian War," *Historia* XX (1971), 405–417.

Raubitschek, A. E. "War Melos tributpflichtig?" *Historia* XII (1963), 78–83.

Romilly, Jacqueline de. *Thucydides and Athenian Imperialism*, tr. Philip Thody. Oxford, 1963.

——. "Thucydides and the Cities of the Athenian Empire," *Bulletin of the Institute of Classical Studies of the University of London* XIII (1966), 1–12.

Ste. Croix, G. E. M. de. "The Character of the Athenian Empire," *Historia* III (1954), 1–41.

——. *The Origins of the Peloponnesian War*. London and Ithaca, 1972.

Schmid, W., and O. Stählin, *Geschichte der Griechische Literatur*. V:2. Munich, 1948.

Schwartz, E. *Das Geschichtswerk der Thukydides*. Hildesheim, 1960, reprinted from edition of 1929.

Sealey, R. "Athens and the Archidamian War," *PACA* I (1958), 61–87.

——. *Essays in Greek Politics*. New York, 1967.

Stahl, Hans-Peter. *Thukydides*. Munich, 1966.

Stevenson, G. H. "The Financial Administration of Pericles," *JHS* XLIV (1924), 1–9.

Thomsen, R. *Eisphora*. Copenhagen, 1964.

Thompson, W. E. "The Athenian Treaties with Haliai and Dareios the Bastard," *Klio* LIII (1971), 119–124.

Thucydides. Text and translation by Charles Forster Smith. I–IV (Loeb). London and Cambridge, Mass., 1919–1923.

Thucydidis Historiae. H. S. Jones and J. E. Powell. Oxford, 1942.

Thucydide, La guerre du péloponnèse. Texte établit et traduit par J. de Romilly, Livres I² et II, III par Raymond Weil et J. de Romilly, IV–V par J. de Romilly (Budé). Paris, 1958, 1962, 1967.

Thucydidis Historiae. Post Carolum Hude edidit Otto Luschnat, (Teubner). Leipzig, 1960.

Thukydides. J. Classen, bearbeitet von J. Steup mit einem nachwort und bibliographischen nachträgen von Rudolf Stark; 5th ed. Nachdruck, Berlin, 1963.

Treu, M. "Athen und Melos und der Melierdialog des Thukydides," *Historia* II (1952/3), 253–273.

——. "Der Stratege Demosthenes," *Historia* V (1956), 420–447.

Vischer, W. *Kleine Schriften*. I. Leipzig, 1877.

Wade-Gery, H. T. "Two Notes on Theopompos, *Philippika*, X; I: Kleon and the Assessment," *AJP* LIX (1938), 129–131.

——. *Essays in Greek History*. Oxford, 1958.

Walker, E. M. "Athens and the Greek Powers, 462–445 B.C.," *CAH* V (1940), 68–97.

Wasserman, F. M. "Post-Periclean Democracy in Action: The Mytilenean Debate (Thuc. III 37–48)," *TAPA* LXXXVII (1956), 27–41.

Wentker, H. *Sizilien und Athen*. Heidelberg, 1956.

West, A. B. "Notes on Certain Athenian Generals of the Year 424–3 B.C.," *AJP* XLV (1924), 141–160.

——. "Pericles' Political Heirs," *CP* XIX (1924), 124–146, 201–228.

——. and B. D. Meritt. "Cleon's Amphipolitan Campaign and the Assessment List of 421," *AJA* XXIX (1925), 54–69.

——. "Thucydides, V, 18, 6. Sane or Gale," *AJP* LVIII (1937), 166–173.

Westlake, H. D. *Essays on the Greek Historians and Greek History.* Manchester, 1969.

——. *Individuals in Thucydides.* Cambridge, 1968.

Wet, B. X. de. "The So-called Defensive Policy of Pericles," *AClass* XII (1969), 103–119.

Wilamowitz-Möllendorf, U. von. "Sphakteria," *SB Ak. Berlin,* 1921, 306–318.

Will, E. "Histoire grecque," *Révue historique,* CCXLV (1971), 85–150.

——. *Le Monde grec et l'Orient, I, Le Ve siècle (510–403).* Paris, 1972.

Woodcock, E. C. "Demosthenes, Son of Alcisthenes," *HSCP* XXXIX (1928), 93–108.

Woodhead, A. G. "Thucydides' Portrait of Cleon," *Mnemosyne* XIII (1960), 289–317.

——. *Thucydides on the Nature of Power.* Cambridge, Mass., 1970.

General Index

❦

Acanthus: Brasidas at, 291, 293, 296, 316; restored to Athens, 347; revolts from Athens, 310, 343, 344

Acarnania, 33-35, 68, 73, 115, 138, 209, 216, 220, 280-281, 357; allied to Athens, 25; Athenian campaign in, 59, 62; attacks Anactorium, 256; Demosthenes' expedition aided by, 201, 202, 356; Demosthenes' Aetolian campaign not aided by, 203; Phormio expedition to, 122; Spartan attack on, 107-109, 210-214

Achaea, 19, 110, 185, 235, 344

Acharnae, 51, 52, 53, 96

Acheson, Dean, 159

Acte (Argolis), 73, 74

Acte (Chalcidice), 302

Aegalius, Mt., 49

Aegean Sea, 17, 21, 29, 115, 150, 156, 180, 187, 199, 256, 257, 278, 292, 302, 364

Aegina, 40, 58, 82, 83, 85, 97, 157, 193, 232; occupied by Athens, 64, 69; population expelled by Athenians, 62; population settled in Thyrea, 63, 264

Aegitium, 204, 205

Aegospotami, 82

Aenos, 241

Aeolia, 149

Aetolia, 245, 268, 289, 356; attacked by Demosthenes, 202-209; threatens Naupactus, 201

Agis, King of Sparta, 147, 193, 219, 223, 224

Agraea, 214, 215, 217, 281

Alcibiades, 91, 125, 238, 286, 301, 342, 356

Alcidas, Spartan navarch, 146, 147, 148, 150, 151, 153, 171, 175, 180, 197, 199

Alcmaeonidae, 125

Alexander of Macedon, 283

Ambracia, 121, 201; allied to Sparta, 19; attacks Amphilochian Argos, 94, 96; joins Spartan expedition to Corcyra, 180; provokes Spartan attack on Acarnania, 107-108; provokes second Spartan campaign in northwestern Greece, 210-217

Ameinias, 314

Amphilochia, 83, 210, 215, 216

Amphilochian Argos, 94, 96, 108, 210, 211, 212

Amphipolis, 185, 303, 310, 315, 316, 319, 333, 336, 338, 341; attacked by Brasidas, 291-300; defended by Eucles and Thucydides, 290; Cleon's attempt to recover, 321-330; founded by Hagnon, 55, 121; and Spartan promise to restore to Athens, 342, 346, 348; strategic importance, 288

Amyntas, 119

Anactorium, 19, 108, 256, 342, 348

Anaea, 278

Andros, 252

Aneristus, 94

Antandros, 278

Antirrhium, 109, 113

Antissa, 133, 142

Apodoti, 203

Apollonia, 256

Apragmosyne, apragmones, 88-90

Archestratus, Athenian general in 433/2, 38, 318

Archidamus, King of Sparta, 20, 24, 40, 67, 70, 74, 84, 99, 107, 331, 352;

Index of Modern Authors

❦

Index of Ancient Authors and Inscriptions

✿